Broadcast Journalism
Techniques of Radio and Television News

Fifth Edition

Andrew Boyd

Focal Press

OXFORD   AUCKLAND   BOSTON   JOHANNESBURG   MELBOURNE   NEW DELHI

Focal Press
An imprint of Butterworth-Heinemann
Linacre House, Jordan Hill, Oxford OX2 8DP
225 Wildwood Avenue, Woburn, MA 01801-2041
A division of Reed Educational and Professional Publishing Ltd

A member of the Reed Elsevier plc group

First published 1988
Reprinted 1990
Second edition 1993
Reprinted 1993
Third edition 1994
Reprinted 1995
Fourth edition 1997
Reprinted 1998 (twice), 1999
Fifth edition 2001

British Library Cataloguing in Publication Data
A catalogue record for this book is available from the British Library

Library of Congress Cataloguing in Publication Data
Boyd, Andrew, 1956–
    Broadcast journalism: techniques of radio and television news/Andrew Boyd – 5th ed.
    p.cm.
    Includes bibliographical references and index.
    ISBN 0-240-51571-4 (alk. paper)
    1. Broadcast journalism.   2. Broadcast journalism – Great Britain.   I. Title.
    PN4784.B75 B69 2000
    070.1'94–dc21   00-064672

ISBN 0 240 51571 4

Composition by Genesis Typesetting, Rochester, Kent
Printed and bound in Great Britain

FOR EVERY TITLE THAT WE PUBLISH, BUTTERWORTH-HEINEMANN
WILL PAY FOR BTCV TO PLANT AND CARE FOR A TREE.

To Michael and Laura and all my students
– the voices of tomorrow

Our success is measured by the success of our successors.

Contents

Foreword

More than 60 years have passed since broadcast news began to take over from the press as the prime source of up-to-date information about current events in the world at large. The turning point was almost certainly the European crisis which culminated in the Munich agreement of September 1938. Then war seemed inevitable and radio, for the first time, showed that it could deliver news to an anxious audience faster and with more immediacy than the best-run newspapers. The Second World War confirmed the trend, not just in Britain itself, where the nation gathered each night round its wireless sets to listen to the *Nine O'Clock News* for an authoritative account of the swaying fortunes of war, but more widely through the BBC's European and Overseas Services, which then established standards of reliability and professionalism which have been maintained to this day.

Yet the BBC, then a monopoly, had been slow in appreciating the importance of broadcast news. Reith, its founder, and his senior colleagues were deeply suspicious of journalists, and it was not until 1937 that the BBC appointed its first professional, R T. Clark, to be its News Editor. The previous year, a proposal by a young, newly recruited Topical Talks Assistant, Richard Dimbleby, for the creation of a team of BBC reporters and the introduction of voiced reports in bulletins had fallen on deaf ears. So had a proposal for the setting up of a corps of BBC correspondents put forward by Commander Stephen King-Hall, a noted broadcaster of the period.

Andrew Boyd's book vividly reflects the distance travelled since those early days and graphically portrays the vast new industry which the growth of the broadcast news media has brought into being. It is not just that news has become the staple ingredient *par excellence* of both radio and television. Nor is it just that nowadays far more people get their daily ration of news from hearing it or seeing it than from reading it. It is also that the number of sources of broadcast news has greatly increased with the proliferation of radio and television channels, and that technological advances have brought the gathering, processing and presentation of news to a remarkably high pitch of speed and sophistication.

Andrew Boyd rightly focuses on the skills required in a profession which long ago ceased to be the province of talented amateurs. Young people who read his book will find in it not only a profusion of first-hand information about what it is like to work 'at the coal face' in this demanding trade and on how news is gathered, processed, edited and packaged in the various sectors of the television and radio industries, but also a great deal of practical instruction on the craft of television and radio news broadcasting, from the first indications of a breaking story to the full treatment in a news programme. But behind the hard-nosed, down-to-earth approach of the experienced news editor there is the frequently reaffirmed awareness of the special responsibilities of broadcasting journalists and the fundamental values – independence, integrity, dedication to the truth – without which there can be no good journalism, however well developed the skills.

Gerard Mansell
Former Deputy Director-General of the BBC;
Managing Director of BBC World Service and Chairman of the Joint Advisory
Committee for the Training of Radio Journalists, now BJTC
(Broadcast Journalism Training Council)

How to use this book

The pace of change is hotting up. New technology and new techniques are turning broadcasting inside out. Thousands of broadcasters – myself included – have benefited from changes we might have dreamt, but never imagined we would actually see.

Thanks to new technology, I have been able to travel to far-flung nations with a videocamera small enough to hold in one hand, but capable of recording pictures deemed fit for broadcast and sounds that are crisper than any machine I used in radio.

At home I have a computer capable of editing video and putting together radio packages. With this and my single camera I can produce professional reports for TV and radio. And thanks to the web, I could, if I chose, become a one-man TV network.

That I can afford such kit as a freelance is nothing short of staggering. A few years ago equipment capable of producing similar results would have cost me my house. A decade earlier it would have cost me a row of houses. Today, low-cost, high-quality technology means I can indulge my passion for human rights reporting with impunity.

So this fifth edition of *Broadcast Journalism* reflects the incredible changes that have occurred in a few short years: the rise of the videojournalist; multi-skilling, the web and 24-hour news, to name a few.

As ever, *Broadcast Journalism* continues to be a practical manual for reporters eager to make a career in the hectic world of broadcasting. It offers a clear insight into the arena of electronic news and, with extensive illustrations, offers step-by-step practical instruction in all the essential skills of reporting for radio and TV.

The three main parts – Broadcast Journalism, Radio, and Television – systematically lay the foundations required by the aspiring broadcast journalist.

Part One looks at the growing career opportunities in broadcasting and offers a plan of campaign for anyone determined enough to break in. It goes on to deal with the business of newswriting, newsgathering, interviewing, programme making and presentation; focusing on the common ground between radio and television.

Parts Two and Three place those skills firmly in the context of the radio and TV newsroom. Each begins by taking the reader behind the scenes, first to experience the atmosphere in the internationally respected newsroom of the BBC World Service in London and then to the fast-changing world of ITN.

How the equipment works and how the reporter should use it is clearly explained in the sections on television and radio, which offer instruction in the basics of camerawork, recording and editing pictures and audio, using the latest digital technology – and TV scriptwriting. New for this edition are extensive chapters on the emerging worlds of videojournalism and the Internet.

Each chapter ends with a set of practical suggestions for developing the skills outlined. These form the basis of a training course, which you can use to teach yourself or others. Lastly, a preliminary list of training contacts is included.

The aim has been to produce a comprehensive manual – a tool – to be grasped and used by students, teachers and practitioners of broadcast journalism alike.

My thanks to the readers of the previous four editions for making this the standard textbook on broadcasting. I hope this fifth edition – which represents a major revision – will ensure *Broadcast Journalism's* popularity in the years to come.

Andrew Boyd

List of illustrations

Acknowledgements

Sincere and grateful thanks to all who have borne with me, opened their doors to me, put themselves out for me, supplied pictures, information and advice, and managed to keep smiling throughout my barrage of foolish questions. Without your help and support this book would not have been possible.

ITN: Nigel Dacre; Stewart Purvis; Jonathan Munro; Malcolm Munro; Robin Elias; Phil Moger; Fergus Sheppard; Emma Hoskyns; Shiulie Ghosh; Rachel McTavish; Eddie Botsio; Mike Inglis; Mike Parkin; Roger Lorenz; Dave McDonald; Anne Were.

BBC World Service: Bob Jobbins; Keith Somerville; Peter Brooks; Ian Richardson; Ian Miller; Jenny Cole; John McLean; Julie Candler; Andrew Whitehead; Lawrence Reeve-Jones and Paul Jenkinson.

Thanks also to Mike Dodd; Kim Sabido; Anya Sitaram; Judith Melby, CBC; Harry Radcliffe, CBS; Freda Morris, NBC; Malcolm Downing, Pepita Conlon, Paul Cleveland and Ian Henderson, ABC; John Rodman and Annette Bosworth, WEEI; Broadcast News, Canada; Federation of Australian Broadcasters; Canadian Bureau for International Education; Scottish Television; Broadcasting Corporation of New Zealand; Simon Ellis, BBC Essex; Katrina Balmforth, Chiltern Radio; Penny Young, BBC Northampton; Gerry Radcliffe and Tony Delahunty, Pennine Radio, Henry Yelf; BBC Radio Solent; Jim Greensmith, Radio Hallam; Richard Bestic; Rob McKenzie; Capital Radio; BBC Southern Counties Radio; Peter Everett; BBC; LBC/IRN; BBC General News Service; Reuters News Agency; Media Touch Systems Inc.; Reuters TV; WTN; Tyne Tees TV; HTV; Grampian TV; County Sound; Uher; Marantz Audio UK; EDS Portaprompt; Nagra Kudelski SA; E.W.O. Bauch Ltd; Sony Broadcast Ltd; UK Press Gazette; British Rail Press Office; Panasonic; Avid; ASC; Digital Audio Labs Inc.; Miles Kington, Writer and Posy Simmonds, Cartoonist.

Special thanks to Gerard Mansell, former Managing Editor, BBC External Services. Whilst every effort has been made to contact copyright holders, the publisher would like to hear from anyone whose copyright has unwittingly been infringed.

Part One

BROADCAST JOURNALISM

'The quintessence of journalism as high art: filling the void at zero hour on a subject you know absolutely nothing about.'

TONY SAMSTAG, BBC WORLD SERVICE STRINGER, OSLO

Figure 1 Going live . . . producing upwards of 100 hours of news programmes each week for 143 million listeners. No other station comes close. The BBC World Service. (*Andrew Boyd*)

NEWS GATHERING

1 The best job in town

> 'Practically everyone works at high speed. Telephones ring, people shout, crises pop up all the time, and deadlines keep thundering down. It's not an environment for the weak of heart.' — PHILIP O. KIERSTEAD, ALL-NEWS RADIO*

Ask most journalists what they think about their chosen profession and the chances are they will bemoan the anti-social hours, unreasonable stress, flogging to meet constant deadlines, time wasted draped over the telephone, destruction of family life and home existence, but when the griping is over and you ask them what else they would rather do, the chances are they would shrug, smile and tell you, 'nothing'.

Few professions can match broadcast journalism for its rewards in terms of job satisfaction, interest, variety, sheer challenge – and for the select few – fame and wealth.

So what does it take to become a player in the world of broadcasting?

Personal qualities

> 'The only qualities for real success in journalism are ratlike cunning, a plausible manner and a little literary ability. The capacity to steal other peoples' ideas and phrases . . . is also invaluable.'
> — NICHOLAS TOMALIN, BRITISH JOURNALIST
>
> 'The qualities I look for in a radio reporter are: a good nose for a story, a determination to ferret out the details despite the obstacles, an interest in, and genuine awareness of, current news and issues, a lively imaginative mind, and a sense of humour.' — SIMON ELLIS, BBC LOCAL RADIO NEWS EDITOR
>
> 'A good reporter is someone who is up-front with self confidence, bright, and who knows what a story is . . . the reporter you send out on one story who comes back with two others as well, and who can find the offbeat in the run of the mill event. Those people will always get to the top very fast.'
> — PENNY YOUNG, NEWS EDITOR BBC LOCAL RADIO

* *All-News Radio*, TAB, 1980.

Employers and training courses alike are looking for special personal qualities from people who think they have what it takes to make a broadcast journalist.

Top of the list is commitment. Reporters must have the stamina to cope with shift work whose varying patterns could take them from three in the morning one day for a 12-hour shift, to from 10 at night a couple of days later.

Perhaps that is why the typical British radio journalist is a stressed-out thirtysomething. A union survey found that specialist journalists in the BBC regions worked an average of 57.3 hours per week and suffered from 'gross overwork and stress'.*

So, the reporter who displays the right stuff must be able to deliver peak performance even in the face of deep-set fatigue, and still remain a cheerful team member. Prima donnas and fragile personas that need nannying and constant encouragement will last only a short while in the brusque atmosphere of the newsroom with its relentless deadlines. He or she should also be self-reliant and capable of working with a minimum of guidance and supervision.

Intelligence, curiosity, creativity and writing ability are basic qualities. Added to this, our paragon will need that essential spark. Vitality, vivacity, energy, drive, enthusiasm – call it what you will – news editors are looking for that extra something that will set one applicant above all others.

For those that do manage to climb the greasy pole, the rewards can be high. An on-screen reporter at ITN can expect to earn upwards of £30 000. To deserve that they will need special qualities, as ITN's Editor-in-Chief, Nigel Dacre explains:

'It's getting tougher to break into the top jobs. You need an ability to perform well on camera that wasn't such a requirement in past years. These days you are expected to do a lot of live two-way work, such as interviews with a newscaster. The ability to grapple with complicated stories at short notice continues to be a very big requirement. Thirdly, we need people who can really make a difference to a story by making it distinctive. It's that combination of on-screen abilities, a sophisticated approach to difficult stories and a creative spark that is important for an on-screen reporter. For off-screen reporters – production staff – it's probably the other two.'

Malcolm Downing, of the Australian Broadcasting Corporation looks for a quality that is rarer still, especially when coupled with these other virtues. *'Humility – the opposite of the assumption that you know it all.'*

Jobs in broadcasting

Will Glennon worked on a student newspaper and in local radio before taking unpaid work experience with the BBC. After a postgraduate course in journalism he joined the BBC Regional Journalism Trainee scheme, before becoming a bi-media Broadcast Journalist.

'I've found that I need stamina and perseverance to progress. Whatever your particular experience, the key to being successful in journalism is the ability to understand people. The stories you tell are always about somebody and are always directed to people as well. Creativity is important. If you have a good idea, finding a fresh way of telling an old story can work just as well as discovering a completely new one.'†

* *NUJ survey*, June 1995.
† www.bbc.co.uk/cgi-bin/education/betsie/parser.pl

The largest newsgathering organisation in the world, the BBC, offers careers in network and regional TV; *News 24*, the continuous news service; network, regional and World Service radio; Online and Ceefax.

All radio and television stations belong in one of three leagues: *local, major market* (big city or regional), and *national* (network). TV usually pays better than radio, and as one might expect, the higher the profile and the bigger the audience, the greater the salary.

But there are many more jobs for journalists in broadcasting than the coveted role of on-air reporter. Positions range from behind-the-scenes writers and producers, to newsreaders and presenters. Network and bigger stations offer more scope for specialization, while smaller stations, like those in remote parts of America and Australia, often employ a jack-of-all-trades who can turn a hand to everything from reading the news to selling advertising and handling the payroll.

And broadcasting is on the move. Developments in cable and satellite TV open the door to even more opportunities. Radio is branching out into smaller, leaner and more specialized units. There are new national stations in Britain and potentially hundreds more on the way, thanks to developments in data compression technology.

Radio

Rob McKenzie gave up a career as an engineer to train as a broadcaster on the radio journalism course at the London College of Printing before joining one of Britain's biggest independent stations, Capital Radio.

'*It's an exciting life I'm sure thousands would envy because of the opportunities I get to do things. Getting in is a matter of luck – being in the right place at the right time and being good at your job. There also has to be a spark inside you which says, "I'm determined to do this." I think you've got to be able to grasp a subject quickly and be able to put it across in a simple, direct, manner.*'

For the radio journalist the career path is likely to run from reporter to producer and into management as news editor, though some organizations rank reporters above producers. Higher-level management includes programme organizer or station manager, or equivalent. For those who prefer to remain in the field as reporters, finding a specialism such as industrial, political or foreign correspondent is often the answer.

The larger the station, the more opportunity there is to specialize and the greater the variety of positions available. Some network and larger stations employ announcers and newsreaders who do nothing else, writers who only rewrite other people's copy and current affairs reporters who specialize in making documentaries.

'*Even more than print reporters, radio journalists need to be able to interact with a lot of different types of people in rapid succession. They need to gain people's co-operation quickly and get them to talk in easy-to-understand terms.*

'*They also need the indefinable "it" factor, which allows them to project their personality and sound credible.*

> *'And because increasing amounts of radio journalism goes to air live – with reporters frequently being interviewed themselves as well as asking questions of others – radio journalists need to maintain high standards of accuracy while thinking on their feet and talking without a prepared script. In this respect they need the skills which good sporting commentators have always had.'*
> – MICHAEL DODD, EX-ABC, NOW RADIO TRAINER AND
> FREELANCE FOREIGN CORRESPONDENT

Television

> *'In American television there is more opportunity for training than in British TV. Any major market station will have at least an hour's news broadcast preceding or following the network newscast. People get out of university and go to work on small stations where they can afford to make mistakes covering things that are not earth shattering, then they go on to bigger markets and some of them end up in the networks.'*
> – PAUL CLEVELAND, ASSIGNMENT MANAGER, ABC NEWS

Television is usually seen as a natural progression from radio. TV journalists often start as sub-editors, writing and re-writing copy, and may move up to become reporters. From there they can follow a similar career path to that of radio, into speciality reporting, production or management.

Some reporters and presenters start out as researchers, the unsung heroes of television, whose job it is to come up with programme ideas, set up interviews, collect background information, hunt for archive material and possibly write scripts.

Kim Sabido began his career in local radio, progressing to become a network reporter with Independent Radio News. He covered the Falklands War for IRN, sending back vivid accounts of the fighting, before moving into television as a reporter with ITN:

> *'There's a lot more independence and personal freedom with radio and in a way it's more rewarding. In Independent Radio as it was then, I was given total freedom as a respected reporter. On television you have a lot of masters and your material can be seen, reprocessed, packaged and edited by other people beyond your control.'*

The multi-skilled broadcast journalist

In the BBC and beyond, it is becoming common practice for journalists to be multi-skilled – able to produce reports for radio, TV and increasingly the web. According to the BBC, the three for the price of one policy is proving successful:

> *'The purpose of bi-media and multi-skilling is to reduce staff, to save money and to improve job satisfaction. It has been an eye-opener how popular it has been.'* *

Not all journalists agree. As one union organizer complained: 'I already carry a recorder, a telephone and a notebook. The last thing I want is to go into a difficult situation carrying that lot plus a camera with one eye shut and the other looking through a viewfinder.'†

---

* *The Guardian*, 5 April 1993.
† *The Journalist*, June 1993.

> *'New technology allows you to change the way you work and the way you spend your time. Journalists will increasingly do more graphics, editing, audio editing and video editing. The future for journalists is greater multi-skilling.'*
> – BBC NEWS AND CURRENT AFFAIRS DIRECTORATE

The BBC is sold out on the idea of the multi-skilled broadcaster. New recruits usually begin reporting and working on bulletins in radio, and in regional TV as newsroom-based journalists. Their work also takes in Online, CEEFAX (teletext) and subtitling.

The BBC describes an entry-level career in broadcast journalism as the ideal environment for developing interviewing, newswriting and newsreading skills, getting to grips with the equipment and learning to produce programmes. Two of the Beeb's most distinguished journalists, Michael Buerk and Kate Adie, began their careers in local radio. Most BBC journalists would follow a similar path, working their way from local newsrooms to network news, perhaps via *News 24*. They say a formal journalism qualification helps, but is by no means a necessity.

What the Beeb does want to see is evidence of commitment to journalism, in the form of articles published at school, university or in the press. Relevant work experience in radio or on newspapers is also an advantage.

The skills the Beeb is looking for include:

- Strong interest in news and current affairs
- Sound news judgement
- Writing ability
- Communication skills
- The ability to generate and develop ideas
- The ability to work well in a team in a variety of roles
- Confident IT skills, including word processing

Personal qualities include:

- Initiative, commitment, motivation and energy
- Drive and resilience under pressure
- Flexibility and adaptability to cope with changing priorities
- Ability to be a good editorial all-rounder

Freelancing

> *'Freelancing, especially foreign freelancing, is for the birds. It is a profession without security, grossly, almost laughingly, underpaid. It is the province of maladjusted freaks, outsiders who cannot work in the system back home, characters who inhabit a twilight, pension-less world . . .'*
> – KIERAN COOKE, BBC STRINGER IN ATHENS*

* From 'Twilight, underpaid world of freelancing abroad', *UK Press Gazette*, 30 March 1987.

Freelances travel the country or work a region, filling in for newsroom staff who are sick or on leave, or filing reports and stories on a commissioned or casual basis. They are paid a daily rate or by the item.

Freelancing offers a greater variety and range of experience to newly trained reporters, and is the most effective foot-in-the-door method of getting employment. When a job comes up, the good freelance becomes the benchmark against which all other applicants are judged. He or she has been tried and tested, is familiar with the radio or TV station and its patch and already knows many of its news contacts. Vacancies are not always advertised. Many stations prefer to invite known contacts to apply. News editors often cultivate freelances to provide a steady supply of replacement staff.

A good freelance can earn more than a staff reporter, but the drawbacks are insecurity, no sick pay, paid holidays or perks, living out of a suitcase, constantly having to work flat out to prove yourself to a prospective employer and putting up with stations which can take months to settle their accounts. If you decide to follow the freelance path, make sure you keep meticulous accounts, send regular invoices (be prepared to send reminders) and can call on the services of a good accountant.

Union membership

Freelances would be well advised to join a recognized union prepared to fight on their behalf if a station is reluctant to pay the going rate, or if it tries to take in too many 'volunteers' who could dilute the freelance pool and affect their chances of getting shifts.

Some stations will refuse to employ non-union members, and may be reluctant to buy stories and tip-offs from someone not registered with the union.

PAY – THE GOOD NEWS OR THE BAD?

According to the industry training organisation, Skillset, fewer than 4 per cent of broadcast journalists earn less than £20 000. 40 per cent earn between £20 000–£30 000 and even more – 43 per cent – earn between £30 000 and £40 000. The bad news is that almost half worked more than 45 hours a week and the poorest paid are in radio.

'There has been a steady decline in the training, pay and conditions of UK radio journalists since 1987 . . . The real value of salaries is 50 per cent, sometimes even 40 per cent, of the scale 10 years ago. Freelance budgets for contributions are derisory or non-existent . . . expansion in the number of radio stations has not been met by expansion in salaries and newsroom staffing.'
– TIM CROOK, INTERNATIONAL RADIO JOURNALISM*

Industry training

'What we want are people steeped in news. As long as they've got good writing ability and a nose for news we can quickly teach them the video part. Radio is fantastic training ground, perhaps the best place to begin.'   – SIR DAVID NICHOLAS, FORMER EDITOR-IN-CHIEF, ITN

* *Press Gazette*, 9 January 1998.

The industry's training commitment in Britain ranges from weak to variable. On-the-job training is usually for the fortunate few taken direct from school or university. Bigger organizations such as the BBC and ITN operate highly selective graduate trainee schemes, for which they pick only a handful of candidates from the thousands who apply.

The BBC pays its Broadcast Journalist Trainees a salary of £15 500, plus London weighting during their year-long cadetship. The prospect of a salary, training by the top

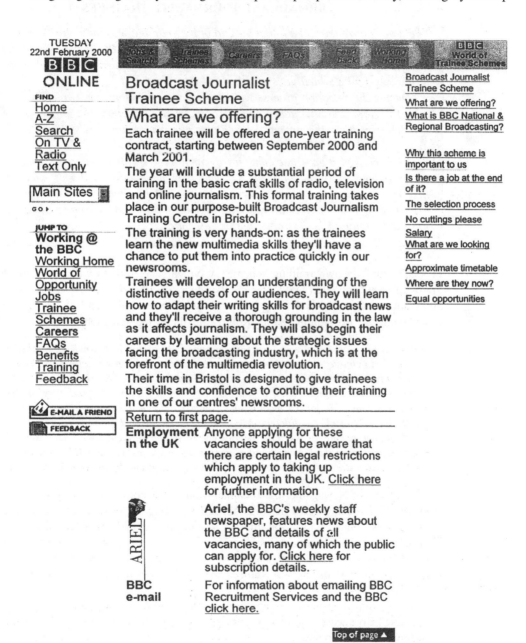

Figure 2 Find out from the web what work is available – job prospects for aspiring journalists on the BBC's Broadcast Journalist Trainee Scheme. (*Courtesy BBC*)

name in the industry, and a prospective career with the world's biggest broadcaster make this the most sought-after training scheme.

After a formal training at the BBC's purpose-built centre in Bristol, trainees will move on to one of the Beeb's 14 regional newsrooms.

BROADCAST JOURNALIST TRAINEES

'We don't guarantee you a job at the end of the year, but we aim to give you the skills and experience to compete for jobs leading to a career in BBC journalism throughout the UK. You will need to convince us that you have an enquiring mind and an interest in current affairs which goes well beyond the superficial.

'During the selection process we'll be assessing whether you can spot and tell a story; whether you have ideas and the confidence to express and pursue them; and whether you have the potential to adapt your communication skills to broadcast news.

'It's likely you'll have had some involvement in journalism – maybe as paid work, or at college or as a volunteer. Or you may have other skills of value in our newsrooms. Whatever your background, you will be able to show, through your experiences, that you have the qualities needed to be a BBC journalist. An education to degree standard is desirable, but not essential.'*

ITN also runs its own training scheme. A typical ITN trainee will be 24 to 25 and a graduate, well travelled with some experience of life. There are up to a thousand applicants for just six or fewer places. To say ITN can pick and choose would be an understatement! Programme editor Robin Elias is on the selection panel:

> *'I don't see any applicant who hasn't had a good background in journalism, not necessarily from a media course, but who has demonstrated initiative and practical experience by being editor of the university magazine or working for hospital radio. We ask them to do about 500 words on a media topic to show they are well versed in the area and that they can write.*
>
> *'Our scheme lasts for 18 months and you get a tremendous grounding in all areas – production, technical, the different newsrooms, radio work and in the bureaux.*
>
> *'What I am looking for is a lot of energy, vitality and an up-beat nature; enthusiasm for the news, the ability to think clearly and a passion and excitement. You will be working a lot of the time under stress, so you must be able to show you are able to mix in and muck in.'*

ITN's Head of Newsgathering, Jonathan Munro, has come a long way since graduating from the ITN scheme. Now he finds himself selecting the next generation of wannabes. This is what annoys him the most: *'talking to candidates who haven't seen the programmes and can't name our top correspondents.'* Things have changed since his day: *'They have to be increasingly willing to be multi-skilled. When I joined there was no requirement to work online, but trainees now have to learn how to operate a website and how to edit.'*

Coming from newspapers is another way into radio or television at a writer or sub-editor level. Broadcast newsrooms look favourably on trained reporters from local papers who know the station's area.

* www.bbc.co.uk/jobs 11 February 2000.

Network TV and radio recruit heavily from local and regional stations. During holiday times promising scriptwriters step into the front line and amass some airtime, putting themselves in pole position for a reporting job when one comes up.

Many newsroom secretaries or technical assistants go on to make excellent journalists with the benefit of this head start.

STARTING OUT IN AUSTRALIA

'Most people who get into broadcasting in Australia have completed a media or journalism degree. Most have also worked at a community, local or narrowcast radio station. Others come in after working as print journalists.

'The Australian Broadcasting Corporation has a federal radio training department based in Sydney, and regional training managers in Perth, Brisbane, Melbourne and Sydney. Courses are offered in all areas of journalism and programme making, as well as management and operations. ABC Television has its own training department.'

WHAT ARE YOU LOOKING FOR IN A TRAINEE BROADCASTER?

'As well as some formal media skills and passion, an interest in radio or television and an acceptance that they haven't got it all yet.'

– PEPITA CONLON, ABC RADIO TRAINING

Training courses

'I took a journalism course once. They told me if I put everything in a certain order I would be a journalist.'   – WELLS TWOMBLY, US SPORTS JOURNALIST

'I think you've got to go on a course these days, if you want to be good. A course gives you a far greater breadth of ideas and gets rid of bad habits before you start.'
– ROB MCKENZIE, PRODUCER/PRESENTER CAPITAL RADIO

One survey has found that half of all UK undergraduates now want to be journalists. With so many hopefuls chasing every available job that makes it a buyer's market.

Increasingly, news editors are recruiting only people who have had substantial experience or professional training. Courses are available, but there are some clear indicators that will tell you whether a course is worth applying for.

First, it should offer a thoroughly practical training, with as much hands-on experience of broadcast equipment and practical reporting as possible. The course should possess at least one studio, ample editing equipment and enough portable recorders to issue one per student. It should also offer access to the latest digital technology.

Second, the course should see itself as vocational first and academic second. Academic areas that have to be covered are law, ethics and public administration, but these should be closely integrated into the practical side of the course. Chief among these is law for journalists, as no news editor would chance their reputation with a reporter who might land them with a libel suit or a prosecution for contempt of court.

Figure 3 There are many routes into broadcasting, but one of the best is the one-year vocational course. Here, a radio journalism student presents a programme in the training studio at the London College of Printing. (*Andrew Boyd*)

The third indicator of a good course is its record. What jobs are past students now doing and how long did they have to wait to get them?

But perhaps the most telling test is to ask prospective employers for their recommendations and look for courses that have been recognized by the industry. It is useful to have the backing of the major journalists' union, which should produce a current list of approved courses.

Ideally, begin by looking for a course that is run by a radio or TV station, and preferably one which pays the trainee a wage while he or she is learning the ropes. An alternative is to seek sponsorship from a broadcast company to pay for your training at college. But a word of warning – it could be easier to win the lottery.

Courses range in length from a weekend to several years, from part-time to full-time. Be warned – the cost of a course will not always be an accurate indication of its value to the student. Conversion courses also exist for newspaper reporters who want to move into broadcasting.

A list of training contacts is given in the Appendix.

Degree, or not degree . . .?

Broadcasters with a degree are now in the majority, and as graduate entry is becoming the norm the best advice is for school leavers to take a degree before beginning their careers. Even if you don't need one to start with it can be useful when it comes to promotion.

Many training courses also require a degree, and academic selection panels and employers alike look for evidence of commitment to your chosen career in the form of broadcasting experience. A good deal of the right kind of experience can sometimes override the absence of a degree.

A *practical* degree in journalism or media can provide an interesting overview of broadcasting. If the course also offers an attachment to the broadcasting industry that could give you a head start later when applying for vocational courses or jobs. But avoid academic courses of the media-watching variety, which often frustrate and disappoint students who would rather work within the media than stand on the sidelines and criticize.

A good general-purpose degree would be in English – preferably at a university or college with campus radio and TV. ITN's Jonathan Munro believes a degree in a second language is even better: *'I always recommend school-leavers to get a degree in languages, as this is the most useful tool you can have, far more useful than media studies.'*

Getting a foot in the door

Assuming you have taken your training course and passed with flying colours, you now need that all-elusive job in journalism. The first thing you have to do is get your foot in the door.

The following stark advice is often given to wannabe Walter Cronkites and prospective Jeremy Paxmans: the industry has never heard of you, and right now, it neither needs you nor wants you. Being brilliant is not enough. You have to *prove* how good you are: market yourself, persuade them they will miss out if they don't agree to see you. To succeed you need wit, charm, subtlety, persistence – and heaps of talent.

The saying it is not *what* you know but *who* you know that counts is probably truer of broadcasting than many other professions. Broadcasting is a village industry. By the time a job is advertised the news editor might already have a candidate lined up, so you should make your play before the job ads appear.

The best way to put yourself in the running is to visit news editors and talk to them for twenty minutes to find out what they are looking for, tell them what you can do and see what opportunities are coming up.

Plan your campaign. Begin by sending a demonstration recording of your work and curriculum vitae, and follow these up within a week with a phone call asking for a meeting.

Your demo should be short, succinct and superb. For a job in radio news it should be on a single side of a cassette or on CD and comprise a three-minute bulletin with actuality clips (interviews with household names preferably, and all your own work) followed by a gripping interview of not longer than two and a half minutes and a sparkling package of the same length. It should be professionally presented and labelled. For TV send a short demo of your work on videocassette (VHS).

Your CV should be printed and well laid out. It should give your name, address, phone and e-mail numbers, date of birth, relevant broadcast experience (including freelance work), broadcast training, educational qualifications (briefly), language skills, brief relevant details of previous employment, whether you hold a driving licence, a note of *interesting* personal hobbies and achievements, and the names and addresses of two referees. Put your CV on a word processor and tailor it to suit each application.

'When I get your application form, the first thing I look at is your previous experience,' says former BBC World Service Editor, Terry Heron, *'what you have done, where you have been. That is the priority. **Then** I look at the panel that shows your educational achievements.'*

The interview

Preparation is everything, whether you are applying for a job or work experience. Know your station, be familiar with its output, its style. Know about the area – its industry, politics, and stories. Be familiar with the news the station is running that day and have constructive comments to make about its output and ideas on how to develop those stories. Be well briefed in current affairs. Be prepared to face newsreading, news writing or screen tests. Be early. Be smart.

The best way to get briefed is to talk to staff members who are doing the job you have applied for. Be prepared for standard interview questions:

- Why do you want to work here?
- What can you offer us?
- What do you think of the station's output?
- What do you see yourself doing in five years' time?
- Do you work well in a team?

Come over as confident, positive, lively, interesting and above all, enthusiastic.

THE CASE FOR STARTING SMALL

BBC World Service newsreader Julie Candler took a post-graduate diploma in radio journalism at Highbury College in Portsmouth, England, which she describes as 'good fun'. Then she joined BBC Radio Leicester as a producer, before becoming an announcer with the World Service. Why the switch?

'Well, you can't get a bigger audience – 140 million. I'm lucky, because we do so many different things here. We don't just do the news; we do continuity and take part in other programmes for other services.

'But I would always start in local radio. It's a very good training ground. I've done my fair share of squatting in telephone boxes, watching police sieges. You get such a breadth of experience in local radio because you get to do everything. I was the first at the scene at an air crash in Kegworth. I was still in my pyjamas. I'd only just got there. There had been lots of bomb threats and I was going round the world to ABC in America: "Julie, do you think this is a bomb?" And I would say, "Well, we're not sure at this stage . . ." It was a good training to be able to think on your feet.

'If you start off in a larger news organization you won't get to do the big stories. But there's a big story happening somewhere around the country all the time, and if you're in local radio it will probably be you who will be there.'

A level playing field?

Women

Most jobs in BBC Radio are held by women, yet the same is true of only three per cent of the top posts in the BBC's Regional Broadcasting Directorate. And women occupy only 16 per cent of positions in the next grade down. It's a situation BBC bosses agree is 'frankly unacceptable'.

And it is not only in the BBC that opportunities for women are restricted. In pan-European broadcasting, women occupy just six per cent of management posts, hold only 11 per cent of senior executive positions and make up a mere seven per cent of technical staff.

*'I think there **is** discrimination,'* says BBC local radio news editor Penny Young, *'and another problem is that women tend to get diverted because they get married and have kids, but if they really want to succeed, the opportunities are there.'*

Newsreader Julie Candler used to be a sports journalist in the mid-1980s. In those days, she says she was one of only two women reporting on sport for local radio. *'I would go down to the local football club and try to do an interview and the Leicester City manager would say: "Oh, I can't talk to a woman about football!" and pack me off. And in the Leicester Tigers rugby ground, women were not allowed in the commentary box. So I would have to sit outside.'*

But she believes opportunities today for women are levelling out. Could the same be true for black journalists?

Figure 4 BBC World Service newsreader Julie Candler, a post-graduate trainee: *'I would always start off in local radio. In a larger news organization you won't get to do the big stories.'* (*Andrew Boyd*)

Black journalists

> '*Despite the growing number of black faces on screen, among the hundreds of TV programme executives who wield power in the BBC, ITV and Channel 4 there are only four non-whites – and two of those deal exclusively with programmes for minorities ... For there to be fewer minority figures at the top of our major broadcasting organisations than there were ten years ago is a disgrace.*'
> – TREVOR PHILLIPS, HEAD OF CURRENT AFFAIRS, LWT

While more than five in a hundred in Britain are classified as of ethnic origin, only one in a hundred is thought to be employed in the media. The BBC has been criticized for recruiting too few black reporters, but has altered its recruitment policies to help redress the balance. Even so, across the networks and in the upper echelons there would appear to be some way to go.

Trevor McDonald was Britain's first black newscaster and is widely thought to be the most popular in the nation. He began his career in Trinidad in 1962 as an interviewer for local current affairs programmes. Five years later he joined the BBC in London and today is the senior anchorman at ITN. In a moment of reflection, he wondered whether he had become a token black face on British TV: '*There is a complacency here. "Look, there's always Trevor McDonald," they say. Sometimes I wonder if I have done a great disservice.*'*

McDonald's advice for anyone starting out in journalism – black, white, male or female – is: '*Come equipped with the best qualifications you can get, such as a good degree in English, and then read voraciously – the information will stick and you will be more confident about going out into this curious world of journalism.*'

Thirty-eight-year-old Eddie Botsio is another black journalist who shows that tenacity – and flexibility – can pay off. Botsio was turned down by the BBC's own training scheme, so he took a postgraduate diploma in radio journalism at the London College of Printing, which included an attachment to BBC Radio 4.

He went on to work as a reporter at BBC Radio London and got two major stories under his belt – a huge fire in the London Underground and a hurricane. After that, the BBC accepted him for further training under the Asian Afro-Caribbean Reporters' Trust.

During an attachment to BBC Belfast he was mistaken for a British soldier and threatened, and covered a bomb explosion in a swimming pool. He recalls: '*I went to the hospital and interviewed a woman who was covered from head to foot in blood. She didn't know what had happened to her little child, but as we were filming the girl turned up and there was a reunion. The only skill involved was when to shut up and let her tell her story.*'

Botsio became a staff reporter for the BBC in Southampton, and was involved in the launch of the award-winning series *Black Britain*, presenting, producing and reporting. Further stints with the BBC and ITN followed, which included coverage of the Paddington rail crash for Channel 5.

So are things evening out for black journalists? '*People are still saying things have to improve. I know a number of black journalists who are frustrated. I hope when my daughter is applying for jobs that I'm not still hearing, "Oh, we need to do something about this."*'

'*I would be the last person to cry discrimination, because I've had fantastic opportunities, but there are limits. They can be overcome if you've a will.*'

* *1999 Media Guide*, Fourth Estate, p. 78.

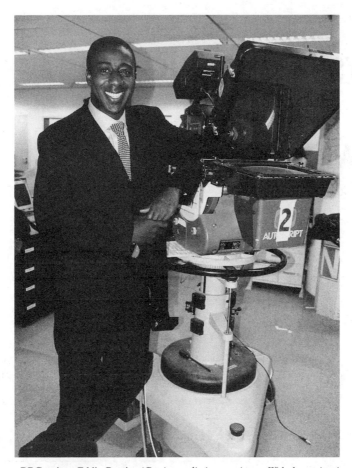

Figure 5   Former BBC trainee Eddie Botsio: *'Get journalistic experience. With determination you can break into broadcasting.'* (*Andrew Boyd*)

His top tip to would-be reporters? *'Get journalistic experience. When I first applied to the Beeb they said, "You haven't got experience." So I went away and did a course. When I went back they said, "You need more experience." So I got it, came back and got on the scheme. With determination you can do it.'*

What didn't they teach him in college? *'How to keep warm on a stakeout!'*

> *'The most important thing for any would-be journalist is not to be put off by initial rejection. Persevere with applications and don't be afraid to knock on doors to ask for work experience or simply the chance to look round. Most broadcasting organisations are far less intimidating than they would appear – and remember, everyone is always on the look-out for talent.'*
> — IVOR YORKE, THE MOVING IMAGE SOCIETY
>
> *'A career in broadcast journalism is at the very pinnacle of trendiness.'*
> — *THE MEDIA GUIDE*

NEWS GATHERING

2 What is news?

> 'Tidings, new or interesting information, fresh events reported.'
> – CONCISE OXFORD DICTIONARY
>
> 'News is the first rough draft of history.' – BEN BRADLEE
>
> 'News is the immediate, the important, the things that have impact on our lives.'
> – FREDA MORRIS, NBC
>
> 'When a dog bites a man, that is not news, but when a man bites a dog, that is news.'
> – CHARLES DANA
>
> 'News is anything that makes a reader say, "Gee Whiz!" ' – ARTHUR MCEWEN

Whatever news may be, there is more of it about than ever before – on the Net, on the growing myriad TV channels, and squawking out of the tinny speaker in the corner of the kitchen.

Survey after survey finds more people are abandoning their newspapers and turning to TV to find out what is going on in the world. More than 70 per cent now say TV has become their main source of domestic and international news and TV has finally outstripped newspapers as the primary provider of local news.*

So broadcast news rules. But what are the rules that govern the news?

Most editors would agree that newsgathering is more of an art than a science. But ask them to agree on today's top stories and many would come to blows. To select stories to satisfy a given audience you are said to need a 'nose' for news.

But if it were all a matter of nature rather than nurture there would be no excuse for a textbook like this. So let's look at the elements no self-respecting news story can be without.

---

* *Independent Television Commission Survey, 1998*. Only one in ten give local radio as their primary source of news.

Figure 6 Hunting down the news wherever it happens, then getting it out to the network. Inside the news factory at IRN. (*Courtesy IRN*)

Proximity

SMALL EARTHQUAKE IN CHILE – NOT MANY DEAD

This headline was a little joke by a *Times* sub-editor and has all the resounding impact of a damp squib. It was intended to be everything news is not – undramatic, remote and unimportant – though the irony would have been lost on anyone living in Chile.

Yet this spoof has something to say about the nature of news. For a story to have impact, it has to be relevant. For news to be relevant, it has to have proximity. Huge problems for *them* are less important than small problems for *us*.

Relevance

Even when the proximity gap is narrowed, a news item may fail to interest different groups within the same country. A surge in the price of coffee might shake up the businessmen of Nairobi, but fail to stir the fishermen and woodcarvers of Mombasa. But if the price of coffee crashed, the item would come home to everyone in Kenya – the economy would slump and they would all be affected.

But even when a story contains both touchstones of proximity and relevance, the reaction it provokes in you will depend on your upbringing, environment, education, background, beliefs, and morality. In other words, news values are subjective and newsgathering is an art, rather than a science.

Despite that, every editor would agree that the greater the effect of a story on listeners' lives, their income and emotions, the more important that item will be. And every editor knows that if a news service is to win and hold an audience, the bulk of its stories must have impact on most of the people most of the time.

Immediacy

'Yesterday's newspaper is used to wrap fish and yesterday's broadcast does not exist at all.'   – MARTIN MAYER

'The strength of radio is its immediacy. Exploit that by constantly up-dating stories and keeping them fresh. We're telling people what's happening now.'
– MALCOLM SHAW, NEWS EDITOR, INDEPENDENT RADIO

'Radio news is what happened five minutes ago and its impact on what is going to happen in the next five minutes.'
– RICHARD BESTIC, PARLIAMENTARY CORRESPONDENT

News is about what is happening *now* – or the first inkling of something that happened earlier but was hushed up. And nowhere is news more immediate than in the electronic media. *'You catch it live!'* used to be the catchphrase of one radio station's sports service. It is a boast the printed word can never match.

To the broadcast journalist, what happened yesterday is dead and buried. There has to be something new to say, some fresh angle. And with hourly headlines, even what went on at 11 will have to be updated for noon.

To put it another way: *news is only news while it is new.*

Interest

'Journalism largely consists of saying "Lord Jones dead" to people who never knew Lord Jones was alive.'   – G. K. CHESTERTON

'Worthy, but dull' is one of the most damning indictments you could make about a news report. News should make you suck in your breath and exclaim, sit up, take notice and listen.

Broadcast news is often criticized for pandering to the popular taste, but by its very nature, broadcasting caters for the mass interest, rather than that of a minority. Stories must have a wide appeal or most of the audience will change channels.

The skill of the newswriter comes in drawing out the relevance of a story and presenting it clearly and factually while making the most of every scrap of interest. This way the newswriter can give the audience what it *needs* to know – as well as what it *wants* to know.

The most interesting element in news is often people – showbusiness personalities, celebrities, big-name politicians, royalty – elite people, who we know only from a distance

Story Slug	Segment	Summary	Reporter	Background
HOME STAFFING				1
WHOWHERE		LAS VEGAS: MATES/SHAND/SAMPY/THOMPSON MAPUTO/S. AFRICA: EWART/ANSTEY/REX/SQUIRES MOSCOW: WEBSTER/OLEG/KNAPMAN JERUSALEM: MANYON/STEELE TURKEY: NEELY/PHIPPS/NERAC HONG KONG: NICHOLAS (BRADBY) BEIJING/HONG KONG: GATZ (non coverage) LONDON/SKOPJE: DAVIDSON (photographer)		
QUAKE		Death toll expected to rise way beyond the 374 so far. Clinton arrives in Arkara today, before going onto Istanbul Tuesday for the OSCE summit. . Experts also warning that the pattern of aftershocks strongly suggest that the next big quake will hit Istanbul. Neely heading to country to see damage. For EN	NEELY EX RTV dish for EN	1
IRELAND		All parties in the peace process meet at Stormont. Trimble will probably try and buy more time to get UUP support for the proposals on the table.	IRVINE	3
FAYED		Start of libel trial in which former MP Neil Hamilton is suing Mohamed Al Fayed over cash for questions allegations . Listed for four weeks , Fayed to take the witness stand this week. NOTE:Fayed, as defendant will give evidence before Hamilton. Also Fayed Will enter court via side door to avoid scrum. There is a chance of an out of court settlement. Legal arguments all am. Court 13. GHOSH/HOSKYNS/PRISCILLA.0800	GHOSH x SIS/ED	
BEEF		EU Agriculture Ministers meet in Brussels for monthly committee. Nick Brown comes face to face with his counterpart, Jean Glavany. Beef not " officially" on agenda, Brown to present papers to the Commission calling on legal action against French - who may decide their move today	SMITH	2
AIR SEX		Couple accused of having sex on a trans-Atlantic plane due at Manchester magistrates court	BAKER x SISMAN	
GLITTER		The woman at the centre of the Gary Glitter case breaks her silence and drops her anonymity when she gives an interview to Talk Radio. Appears with Derek Hatton between 1100-1200. Details in dayfile	REPORTER TBA on merit	
ROYAL TOUR		Queen arrives Mozambique 1200 local.(1000G) Met by President Chissano. In PM Queen opens trade exhibition. Duke visits malaria control project. Banquet in eve. Then depart for Uk.	EWART EX MAPUTO Booked ex Newsforce 1745-1815/2150-2210G	
BUS SUMMIT		Prescott meets leaders of Britain's bus industry. Among the issues likely to dominate are the running-down of rural services and deregulation. Starts at 0900; Prescott speech 1000. Runs until 1500. WESTHEAD producing. (Poss LTN live with Lord McDonald - Millbank to confirm	CHOI + LTN LIVE	1

Figure 7 Newsrooms produce diaries or prospects each day to show the stories they plan to cover and the reporters assigned to them. This ITN list extends to several pages. (*Courtesy ITN*)

and who interest us out of curiosity, envy, admiration, malice or affection; people through whom we live our lives vicariously, or whose actions and decisions influence and shape our existence.

Drama

Dramatic events of the stranger-than-fiction variety make striking headlines. Shotgun sieges, violent crimes, car chases, cliff-top rescues – the greater the drama, the greater its prominence in a bulletin. Excitement, danger, adventure, conflict, have as great an appeal to the newswriter as the novelist or movie-maker. And TV is a slave to dramatic pictures. As far as TV is concerned, no pictures, no story.

The art of newswriting is closely related to storytelling – news items are referred to as stories – but if the news is to maintain integrity and credibility, the temptation to dress up the facts to make them more like fiction has to be avoided.

Entertainment

In some journalistic circles entertainment is still a dirty word, but news and showbusiness often go hand in glove. There is an element of performance in the presentation of news and sometimes pure entertainment in its writing. The *kicker* or *tailpiece* is a prime example. This is the light or humorous story at the end of a bulletin, immortalized in the UK by ITN, whose policy to 'leave 'em smiling' is pure showbiz.

Figure 8 ITN's 6.30 flagship – some say it's no substitute for *News at Ten*, booted off the airwaves to make way for prime-time movies. (*Courtesy ITN*)

Information and entertainment are often held in tension. Where news ends and entertainment begins is more than a matter of house style. It is one of the crucial questions facing the news media today. Where that line is drawn will depend on the target audience for a programme and the priority that is placed on high ratings. The surest way to boost those ratings is to increase the amount of entertainment that goes into the mix.

'Steven McBride is 20 years old.'

So what? It might be information, but it's not news.

'Half his short life has been spent in prisons, borstals and other institutions.'

Well, that's sad and may be of some interest to somebody because it is unusual, but it is still not news.

'Steven McBride is coming out today . . . a free man.'

It is information, it has some interest and it is new because he is coming out today, but it is still not news.

'Three months ago, McBride was sentenced to **life** *for the murder of his parents.'*

His parents. Now this is important. How can a man who has been charged with murdering his parents be let out of prison after only three months?

'New evidence has come to light to show conclusively that McBride did not commit the murders and that the killer is still on the loose and has already struck again.'

The information is new, interesting, and important, but for it to be newsworthy, it would have to be relevant to you, the audience. If the murders were committed in your home town – that is news – and local radio and TV there would almost certainly run it as their lead.

Different types of news

Many first-time visitors to a newsroom ask the same question: 'Where do you get all your news?' The answer is, it may not grow on trees, but there is usually plenty to be found if you know where to look, as the rest of this chapter explains.

'We reflect our audience's real priorities,' says Dean Squire of BBC Radio Leicester, first of the BBC's local radio stations. *'Our aim is to bring people news both from around the corner and around the world.'**

After cutting their teeth on bread and butter stories, many reporters think about moving on to network news or television. But whether a news story is local, national or international, it will usually fall into one or more of the following categories.

Emergencies

The emergency services deal with the high points of human drama – fires, sea or mountain rescues – whenever human life is at risk there is a story.

* '10 Million Listeners and Still Counting', *Radio Times*, 7 November 1992.

Accidents are a steady but unpredictable source of news, but the larger the area covered by the news service, the more serious these would have to be to warrant coverage, otherwise the bulletins would be full of little else, so reporting of accidents is usually confined to death or serious injury.

Crime

Rising crime rates offer a steady source of news. The larger the area, the more crime there will be, so only more serious offences are likely to be reported.

Crime stories have many phases, from the actual incident, to the police raid, arrest, and eventual appearance in court.

> *'Crime is still a big one. People love crime stories, they really do, no matter where in the world you are people want to know about what is happening on the streets; the murder, the rapes, the robberies – that occupies a fairly large chunk of time.'*
> – ANNETTE BOSWORTH, WEEI, BOSTON*

Local and national government

Every action of government – locally or nationally – has a bearing on a potential audience, and whatever affects an audience is news. To prevent bulletins becoming swamped with items from city hall, news policy is usually to report only the stories that have the greatest effect on the largest number of people.

Planning and developments

Building developments are news which is emerging before your eyes. Big plans make big news, and new projects, leisure complexes, shopping malls and housing schemes which impact on an area are certain to be given the big news treatment in any local newsroom. Nationally, the difference is one of scale. Newsworthy developments would include major road-building schemes, new townships, dams and other large projects.

But the concept of developments as news expands beyond public works to mean any form of major change that is happening or is about to happen that will affect a given audience.

Conflict and controversy

> *'Almost inevitably, anything that threatens people's peace, prosperity or well-being is news and likely to make headlines.'* – ALASTAIR HETHERINGTON†

News is about change – events that shape our society and alter the way we live. Conflict is the essence of drama, and the dramatic makes news.

---

* From WEEI, video by Ian Hyams.
† From *News, Newspapers and Television*, Macmillan, 1985.

This can be physical clashes in the streets or a conflict of ideals – a row at the local council or in Parliament. Where actions or ideas mean upheavals in society, then that conflict is news. Every issue in the public eye has those who are for it and those who are against it. Broadcast journalism can cover what is happening, stimulate debate, and bring important issues into sharper focus.

Pressure groups

Pressure groups are people who have organized themselves to stir up controversy. They either want change or are opposed to it, so their demands usually make news. Reaction to government policy, events or developments can make an effective follow-up to a story. The reporter seeks out the players in the underlying conflict, exposes the points of contention and so uncovers the news.

Industry

Employment is a major factor in most people's lives, so developments in industry make big news. Be they layoffs or job recruitment – either way they will affect the workforce and prosperity of an area.

Health

Health makes news, from outbreaks of mad cow disease to a shortage of blood donors.

Human interest

A human interest story may be defined as an extraordinary thing that has happened to an ordinary person. Soft news is lightweight material which people like to gossip about, such as who's won the pools or discovered a Ming vase in their shed. It is the unusual, ironic, or offbeat; the sort of story that people like to swap in pubs and bars.

Personalities

Visiting personalities, royalty or politicians are usually good for a local news item, especially if their visit is linked to a local event or occasion. Nationally, the bigger the name, the more likely it is to make news. The more entertainment a station mixes with its news, the more prominently personalities – especially from showbusiness – are likely to feature.

Sport

Many in the audience tolerate the news only because they know if they stay tuned they will get the latest football, cricket or rugby results. Local teams and clubs often feature strongly in regional news, especially if they are doing well or badly in their leagues, and this is reflected at a national level, where news usually focuses on the promotion battles and relegation struggles that mark the changing fortunes of the top and bottom contenders.

Seasonal news

Seasonal news includes Christmas shopping, January sales, the first cuckoo, the tourist season, seasonal unemployment.

Special local interest

No two news areas are the same. Each will throw up stories peculiar to its own geography and make-up. An area with a car factory will create news about recruitment, layoffs, new models and the fortunes of the company. A seaport with a naval base will produce stories of warships stationed there and naval exercises involving local ships and men. A mountainous region will generate items about missing climbers and mountain rescues.

Distinguishing features give an area its identify. Audience loyalty is built when a station is seen to be providing a truly local news service.

Weather

Regular weather updates are one of the main features in the local news. TV companies spend a great deal of money providing a high-quality weather service. On the national news satellite pictures are often combined with detailed graphics and elaborate weather maps.

Weather normally follows the news, but at times of extreme conditions, the weather itself will make headlines. Radio comes into its own when there are flash floods, droughts

Figure 9 No news programme is complete without a weather report. The BBC weather centre is linked to a computer at the Met Office. The weather map is electronically inserted into the picture. The weathercaster sees a faint image projected from behind – just bright enough to show her where to point. She uses the remote control in her hand to switch to the next picture. (*Courtesy BBC*)

or serious snowfalls. Local radio in Wales picked up huge audiences one severe winter by running a snowdesk. Residents and travellers were snowed under and cut off for days at a time. The station put out a constant stream of information and gave advice by telephone. The service was a lifeline. Few things can touch radio for its immediacy in times of crisis. Couple the radio with the Internet and you have the potential for a first-rate emergency information service.

Traffic

Next to the weather, the first thing many people want to know in the morning is whether the roads will be clear for getting to work. Radio is the only medium motorists can safely take in while driving. In car-orientated societies where large numbers commute to work, traffic and travel news can pick up big audiences. These periods are known as *drive-time*. Radio stations can give up-to-the-minute information on which roads are blocked and where there are traffic jams.

Some car radios can automatically scan channels and seek out the latest traffic reports. In Britain, the Automobile Association (AA) has its own reporters who go live into local radio drive-time programmes from AA offices around the country.

Some larger stations, such as Capital Radio in London, have their own aircraft scanning the roads for traffic snarl-ups, with a reporter on board who can send back live updates over a radio link.

Mobile phones are also frequently used to get a first-hand picture of the build-up of traffic from the motorists who are trapped in it. Many stations extend their service to cover all types of commuting by providing drive-time reports about buses, trains, ferries and flights.

Animals

Few items prompt greater reaction from the legions of pet lovers than shaggy dog stories. Men, women and babies may die in fires but fail to provoke a murmur, but if anyone tries to poison a poodle, the switchboards are likely to be jammed with calls.

---

200 000 news bulletins a year; 140 000 Met Office weather reports; 90 000 AA Roadwatch updates; 200 000 hours a year of programming; 10 000 000 listeners each week.   – BBC LOCAL RADIO

Checklist

For any item which does not fall into the above categories, the test of whether or not it is news to a given audience is:

Is it:

- Relevant?
- Important?
- Tragic?
- Unusual?

- The last?
- The most expensive?
- Immediate or imminent?
- Interesting?
- Controversial?
- The first?
- The biggest?
- Funny, or ironic?

But the first question an editor will ask is: *Does it affect **our** audience?*
And for the local newsroom that means: *Is it local?*

> *'News is something someone, somewhere doesn't want you to print. The rest is advertising.'*
> – ANON

Fieldwork

1 Video record a local TV news programme and list the stories that appear. See if each of the items will fit into one or more of the categories in the summary above. If you cannot place any of the items, work out suitable new categories into which they will fit.

2 Record national and local radio bulletins of comparable lengths on the same day and list the stories in each.

   Go through each story to see how it rates in your view in terms of *relevance*, *significance*, *immediacy*, *interest* and *entertainment*. Award each story points out of three under each category, where three is the maximum score (*Very important*, etc.) and zero is the lowest. Add up the totals and see which bulletin scores the highest overall. Is that the one you preferred? If not, why do you think it rated so highly?

3 Which stories did you find the most relevant and why? In what way is the relevance of those stories determined by their geographical proximity to you?

   Which stories did you find the most important and what made some stories more interesting than others? Why?

   Decide which you think is the most controversial story in each bulletin and why.

4 Focusing on the idea that News = Change, work out what are the biggest changes happening in your local area at the moment that might find their way into a news bulletin.

5 News has just come in of a big fire in a chemical warehouse in the centre of town. Some of the chemicals are highly explosive. Police say the whole warehouse is like a giant bomb and are evacuating the area. Given unlimited resources, how would you cover the story for TV? (Split into teams of four if you are in a class and discuss.)

NEWS GATHERING

3 News sources

'Journalism – an ability to meet the challenge of filling the space'
– REBECCA WEST, *NEW YORK HERALD TRIBUNE*

There are some days when news just seems to fall into your lap. Everywhere you turn another story is breaking. Days like these are a journalist's dream.

The nightmare begins in the holiday season when nothing seems to happen. Local check calls to the police elicit jokey offers from bored constables to *'go out and bite a dog for you'*.

And so the media resort to clutching at flying saucers and running items about nude bathing on the beaches. This is known as the *silly season*.

Most times the newsperson's lot is somewhere between these extremes. What stories there are have to be dug for. Graft is required to turn a tip-off into hard facts.

Reporters

The biggest source of news for any radio or TV station should be its reporting staff. Many local stations rightly insist that their journalists live in the community to which they are broadcasting. Through everyday contact with people in the area, from their observations as they shop or drive to work, will come ideas for stories.

From the car window the reporter notices that the construction of a new factory seems to be behind time. There has been little progress for almost a month; so the reporter pulls in at the roadside and asks the foreman why. Closer to the station, rows of publicly owned houses on an inner-city site seem to be rotting away; what can the authorities do to make them habitable? Squatters are moving in; are the neighbours concerned? Would the squatters resist attempts to evict them? Reporters need to keep their eyes and ears open.

Wealthier stations are able to employ *specialists* – reporters who are experts in certain areas, with experience behind them and a key set of contacts. Chief fields are local government, industry, or crime.

The job of the *investigative journalist* is to find something wrong and expose it. He or she is a positive force for change, a professional with the ability to penetrate the closed ranks of vested interests and free imprisoned information from behind enemy lines. Investigative reporters may also work in teams on projects such as documentaries.

Figure 10   Listening room of the BBC's news monitoring service at Caversham. The BBC tunes into the radio, TV and news agencies of some 140 countries, transmitted in around 70 different languages. Information is fed to the BBC, government and the press. (*Courtesy BBC*)

Not every station can spare the time or has the scope to permit an ordinary reporter to develop into an investigative journalist, but all reporters have to be investigators at heart.

Contacts

When the big story breaks, the first thing a reporter reaches for is the contacts book – their most valuable resource. It contains the names and phone numbers of everyone in the area who regularly makes or comments on the news, plus national figures whose sphere of influence may include the reporter's own 'beat'.

The relationship between reporters and their contacts is doubled-edged. The newswriter needs a story, the newsmaker needs publicity. Clearly, a line has to be drawn, and the place to draw it is well before the point where editorial freedom and integrity begin to be compromised.

After a while, reporters may find that some of their regular contacts become friends. That may be fine when there is good news involving that contact, but if the news is bad, it still has to be reported. In the end, reporters must maintain their independence. They can never afford to owe anyone favours.

Newsroom diary

Newsrooms keep a diary, which is made up each day by the news editor. It gives details of stories the newsroom will cover, the times of events and the reporters allotted to them.

The diary, or a list of prospects drawn from that diary, is the first thing reporters look at when they arrive on shift. It is the day's plan of action; the newsroom route map, and it will probably be stored on computer.

The editor makes up the diary from information in the post, tips from reporters and stories that are known to be breaking. Files are usually kept on major stories containing up-to-date cuttings and background information. Bigger stations have libraries and news information services to help with more extensive research.

Files

In its simplest form the futures file can be a single drawer in a filing cabinet with drop-files numbered 1 to 31, one for each day of the month. These days it would typically be a folder in the newsroom computer. Selected news releases about events at some future date are noted in the diary and put on file. Court appearances of newsworthy cases are filed ahead, with copy relating to earlier hearings.

An *archive* may be developed by transferring the month's files to an identical filing drawer with all the copy used and possibly recordings of the output. Bulletins and news programmes may also be stored in the archive, either as hard copy or as digital recordings.

All incoming copy of interest, but which failed to make the bulletins, is kept on file. Where hard copy is used it will probably be impaled on a spike or kept in a basket.

The trouble with storing information on paper is that it takes too much space to allow files to go back a long way, and increasingly stations are keeping their files on computer databases.

Stories can be instantly recalled, even if the computer operator has forgotten the date or author of the copy. One or two key words are typed in and, providing those words featured in the story, the copy will quickly come up on the screen.

The WPB is often the biggest file of all. Newsrooms get flooded with useless information and propaganda, most of which ends up, with scarcely a glance, where it belongs, in the waste paper bin.

Check calls

A story that is happening right *now*, such as an armed robbery, fire, or air crash, is known in Britain as *breaking news* and in America as a *spot story*. Prime sources of breaking news are emergency services – fire, police, ambulance, coastguard, etc. – which are contacted regularly. These inquiries are known as *check calls*. Often they begin by dialling a number and listening to a recording of the events the emergency services consider most important. Such recordings are usually updated several times a day, but they will often bear little relation to your deadline and leave you at the mercy of a non-journalist's news judgement. So reporters often prefer to get through to a living, breathing officer.

The problem is that in an area rich in news media, the overworked emergency services may be tempted to shake off callers by saying nothing is happening even when it is. Shift changes may mean a call is made before the new duty officer has managed to catch up on his/her paperwork, so he/she is unaware of the events of the previous few hours and gives the reporter a false impression.

A common mistake is for the reporter to try to get information from the wrong person. In provincial British police stations constables are rarely authorized to talk to the media, who should instead refer inquiries to duty inspectors or station sergeants. If a serious crime has been committed, a station sergeant may know little about it, so the best contact would be the detective from CID (Criminal Investigation Department) or equivalent, handling the case.

Constabularies may be organized on a county basis, each with its own press officer whose task it is to collect important news from police stations and release it to the media. They can overlook the bread and butter items and be too slow off the mark with breaking stories.

Press officers are distant from the scene of the crime, so information can take some time to get to them. To make matters worse, local police, who *do* know what is happening, are often instructed in major crimes to redirect all inquiries to the press office.

Often the police need the media as much as the media needs the police, for making appeals for witnesses and help in tracing missing persons. Reporters are not obliged to cooperate, but goodwill is often the best way of ensuring a steady flow of information.

Emergency services radio

The surest way to keep in touch with major breaking news is to tune in to emergency services radio. By monitoring the transmissions of police and fire services you can hear the news as it is actually happening, instead of waiting for the official version to be collated and sanitized by a spokesperson.

In Britain it is illegal to listen to police radio and take action as a result of that information. The law is intended to deter criminals from listening to police activity. To make it harder, messages from base are given on one frequency and mobile units reply on another, so only half the conversation can be heard at one time.

Figure 11 Media feeds off media . . . monitoring TV coverage of local elections at a London radio station. (*Andrew Boyd*)

In America it is common for reporters to turn up at an incident before the police, but British law means that writing a story from a police broadcast or sending a reporter to the scene could result in a prosecution. In practice it would be difficult to prove the reporter had been listening to police radio.

A more likely outcome would be the straining of relationships between the newsroom and the police, which could result in a loss of goodwill and stem the flow of official information.

In places where listening in is legal, newsrooms commonly use radio *scanners*. These monitor the emergency airwaves for a transmission and home in on the conversation.

The 10 code

In many countries the police talk to one another in a code designed to help them communicate clearly and rapidly over the air, while at the same time mystifying unauthorized eavesdroppers.

Frequently the code used is a variation of the 10 code. Instead of saying *'Fight in progress'*, for example, an officer might say *'10–10'*, followed by the location. Each force may have its own version of the code where the numbers mean something different.

Some of the key messages in one variation of the 10 code are:

10–31 Crime in progress
10–32 Man with a gun
10–33 Emergency
10–34 Riot
10–35 Major crime alert
10–50 Accident
10–57 Hit and run
10–79 Notify coroner

Whatever is heard over police radio *must* be checked before use. 'Emergencies' can turn out to be a storm in a teacup – or something else. People rushed to a field in Cheshire after police messages warned that a flying saucer had crash-landed. When they turned up they were promptly arrested by little blue men who charged them with listening illegally to police radio.*

Politicians

'Too much of what I see is press release broadcasting. You automatically go and get a ministry, then somebody from the opposition. All these people do is give you party political statements. I find that boring and can't believe the public learns anything. You already know what the political parties are going to say, and I can't see where any of that does a damn thing to improve the quality of our understanding.'
    – HARRY RADLIFFE, BUREAU CHIEF, CBS NEWS

* *The Guardian*, 23 March 1993.

Figure 12 Chasing contacts under pressure . . . if the computer database goes down the writing's on the wall at BBC Southern Counties Radio. (*Andrew Boyd*)

Local politicians are a prime source of news for the regional newsroom. Usually they are happy to oblige as this raises their profile and may win votes. A reporter should be wise to that and make sure legitimate news, rather than vote-catching rhetoric, gets on air.

Every journalist should know the names of the area's representatives in both local and national government, and should have contact numbers for them at work and at home as well as their mobile phone numbers.

When politicians are not making news themselves, they are usually good for a comment or reaction to stories that affect their constituencies or wards. Political comment is cheap and readily available and this type of reaction can be overdone, lead to accusations of political bias, and leave a bulletin sounding as dull as a party political broadcast. Use sparingly.

Pressure groups

A similar warning applies to using pressure groups for reaction and comment: beware of vested interests. Big pressure groups include trades unions and employers' organizations. Smaller groups abound such as the Jubilee Campaign, which is pressing for the forgiveness of the Developing World's debt, and the Animal Liberation Front, which sometimes takes criminal action against vivisection laboratories. Many charities also act as pressure groups.

Beware of unrepresentative groups with only a handful of members. Bona fide pressure groups have an important contribution to make to public debate.

Staged events

Staging a news event is the pressure group's ultimate way of winning attention. These usually fall into one of three categories: *protest*; *announcement* and *set-piece*.

The protest

This is the pressure group trying to give its voice as wide a public hearing as possible. A three-lane highway is to be constructed across green fields to run alongside a housing estate. Residents, environmentalists, and opposition politicians form an action group to stage a march on the town hall. To make sure the cameras are there they make the event as visual as possible, with people dressed in fancy costumes and carrying banners. To ensure radio coverage they chant and sing specially written protest songs.

The announcement

This is more formal, and often takes the shape of a news conference. When the town planners announce their three-lane highway they do so with a lavish presentation. All the media is invited to a conference in the chandeliered opulence of the town hall banqueting room. Drinks are laid on and a buffet provided.

When reporters have been wined and dined and their journalistic sensibilities submerged beneath a stupor of alcohol, the mayor and other senior officials are ceremoniously invited to make their presentation. The road scheme is flourished with neat and convincing rhetoric about better traffic flow, reduced accident figures and the positive effect on trade in the town. For the cameras, there are stylish mock-ups of the road and artists' impressions. For the media, press packs are provided with slickly written articles the organizers hope will be published unaltered. Key speakers are available immediately after the presentation for photocalls and interviews.

The set-piece

This is usually staged simply for publicity. The new highway has been built, and a TV personality hired to open it by leading a cavalcade of vintage cars along its length – very visual and almost assured of TV coverage. At its best the set-piece provides a bright and appealing story for the bulletin, at its worst it can be news manipulation of the first order.

A prime example was the funeral of an IRA hunger striker that received widespread coverage on British television. This was largely thanks to the specially constructed grandstand provided by the terrorist organization just for the cameras.

At the other extreme was the 'Great Auk Story'. Reporters from British newspapers and a TV journalist were lured to the remote Orkney Islands where a team of five eccentrics was believed to be embarking on an expedition to find the Great Auk, a seabird thought to have been extinct for 150 years. Hopes were fuelled by reported sightings by islanders. When the bird eventually did make an appearance it was not only extinct, it was stuffed. It turned out to be a stunt for a whisky company. It was not wholly successful. At least one reporter, peeved at being taken on a wild Auk chase, refused to name the distillery which had organized the stunt.

Where news events are a lavish attempt at news management by publicity seekers, journalists should be aware of this and not let it influence their news judgement. Money talks, but you don't have to listen.

News releases

Each morning, editors in broadcast newsrooms have a pile of mail dumped before them on their desks. Added to that are yards of curly fax paper and an electronic mountain of e-mails.

Yet most of the items dispatched to the media will end up in the recycling bin after scarcely a second glance. That is because so much is irrelevant and of little interest to the audience. Middle East countries have been known to send regular bulletins on their economic progress and internal politics to small-town radio stations in England.

To sift the wheat from the chaff, incoming news releases are copytasted. To scrutinize each item carefully could take hours, so each envelope (where applicable) is ripped open and its contents hastily scanned. Unless a news angle presents itself almost immediately the copy is filed in the bin.

Most of the material comprises public relations handouts – usually dressed-up advertising the writers hope will pass as news. They are usually disappointed. If the handout is one of the small percentage that does contain a possible story, it will be checked and written up into copy.

Some news releases carry *embargoes*, which means they are not to be used before a certain release date. Public relations people use the embargo to try to control the flow of news, and prevent stories being run in what they would regard as a haphazard fashion. On the plus side, the embargo gives the newsroom time to prepare its report by giving advanced warning of the event.

The Queen's New Year's Honours List is a good example of embargoed material. The list is sent out well before the official announcement. Local stations can then produce stories about people in their area that are ready to run the moment the embargo is lifted.

Syndicated recordings

Among the daily plethora of unsolicited material that arrives in the newsroom may be a number of recorded items sent in by public relations companies. These are often available free of charge and usually have some advertising tie-up.

Tearfund
100 Church Road, Teddington, Middlesex TW11 8QE, United Kingdom

Press Telephone: +44 (0)181 977 6061
Facsimile: +44 (0)181 943 3594
Pager: 0941 100200 184451

Internet: www.tearfund.org
E-mail: media@tearfund.dircon.co.uk

MEDIA RELEASE

Embargoed until 0001 Monday 10th January 2000

Survey reveals public demand for 'ethical tourism'

A majority of British holiday makers would be willing to pay more for their holidays abroad if the extra money ensured good wages and working conditions for staff in resorts and hotels, and preservation of the environment in communities being visited, according to a survey published today (10/1/00) by Christian relief and development agency Tearfund.

As tour companies and travel agents tempt holiday makers with glossy New Year brochures, Tearfund's survey of more than 2000 adults reveals that British travellers do not simply respond to the best holiday bargains on offer. If given a choice they are increasingly willing to take ethical considerations into account when booking holidays.

Nearly half those questioned said they would be more likely to travel with a company that had a written ethical code, which suggests that there is an opportunity for tour companies to gain a competitive edge in the tourism market. More than half said they would pay an average of an extra five per cent - or £25 on a £500 holiday - to guarantee ethical standards like fair wages and reversal of damage to the environment caused by tourism.

"These findings indicate that, in the wake of the rising popularity of ethical investments and fairly-traded goods, there is significant public support for a move towards ethical tourism," says Andy Atkins, Public Policy Advisor for Tearfund. "In the developing world where tourism is rapidly growing, ethical tourism can help to make a difference to the lives of poor people. The extra five per cent which holiday makers say they are prepared to pay may sound small, but in fact it would be the equivalent of adding an extra £100 million to the UK aid budget."

to page 2

A member body of the Evangelical Alliance and Evangelical Missionary Alliance
Tear Fund. Registered office: as above Registered in England: 994339 A company limited by guarantee. Registered charity number: 265464

Figure 13 Embargoed news releases give advanced information on the understanding nothing will be published until the release date, giving the newsroom time to prepare the story. (*Courtesy TEARFUND*)

The video version is known as the *Video News Release* (VNR). This, and its radio equivalent, are more sophisticated variations of the news release which appeal to producers who are slothful or overstretched and who may be grateful to receive something for nothing. But as the saying goes, there is no such thing as a free lunch. The PR company hopes stations will find a slot for the item and play it on air unedited. Used in this way, syndicated recordings are simply free, unadulterated, publicity.

They may be interviews with airline bosses talking about new or cheaper flights; company directors explaining plans for a superstore in the area or even agricultural hints and tips from a government agency.

At best, syndicated items are harmless, even useful, fillers. At worst they can be scarcely disguised adverts or propaganda. No unsolicited recordings should be used without checking for violations of the advertising code, and that journalistically and technically the piece is up to standard and relevant to the audience. Handle with care.

Freelances

Most newsrooms supplement their own material by buying news tip-offs and stories from freelances. Non-staff members who contribute regularly are known as *stringers* or correspondents; working journalists who add considerably to the eyes and ears of a station. Freelances may also be employed to fill for absent members.

Stringers are often local newspaper reporters boosting their incomes by selling copy to other media in the area – with or without the blessing of their editors. Some will make their living this way.

The most organized may band together to form a local news agency. These often specialize in fields such as court, council, or sports reporting – assignments that would often take too much time to make it worth an editor's while to cover. Instead, a stringer will be commissioned to cover the event, and will usually file for a number of stations. Stringers will either be specially commissioned to report a story, or will offer their copy 'on spec.', in the hope that the station will buy it.

Advantages and disadvantages of using stringers

Advantages

- Stringers are cost-effective because they are often paid only for work that gets used on air;
- They enhance a station's 'ground cover', by using local specialist knowledge to get stories that might not be available to staff reporters;
- They can be commissioned to cover stories that would be too time-consuming to warrant staff coverage;
- Experienced broadcast freelances can fill for staff members who are sick or on holiday.

Disadvantages

- Stringer copy is seldom exclusive as their living depends on supplying news to as many outlets as possible;
- Copy may not be in broadcast style, as many stringers are newspaper journalists more familiar with writing for print;

- Stringers have to sell their copy to make a living, so stories may be dressed up to make them more marketable;
- Stringers are less accountable than staffers who can be more readily disciplined for their mistakes.

Tip-offs

Another source of news is the tip-off, from known contacts or members of the audience, who may phone in with what they consider to be news items. In the USA, where union regulations permit, some stations appoint a number of authorised tipsters from the audience who call in when they spot a possible story. One station in Atlanta, Georgia, even went to the length of issuing tipsters with car stickers and giving a cash bonus for the tip of the week.

Items from tipsters cannot be given the same weight as tip-offs from bona fide stringers or correspondents: the information is not from a trained journalist, the source may be unreliable, the facts confused or even libellous. Also, every station has its time wasters and hangers-on who phone in or call round out of sheer self-importance. Worst of all, the tipster may be malicious, and the information a hoax.

Hoaxes

MISSING ARISTOCRAT LORD LUCAN SPOTTED IN SOUTH AFRICA

GADAFFI ORDERS DEATH OF EXPELLED DIPLOMATS

PRINCE CHARLES ATTACKS ARCHITECT

ROBERT DE NIRO TO STAR IN YORKSHIRE RIPPER MOVIE

'I conned CNN into believing Gorbachev was resigning, long before he did . . . billions were lost on foreign exchanges.'

– All his own work – mass-hoaxer Rocky Ryan.

'Ryan is a pain in the rear but knowing there are hoaxers like him about ought to make all of us more careful about thorough checking of the facts. In a way he actually might be good for us.'

– NEWSDESK EXECUTIVE QUOTED IN *UK PRESS GAZETTE**

Broadcast news, with its quick-fire deadlines and lack of time for checks and balances, sometimes falls prey to the most elaborate of hoaxes. People ring up claiming to be contacts who are known by the station, such as police inspectors, and offer phoney information.

A person claiming to be a well-known sports commentator telephoned the BBC's national radio newsroom with the snap that a British racing driver had been killed. It was a hoax.

* 'Me, Luciano and the Pope', Rocky Ryan, *The Guardian*, 2 November 1992.

BBC TV news has been hoaxed about an air crash, and a tip-off on April fool's day caused the independent station, Essex Radio, to put out news of an armed man holding a hostage. This tip, on the newsroom's ex-directory hot-line, came three minutes before the bulletin. When the police heard the news they panicked and sent their cars racing to the scene only to discover that they and the radio station had been duped.

If in doubt, check it out. The only sure protection against the hoaxer is a set of sharp wits and the common sense to check the information.

If someone rings up claiming to be a regular contact and does not ring true for some reason, get their number and check it against the known contact's number. Even if it matches, ring them back to make sure they had not simply looked up the number in the phone book. If the caller is genuine, they should not object to the care with which their information is being checked.

Occasionally, a tip-off will yield some useful information, but for safety's sake *all* tip-offs, whether they appear genuine or not, must be checked before running – even if it does mean missing the deadline. In the end, accuracy counts for more than speed – *if it doesn't check out, chuck it out*.

Wire services and news agencies

The major external source of news is the international news agencies. Among the largest is Reuters, with more than 70 bureaux around the world, supplying news by satellite to upwards of 200 broadcasters in 85 countries. Other global giants include the US-based Associated Press (AP) and Worldwide Television News (WTN), which has camera crews in 90 cities supplying news 24 hours a day to more than 1000 broadcasters.

Britain's domestic news agency is the Press Association (PA), whose legion of journalists and stringers provide some 1500 stories a day to most British newsrooms. Commonwealth equivalents include the Australian Associated Press (AAP) and Canadian Press.

Agencies employ correspondents whose reports are relayed directly into newsroom computers or onto wire machines. Audio and video reports are beamed to newsrooms by satellite or piped in by landline, where they are re-recorded for later use.

Agency correspondents can effectively boost even the smallest station's coverage to incorporate national or international news, multiplying by many times the number of reporters at that station's disposal and leaving local journalists free to concentrate on their patch.

As well as news, some agencies offer specialized wires, covering fields of interest such as weather, sport, or business news.

The network

A logical step from relying on the resources of agencies or freelances is for broadcast organizations to pool their news stories and programmes.

This produces economies of scale. If five stations take the same programme, then the costs are spread five ways. When stations work together more cash can be found to produce higher quality programmes. Material formerly beyond the reach of a small station may now be made available under a pooling scheme. This is the principle behind networking.

Networking can take place in a formalized system where all the stations are owned and regulated by a single body, such as the BBC, or in a looser federation, such as Independent

---

WORLD NEWS

POLL – Scots and Welsh unimpressed with parliaments
OUTLOOK – World Business News at 1105 GMT, Feb 22
OUTLOOK – World News at 1100 GMT
Italy's PM talks with Syrians on Mideast peace
Indonesia parliament to quiz Wiranto on East Timor
Myanmar brushes off US retention of sanctions
FEATURE – Home rule will restore N. Ireland potential
FEATURE – Mobile Net players plug content at CeBIT
Prosecutor appeals against genocide suspect's release
Schroeder adviser rejects calls to boycott Austria
S. Korean President Kim praises N. Korean leader
Deadline looms for comment on Pinochet report
Palestinian students, police clash in Hebron
Gucci's Tom Ford says he has no plans to step down
Russia to shut Chechen border for fear of attacks
HK offers residency to remaining boatpeople
Cricket – Sri Lanka board interim committee to resign
Israel court hands two life terms to Arab

Dozens die in Nigeria religious clashes – witnesses

KADUNA, Nigeria, Feb 22 (Reuters) – Dozens of people were killed in fighting in the northern Nigerian city of Kaduna between Christians and Moslems demanding the introduction of Islamic law, witnesses said on Tuesday.

"Police are firing indiscriminately at the rioters but they are refusing to retreat. There are bodies all over the streets," said Reuters correspondent Felix Onuah from the working class Sabo district of the city.

Police said they had picked up 25 bodies from the streets overnight, while fighting continued in parts of the city where fighting flared on Monday after a march by thousands of Christians protesting against demands for the introduction of sharia.

The introduction of sharia in one state and growing clamour from Moslems in other northern states has polarised religious opinion in the oil-producing country of at least 108 million, Africa's most populous nation.

Ethnic and political tension has been on the rise in Nigeria since President Olusegun Obasanjo took office last May to end 15 years of military dictatorship.

"What more can we do? The situation is desperate," said one police officer in Kaduna.

Figure 14 News agencies pump out hundreds of stories each day, considerably adding to the reporting strength of the newsroom. But before agency copy can be used on air stories have to be rewritten to suit the station style. The report from Reuters might have to be boiled down to 90 words or less and rewritten for reading aloud. (*Courtesy Reuters*)

Radio in the UK. A declining number of commercial stations now operate singly. Many are clustered into groups such as GWR, whose members include stations in the Chiltern Radio Network which pool their resources.

Canada and Australia both have their equivalents of the BBC – the Canadian Broadcasting Corporation and the Australian Broadcasting Corporation. In most developing countries the State retains a high degree of control over TV and radio.

The first US national network came into operation in 1928, with 56 stations under the control of the National Broadcasting Company (NBC). Others followed, including ABC (American Broadcasting Company); CBS (Colombia Broadcasting System); MBS (Mutual Broadcasting System) and NPR (National Public Radio). The USA has the largest concentration of TV companies in the world and the most TV sets.

As trade barriers come down and satellites go up broadcasting has gone increasingly global. Moguls like the Italian Silvio Berlusconi and Australian-turned-US citizen Rupert Murdoch are vying for greater control of an increasingly volatile marketplace.

Many networks feed their string of local stations with national news from a centralized newsroom, and those stations in turn send back reports of major stories to the network.

IRN (Independent Radio News) in London is Britain's main radio news agency, providing news bulletins on the hour, as well as copy and audio to most of the 200 plus stations in the independent network. Distribution is via satellite. Stations can take the national news live or assemble and read their own versions of the bulletin. The service is run by ITN (Independent Television News), whose globe-trotting reporters supplement the service by filing radio versions of their TV stories.

Some stations in remote regions such as Scotland prefer to compile their own national bulletins which can be angled to suit their Scottish audiences, rather than settle for news with a London emphasis.

The BBC's network service operates differently, providing copy and audio which are distributed electronically, but not a live bulletin which stations can pipe-in on the hour.

In the USA, regional networks range from groups of stations who exchange reports on a regular basis, to scaled down national networks with a centrally produced bulletin transmitted every hour.

When a station switches over to take the network news, this is called *opting-in* to the network. The process of switching back is called *opting-out*. Where opt-outs are used, bulletins will end with a readily identifiable *outcue* such as a timecheck, which is the presenter's cue for switching back to local programming.

Many radio stations follow the national news with a local bulletin, others precede it with local news, and some prefer to combine the two in a single bulletin, known as a *news-mix*. Many television stations produce their own regional news but take a networked national news service.

Local TV and radio stations will also be expected to contribute to the pool of news stories available to the network. Material is supplied to and from the network along a *contribution circuit*. Stations with similar interests may install their own contribution circuits and supply one another with material, operating like a network within a network.

The EBU in figures

- 117 members in 80 countries (69 active members in 50 countries and 48 associate members in 30 countries).
- Turnover in 1999: 407 million Swiss francs (+/-252 million Euros), including 189 million for sports rights and events and CHF 117 million for the network.
- EBU employs a staff of 252 including 11 in Moscow and 11 in North America – and the headquarters in Geneva hosts around 10,000 visitors and delegates from member organizations every year.
- In television, 20 satellite channels relay 70,000 transmissions per year (including 25,000 news items and 7,700 hours of sports and cultural programmes). Eurovision is received by 255 million homes or a potential total of 640 million viewers.
- In radio, two satellite channels relay 2,000 concerts and operas, 400 sports fixtures and 120 major news events every year. Euroradio has a potential audience of 400 million listeners.

Figure 15   Greater than the sum of the parts? The European Broadcasting Union (EBU), which facilitates the exchange of news items between member organizations. (*Courtesy www. ebu.ch*)

Other news media

Journalists take a professional pride in beating their fellows to a story. Most news editors monitor the rival media to make sure they are ahead with the news and to see if there is anything they have missed.

One of the news editor's first tasks each day is usually to go through the national and local papers to see if there are any stories referring to the area which need to be followed-up.

Figure 16 Sifting through story ideas at ITN, to answer the perennial question – what to cover and what to leave out? (*Andrew Boyd*)

Following-up a news item means checking and developing it to find a new angle. This means much more than just taking a story from a newspaper and rewriting it for broadcast. That would be plagiarism – stealing somebody's work. Facts may also be wrong and errors repeated.

There is no copyright on ideas, however, and journalists often feed on one another for their leads and inspiration, as in this actual example:

'Get the father . . .'

Two rival TV news programmes went on air close to one another in the evening: *Coast to Coast*, the independent programme, between 6 and 6.30; *South Today*, the BBC service, from 6.35 to 7.

Coast to Coast picks up a breaking news story. A local businessman is to be released from Libya. He had been jailed because his boss's company had run into debt there and he was being held responsible. He is to be set free and is flying home tonight. *Coast to Coast* has carried the item as a copy story.

South Today is monitoring the programme and immediately gets a reporter to phone Gatwick Airport to try to interview the father, who is waiting for his son's flight.

Meanwhile *Coast to Coast* has just finished and the opening sequences of *South Today* are going out on air. The presenters are told to stand by for late breaking news.

Minutes later copy comes in saying the businessman is due to arrive within the hour, and a presenter breaks from the script to read the story unrehearsed.

At the airport, public relations staff are busily trying to find the father.

Twenty minutes into the programme and all that remains is the weather and the headlines. The father has not been found and time is running out. The producer takes over the story. He gets through to the father even as the closing headlines are being read.

The director quickly tells one of the presenters through his earpiece that the father is on the phone waiting to be interviewed. The presenter has 45 seconds to ad-lib the interview before the programme ends and transmission returns to the network. It is not possible to overrun by even a second.

The businessman's father says he is delighted his son is returning home. The Foreign Office confirmed the news yesterday. As alcohol was forbidden in Libya, they will crack open some bottles of his son's favourite beer.

The director counts down the closing seconds while the presenter thanks the father for talking to him and wishes the viewers a calm good evening. The programme ends bang on time and as coolly as if it had all been planned from the start. Independent television led the way, but the BBC got the better story.

Shared material

A growing number of BBC TV and radio newsrooms now share the same building, so there is a crossover of ideas. Joint newsrooms take this one step further. Story ideas are swapped and stringer and agency copy pooled.

The BBC increasingly expects its reporters to be able to cover stories for both radio and television, and its trainee journalists are now being taught to be bimedial.

On occasions, radio will use the soundtrack of TV interviews in bulletin, and TV stations may make use of radio reporters to supply phone reports on breaking stories.

In Britain, independent radio sometimes uses material recorded off-air from independent television, although the two have no corporate tie-up. The arrangement usually requires the radio station to credit the TV company for using its audio. Cable television companies have also used reporters from local radio stations to produce and present their news programmes.

At an international level, news services frequently exchange reports with one another to enhance their worldwide coverage. A number of broadcasting unions act as clearing houses.

Fieldwork

1 It is a quiet day on the radio station. No news is breaking; there is nothing to follow up. You are sent out by your news editor to find a story. If you are able to, go out into your neighbourhood and see what you can come up with. (Go in pairs if you are in a class.) If you can't get out, discuss what stories you might cover.

2 You are setting up TV news coverage in a brand new area. Think of ten important contacts you would make in the community. Then find out the name, job title and phone number of the major contacts you would expect to call each day in your area to make the check calls to the emergency services.

3 If it is legal, listen in to the emergency services band on the radio and see if you can work out what they are covering. If they use a variation of the 10 Code, jot down the codes used and find out what they mean.

4 From your own TV viewing and radio listening, which do you think are the most active pressure groups in your area and how do they get their message across to the media? Do they come across favourably or badly? Why?

5 A caller on the line to your newsroom says large quantities of lethal waste have leaked from a nearby industrial plant. The toxic chemical is spilling into a reservoir that directly feeds the local water supply. He says he is the manager at the plant and is urging you to put out a message immediately warning people to stop drinking the water as it could poison them. What do you do?

NEWS GATHERING

4 Getting the story

'I always wanted to be a reporter. There was never anything else, nothing as exciting. The great joy of reporting is going out and coming back with complete chaos. You've got some ideas, a few notes in the notebook, a few rushes in the can – all kinds of different things – and you've got to put it all together to make a story. It's a great feeling of satisfaction.' — STEPHEN COLE, BBC WORLD NEWS

News editors are to broadcast journalism what generals are to warfare. They set the objectives, weigh the resources and draw up the plan of campaign. Under their command are the officers and troops on the ground.

Some news editors prefer to be in the thick of battle, directing the action from the front line, while others favour a loftier perspective, set back from the heat of the action. These will oversee strategy, but delegate a number two to be responsible for tactics. In larger newsrooms, this may be the deputy news editor, senior producer, or bulletin producer. Working to the news editor's plan of campaign he or she will keep in touch with the news as it develops and arrange coverage.

Newsroom conference

In larger newsrooms the plan of campaign is drawn up at the morning conference. Producers and senior staff put their heads together with the news editor to map out the day's coverage.

BBC Southern Counties Radio is based in Guildford but ranges across Surrey, Sussex and Hampshire. Why drag in staff for the 9 am conference when there are stories to be covered on their own patch? Instead Southern Counties carries out the conference via a telephone link to bureaux across the region. Area reporters hook-up to the HQ via studio-quality phone lines and pool their ideas into the central newsgathering operation.*

Many stories will already be in the diary or on the files; some of yesterday's items will still be current and will need to be followed-up to find new angles. The news wires may produce items, which can be used or pursued. Producers and reporters will be expected to come forward with their own ideas, and other leads may come in the post or from rival media.

* *Ariel*, November 1995.

Figure 17   Staffing the news bureaux at BBC Southern Counties Radio. Area reporters hook up to HQ via studio-quality phone lines. (*Andrew Boyd*)

Stories are then ranked in order of importance and in line with station policy and resources are allocated accordingly.

If more stories present themselves than staff reporters can cover, the news editor will bring in freelance support or put some stories 'on ice', to be followed only if others fall down.

On a thin day, the news editor may have to rely on back-up material to fill the programme. Most stations have a small collection of timeless features, which have been kept for such emergencies, called *fillers* or *padding*. Where there is little hard news to cover, reporters and crews may be sent out to get more filler material to top up the reserves.

If the station is running news on the hour, the news editor will attempt to spread coverage throughout the day to provide an even balance, with the emphasis on peak-time listening. For longer news programmes, producers arrange coverage to ensure reports are back in time to make those deadlines.

Copytasting

Each newsroom will have someone in charge of the newsdesk at all times, keeping a close eye on agency material and breaking stories. As news comes in, a senior journalist will copytaste each item to see if it is worth running or pursuing or offers new information on an existing story.

When a good story breaks unexpectedly, the news editor, like the general, must be prepared to switch forces rapidly from one front to another to meet the new challenge.

Figure 18 Where the chase begins . . . setting the news agenda at the editorial conference of the BBC World Service. (*Andrew Boyd*)

Reporters may be asked to drop what they are doing and cover the new story instead; old running orders will be scrapped and new ones devised. This demand for sharp reflexes, total flexibility and all-stops-out performance puts the buzz into news reporting.

Balance of news

Chasing breaking news is only half the story. The news editor or producer also has the overall balance of the programme to consider. In a 30-minute TV programme time will be set aside for regular slots or segments, such as sport, headlines and the weather, and material will have to be found to fill them.

In any audience some would prefer to unwind to light items at the end of a working day rather than endure heavyweight stories; others will prefer national news to local, and commercial stations may be expected to inject enough entertainment into the show to shore-up audience ratings. All these conflicting demands will be brought to bear in shaping the news priorities and arranging coverage at the start of the day.

Visuals and actuality

Getting the story in radio and TV means more than simply gathering the facts. How these facts are illustrated is also important. Like newspapers with their photographs, radio has its sounds, recorded at the scene. These are called *actuality*.

Radio brings a report to life by painting a picture in the imagination of the listener, while TV takes its audience to the scene through the use of film and video footage. And TV can add to its armoury sound effects, graphics and still photographs. The cost of all this artistry is to make TV sometimes slower and less flexible than radio, but attractive visuals and interesting actuality breathe life into the coverage of news. Good illustrations can boost the position of a report in the programme, and poor actuality or footage may make a producer think twice about running it at all.

The brief

The ideal brief would be a printed note giving details of the story, saying whom the interviewee was, the time and place of the interview, with the relevant press clippings, background and a selection of suitable questions. But reality usually falls short of the ideal. News editors are busy people who say the reason they have two ears is so they can perch a telephone under each. Most reporters will be all too familiar with the phrase that greets then when they arrive for work: *'Don't take your coat off . . .'*.

Sometimes 'brief' is the operative word . . . It may go something like this: *'The strike at the car plant – the MD's in his office, he'll see you in ten minutes. Give me holding for 11, a clip for noon and I'll take two and a half for the 1 o'clock.'*

No note; no background list of questions. Not even a *'please'*.

The reporter is already expected to know the strike has been called, the car plant it concerns, where it is, how to get there, who the managing director is, all the necessary background to produce three separate items, and to have the know-how to come up with a line of questioning that perfectly matches the unspoken ideas in the news editor's head. So what's unreasonable about that?

However frantic the news editor may be, the reporter will have to prise out the answers to three questions before setting out on the assignment:

- What do you want?
- When do you want it for?
- How long do you want it to run?

With the car workers' strike, the plant's managing director will be asked: *'What's your reaction to the stoppage? How damaging could it be for the company? Will jobs or orders be lost? How long can the company survive the action?'*. The union point of view will also be required.

Knowing the time of transmission and the length of the item is vital. There would be no point in returning to the newsroom at 3 pm with enough material to make a half-hour documentary when what was wanted was a 20-second clip for the lunchtime news. No one will appreciate this masterpiece if it arrives too late or runs too long to go in the programme.

News reporters usually work to the next bulletin deadline. On some stations deadlines crop up every 15 minutes, so when reporters go out on a story, that story must not vanish with them. Hence the instruction to write *holding copy*. This is a short news item that can be run in the next bulletin or headlines to tide the newsroom over until the reporter returns with the interview.

If the reporter is likely to be out for some time, say, at a conference, he or she may be expected to phone in regular reports from the venue to keep the bulletins topped up with the latest news. Recorded interviews can also be fed back down the phone as a last resort.

The next directive is to provide a clip for noon: that would be the best 20 seconds or so from the interview to illustrate the story.

Lastly, the reporter here has been asked to produce an interview of 2 minutes 30 seconds for the 1 o'clock news programme. The questions above would satisfy that, with any leads picked up from the managing director which give a new slant on the story.

Many news editors would argue that an elaborate brief should not be necessary, as reporters are expected to have a good working knowledge of their area and keep abreast of breaking news. But things are not always so hectic. When reporters arrive on duty, they may be given time to catch up by reading through the output of the previous shift. *Reading-in* helps reporters familiarize themselves with what has already gone on air.

Where more background is required, reporters on small stations would be expected to research it themselves, while those on larger stations may be able to call upon a researcher or the station's news information service or library.

> *'What you need is a wide background knowledge, rather than narrow specialization, and you need to keep it up to date.'*
> – BBC WORLD SERVICE NEWSROOM GUIDE

The angle

Think of a news story as a diamond. A diamond has many facets, and whichever way you hold it, it is impossible to look at them all at once. Some will always be hidden from view. Likewise, it may impossible to cover every aspect of a news story at once – there is seldom the time or space. The reporter will be forced to concentrate on a few of the story's facets. Each facet represents a different angle. The angle is the part of the story the reporter chooses to hold up to the light at any one time. Most stories will have a number of different angles and news editors and producers usually spell out which particular one they want the reporter to focus on.

Take a story about a big new contract at a steelworks: the fact of the contract is the story, but that may not be reason enough for running it. Information only becomes news when it affects a given audience. If the contract is big enough, it might make national news, but the editor in a local newsroom would run the story only if the steelworks were in his or her area. The story would then have a *local angle*. With national news, the main angle is often the importance or significance of the story to the nation. At a local level, the importance to the community comes first.

Once the news editor is satisfied the story is relevant to the audience, he or she may want to cover it a number of different ways. The angle will change according to viewpoint, and with the steelworks, the obvious viewpoints to go for would be those of the management and workforce. An interview will be arranged with the company about the size of the contract, the effect on the company's prospects and the likelihood of more jobs.

If the reporter discovers 500 new jobs will be offered over the coming three years, the follow-up angle would shift to the union viewpoint. The major union would be asked to comment.

So far, both interviews have been with spokespeople; one to establish the facts of the story and the other to react to them, and there is a constant danger in journalism of always talking to experts, or *talking heads*, and overlooking ordinary people with grassroots opinions.

Figure 19   To get the story, first get the picture. All eyes on the man in the suit outside the Courts of Justice in London. (*Andrew Boyd*)

Another viewpoint, closer to the audience, would be that of the workers at the steelworks. The reporter would ask some for their reactions to the news and might follow that by talking to several unemployed people who now have their first chance for some time of finding a job.

Workers and unemployed alike are the people whose lives will be affected by the contract, and they and their dependants will probably make up a significant part of the station's audience. In the end, it is their reactions that matter the most.

Using extracts from all the interviews, a comprehensive and well-rounded report could be built up, with background material filled in by the reporter. This is known as a *package*.

A TV reporter will want to illustrate the item with good footage of the steelworks in action. Dramatic images of red-hot molten steel and flying sparks would feature with shots of blue-collar workers with their protective facemasks, contrasting perhaps with images of a be-suited director in a plush office.

Radio will certainly go for the noise of the steelworks, the clashing of metal and the voices of people at work.

Chasing the contact

Once the reporter has been briefed and found out *what* is wanted and *when*, the process of getting the story begins with the contacts file.

Much precious time on a 60-minute deadline can be saved by going for the right person from the start. Go straight to the top. Don't waste time with minor officials who will only refer you upwards. If you are dealing with a company, go for the managing director. Only settle for the *press office* if the MD or secretary insists. A press officer is one step away from the person you want to interview and may have reasons for putting you off.

Some organizations will insist you use their press officers – that is what they pay them for – and it is possible to build up a good working relationship with the best of them, but remember that behind every plausible statement and off-the-record remark there lurks a vested interest.

> *'I don't want any of my journalists talking to press officers. Press officers are paid to conceal the truth, not to tell it.'*   – STEWART STEPHEN, EDITOR

Setting up the interview can be the dullest, most time-consuming chore in journalism. Sometimes the ringing round can seem interminable and more time can be spent waiting for people to phone you back than in reporting.

To save time, the best tip is never to rely on anyone to call you back. If a secretary tells you your contact is speaking on another line and will return your call, politely insist on holding on while he or she finishes the conversation. If you hang up, your name will be added to the list of callbacks, and that list could be a long one. Also, if the story might mean adverse publicity, you could find yourself waiting by the phone forever.

If your contact is out, ask for their mobile phone number. Failing that, leave a message stressing the urgency of your business, and ask if there is someone else who could handle

Figure 20 News quarry cornered . . . no escaping the camera, the light and the reporter in this interview for ITN. (*Andrew Boyd*)

your inquiry. If they try to put you off, be polite but persistent, and if that fails, go above their heads to someone more senior. If no one can talk to you, find out where your contact is and call him or her there. Don't be fobbed off. Remember, every minute wasted brings you closer to your deadline. The approach should be assertive rather than aggressive and tenacious but always polite.

If after that your interviewee is still playing hard to get, then put that angle 'on hold' and approach they story from another direction.

With the steelworks item, if management is being elusive, go instead for the union line. With a more controversial story, such as plans to build a prison in the area, if those behind the scheme won't talk, go directly to the opposition or the grassroots and interview residents who may be frightened about the prospect of prisoners escaping near their homes.

All too often, despite your best endeavours, you will find yourself staring at the telephone, willing it to ring, while messages and repeated messages lie neglected in a heap on your contact's desk.

At this stage, you are wasting time and should go back to your news editor. Say what steps you have taken, and seek further direction. Should you continue to wait by the phone, firing off still more messages, or should you cut your losses and try a different angle or abandon this and get on with another item?

Staged news conferences

News conferences can be a time-consuming way of getting a story. Having sat through a 40-minute presentation, when questions are invited from the floor the tendency is for reporters to talk over each other and fire their questions at once, often in pursuit of different angles. This kind of anarchy may be induced by approaching deadlines or the latest newsbiz trend for *'correspondent's presence'* – where the reporter is placed centre stage and shown conspicuously chasing the news. Either way, the scrum can make for a garbled recording.

Set presentations can be difficult to record if the speakers are some distance from the microphone and much of the material may ramble on irrelevantly, which makes for troublesome editing. Always pack more than enough recording medium and make a clear note of when the interesting points were made.

Press conferences generally live up to their name. The format was devised for print journalism and is largely unsuited to the electronic era. The opportunity to record interviews usually comes *after* the conference. Some newsrooms refuse to give coverage unless the main speakers make themselves available for private interviews well in advance and provide copies of speeches so questions can be prepared.

The alternatives are to hang around for interviews until the conference is finished, or record them on location before the conference gets under way, but there may well be a queue of other reporters with the same idea.

Radio has an advantage. When TV moves in to do an interview, the crews usually take a little time to set up their lights and cameras, so radio reporters are advised to be assertive and to get in first, pleading that the interview will take only a few minutes. Cooling your heels while TV completes the cumbrous operation of lights, colour check, pre-chat, interview and cutaways, will only push you closer to your deadline.

Beating the clock

The fastest way to get a report on air is via the telephone, and live pieces can be taken directly into news programmes and bulletins. But telephone items (*phonos*) are mushy in quality and for TV lack that essential visual element. Mobile phones may have liberated reporters from playing hunt the payphone and leave us free to stay at the scene of the story, but well before you go live make sure to check your signal is strong and clearly audible.

Stations with few reporters will often rely on interviewees to come to them. Alternatively, your interviewee could remain at the office and talk to you in studio quality along a digital phone line. Either practice frees the journalist to remain in the newsroom and chase more stories, but both are better suited to radio than TV where the choice of location is often determined by the need for interesting visuals.

If time is short and the reporter has to travel to the interview, precious minutes can be clawed back by planning the route. Rush-hour delays should be taken into consideration. Detailed street maps or some kind of electronic navigation system are essential. Another option is to travel by cab and put a taxi driver's expert knowledge at your disposal. This also gives you time to plan your interview on the way there and check your material on the way back.

If the station has a radio car or outside broadcast vehicle, live reports can be sent back which save time and add considerably to the sense of urgency and occasion.

Work to sequence

Another way to claw back precious minutes is to arrange to do your interviews in the order in which they will appear on air. This keeps the recordings in a logical sequence and helps with the preparation of questions.

Make sure all the key phrases and quotes you intend to keep are noted either during the interview or after it, and log the points where those quotes occur. This can be done from a stopwatch, or by using the counter on the recorder. Jotting down single trigger words such as 'angry' or 'delighted' can help you plan your editing.

Many radio reporters listen to their interviews in the car going back to the station and the editing process is well advanced in their minds even before they return.

Don't panic

In the editing room, many inexperienced journalists, sweating against the clock, let circumstances panic them. There is always the hope that you *will* be able to turn round that three-minute package in the last moments before the programme, and an experienced hand will have little trouble in doing just that. But the old adage about more haste less speed is especially true in broadcasting.

Be realistic. If you doubt your ability to get the piece on air by the deadline, then warn the producer or news editor that it may not be coming. Give them time to prepare a standby. Whatever you do, don't leave them without that safety net. If they are banking on your item and it fails to turn up, at best you will try the patience of your colleagues, and at worst you will leave a hole in the programme that could prove impossible to fill, throw the presentation team into confusion and lead to a disaster on air.

Similarly, by rushing your piece you could easily make a mistake and the first time you realize your blunder may be when you see or hear it going on air. When a deadline is rapidly approaching, the temptation to run the piece without checking it through can be almost irresistible.

If mistakes do appear, the station's credibility takes a nosedive, and the authority of that bulletin is knocked. The audience and your colleagues will judge you, not by the amount of well-intentioned effort that went into your work, but by the results as they appear on air. In the end, that is all that really matters.

> *'The most important thing about news is the listener – most radio journalists think getting the last-minute story into the bulletin is more important than presentation, and getting the facts absolutely right – they are mistaken.'*
> – SIMON ELLIS, BBC NEWS EDITOR

Fieldwork

1 Find out the names of the news editors at your nearest radio and TV stations and ask if you can visit their newsrooms for a day (longer if possible) to observe what goes on. Talk to the journalists about their jobs without getting in their way and ask if you can go with any of the reporters on a story. Watch how the news develops from an idea to a full-blown report.

2 Listen to the main local news programme on the radio and see if you can work out which, if any, of the stories are being used as padding or fillers. Listen especially to any actuality in the bulletin and discuss whether it added anything to the story, or if the story would have been clearer without it. Was there too much or too little actuality in the bulletin?

3 Read through a local newspaper and make a list of stories that could be followed-up. Think about the angles you could take to develop the story further. Then plan your coverage for each of them. Work out contacts and questions and draw up briefs for your reporters.

4 For TV, work out what footage you would want to take to illustrate those different stories. Go for a good a mix of coverage with plenty of variety. Be creative.

5 If you have access to radio or TV recording equipment, find a contact involved in one of the stories who is willing to be interviewed. Compare your finished report with those in the next radio and TV bulletins and discuss how your own work could be improved.

5 Conversational writing

'Writing, when properly managed . . . is but another name for conversation.'
– LAURENCE STERNE

'For years, editors told reporters: "Don't tell me about it, write it." Turn that around, and you have a good rule for the broadcast journalist: "Don't just write it, TELL ME ABOUT IT." ' – BROADCAST NEWS OF CANADA, STYLE BOOK

Anyone with ambition towards writing will probably appreciate a lively piece of prose. We all have our journalistic giants and literary heroes. But what may be clear and sparkling to the eye may be confused and baffling to the ear. It may also prove impossible to read out aloud. The following is from Hemingway's *For Whom the Bell Tolls*. A Spanish gypsy, Rafael, is describing a machine gun attack on a Fascist train. Read it out loud and see how you get on:

'The train was coming steadily. We saw it far away. And I had an excitement so great that I cannot tell it. We saw steam from it and then later came the noise of the whistle. Then it came chu-chu-chu-chu-chu-chu steadily larger and larger and then, at the moment of the explosion, the front wheels of the engine rose up and all of the earth seemed to rise in a great cloud of blackness and a roar and the engine rose high in the cloud of dirt and of the wooden ties rising in the air as in a dream and then it fell on to its side like a great wounded animal and there was an explosion of white steam before the clods of the other explosion had ceased to fall on us and the maquina commenced to speak ta-tat-tat-ta!' went the gypsy, shaking his two clenched fists up and down in front of him, thumbs up, on an imaginary machine gun.'*

Breathless? Punctuation is minimal to drive the speech forward and convey a sense of excitement, but although it makes compelling reading on paper, it is almost impossible to read aloud without suffering from oxygen starvation. Even conventional prose can cause problems, because the writing obeys the rules of the written, rather than the spoken word.

Writing for broadcast can mean tossing away literary conventions, including the rules of grammar, if the words are to make sense to the ear, rather than the eye. In print, shades of meaning are conveyed with choice adjectives and skilful prose, but the spoken word makes use of a medium, which is altogether more subtle and powerful – the human voice.

* Penguin, 1969, page 31.

Figure 21 Keeping a straight back and a stiff sheet of paper. Reading the news at BBC Radio Solent – note the old-fashioned ribbon mike in the centre of the table. (*Andrew Boyd*)

Telling the story

> '*If you find it difficult to put your thoughts down on paper clearly and simply, use the trick of telling someone out loud what you want to say, Your brain will throw out most of the padding automatically. People talk more clearly than they write; so make your writing more like your talking and your viewers will understand you better.*'
> – HARRIS WATTS*

An accomplished reader can breathe life into the flat black marks on a page, investing them with shades of light and dark, irony, pleasure or distaste with nothing more than a minor variation in the pitch or tone of his or her voice.

For print journalists making the crossover into broadcasting and graduates embarking on a career in radio or TV, the hardest adjustment can be to break out of the literary mould imposed on us since our schooldays. All the emphasis then was on the written word, but everything in broadcasting is written to be spoken.

For many years BBC World Service journalists dictated copy to secretaries to be sure their reports were in a conversational style. Staffing cuts and computers put paid to the secretaries, but good broadcast journalists everywhere give the lie to the saying that

* *On Camera*, BBC, 1995.

talking to yourself is the first sign of madness by muttering stories under their breath before committing them to the computer screen. A piece of broadcast copy should sound natural to the ear and be easy to read out loud, without causing the reader to stumble over words and gasp for breath.

Newswriting, which may look fine in print, can often *sound* stilted and peculiar:

> *'Judge Theodore T. Townshend (43), of 17 Withy Grove, Edmonton, Alberta, has been found guilty of being in charge of a motor vehicle whilst under the influence of alcohol.'*

Picture yourself leaning on a bar telling the same story to a friend. Chances are you would say something like, *'Hey, did you hear about the Alberta Judge who's been found guilty of drunken driving?'*

Without realizing it, you would have translated the written word into the spoken word, and the broadcaster would do the same, leaving out, of course the *'Hey, did you hear . . .?'* The broadcasting equivalent of this attention grabber is the *jingle* (*sounder*, US) into the news bulletin.

The conversational approach would continue for the rest of the item: *'Judge Theodore Townshend, who's 43 and lives at Withy Grove, Edmonton . . . etc.'* The middle initial and road number only clutter up the story and so have been dropped. Any facts that are not vital should be scrapped.

Similarly, broadcast news has no need of a mass of adjectives. For television, the saying *'a picture is worth a thousand words'* holds true and the images presented by the cameras will tell the story more effectively than any description. Where there are no accompanying illustrations, the nuances of inflection in the newsreader's voice will paint a picture as colourful as the most purple of prose.

Writing for a mass audience

> *'At all times remember you are communicating with ONE person. ONE-TO-ONE means YOU and just ONE listener.'* – COUNTY SOUND RADIO STYLEBOOK

For the professional broadcaster there must be no such thing as *'the masses out there'*. Images of a sea of upturned faces somewhere beyond the studio lead only to megaphone newsreading and a style of writing, which turns every story into a proclamation.

The secret of communicating with an audience, however large, is to write and speak as though you were talking to only one person, and it helps if that person is someone you know and like, rather than your worst enemy or boss.

Visualizing a single well-disposed listener warms up the approach, makes it more personal, and avoids the trap of sounding patronizing. Aim to talk *to* the audience and not *at* them.

The most important technique in communication is to meet people where they are – at their level. Nothing enrages an audience more than being talked down to, and few things bore them faster than hearing talk which is above their heads. *Broadcasting* means just that: reaching out to a broad cross-section of the community, and the skill lies in pitching it so what you say satisfies roadsweepers and university dons alike – no mean task.

When reporters learn to *tell* the story rather than write it they are halfway there. The next stage is to realize that the broadcast audience has different needs from the newspaper reader, and that those needs differ again between radio and television.

No second chance

Newspaper readers have one big advantage: they can read and re-read the same item until they can make sense of it. But broadcasters have only one chance to score with their audience. The information is fleeting. As soon as it has passed, it has vanished into the ether and is lost until the broadcast is repeated the following hour – if it is repeated at all.

The onus on making sense of the news lies always with the newswriter and newsreader, never with the audience. This means the broadcast story has to be crystal clear the first time of hearing. Clutter has to go and convoluted writing has to be ironed out; clauses and sub-clauses dismantled and reconstructed as new sentences if necessary.

The writer has to wield a ruthless logic in the way the story is explained, moving the information unswervingly forward from point to point. Mark Twain described the way a good writer constructs a sentence:

> *'He will make sure there are no folds in it, no vaguenesses, no parenthetical interruptions of its view as a whole; when he has done with it, it won't be a sea-serpent, with half of its arches under the water; it will be a torch-light procession.'*

What do you think Mark Twain would have made of the following?

> *'The docks' dispute, which is now in its 17th day, as 300 members of the Transport and General, Britain's largest industrial union, take strike action, because of an overtime ban which has been in operation since February 9, as well as unsocial hours, shows no sign of letting up, despite warnings by the T&G that lorry drivers could be asked to black the port.'*

Chances are you would have to read that through twice to be clear about it, which means the story would have failed on radio or TV. Yet all it needs is a little unravelling:

> *'There's still no sign of a let-up in the docks' dispute, now in its 17th day. This is despite warnings by the Transport and General, Britain's biggest industrial union, that lorry drivers might be called on to black the port. 300 members of the T&G have walked out in protest at unsocial hours and a ban on overtime. The ban was imposed on February the 9th.'*

In this written version, the one sentence of the original has become four. The tangle of subsidiary clauses has been unravelled and chopped into three short sentences. The story progresses logically and the only kink which remains is the brief subsidiary clause, *'Britain's biggest industrial union,'* which is too small to restrict the flow of the sentence.

Notice too, that *'February 9'* which is standard newspaper style, has been changed to the slightly longer, but more conversational, *'February the 9th'*.

Sentences for broadcast need to be clear and declarative, containing a minimum of different ideas. Simplicity and conciseness are the watchwords, yet that does not mean that writing for the voice should be devoid of style, energy or colour. Poetry, which is intended for reading aloud, is often vivid and bursting with life.

Figure 22 Other side of the autocue . . . an operator checks the script before the ITN evening news. The writing style is conversational and the pace is set to match the reading speed of the newsreader. (*Andrew Boyd*)

Canada's Broadcast News organization recommends a sentence length of 20 to 25 words with one thought per sentence, but recognizes the danger that, *'strings of short sentences can be just as deadly as overlong sentences, because they produce a staccato effect.'*

Newspaper readers have the food in their own hands, they can feed themselves and decide how long they want to spend chewing over an item. But radio and TV audiences have to be fed the news. Many stations assume an average attention span of about three minutes; some rate it even shorter – around 90 seconds – but for even three minutes of spoken information to be digested it has to be chopped up into small chunks which are easy to swallow.

> *'A high school teacher of mine once said short declarative sentences are the best kind of writing. Writing should be as concise and clear as possible.'*
> – PAUL CLEVELAND, ABC ASSIGNMENT MANAGER,
> ABC NEWS (US) LONDON

Confusing clauses

An item that makes sense on paper where the punctuation is visible can have an altogether different meaning when read aloud:

'Ethiopia said the Eritrean leader had started the conflict.'

Just *who* is being accused and *by whom* comes down to a little matter of punctuation, or lack of it, which can completely alter the sense of the story:

> *'Ethiopia,' said the Eritrean leader, 'had started the conflict.'*

For broadcast, the copy style has to be unambiguous. Assuming the second version of this hypothetical story is the correct one, it should be rewritten as follows:

> *'The Eritrean leader said Ethiopia had started the conflict.'*

Inverted sentences

Because listeners have to hold in their memory what has been said, inverted sentences such as the one you are reading are to be avoided.

An inversion often demands that listeners retain information that is without meaning until it is put into context. By the time that context comes listeners may have forgotten what they were supposed to remember or be terminally confused. This is how *not* to do it:

> *'Because of the fall in the mortgage rate, which has stimulated home buying, house prices are going up again.'*

> **Rather**: *'House prices are going up again. The fall in the mortgage rate has led to an increase in home buying.'*

State the point to begin with and then explain it, not the other way round, and avoid beginning a sentence with 'Because' or 'According to'. Listeners can never refer back.

Plain English

> *'Journalism – a profession whose business is to explain to others what it personally doesn't understand.'* — LORD NORTHCLIFFE

Plain English should not be confused with dull language; the English tongue is too rich and varied for it ever to need to be boring. Plain English does away with woolliness, wordiness, officialese and circumlocution and replaces it with words and descriptions that are concrete and direct.

Plain English is about rat-catchers and road sweepers, never rodent operators or highway sanitation operatives. It is about straightforward writing using commonly understood words, rather than high-faluting phrases intended to impress. As journalist Harold Evans put it, plain English is about calling a spade a spade and not a factor of production.

The enemy of good writing is the official, the bureaucrat and the so-called expert who uses words as a barrier to understanding instead of as a means of communication. Their aim is to mystify rather than enlighten. A good deal of the journalist's time is spent translating their gobbledegook into plain English so ordinary people can make sense of it.

The danger is that some reporters, out of deadline pressure or laziness, may put something down on paper which they don't really understand in the hope that those who hear it will. They won't.

Never run anything on air that does not make complete sense to you. You will lose your audience and be playing into the hands of the exponents of gobbledegook, who will chalk up another victory.

> *'We use too much jargon. We're like doctors who don't know how to explain things to their patients.'*
> – REPORTER, CANADIAN BROADCASTING CORPORATION*
>
> *'Our job is to dejargonize, to declichefy, to make everything clear, simple and concise.'*
> – BBC BUSH HOUSE NEWSROOM GUIDE

Familiar words

Speaking the layperson's language also means using familiar words. Prefer:

- Cut out   to   Excise
- Destroy   to   Obliterate
- Against   to   Antagonistic to
- Talkative   to   Loquacious
- Truthful   to   Veracious
- Cancel   to   Abrogate
- Poverty   to   Penury
- Highest point   to   Zenith

If you use a word your listeners may not immediately understand, while they are puzzling over its meaning the information that follows will vanish into the ether. By the time they reach for a dictionary or more likely shrug and give up they will have missed the rest of the news.

Easy listening

American broadcaster Irving E. Fang has researched into what makes broadcast copy easy or difficult to understand. He devised the Easy Listening Formula, which is based on the length of words in a sentence. The idea is to add up all the syllables in a sentence, then subtract from that the number of words. If the final score is higher than 20, the sentence contains too many long and abstract words that would make it hard to understand, and it should be subbed down.†

For example:

> *'The British-based human rights organisation, Christian Solidarity Worldwide, is accusing the Sudanese government of using outlawed chemical weapons and breaking the ceasefire in the*

---

* *The Independent*, 30 June 1993.
† *Television News*, Hasting House, 1972, p. 176.

long running civil war with the South in an offensive to clear civilians from oil fields where the first supplies of crude are beginning to flow.' (Score 36)

Rewrite: *'The Sudanese government has been accused of using banned chemical weapons and breaking the ceasefire in the long-running civil war with the South. (Score 13) The British human rights organisation, Christian Solidarity Worldwide, says Khartoum has launched an offensive to clear civilians from oil fields which are just beginning to produce oil.' (Score 20)*

As you can see from this, lengthy attributions stand in the way of easy listening.

Accurate English

Taking shades of grey and turning them into black and white for the sake of simplifying an issue is often the mark of an inexperienced journalist. Some precision might have to be sacrificed for the sake of simplicity, but the final story should still give the facts accurately. How would you translate the following ghastly, but typical, example of officialese?

'The Chairman observed that the Government loan of one million dollars may serve to obviate the immediate necessity for the termination of the contracts in question among non-full time ancillary staff, but that this contingency could not be discounted at a later period in the financial year in the event that funds became exhausted.'

The following version, distilled from the facts above, may look plausible, but would be completely misleading:

'The Chairman said the jobs of support staff had been spared for the time being thanks to a million dollar handout by the Government, but when the cash runs out later in the year, their jobs will have to go.'

The above 'translation' makes the following fatal errors:

- First, the staff are part-time and on contract, which makes the stakes arguably less high than if they had been full-time employees, as the rewritten version implies by omission.
- Second, there is nothing definite about these contracts being spared; '*may* serve to obviate', were the Chairman's words.
- Third, the 'Government handout' is not a handout at all, but a loan, and loans unlike handouts need repaying.
- Fourth, it is not certain the cash will run out later in the year, and,
- Fifth, even if it does, it is by no means definite that those contracts will be cut.

Below is a more accurate translation:

'The Chairman said the jobs of part-time ancillary staff, whose contracts have been under threat, may be safe for the time being, thanks to a million dollar loan from the Government. But he added that job cuts could not be ruled out later if the money ran out.'

If you really want to bewilder your listeners, try sprinkling in the odd word that means something other than most people imagine:

'When asked about the road building, Councillor Joe McFlagherty said he viewed the scheme with complete disinterest.'

To translate that as, *'Councillor Joe McFlagherty said he could not care less about the scheme'* would be to get the wrong end of the stick. Disinterested should not be confused with *uninterested* which suggests a lack of concern. 'Disinterested' means he had no personal or vested interest in the project.

'His alibi was that he had no reason to kill his own mother' does not make sense. *Alibi* means a plea that someone was somewhere else at the time. *Alibi* is not synonymous with *excuse*.

Keep it concrete

The fleeting nature of broadcasting means that information tends to be impressionistic, and radio in particular finds it difficult to convey technical details or abstract ideas. Precise instructions, complex abstractions, ideas or statistics – anything, in fact, which is hard to picture in the mind – do not come across well. Television has the powerful advantage of being able to use graphic illustrations to bring home a point, but even then it is easy to overload the medium with too much information. What it boils down to is that broadcasting is a pretty poor medium for analysis, compared with hard copy, written at length, in print where it can be pored over and digested. As somebody once said: *'Half of what you say is forgotten; the rest gets twisted.'*

The way to use the medium successfully is to keep statements simple, direct, concrete and to the point, and to express them in a way that everyone will readily understand.

Colloquialisms are acceptable for bringing home the meaning of a story, but in-words and slang that have grown stale through overuse will irritate listeners and should be avoided.

Metaphors and examples also help in putting over an idea. Radio paints a picture in someone's mind, but you cannot paint a picture of an idea, a concept or an abstraction. You have to relate that to things people are already familiar with, and that means using illustrations. For example:

Not: *'The Chancellor is increasing taxation on spirits by imposing a 5 per cent increase in prices from midnight tonight.'*

But: *'A bottle of whisky will cost around 60 pence more from midnight tonight. The Chancellor's putting 5 per cent on all spirits, which will push up the price of a short by about five pence.'*

Not: *'The Government's given the go-ahead for a massive new tower block in the centre of Wellington. Crane Towers is to be 297 metres high.'*

But: *'. . . Crane Towers is to be almost 300 metres high . . . that's taller than the Eiffel Tower and almost three times the height of St Paul's Cathedral.'*

The more abstract the words, the harder it becomes to visualize what is meant by them and the more likely we are to end up with a different picture to the one the writer had in mind.

S. I. Hayakawa explains this with his ladder of abstraction idea, which uses Bessie the cow as an example.* To the cowhand, Bessie is a loveable old friend who gazes at him with her big brown eyes while she chews the cud. To a visitor she is merely an old brown cow. To the farm manager every cow on the farm is an item of livestock. To the

---

* *Language in Thoughts and Action*, Harcourt Brace and World, 1964, pp. 176–9, quoted in *Television News*, p. 176.

bookkeeper, livestock comes under the heading of farm assets. To the accountant, assets are synonymous with wealth. Each step up the abstraction ladder takes us one step further from faithful old Bessie.

Ask someone to imagine a cow and they might picture a beast very different from Bessie; tell them 'livestock' and they could imagine a pig or a sheep; 'farm assets' could be tractors or ploughs; 'assets' could be anything saleable and 'wealth' might simply conjure up a picture of a wad of notes. Poor old Bessie!

Make it interesting

The journalist has something the audience wants – information. They want it because it is new, important and relevant. But however much they need this information, they will receive it only if it is presented in a way that is both interesting and entertaining.

At times, broadcasters will be required to tell their audience not simply what they want to hear, but what they need to know. In newsroom parlance, not every story is 'sexy' with instant audience appeal. Some have to be worked at to draw out the point of interest.

The goings-on in the European Union, debates in the Commonwealth or Congress and the workings of local government are important areas which traditionally turn off a mass audience. The challenge to the broadcaster is to demystify those issues by pointing up their relevance in concrete terms that people can readily grasp and relate to. To get that far, you have to begin by capturing audience interest.

Turn people off, and they will simply turn *you* off. Hold their interest, and you will help bring issues home to people they affect, and, by raising public awareness, increase the accountability of those who make the decisions.

Contractions

One of the most obvious differences between written and spoken English is the use of contractions. Words like *can't, couldn't, wouldn't, shouldn't, we'll, she'll, they'll, wasn't, didn't*; and even *shouldn't've* and *can't've* might look peculiar on paper, but are the substance of spoken English. In your next conversation, try to avoid contractions and see how difficult you find it and how stilted it sounds. Broadcasting is about conversation, so contractions are a must.

> *'The Fire Chief said that they had tried everything but had not succeeded in rescuing the mother and her child from the upper window. "We are giving it all that we have got, but we cannot do miracles. There has been no sign of them now for some time, and we are afraid that it is probably already too late." '*

This might pass in print, but read out loud it becomes obvious the story would not work on radio or TV. All it takes is a few deletions and a smattering of apostrophes:

> *'The Fire Chief said they'd tried everything but hadn't succeeded in rescuing the mother and her child from the upper window. "We're giving it all we've got, but we can't do miracles. There's been no sign of them now for some time, and we're afraid it's probably already too late." '*

Figure 23 Write it as you intend to say it. Use contractions – they'll sound more natural. Write in pauses . . . they help your copy – and you – to breathe. (*Andrew Boyd*)

A little contraction can be a dangerous thing. The shortened form can confuse the ear and be misleading to the listener. 'He *couldn't* agree to the proposal', sounds very much like, 'He *could* agree to the proposal' and 'She *didn't* know who committed the murder', could, to someone listening with half an ear, sound like 'She *did* know who committed the murder.'

There are times when NOT is too important a word to risk skipping over it with a contraction. Put it in CAPITALS.

Rhythm

Spoken English has a rhythm of its own that differs from the written word. The simple reason is that, with the exception of Hemingway's gypsy quoted above, people have to come up for breath every now and again.

Sometimes sentences which look fine in print sound unfinished when read aloud because they stray from the conventional rhythms of speech. Usually with spoken English sentences rise and fall and end with the voice turned down; unless that sentence is a question, when the voice will rise at the end.

While print journalists concentrate on cutting words out, broadcasters sometimes extend sentences to make them sound more natural:

'The trial resumes at one,' may sound unfinished, while 'the trial is due to resume at one o'clock' is longer but more rhythmic with a more definite shape and more emphatic conclusion.

The only rule, which supersedes most rules of grammar, is, if it *sounds* right, it probably *is* right. In the end the copy has to communicate, and if that means driving a coach and horses through the flowerbeds of the Queen's English, then so be it.

Another problem, which can often show up only when the copy is read out loud, is that of the unintentional rhyme:

> '*Defence Counsel Simon Crayle said the jury could not fail to set these men free on their not guilty plea, but the judge gave them three months in jail.*'

> '*One defendant, a stocky Croatian, yelled no justice was done in this nation. For disturbance in court, the judge said he ought to serve six further months on probation.*'

Jarring clashes of sound and potential tongue twisters should also be avoided:

> '*At election offices throughout Throstlebury today, each party is preparing to grind into gear for the great haul towards the imminent general election.*'

A little alliteration may occasionally be acceptable, but sometimes several similar sounds spoken aloud sound stupid, while a superfluity of hissing *s* and *c* sounds sound sibilant. Say these sentences yourself and see.

Fieldwork

1 Take two daily newspapers, one popular, the other serious, and read some of the stories out loud. Which newspaper style sounds more like conversational English – the popular style or the serious style? What makes the difference?

Take the hardest story to read aloud and go through it using Fang's Easy Listening Formula and give a score for each sentence. Then rewrite the story using shorter sentences and words with fewer syllables until it satisfies the Easy Listening Formula. Now read it out loud and see how it sounds. Is it any better? Can it still be improved?

2 Find a better way to write this story and to bring the point home:

> '*The rate of inflation has continued to rise over the past 12 month period, according to today's figures, which show that the retail price of staple foodstuffs has increased by 10 per cent – 5 per cent higher than the average inflation rate.*'

3 Discuss the differences between:

Assassinate and Execute	Imply and Infer
Billion and Million	Fewer and Less
Injured and Wounded	Black and Coloured
Claim and Say	

4 A new agricultural strategy for the country has been launched which requires increased productivity by farmers. How would you cover the story to make it sound interesting to a typical audience?

5 Translate the following gobbledegook into plain English:

> '*The Managing Director unequivocally reiterated his observation to the Board that there was an immediate necessity for the augmentation of differentials within the company to offer an extended programme of pecuniary incrementation for senior executives, for the prevention of the continuing and increasing recruitment of not inconsiderable numbers of personnel in higher management by overseas companies currently offering enhanced salaries and more attractive inducements.*'

WRITING FOR BROADCAST

6 Newswriting

> 'When you've got a thing to say,
> Say it! Don't take half a day . . .
> Life is short – a fleeting vapour –
> Don't you fill the whole blamed paper
> With a tale, which at a pinch,
> Could be covered in an inch!
> Boil her down until she simmers,
> Polish her until she glimmers.'
>
> – JOEL CHANDLER HARRIS

Hard news is new and important information about events of significance. Soft news and human interest items are stories run for their entertainment value first and their information second.

In the hard news story for broadcast there is no room for padding. The information must have the impact of an uppercut and connect with the audience in the first sentence.

The news angle

Before so much as rattling the keyboard, the journalist has to be clear about which angle to take on the story. This will depend on where the story occurred, what has been reported already, and what new facts have emerged.

Take the example of an air crash. All 329 people on board were killed when an Air India jumbo jet crashed off the west coast of Ireland. The disaster made headlines throughout the world, but had special significance in India and Canada. The Indian national airline was involved and the plane had taken off from Toronto, bound for Bombay.

Apart from the international importance of the event, news media of both nations had major *local* stories on their hands. The local angle resurfaced time and again in India, Canada and around the world in the villages, towns and cities where the passengers and crew had lived.

A number of different angles would have to be pursued. The first is the fact of the crash, and the questions, *'When, where, why* and *how many dead?'*

That same day two people die when a bomb explodes in a suitcase unloaded from another Canadian flight, from Vancouver. The events are too similar to be a coincidence. So the next angle is *who planted the bomb*? Two militant groups claim responsibility – the Kashmir Liberation Army and the Sikh Dashmesh Regiment.

A reporter is assigned to produce a background item about terrorism in the sub-continent, looking at the history of these groups and their possible motives.

As the names of local people on the passenger list filter back to newsrooms stories would be prepared about the deceased, to be followed perhaps by interviews with relatives.

Meanwhile, a new angle comes into play when search teams set out to recover the wreckage. Eighteen days after the crash, the digital flight recorder is found, putting the story back in the headlines. Three months to the day after the plane went down, it makes big news again when the inquest takes place at Cork, in Ireland.

Developing stories, which constantly throw up new angles and call for different versions, are known as *running stories*. When a major running story breaks, it will often be more than a single reporter can do to keep up with it, so a team is usually assigned to cover every possible angle.

Multi-angled stories

Broadcast news can handle more complex stories by breaking the information down point by point and giving it out in a logical sequence. But another problem can arise when the story has two angles of near equal importance which both deserve a place in the introduction. This is known as the *multi-angled* or *umbrella* story.

The way to tackle this is with a double intro – which is not to say the intro should be double the length:

> *'Today's record crime figures reveal violence and sex attacks at an all-time high . . . Police chiefs say the streets are turning into no-go areas because of the shortage of trained officers.'*

Here we have two stories, the first the escalating crime figures and the second the equally dramatic police reaction to them – both would be developed in the rest of the report.

Multi-angled stories may arise from one good story leading to an equally good follow-up which beg to be combined. These can be refreshed and kept running by updating and emphasizing different angles in subsequent bulletins. Sometimes two stories arise separately, which need to be run together under an umbrella:

> *'Sport . . . and it's been a tremendous day for New Zealand's athletes, with success in the hundred metres at home and a swimming triumph in Europe.'*
> **Or**: *'More bad news for industry . . . A smelting plant in Tema is to close with the loss of more than 130 jobs, and 50 workers are to be made redundant at a nearby steelworks.'*

Both examples begin with an umbrella statement, which covers the two stories in each and signposts what is to follow.

Hard news formula

There is a tried and tested hard news formula which is used in newspapers, radio and TV. It constructs the story by asking who, what, when, where, why and how questions. Answers to these should give most of the information required.

- **What** has happened?
- **Where** did it happen?
- **When** did it happen?
- **Who** was involved?
- **How** did it happen?
- **Why** did it happen?
- **What** does it mean?

Plus extra information, if there is time.

The news story begins with the most important facts, and backs those up with detail, background and interpretation, constructed to get the story across in a logical way that is clear and commands attention. Newswriters for the BBC's World Service are advised to tell listeners all they need to know to understand the story and to stop there. No question should be raised that cannot be answered.

The intro

> *'The first sentence in a radio news story is all-important. It must have, partly, the character of a headline. It must instantly establish the subject in the listener's mind, show him why the story is worth hearing and signpost the direction it is going to take. But it should not try to say too much.'*
>
> – BBC BUSH HOUSE NEWSROOM GUIDE
>
> *'The story should "**sell**" itself in the first line, which should be simple and punchy. My philosophy is that news should be lively rather than worthy. Even if it's serious it doesn't have to be boring. The key is . . . if you enjoy the story, so will the audience.'*
>
> – KATRINA BALMFORTH, NEWS EDITOR, COMMERCIAL RADIO

Once the angle is established, the writer has to work out the introduction (also known as *intro* or *lead* – UK, or headline sentence – USA). This is the first sentence or paragraph of the story and also the most important. Its function is to:

- State the most significant point.
- Grab attention.
- Whet the appetite.
- Signpost the way into the rest of the story.

The first twenty or thirty words are like the ornate fly that an angler uses to lure the fish. The story opening has to be bright, attractive, skilfully constructed and worthy of further investigation. Once listeners are interested and take the bait you can reel them in with the rest of the story.

The intro contains the most important point. If there has been an art auction at which a masterpiece by Rubens has fetched a record price, the main point will be the record sum paid for the painting.

To make it easier to select the main point, it can help to choose a key word or short phrase that sums up whatever is most important about the story.

The key word in the art auction story is 'record'. If the story concerned a car crash that had killed 16, the most important point would be the 16 deaths, not the crash. Car crashes happen all the time, but they seldom claim so many lives, so *'16 dead'* becomes the key phrase.

To build up the story, it may help to imagine a newspaper headline, which could be worked up into an introduction. So, *'Record price for masterpiece'* would be the starting place for the art auction story, and *'Car crash kills 16'* would do for the other.

Both stories would probably make national news, and would lead a local news bulletin if they happened in an area covered by a radio or TV station. The locality would become central to the story and the line would change to *'Record price for masterpiece at New York art auction'*, and *'Car crash in Lagos kills 16'*.

Some stations also require the *today* angle to be pointed up in the intro to heighten the immediacy of the story.

Lastly, as it would scarcely do for broadcasters to speak in headlines, these stories need reworking to turn them into conversational speech, which is easily done.

'The highest price ever paid for a masterpiece has been reached at an art auction in New York.'

'A multiple car crash in downtown Lagos has this morning claimed the lives of 16 people.'

The ideal hard news intro or headline sentence should be short – no longer than twenty to thirty words; uncluttered and without unnecessary detail; simple; direct and capable of grabbing and holding interest.

Placing key words

Looking more closely at the second example above, it might seem more direct to say *'16 people were killed this morning in a multiple car crash in downtown Lagos'*. This would get over the important information and communicate well enough in print, but for broadcast news, putting the main point right at the beginning of the story could create a problem.

The reader of a newspaper is led around the printed page by its layout. Each story is clearly separated from the one before and the reader can choose which items to look at and which to ignore from the headlines, which also prepare the reader for the information to come. Television approaches this with its graphics and strong visual element, but in radio the layout is invisible and sometimes inaudible. Stories are separated by pauses and there is only the reader's voice and the writer's ability to help the listener tell where one story ends and the next begins.

With radio the problem is compounded because people tend to listen with half an ear while they tinker with the car, splash paint over the ceiling or shout at the children. Absolute attention is usually reserved for times of national crisis when families huddle in silent anticipation around their receivers.

COUNTY SOUND RADIO				News Cue Sheet				

Title	Musician				Bulletin/tick/notes:::::::::::Bulletin/tick/notes			
Date	29.9.—	Time	12.10	06.00		14.00		
				07.00		15.00		
Credit		Copy taken by		08.00		16.00	/	
				09.00		17.00		
Words	Natalie	Audio	Natalie	10.00		18.00		
				11.00		19.00		
For broadcast	today – lunch			12.00		22.00		
				13.00	/	24.00		
Cut taken from				Quality: Studio ☐ Location ☒ Phone ☐				

Detectives hunting the triple railway killer – who murdered HORSLEY schoolgirl MARTY TAMBOEZER – are fiercely denying reports the man they want to trap is a musician.

And they say he didn't kill all THREE victims by tying guitar string arund their throats and throttling them to death.

SUPERINTENDENT JOHN HIRST at GUILDFORD CID says the article in a SUNDAY newspaper is totally inaccurate . . .

CUT	Musician	SPECIAL INSTRUCTIONS
DUR	19	
OUT	Irresponsible	
Total	40	

Figure 24 Some news editors insist copy is prepared on special cue sheets. This example gives detailed information about when the story was written, when it was intended for use and when it was actually broadcast. It also shows the recording was made on location rather than in the studio or over the phone. This helps the producer avoid putting too many similar-sounding items into the bulletin.

The box at the bottom left of the sheet gives the title of the recording accompanying the cue, its duration and last words, and the combined duration of the cue and audio. The cue itself points up the local angle in the introduction and stress words are marked by putting them in capitals or in bold. (*Courtesy County Sound*)

Under normal circumstances, the first few words of a news item may easily slip by unnoticed. If the main point does escape the audience, then by the time their attention is drawn back to the story, the whole meaning of the piece may be lost. So avoid putting key words right at the beginning.

Feature openers

> '*A good radio news story takes the listener immediately to the heart of the latest development in terms which anyone with a little intelligence can understand. The story should be told in a way that reflects the tone of the news – whether it's tragic, exciting, amusing or whatever.*'
>
> – MICHAEL DODD,
> ABC (AUSTRALIA) FREELANCE FOREIGN CORRESPONDENT

Not all opening sentences follow the hard news formula. The feature, human interest or soft news story is primarily for entertainment, so the order in which the information is given becomes less important. What matters most is that the story brings a moment of light relief to the audience, and this calls for a different writing technique:

> '*If you've got a thing about creepy crawlies and the thought of stepping on a snake makes you sick, then spare a thought for Jeb Winston from Canberra.*
> '*Jeb's going to be surrounded by snakes . . . many of them poisonous . . . for up to a fortnight. He's planning to sit cross legged in an eight by six tank with more than forty serpents to keep him company in a bid to break the world record for snake-sitting.*'

The hard news formula calls for the meat of the story in the first line, but the introductory paragraph here teases the audience into wanting to get to the bottom of the matter by beginning with a tantalizing appeal to the emotions.

The style is conversational, even anecdotal, and contrasts with the brisk formality of hard news. The story is relaxed, and so is the style of its writing and delivery. This easy-going and informal approach is often used for cheerful end-of-bulletin items.

Most bulletin stories will be written in the straight-backed, concise, hard news style. But the same story can undergo a revolution in style when written in greater detail for a longer programme. Where the presenter is given room to be a 'personality', the writing will often loosen up to take on a chattier, more relaxed and discursive approach:

> **Bulletin intro**: '*Three counties in New Mexico have been declared disaster areas after a winter storm claimed the lives of five people.*'
> **Programme intro**: '*The weather continues to make big news. Some places have more snow than they can handle and others, it seems, can't get enough of it. While St Paul in Minnesota is having to import 600 tons of snow before it can stage its Winter Carnival, elsewhere snowdrifts of up to seven feet are paralysing whole areas and claiming lives. In New Mexico, three counties have been declared disaster areas, after being hit by savage winter storms which killed five people.*'

The feature style, which leads the audience into the story rather than presenting them with the facts in the first line, is used more freely wherever greater emphasis is placed on entertainment and a lighter touch than on straightforward and sometimes impersonal, hard news.

Developing the story

> *'A story has to be built up logically. Start with an attention-grabbing development – something new. Then give the story a beginning, a middle and an end. You have to tell a tale.'*
> – MALCOLM DOWNING, AUSTRALIAN BROADCASTING CORPORATION

Finding the intro is the hardest task in newswriting. Once that is settled the rest of the item will usually fall into place.

The next step is to list the points in their logical order, constructing a story that progresses from point to point without running back on itself or leaving the listener dangling for an explanation.

Explanation usually follows the introduction, and after that comes more detail (beware of clutter), and the tying up of loose ends. This has been described as the *WHAT formula*:

The WHAT formula

W   What has happened? The introduction tells the story in brief.
H   How did it happen? Explain the immediate background or context.
A   Amplify the introduction. Flesh out the main points in order of importance.
T   Tie up loose ends. Give additional background material.

The final story should answer the questions, *who*, *what*, *when*, *where*, *why* and *how*, though not necessarily in that order.

Figure 25   Writing the script isn't always done at the wordprocessor. Reporter Shiulie Ghosh (centre) handwrites the links for her TV news package on location in the editing van. (*Andrew Boyd*)

The trickiest part is deciding which facts to include and which to leave out. A 20-second story is only 60 words long, which leaves no room for superfluous detail. Frequently, important points have to give way if vital points are to remain.

The test of non-essential information is, does the audience need it to make sense of the story, or will the story stand up without it?

In the case of our snake sitter above, his name and where he comes from are important, but his middle names, the name of his road and the number of his house are irrelevant. The details of how he and the snakes will be fed over the fortnight might be interesting, but could be dropped if space is short, while his chances of surviving unbitten and what would happen if a snake did sink its fangs into him would be well worth a mention.

Simply stated, the skill is to write up the information in order of importance until space runs out and then leave the rest.

> *'Tell us why a story is significant, make the connections for us, don't use the language of the insider. Above all don't "dumb down" . . . If people don't make the connections between their own lives and events in the world beyond, then it's partly because we are failing. Failing to understand what moves them, failing to explain the relevance of that issue or event.'* — TONY HALL, CHIEF EXECUTIVE, BBC NEWS

Signposting

> *'Tell 'em you're gonna tell 'em; tell 'em you're tellin' 'em, and tell 'em you've told 'em.'* — ANON

Broadcasting has one major limitation – it is a medium of impressions. The spoken word has an infuriating habit of going in one ear and out the other. Research has shown that people can only recall about two items in eight from the previous night's TV news.*

So to beat these odds, the journalist has to work with the medium and write to create an impression – rather than trying to force-feed an audience with facts that are no sooner heard than forgotten. The art is to decide on the one lasting impression you want to leave your audience, which will usually be the main point of the story, and then to reinforce that by subtly pushing the point home throughout. This is called signposting, and it works like this:

> *Murder charges are being drawn up after a prisoner accused of blasphemy was allegedly tortured to death in police custody in Pakistan.*
> *Under Pakistan's Sharia religious law the penalty for blasphemy is death. But Mukhtar Masih was killed before his case could come to court.*
> *Masih – a Christian – was charged with sending a blasphemous letter to the leader of a mosque.*
> *The note bore his name and address. If he had written it himself he would have been signing his own death warrant.*

* Laurie Taylor and Bob Mullen, *Uninvited Guests*, Chatto and Windus, 1986.

> *Masih died within 24 hours of being taken into police custody. An autopsy showed he had been beaten with a blunt instrument.*
> *Lahore's High Court Prosecutor, Naeem Shakir, is filing a murder charge against two police officers.*
> *Opponents of the Sharia law say the case is another example of an individual being falsely accused of blasphemy to settle a grudge. They're calling for the law to be changed.*

There are three key elements to this story: murder, blasphemy and their location – Pakistan. There is also a twist – the allegation that the police themselves committed the crime. All four points are combined in the intro, which sets the scene for the story.

The story is complicated and needs some explaining. So the second paragraph places the events in context. It takes care to explain that the Sharia is the religious law. Then it contrasts the legal death penalty with the unlawful killing.

The next two paragraphs explain why Masih was suspected of blasphemy – then raise an important question about the evidence.

The following paragraph returns to his death in police custody and explains why murder charges may be brought.

By creating contrasts these four paragraphs help us to see the wood for the trees.

Then we are brought up to date by returning to the main angle of the story, which was signposted in the intro: the charges against the police. That fact is amplified to tell us who is bringing the charge.

Finally the story is rounded off by placing the whole event in a wider context to illustrate its significance.

The aim is to make the message of the story inescapably clear. Signposting picks out the thread of the argument without requiring the audience to backtrack, which is impossible over the air. The skill lies in highlighting and restating the main points without making them *sound* like repetition.

Last line

The last line should round off the story and point ahead to any next developments. This is the *'tell 'em you've told 'em'* part of the signposting. A story about trouble on the roads could end:

> *'. . . and difficult driving conditions are expected to continue until much later this evening.'*

A story about an unofficial bus strike, could finish:

> *'Bus drivers will be meeting their union leaders this afternoon to try to persuade them to make the strike official.'*

Both closings refer back to the events in question (conditions on the roads; the bus strike) and show the way ahead (difficult conditions continuing into the evening; the meeting with union leaders).

Another way to round off a story is for the presenter to pick up on the end of audio or film footage with a final comment. This is known as a *back announcement* (or *back anno*, *BA*). It is a useful device for giving out phone numbers or updating an item recorded earlier with new information:

> **BA**: *'And we've just heard that the road is now clear and traffic is starting to move. Tailbacks are still expected for the next half hour.'*

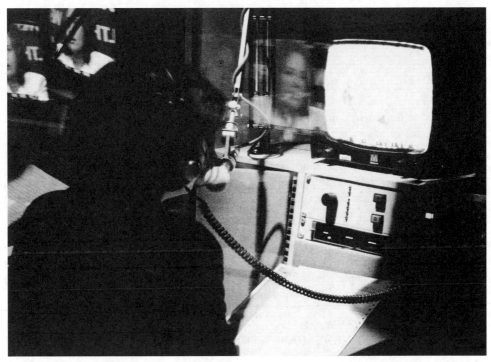

Figure 26   In TV the golden rule is to write the script around the pictures for split-second timing. The next task is to record the narration while the pictures play in the commentary booth. (*Andrew Boyd*)

Back announcements are commonly used in radio to remind an audience who or what they have been listening to and as a bridge between items where some natural link can be found.

> **BA**: *'Mary Fernandez reporting on the growing numbers of teenagers who run away from home . . . Well, one of the biggest dangers to those children must come from the drug pushers, and there's worrying news of yet another kind of drug that is now being sold on the streets . . . etc.'*

Last words

The lasting impression of any programme or item is usually made by the first and last words, and as much care should be taken on ending the story as in writing the intro. As well as beginning strongly, the story should end on a positive note, and not be allowed to tail off weakly or to fizzle out. All writing for the spoken word is a form of poetry so aim to create a pleasing rhythm.

News stories should end with a bang rather than a whimper. Strong, definite and emphatic last words are preferable to limp endings:

> **Prefer**: *'she said the investigation would be launched at once.'*
> **To**: *'. . . the investigation would be launched at once, she said.'*
> **Weak**: *'. . . the gunmen are threatening to shoot the hostages at midnight unless the Government gives in to them.'*
> **Stronger**: *'. . . the gunmen are threatening to shoot the hostages at midnight, unless the Government gives in to their demands.*

The last words are the ones the audience will remember – so make them memorable.

Accuracy

> *'In the case of news we should always wait for the sacrament of confirmation'*
> – VOLTAIRE

'A journalist is someone who finds a story and then lures the facts towards it', and *'Never let the facts get in the way of a good story'*, are cynical quips which, unfortunately, sometimes contain more than a grain of truth.

But nothing devalues a reporter's credibility faster than getting the facts wrong.

Mispronouncing place names irritates listeners and slipping up over someone's name or job title can sour a valued contact. More seriously, an inaccurate court report could lead to a libel suit or an action for contempt. The best maxim for the journalist is *'If in doubt . . . check it out'*.

The main points of the story should always be verified, so no contentious or uncertain points are left to chance. *If they can't be checked out, they should be chucked out.*

The example below illustrates how difficult it can be to get the facts right, especially on a breaking story. This snap arrived on the telex from a news agency:

86626 MYNEWS G
M AND Y NEWSAGENCY, PORTSMOUTH
OIL RIG
A 400 TON SUPPLY SHIP HAS COLLIDED WITH ONE OF THE LEGS OF THE PENROD THREE OIL RIG, 20 MILES SOUTH OF THE ISLE OF WIGHT AND IS TRAPPED IN THE OIL RIG AND SINKING, WITH EIGHT PEOPLE ON BOARD.
IT'S POSSIBLE THAT THE DAMAGE TO THE OILRIG WILL CAUSE IT TO COLLAPSE.
THE SAR HELICOPTER FROM LEE ON SOLENT HAS BEEN SCRAMBLED.
MORE FOLLOWS LATER.
86626 MYNEWS G

A battery of quick-fire calls was made to the coastguard and the search and rescue (SAR) service among others. These threw up the following conflicting information:

Name of oil rig	*Name of ship*	*Size of ship*
Penrod 3	Spearfish	150 tons
Penrod No. 3	Spearship	400 tons
Penrod 83		500 tons
Penrod 85		
Penrose 85		

Number of crew	*Damage to rig*	*State of ship*
6	Slight	Sunk
7	In danger of collapse	Not sunk
8		Partially sunk
		Being towed ashore
		Scuttled

Method of scuttling	*Number of helicopters at scene*	*Location*
Blown up	1	10 miles south of island
Shot out of the water	2	15 miles south of island
		20 miles south of island

Figure 27 Presenting the news on a journalism degree course at the Surrey Institute of Art and Design. The radio script incorporates details of audio inserts to be played in the news bulletin. (*Andrew Boyd*)

Fast-moving events, inaccessible location and lack of official comment from experts too tied up in the operation to talk made the facts difficult to establish.

In the end, the story was that the 143-ton trawler *Spearfish* had become entangled in one of the legs of the *Penrod 85* oil rig when it was trying to land supplies. The six-man crew was winched to safety by *one* helicopter before the ship was towed clear by a frigate and sunk by *anti-aircraft fire*.

The best angle did not emerge until later, when an inspection of the helicopter rotors revealed they had flown so close to the rig that the blades had clipped the superstructure. A couple of centimetres closer and the helicopter would have crashed.

With news flashes and breaking news some reshuffling of the facts is expected as the story becomes clearer. But there are times when getting the facts wrong can have disastrous consequences.

Reports of accidents, air crashes and loss of life must be handled with utmost care. If a crowded passenger train has been derailed and passengers killed, there can be no excuses for confusing the time of the train with that of another. A slip of the eye or stumble on the keyboard can render numbers wildly out, which can have a dramatic effect on a story and create widespread alarm.

> During a severe earthquake in Turkey, Faika Yertutan was travelling on a bus back to her home town, Izmit. Over the bus radio crackled a news flash announcing the quake and declaring: 'Izmit is no more'.
>
> 'It was a 12 hour journey that felt like 12 days,' said Faika, who expected to find her family and friends buried beneath the rubble. Mercifully, they survived, as had most of Izmit. The radio announcer had exaggerated, leaving Faika and others like her to cope with their anxiety.

Unnecessary stress and panic can be prevented by giving specific and accurate details, and with an air crash, by broadcasting the flight number.

When names of the dead are released, those names have to be got right, and if the name is a common one, like Smith, Brown or Patel, details of the address should be given to avoid needless worry.

> *'A newswriter is a man without virtue who writes lies for profit.'*
> – ADAPTED FROM SAMUEL JOHNSON

Fieldwork

1 Put the hard news formula to the test. Go through a couple of meaty newspaper stories marking out where the story answers the questions, *who*, *what*, *when*, *where*, *why* and *how*. Then list the order in which those answers appeared.

2 Sum up the main point of each story in a key phrase of five words or less. Then compare your key phrases to the newspaper headlines. How similar are they? Do the headlines home in on different points? Why?

   Next develop your key phrases into an intro for each story. Keep each intro down to thirty words at maximum. Then compare your intros with the ones used by the newspaper. What are the differences?

3 Construct a hard news story from the following collection of facts:

The Bantry Bay Company employs a workforce of 3000.
There are no plans to cut shopfloor workers.
The company makes widgets.
10 per cent of the clerical workers are to lose their jobs.
The company lost £2 m in the first half of last year.
The cuts are to try to improve efficiency and reduce costs.
There are 1000 white collar (clerical) workers.
The company says that early retirement and voluntary redundancies should account for most of the job cuts.
The last redundancies at the Bantry Bay Company took place five years ago.

4 Now put together a soft news feature from the following facts. Remember, the style ought to be less terse and more entertaining. You will need to think of livelier ways to report the facts than they are given here and should try to avoid repeating the word 'alligator' too often.

The trapper's name was John Tanner.
The alligator weighed 150 pounds.
Mr Tanner took with him only a rope lasso and miner's lamp.
The alligator tried to bite through the noose. With moments to spare, Mr Tanner managed to bind its jaws with electrical tape.
The alligator was caught in the sewers beneath Orlando, in Florida.
Alligator meat is a local delicacy. He could have sold it for its meat and its hide.
He wrestled with the alligator and managed to slip the noose around its neck.
He did not get any money for his efforts. 'It wasn't hurting anybody,' he said.

He got the alligator to come to him by imitating the mating call of the female alligator.
The authorities sent for Mr Tanner after state trappers had failed to catch the reptile, which had tried to bite four drainage inspectors.
He took it to a remote part of the country and let it go.

5 Now turn that feature item into a hard news story of fewer than 100 words. Then go back over your stories and check they are well signposted, end strongly and are easy to read out loud. Finally, if you are in a class, swap your work with someone else, and sub-edit their versions, making any alterations you think are necessary.

WRITING FOR BROADCAST

7 Broadcast style book

> **Good style:**
> *'If I had a donkey as wouldn't go,*
> *do you think I'd wallop him? Oh no.*
> *I'd give him some corn and cry out 'Whoa,*
> *Gee up, Neddy.'*
>
> **Bad style:**
> *'If I had an ass that refused to proceed,*
> *Do you suppose that I should castigate him?*
> *No indeed.*
> *I should present him with some cereals and observe proceed,*
> *Continue, Edward.'*
>   – HAROLD EVANS*

Most broadcast organizations have a view about good style, and though they differ in detail, most would agree that good style is usually whatever makes good sense.

George Orwell wrote *Politics and the English Language* in 1946, but his advice still holds true today;

- Never use a metaphor, simile or other figure of speech which you are used to seeing in print.
- Never use a long word where a short one will do.
- If it is possible to cut out a word, always cut it out.
- Never use the passive where you can use the active.
- Never use a foreign phrase, scientific word or a jargon word if you can think of an everyday English equivalent.
- Break any of these rules sooner than say anything outright barbarous.†

* *Newsman's English*, Heinemann, 1972.
† George Orwell, *Politics and the English Language*.

Clichés

Eric Partridge, in his *Dictionary of Clichés*, defines the cliché as 'a phrase so hackneyed as to be knock-kneed and spavined.'*

They not only fail to enliven dull copy, clichés make even the most significant item sound trite. If we accuse council tax payers of taking up cudgels against city hall whenever they write a letter of complaint, what are we to say the day owner-occupiers really *do* drive nails through wooden clubs and set about their elected representatives?

What will be left to say when war *is* declared?

Hyperbole and clichés are for hacks. This, then, is a dictionary for hacks:

absolute farce	headache	paid the penalty
acid test	heart of gold	painted a grim picture
all-out-effort	heated debate	part and parcel
anybody's guess	high-ranking	picking up the pieces
around the table	horror	point in time
as sick as a parrot	how does it feel?	pool of blood
at this point in time	in a nutshell	pride and joy
balanced on a knife edge	in due course	probe
beat a hasty retreat	in full swing	pull out the stops
bid (for attempt)	iron out the problem	put into perspective
bitter end	jobless youngsters	quiz (for question)
bolt from the blue	lashed out at	rushed to the scene
bombshell	last but not least	selling like hot cakes
boost	last-ditch effort	shock
boss	last-minute decision	short and sweet
brutal reminder	leading the hunt	shot himself in the foot
calm before the storm	leaps and bounds	shot in the arm
calm but tense	leave no stone unturned	show of force
cash boost	limped into port	sitting on the fence
chequered career	loud and clear	sitting on a goldmine
chief	lucky few	$64 000 question
clampdown	luxury liner	square peg in a round
crackdown	major new development/	hole
daylight robbery	project	still anybody's guess
deciding factor	marked contrast	stuck to his/her guns
desperate attempt/bid	mercy dash	sweeping changes
doctors fought	miracle cure	up in arms
drama	mindless vandals	up in the air
dramatic decision/new move	mine of information	vanished into thin air
dug in their heels	news leaked out	vast amount
effortless victory	nipped in the bud	virtual standstill
fell on deaf ears	none the worse for wear	voiced his approval
gave as good as he got	not to be outdone	weighty matter
get under way	one in the eye	what of the future?
given the green light	over and above	whole new ball game
going walkabout	over the moon	wreak havoc
got the message	own goal	writing on the wall

No doubt you will have your own favourites to add to the list. With technology making strides, it may soon be possible to program into a computer an elaborate lexicon of clichés,

* Routledge, 1940.

enter the type of story, say, *murder*; key in details such as the name of the victim, and within a matter of seconds, we could be reading printouts of sparkling news copy, such as the following:

> *'Police are hunting a vicious killer following the brutal murder of (FILL IN NAME) in his opulent country house in the secluded backwater of (FILL IN NAME) this morning.*
> *'(FILL IN NAME)'s mutilated body was found lying in a pool of blood in the bedroom. A sawn off shotgun lay nearby. Police discovered the corpse after a dawn raid on the mansion in the early hours of the morning, following a tip from an underworld supergrass.*
> *'Detective Inspector (FILL IN NAME) who's leading the hunt, said the killer had vanished into thin air. Police with tracker dogs were now combing nearby woods, and pledged to leave no stone unturned until the butcher of (FILL IN NAME) had been brought to justice.*
> *'(FILL IN NAME) was described by stunned and grief-stricken neighbours as "a pillar of society".*
> *'(FILL IN NAME)'s widow, shapely blonde (FILL IN NAME) told us how she felt . . .'*

Journalese

The cliché owes much to journalese, described by writer John Leo as the native tongue of newsgatherers and pundits. It is the language of the label and instant metaphor, drawing its inspiration from space-starved newspaper headlines to make pronouncements of stunning clarity over matters which to everybody else appear decidedly muddied.

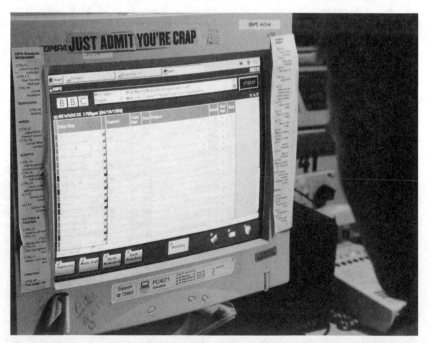

Figure 28 *'Just admit you're – what is house style for "crap"?'* Preparing a news programme on the BBC's Electronic News Production System. How long before someone programmes the computer to sound the alarm if the house style is broken? (*Andrew Boyd*)

> *'Every cub reporter ... knows that fires rage out of control, minor mischief is perpetrated by Vandals (never Visigoths, Franks or a single Vandal working alone) and key labour accords are hammered out by weary negotiators in marathon, round-the-clock bargaining sessions, thus narrowly averting threatened walkouts.'*
>
> – JOHN LEO*

More disturbingly, an evening's sport of name-calling, stone-throwing and petty crimes against property by rival gangs of schoolboys in Northern Ireland (which is divided along sectarian, religious, tribal and political lines) becomes a *'fresh outbreak of violence between loyalists and republican supporters ...'*

Clichés and journalese are devils disguised as angels. They lie in wait for the moment Inspiration turns her back, before overpowering her, stealing her clothes and sneaking up on the reporter as a deadline approaches.

Hapless hacks are usually so intent on beating the clock that they fail to see through the disguise and welcome these saboteurs as saviours. So resigned are reporters to their infiltration and so dependent on their support that, even when their disguise wears thin through over-use, the two are often left to wreak their havoc unchecked. The alternative is to waste precious minutes attempting to revive Inspiration, who has an infuriating habit of succumbing whenever deadlines draw near.

Even books are written to deadlines, and it is not inconceivable that you may unmask the odd cliché within these pages. Feel free to strike the offender through with a biro and, if you find Inspiration at her post, make some suitable correction.

Hyperbole

> **Definition of hype**
> *'Exaggerated statement not meant to be taken literally.'*
> – *CONCISE OXFORD DICTIONARY*
>
> *'Headlines twice the size of the events.'* – JOHN GALSWORTHY

Another blood relation of journalese is hype. Hype can be found scattered throughout the media, and in especially large concentrations wherever advertising copywriters gather.

Many journalists readily call on hype's assistance to lend support to a flaccid story on a quiet news day.

> *'Children's lives could be at risk if they swallow quantities of a lethal drug which have gone missing in Harare.'*

Translated: Somebody dropped their sleeping tablets on their way home from the shops.

> *'A man has been arrested in Perth after an appalling and unprovoked sex attack on a defenceless three-year-old girl.'*

---

* 'Journalese for the lay reader', *Time*, 18 March, 1985.

But: All sex attacks are appalling:
    NO three-year-old girl is likely to provoke such an attack
    ALL small girls are defenceless.

Hype of this order is unpleasant, distasteful and unnecessary. If the story can't stand up without it, it should not be run.

If the news is to remain a reliable source of factual information, hype should be kept within the confines of the commercial break.

Adjectives

> *'I will rarely use an adjective and only because I think it's important, and then I will ask for it to be taken out in the next bulletin.'*
> — PENNY YOUNG, BBC NEWS EDITOR

How many adjectives you use will depend on your house style and whether the station's image is 'quality' or 'popular'. Contrast the versions below:

> *'Firemen with oxy-acetylene cutters took three hours to free the body from the wreckage. They said it was one of the worst crashes they'd seen.'*

> *'Firemen with oxy-acetylene cutters struggled for three hours to free the mangled body from the shattered cab. They said the horrific crash was one of the worst they'd seen.'*

Most stations would think twice about the tasteless 'mangled'. Adjectives add colour but too many make the piece sound like an extract from a lurid novel. Remove them all and the item can sound dull or bland. Handle with care.

Quotations

A choice quotation can add considerably to the flavour of a report, but there are hazards in using quotes in broadcasting.

In print a quote is immediately obvious because of the quotation marks, but broadcast audiences cannot *hear* when a quote begins and ends, so they should be kept short and clearly attributed:

> *'The Prime Minister rounded on the protesters, accusing them of "behaving like a bunch of anarchists".'*

The newsreader can help with the signposting, by pausing for a fraction of a second before reading the quote.

Attribution

Information should be attributed clearly to leave the audience in no doubt about who is speaking – remember, listeners can never refer back. This said, attribution can be overdone and badly clutter a piece of copy:

> *'The honourable Peter Threeple, Junior Minister in the Department of Health, said today than an injection of 20 million pounds would be made available to improve wages in the National Health Service.'*

Not exactly an attention grabber, so the sentence should be turned around to put the facts before the attribution, and the attribution shortened to be still accurate, but much more manageable:

> *'A cash injection of 20 million pounds is to be made available to improve wages in the Health Service.*
> *'Health Minister Peter Threeple told the Commons today that the money . . . etc.'*

The message is often more important than the messenger. In this case the news of the funding is more important than the name of the minister, so the information should be run before the attribution.

Stories should begin with a person's name only when that name is widely known. If the audience cannot immediately identify the person, this becomes a point of confusion at the start of a story.

To avoid cluttering an introduction it is sometimes necessary to choose between giving a person's name or title in the first line. If their name is better known than their job or organization, then the name should be given before the title, and vice versa.

> *'The Director General of the CBI, Digby Jones, has called on the Bank of England to hold down interest rates.'*

This might work satisfactorily in print, but spoken out loud the first line becomes cluttered and the title CBI may not be universally understood. The attribution should be spread over two sentences and some clear signposting provided:

> *'The leader of Britain's employers is calling on the Bank of England to hold down interest rates. Digby Jones, Director General of the Confederation of British Industry, wants the Bank to . . . etc.'*

The art is to attribute a statement clearly without letting the attribution get in the way. Television has a major advantage over radio – interviewees can appear without a verbal introduction because their names and titles can be displayed on the screen over the pictures.

Contentious statements

When statements are controversial or contentious the attribution has to be made clearly and cannot be held back until the second sentence:

> *'America's unemployed are a shiftless, lazy bunch of spongers, who should be forced to sweep the streets until they find a decent job.' So said Governor Richman at a news conference today . . .'*

This first sentence has turned a highly debatable assertion into a statement of fact, and the danger is that the audience may miss the attribution that follows and identify the opinion with the newsreader. The station could lose a large section of its audience – the unemployed. Maintain impartiality by keeping a safe distance from such statements.

This problem is avoided by giving the attribution in the same sentence and signposting that this is a matter of opinion and not facts:

> *'Governor Richman launched a scathing attack on America's unemployed today . . . calling them a shiftless, lazy bunch of spongers. And, speaking at a news conference, he said they should be forced to sweep the streets until they could get themselves decent jobs.'*

This gets the broadcaster off the hook and leaves Governor Richman dangling firmly *on* it.

Careful attribution is crucial where facts are being asserted which have yet to be proven true. It is not uncommon with war reporting to find both sides claiming substantial victories over each other at the same time. Unless the facts can be confirmed from independent sources, such statements should never be given without qualification:

> *'Cornish and Devonian forces are both claiming significant victories today. The Cornish airforce* **say** *they shot down 14 Devonian bombers with no losses of their own and the Devonian airforce is* **claiming** *to have destroyed every Cornish airfield. Both sides now* **say** *they have total air superiority and in official statements today each side* **alleges** *the other is lying.'*

Say, claim and *allege* are useful qualifications for suspect information and distance the newsreader enough to avoid sounding like a propaganda mouthpiece. *Claim* and *allege* should be avoided where no doubt is meant to be implied, and repetition of the word *'said'* can be avoided by using phrases like *'he added'* or *'pointed out'*.

Immediacy

One of the great strengths of broadcast news is its immediacy. It wipes the floor with newspapers when it comes to reacting quickly to changing events. The Cuban missile crisis in 1962 when the world stood on the brink of nuclear war has been accredited as the catalyst which caused the switch from papers to TV as the prime source of news.*

Broadcasters are able to follow events as they unfold. They understandably play to their strengths, and most newsrooms heighten the sense of immediacy in their copy by using the present or perfect tenses. While tomorrow's newspaper will tell us:

> *'Victory celebrations took place yesterday in both India and Pakistan over the agreement to end the fighting in Kashmir.' (Past tense)*

Today's bulletin might say:

> *'Indian and Pakistan have both claimed victory over the agreement to end the fighting in Kashmir.' (Perfect tense)*

To use either of these backward-looking tenses is to retreat from the immediacy of the action. The present tense is even more up-to-the-minute:

> *'Thousands of Angolans are fleeing into Zambia to escape fighting which is erupting again in Angola's eastern province.'*

---

* Anthony Davis, *Television: Here is the news*, Independent Books Ltd, 1976, p. 23.

The word 'yesterday' is taboo in broadcasting. Nothing sounds more incongruous than a station with hourly bulletins giving a time reference that harks back 24 hours. If 'yesterday' or 'last night' have to be used, they should be kept out of the opening sentence and buried further down the story.

Similarly, phrases such as *'this morning', 'this afternoon'*, or *'this evening'* can date copy. So, for inclusion in the 6 o'clock news, the following story would have to be rewritten:

> *'The chief prosecutor for the Rwandan genocide tribunal pledged this morning to re-arrest a key suspect if he is released . . .'*

The phrase *'pledged this morning'*, which would stand out like a sore thumb by the evening, would be replaced with the words *'has pledged'*. Some news editors object to prolific use of the word 'today' arguing that all broadcasting is about what happened today, so the word is redundant and can be omitted.

Similarly, exact times, such as *'at seven minutes past twelve'* should be rounded off to *'just after midday'*, and specific times should be used only if they are essential to the story or heighten the immediacy of the coverage:

> *'News just in . . . the President of Sri Lanka has been assassinated in a suicide bomb attack. The bomber struck within the past few minutes at the head of the Mayday parade in Colombo . . .'*

For those listening in the small hours of the morning, references to events *'last night'* can be confusing, and should be replaced with *'overnight'* or *'during the night'*.

Time references have to be handled even more carefully when a station is broadcasting over several time zones. Canada, for example, spans seven such zones. To avoid confusion over their copy, news agencies that file stories over a wide area usually include the day of the week in brackets.

Active

News is about movement, change and action. Yet too often newswriting is reduced to the passive voice – instead of actions that produce change, we hear of changes that have occurred as a result of actions. *'The car smashed into the brick wall'* becomes the limp and soft-centred *'the brick wall was smashed into by the car'*.

Hickory Dickory Dock	Hickory Dickory Dock
The clock was run up by the mouse	The mouse ran up the clock
One o'clock was struck	The clock struck one
Down the mouse ran	The mouse ran down
Hickory Dickory Dock	Hickory Dickory Dock.

The passive version on the left could be said to be lacking something of the snap of the original. The active voice is tighter, crisper and more concrete.

Positive

> *'Good style is when you can see pictures in your writing, but just as important is a good grasp of the English language – and that's getting rarer and rarer to find.'*
> – JUDITH MELBY, NETWORK PRODUCER,
> CANADIAN BROADCASTING CORPORATION

News is about what is happening, so even what is *not* happening should be expressed in an active, positive way. *'He did not succeed'*, becomes *'he failed'*; *'He was asked to move, but didn't'*, becomes *'he refused to move'*; *'Plans for the hospital would not go ahead for the time being'*, becomes, *'Plans for the hospital have been shelved'*.

Double negatives should be unravelled; *'Doctors say it is improbable that the illness will not prove terminal'* becomes *'Doctors admit the patient will probably die'*.

Redundancies

Redundancies are words that serve only to clutter up the copy. They should be ruthlessly eliminated:

> **Check *out***
> ***End* result**
> ***Period* of a week, etc.**

One of the worst offenders is the little word *'that'*, which can straddle the middle of a sentence like a roadblock:

> *'Rugby, and New Zealand's All Blacks say* **that they are** *set to trounce arch-rivals Fiji in the World Sevens Series.'*

Dump 'that' and contract 'they are'. It slips off the tongue much more smoothly: *'The All-Blacks say they're set to trounce . . .'*

Like that, *the* can also be a pain. To be extreme about them both:

> *'When asked about* **the** *possible strike action,* **the** *dockers' leaders said* **that** *they hoped that* **that** *would not be necessary.'*

Now read the sentence again and leave out the words in bold.

Every word should earn its place in the copy. Newswriting is too streamlined to carry any passengers. Modifiers such as *'very'*, *'quite'*, and *'almost'* are excess baggage and should be dumped.

Repetition

> *'The obvious is better than the obvious avoidance of it'*
> – *FOWLER'S MODERN ENGLISH USAGE*

Unnecessary repetition of words can jar the ear and should be avoided, but if no alternative can be found, and if it *sounds* right, then don't be afraid to repeat. No one has yet come up with a way of avoiding saying 'fire' in a story about a . . . well, a conflagration, without sounding absurd. Common practice is to alternate the words 'fire' and 'blaze'.

Where a *proposal* is involved, alternatives such as *scheme*, *plan*, *project* or *programme* may be used.

Homonyms

Homonyms are words that sound like others with different meanings:

Bare	and	**Bear**
Blight	and	**Plight**
Ate	and	**Eight**
Billion	and	**Million**
Fatal	and	**Facial**

Confusing fatal and facial injuries in an accident report could give somebody's mother a heart attack! Usually the context will make the meaning of the word clear, but beware of baffling the listener.

Singular or plural?

Should it be the Government *says* or the Government *say*? Opinions differ and many newsrooms settle the issue by writing whatever sounds right to the ear. The trouble starts when inconsistencies creep into the copy:

> *'The Conservative party say their policies will defend Britain's position in Europe. The party wants an end to what it describes as "European meddling" in Britain's affairs.*

'The Conservative party says' and *'The party wants'* may both sound right individually, but they do not sound right together. Journalists must make up their own mind.

Pronouns

Using pronouns in broadcasting requires a special discipline to get round the problem of muddling the listener who can't go back over what has been said:

> *'Film star Richard Cruise was involved in an ugly scene with fellow actor Tom Gere outside a Hollywood restaurant today. Cruise called Gere a has-been, and Gere responded by casting doubt on Cruise's parentage. He said he would sue.'*

Is Gere suing Cruise or is Cruise suing Gere? The way around this is to swap the pronoun for a name:

> *'Cruise said he would sue.'*

Punctuation

Writing for broadcast is writing to be read aloud. Sentences should be broken into groups of meaning and these should be separated by a visible pause. Semi-colons and colons do not work well because they are visually too similar to the full stop (period) or comma.

Pauses that are intended to be longer than a comma can be indicated by the dash – – hyphen - ellipsis . . . or slash /. The ellipsis or dash (double hyphen) are perhaps the most effective indicators of pauses because they create more physical space between words than other forms of punctuation. Each new idea should be separated by a longer pause, and the best way to indicate this is to begin a new paragraph.

Capital letters can be used for names or to create emphasis, but if the story is written entirely in capitals, as is often the case (*sic*), the emphasis and visual signal at the start of the sentence is lost.

Spelling

> *'The names of people represent an enormous threat, particularly if they're foreign names that you suddenly see for the first time.'*
> – ANNA FORD, UK NEWSREADER AND PRESENTER
>
> *'If you get a difficult name to pronounce and you're fairly uncertain in your own mind about it, there's one golden rule – look the viewer straight in the eye through the camera lens, and say the first thing that comes into your head.'*
> – ANDREW GARDNER, BRITISH NEWSREADER*

Some people say spelling is irrelevant in broadcasting, but that is not strictly true. The listener may not know if the wurds are speld gud, but misspelled words can act like banana skins beneath unwary newsreaders and cause them to stumble or trip.

Foreign or unfamiliar names can also be a problem. The solution is to spell them *fon-et-ik-lee* (phonetically) – as they sound. It is also a good idea to warn newsreaders of a pronunciation trap by marking the top of the page. They can then rehearse the troublesome word.

Abbreviations

Abbreviations generally make sense to the eye, but not to the ear. All but the most common, such as Mr and Mrs and USA, should be avoided.

Names of organizations should be spelled out unless they are commonly known by their initials, such as the BBC. Never use abbreviations that the newsreader would have to translate, such as C-in-C for Commander in Chief. The newsreader may be thrown for a second or get them wrong.

Some stations require abbreviations to be hyphenated, for example P-T-A, A-N-C, unless they form recognizable words (acronyms), when they should be left intact, for example NATO.

---

* *It'll Be Alright on the Night*, London Weekend Television.

Figures

Nothing clutters copy quicker or confuses the ear more than a collection of figures. Even a short figure on a piece of paper can take a surprisingly long time to read aloud.

A single story should contain as few figures as possible, and within the bounds of accuracy numbers should always by rounded up or down to make them easier to take in: for 246 326, write 'almost 250 000' or, even better, 'nearly a quarter of a million'.

Broadcast stations vary in their approach to figures, but whatever the house style, clarity is the aim, for the sake of the newsreader as well as the listener. Resist the temptation to use *'a million'* instead of *'one million'*, as listeners could easily confuse it for eight million. *'Billion'* should also be avoided at this means different things in different countries. Refer to so many thousands of millions instead.

Proof reading

Copy should always be read out loud, to check for the sense and make sure no traps lie in wait for the unwary newsreader. Never leave it to the reader to check the copy through. A sudden rush before the bulletin could leave no time to prepare. The acid test of good copy is whether someone else could read it out loud, having never before clapped eyes on it, and get through without tripping over his tongue.

Below are some examples of hastily written copy which were actually submitted to be read on air:

> **HEALTH OFFICERS THROUGHOUT THE COUNTRY ARE BEING PUT ON THE ALERT FOR TYPYOID CASES ... AFTER SIX PEOPLE RETURNING FROM A GREEK HOLIDAY WERE FOUND TO HAVE THE DISEASE TAKES TWENTY ONE DAYS TO INCUBATE AND IT'S THOUGHT MORE CASES COULD DEVELOP IN THE NEXT FEW DAYS.**
> *****
> **ENGLAND BEAT THE REPUBLIC OF IRELAND TWO NIL LAST NIGHT AT WEMBLEY. IT WAS AN EASY WIN, AND ENGLAND WERE ON TOP UNTIL THE CLOSING MINUTES WHEN BRADY SCORED FOR IRELAND.**
> *****

Apart from the spelling mistakes, these stories may look feasible at first glance. Only when they are read through do the problems become obvious.

Even the most innocent words and phrases can sometimes conspire to trap you. Find another way of saying it *before* you go on air:

> *'Avon's ambulamencement ... Avon's ambulaments ... Avon's ambulen ... Avon's ambewlamence ... (Pause. Deep breath) The ambulancemen of Avon ...'* – British TV.

Ambiguity

Ambiguity offers the audience a rich source of humour at the newsreader's expense. Howlers can range from the simple snigger:

> *'Orchestra musicians at the Royal Opera House are threatening to strike next week, if the management turn down a 10 per cent no-strings pay rise.'*

to the cringingly embarrassing:

> '... the batsman's Holding ... the bowler's Willey ...'

Here are some other examples which might have been caught in time if the writer had troubled to read them through:

> 'Teams of traditional dancers from various parts of Kenya exposed themselves to world scouts delegates in a grand performance.'

> 'About 50 students broke into the college, smashing glass and chanting, "No cuts, no cuts". A porter had his hand injured ...'

> 'During evidence PC John Wilkinson said that John Depledge had given him a violent blow to the testicles. They both fell to the ground ...'

Fieldwork

1 Compare two radio bulletins on different stations that vary in style. Which do you prefer and why? Jot down the clichés and journalese that appear in each. See if you can come up with less hackneyed ways of saying the same thing.

2 Scan the pages of a popular newspaper for examples of journalese. How many of these phrases do you occasionally hear in radio or TV news broadcasts? Again, see if you can come up with alternatives.

3 The following story needs rewriting to clarify it, tidy up the attribution, simplify the figures and generally knock it into shape. Have a go.

Flagham Council leader and Housing Chairman, Councillor Fred Bunter MA, has dismissed opposition plans to cut council rents as 'absurd'. Rent cuts of up to 19 per cent had been suggested to help out the 6883 tenants who had fallen badly into arrears. Councillor Bunter said the rent cuts would penalise the council's other 63 722 tenants who had managed to keep up with their rent. The cut price rents scheme was proposed by opposition spokesman on Housing, Councillor Bob Taylor, who said, 'Many of these tenants have no way of paying their rent. They are in severe difficulties, often through no fault of their own, and must be helped.'

4 Rewrite the following headlines into a more immediate, direct and active broadcast style:

In connection with the Security Holdings armed robbery in Parkerville last month, four men appeared briefly in court today. An adjournment was granted for a week.
The search for twelve fishermen from a Danish trawler in the North Sea ended when they were found safe and well drifting on the sea in a small boat.
Three schoolchildren died after their school bus was hit by a car on the M1. Other vehicles were not involved.

5 The following story is a complete mess. Whoever wrote it should fear for his/her job. The angle needs pointing up, it has unnecessary repetition, redundancies, convolution, singular/plural problems, hopeless punctuation and too many adjectives. Hammer it into shape and rewrite it to broadcast style.

The Police Department is urgently calling for eye-witnesses following a tragic and fatal fire at hospital in Brunton. The fire broke out in the third floor laundry room at the modern 300-bed General Hospital in Brunton and quickly spread to the casualty ward. Frightened patients in the casualty ward hastily raised the alarm and worried doctors and nurses had to evacuate them from the ward along with all the other patients in the rest of the hospital who later heard the distressing news that an ancillary worker in the laundry room where the fire began was overcome by the fumes and sadly died in the horrific fire which is still burning fiercely as firemen continue bravely to fight the flames which are still lighting up the night sky. The police say that they think the fire may have been started on purpose. The flames have badly damaged about half of the hospital. No other patient or member of staff was injured in the fire.

INTERVIEWING

8 The interview

> *'He puts his blunt, loaded questions with the air of a prosecuting counsel at a murder trial. As he swings back to face the camera, metaphorically blowing on his knuckles, one detects the muffled disturbance as his shaken victim is led away.'*
> – SIR ROBIN DAY – THROUGH THE EYES OF A CRITIC
>
> *'It's marvellous! I have the opportunity to be impertinent to people I'd never normally meet and I can say what would be considered rude things and they have to answer. It's a position of great responsibility and I'm privileged to do it.'*
> – RICHARD BESTIC, PARLIAMENTARY CORRESPONDENT

Every scrap of information that reaches the airwaves stems from an interview of some sort – a chat in a bar to get some background, an informal phone call to clear up some details, or a recording for transmission.

Broadcasting's great appeal is that the audience can hear the facts straight from the horse's mouth. The speaker's own words lend greater authority to a report than any number of quotes in next day's newspaper. Listeners can follow events as they happen – live.

The interviewer's skill

Interviewers are brokers of information. Their skill lies in matching the goods on offer with the needs of their customers. Their art is to tease out the story in the teller's own words, while making sure every word will be clearly understood by the audience.

Listeners can then make up their own minds about whether to believe what is being said. The function of exposing the viewpoints of the powerful and influential to public debate and criticism is one of the major planks in the argument that a free news media is essential to democracy.

To the best of their ability, reporters must lay aside their own interests, points of view and prejudices. The reporter's job is not to produce propaganda, however noble the cause: that is the task of the politician and public relations officer. Reporters are watchdogs for their audience, and it is with them that their loyalties must lie.

Figure 29 The art of the interview . . . maintain eye contact while simultaneously reading the questions, working the control desk and listening to your producer in the headphones. (*Andrew Boyd*)

Reporters' skills, their knowledge of the subject, and their access to the interviewee give them the means and the responsibility to ask the sort of 'Yes, but . . .' questions their audience would love to ask in their place. The reporter is the bridge between the layperson and the expert, the person in the street and the official, and a good interview will often test the validity of an argument by exploring its points of tension or controversy.

Different types of interview

> '*Australian broadcasting tends to exhibit the directness of approach that is a key national characteristic. This means that broadcasters often tend to be very tough on politicians and other decision-makers when they won't address the point in question. When done well, this can only be a plus for the listener.*'
> – AUSTRALIAN FOREIGN CORRESPONDENT, MICHAEL DODD

The BBC tells its trainees that there are three basic types of interview:

1 The *hard exposure* interview which investigates a subject.
2 The *informational* interview which puts the audience in the picture.
3 The *emotional* interview which aims to reveal an interviewee's state of mind.

These three paint a broad picture of the art of the interview, which we can develop further into twelve different types, all with special functions:

- Hard news
- Informational
- Investigative
- Adversarial
- Interpretative
- Personal
- Emotional
- Entertainment
- Actuality
- Telephone or remote
- Vox pop and multiple
- Grabbed

A disaster story?

The following extraordinary interview is something of a classic. It was broadcast on the British network news service IRN (Independent Radio News) during a long and bitter strike. The man facing the microphone was militant miner's leader Arthur Scargill, a Yorkshireman not known for his gentle touch with interviewers, or for giving any ground in an argument. But this reporter thought he could take him on and beat him at his own game – live on peak-time radio. Decide for yourself whether he succeeded and whether the result made good or bad radio.

The first major stumbling block came near the beginning when the interviewer asked the militant miner's leader to admit defeat:

> *'Five weeks into the dispute the membership . . . is still divided over whether to follow your call. Would you concede that the strike is a bitter one and that like never before miner is pitched against miner?'*

Which prompted the swift response:

> **Scargill**: *'. . . now I'm not going to correct you again, I hope . . . If people misinterpret what we're doing the way you're doing, then clearly it's little wonder the British people don't know the facts . . .'* (He then proceeded to reiterate a point he had made earlier)
> **Interviewer**: *'We'll deal with those points later . . .'*
> **Scargill**: *'No, I'm sorry, you'll not . . .'*
> **Interviewer**: *'Mr Scargill, could you please answer my question . . .'*
> **Scargill**: *'No, I'm sorry, you'll not deal with those points later in the programme, you'll either listen to what I've got to say or not at all . . .'*
> **Interviewer**: *'We'll come to those in a minute . . .'*
> **Scargill**: *'No, I'm sorry, you can either listen to the answers that I'm giving, or alternatively, you can shut up . . .'*
> **Interviewer**: *'We'll come to those figures later, Mr Scargill . . .'*
> **Scargill**: *'No, I'm sorry, one thing you're going to learn is that on an interview of this kind, you're going to listen clearly to the things that I want to talk about . . .'* (this gentle banter continued for some time, until)

Scargill: *'Now are you going to listen?'*

Interviewer: *'No, can you please . . .'* (but his voice is drowned out by that of his guest)

Scargill: *'Then as far as I'm concerned we might as well pack up this interview . . . Now it's obvious you're not going to listen, and if you're not going to listen, lad, than there's no point in me talking to you is there, eh?'* (They debated this moot point for a time, until)

Interviewer: (Exasperated) *'Mr Scargill, Mr Scargill, can you please answer the question?'*

Scargill: *'Now are you going to listen to my answers or not?'*

Interviewer: *'If you listen, if you listen to my questions and give answers to them, it's as simple as that!'*

Scargill: *'Quite frankly, either you're going to listen to my answers or not. And if you're not, then you're going to obviously make yourself look a complete fool . . .'*

Interviewer: (Pleadingly) *'Then why don't you give answers to the questions I'm giving, Mr Scargill . . .?'*

Scargill: *'You're either going to let me answer the questions in my way, or if you want, write the answers that you want on a board and tell people that you want me to answer those questions your way . . .'*

Interviewer: (Gathering about himself his last shreds of composure) *'Can you come to the point then, and answer the question?'*

Scargill: (Unrelenting) *'I can come to any point I want providing you'll shut up and let me answer, but if you won't shut up, then I can't . . . If you don't, then this interview is going to go on in this silly way as a result of your irresponsible attitude.'*

Interviewer: (Abandonedly) *'Let's move on to something else . . . (Sigh)'*

But that proved to be a vain hope, and, although the question had long since been forgotten, by the audience at least, interviewer and interviewee continued the same exasperating sparring match for some time, with Mr Scargill repeating the same point again and again, and punctuating his interviewee's unwelcome interruptions with observations that his would-be interrogator was:

● Speaking as a representative of the Coal Board or the Government.
● Trying to make himself a budding Robin Day (a veteran BBC interviewer), which he followed through with stern rejoinder: *'. . . well, tha's not doing it wi' me, lad!'*.
● That his interviewer was an ignorant man who ought to have more sense.
● And that he ought to get out of the chair and let someone else sit there who *could* do the job.

Were his remarks justified? Judge for yourself. Full marks for persistence on the part of the interviewer, but perhaps that persistence could have been better placed in seeking answers to questions designed to elicit information rather than to invoke the other man's wrath. In the end it was a victory on points for Mr Scargill, but one which was unlikely to popularize either him or his cause or do much to enhance the reputation of live broadcasting.

Strangely though; however disastrous it may have sounded, it did make compelling radio . . .

Hard news

The *hard news interview* is usually short, to the point, and to illustrate a bulletin or news item. It deals only with important facts, or comment and reaction to those facts.

Figure 30 (*Top*) Pick a camera, any camera and gaze steadily at it. Whatever you do, try not to stare at the furry condom . . . . (*Bottom*) There are times when eye-contact with the camera is strictly not required, such as for this fly-on-the-wall documentary. (*Courtesy Grampian TV*)

Let's set up a scenario to see how this and other types of interview apply:

A cruise liner is in trouble 80 miles out to sea with a fire apparently out of control in the engine room. You have the coastguard on the phone and he is prepared to be interviewed. Once the name of the ship, the number on board, her destination, her point of departure, and the name of her owners are established for the cue material, the questions to the coastguard would be:

- *How bad is the fire?*
- *How did it start?*
- *How can the fire be prevented from spreading?*
- *How safe are the passengers?*
- *What about the crew?*
- *Are they likely to have to abandon ship?*
- *What steps are being taken to rescue them? etc.*

The answer that will illustrate the news will be the strongest to emerge from these key questions. Important facts and background will be given in the cue, while more detail and explanation will go into the programme-length interview of between two and three minutes.

There is no reason to settle for interviewing the coastguard if there is a chance of raising the crew of the ship by radio telephone. A first-hand account from the people at the centre of a story is always preferable, though here the crew would almost certainly be too busy fighting the fire to talk.

Informational

The *informational interview* is similar to the hard news interview, but need not be restricted to major stories. An informational interview can be about an *event* – something that is happening or about to happen.

It can also provide *background*. Returning to the cruise liner story, an interview could be set up with the station's shipping correspondent, who would probably be a freelance with specialist knowledge. He or she would be asked about the whole issue of accidents at sea, with questions such as:

- *What is the normal procedure for abandoning ship?*
- *How safe is this?*
- *How long before the passengers could be picked up?*
- *Would they suffer from exposure in these weather conditions?*

Broadening to:

- *Just how safe is travelling by sea these days?*
- *How does it compare with air travel? etc.*

Informational interviews go beyond the main point to seek an explanation of the *hows* and *whys* of the story. As such they tend to produce better extended features than short bulletin items.

Investigative

The *investigative interview* aims to get behind the facts to discover what *really* caused events and sometimes what could be done to prevent a recurrence.

This kind of interview can run and run and often forms the basis of a documentary.

Assuming with the above story you discover there has been a recent spate of accidents involving cruise liners, and this is the second vessel belonging to that shipping line to have caught fire within three months; then your next step would be to raise this with the owners.

With investigative interviews it is only sensible not to put your prey to flight by scaring them off with your first question, so the interview would be conducted something like this:

- *How did the fire break out?*
- *How quickly was it discovered?*
- *Why wasn't the crew able to control it?*

Figure 31   Hold the mike lightly but firmly, make eye-contact and animate. (*Andrew Boyd*)

- *When was the ship last checked for safety?*
- *What problems were discovered then?*
- *How would you describe your safety record?*
- *This is your second liner to have caught fire in three months . . . how do you account for that?*

At this stage it is likely the interview will rapidly move from being investigative into the category below.

Adversarial

> **Jeremy Paxman**: *'Did you threaten to overrule him?'*
> **Home Secretary Michael Howard**: *'I was not entitled to instruct Derek Lewis and I did not instruct him. And the truth of it is . . .'*
> **Paxman**: *'Did you threaten to overrule him?'*
> **Howard**: *'And the truth of the matter is Mr Marriot was not suspended. I did not . . .'*
> **Paxman**: *'Did you threaten to overrule him?'*
> **Howard**: *'I did not overrule Derek Lewis.'*
> **Paxman**: *'Did you threaten to overrule him?'*
> **Howard**: *'I took advice on what I could and could not do . . .'*
> **Paxman**: *'Did you threaten to overrule him, Mr Howard?'*
>
> And so it continued, with Paxman fixing the Home Secretary with the same question some 14 times, he later admitted, because his producer said the next item was not ready.
> The Home Secretary later reflected: *'It's not uncommon for a politician not to answer a question directly. It's pretty uncommon for them to be asked the same question [repeatedly].'**

No one likes to be cross-examined or have their motives questioned, so frequently the *adversarial interview* turns into a war of words between the two parties as the interviewer tries to get the other to admit to things that he or she really does not want to say. Our disaster at sea interview might continue:

- *Some people might see two fires in three months as negligence on your part. How would you answer that?*
- *Would you agree that your safety standards need looking into?*
- *What plans do you have for improving those safety standards? etc.*

And if it turned out that the crew had been unable to control the fire because they had set sail five hands down owing to a severe outbreak of flu back in port, the right and proper questions to ask would be:

- *Why was the ship permitted to sail with too few crewmen to deal with an emergency?*

* Newsnight, BBC2, 1997.

- *Some would say this action put your ship and your passengers' lives in jeopardy. How would you answer that?*
- *What disciplinary action do you plan to take against the captain who authorized the sailing? etc.*

But beware ... The adversarial approach should never be seen to be a head-on clash between the interviewer and the interviewee. The reporter is representing the audience or speaking up on behalf of public opinion. Even the question above about risking the safety of passengers and ship begins: *'Some would say ...'*

A verbal assault on an interviewee might result in allegations of victimization and bias (see the interview with Arthur Scargill earlier in this chapter). And if this happens it could shift public sympathy away from the reporter and towards the 'victim'.

Adversarial interviews run the greatest risk of a libel suit. This is where a person who has had something damaging said about them seeks compensation in the courts. As a journalist, opening your mouth before thinking could prove to be your costliest mistake.

By nature, the adversarial interview attempts to undermine or disprove an argument by direct and public confrontation. The atmosphere may get heated, but the professional should always resist getting hot under the collar. In the heat of the moment it is too easy to say something disparaging or harmful to an interviewee.

The adversarial approach comes and goes with fashion, but should only be used where appropriate. There is really no excuse for cross-examining a welfare organization about plans for a new orphanage, unless the proposal really does smack of corruption.

'Never trust a smiling reporter.' — ED KOCH

Interpretative

There are two prongs to the *interpretative interview*: the first is the *reaction* story – a response either for or against what has happened; the second is an *explanation* of events.

Both approaches offer a perspective on what has taken place, and put the event into context. By bringing an issue into the light it is possible to examine it more closely.

Reaction is frequently stronger and more effective when it comes from someone who is personally involved.

Analysis, explanation or *interpretation* comes best from an expert eye far enough away from the story to remain objective.

Our shipping correspondent in the example above fits that bill exactly. He or she could ask:

- *How will this accident affect public confidence in sea travel?*
- *Do the safety laws need tightening up? If so, how?*
- *What provision is there in maritime law for setting sail without an adequate or healthy crew?*
- *What cover does travel insurance offer passengers?*

Personal

The *personal interview* might be a short interview with a celebrity about their favourite subject – themselves, or a longer, more inquisitive and intentionally revealing *personality profile*. Among the best of this breed is Radio 4's *In the Psychiatrist's Chair*. This talks to well-known people from different walks of life, and attempts to get beneath their skins to find out not what they do, but why they do it, what drives and motivates them and what in their past has made them the people they are today? In short, what makes them tick?

The interview is intimate and penetrating. To lower a person's guard to the point where they become vulnerable and yet still secure enough with the interviewer to answer questions such as, *'Do you believe in God?'* and *'Have you ever wanted to take your own life?'* requires the interviewer to combine the insight of a psychiatrist with the empathy of a priest at the confessional. It can make fascinating listening.

Emotional

The *emotional interview* is an attempt to lay bare someone's feelings, to enable an audience to share in a personal tragedy or moving event. The emotional interview springs from the personal interview, above, and is perhaps the most sensitive area of reporting. It is dealing with a subject's inner self, an area into which the media too frequently trespasses uninvited.

Returning to our stricken cruise liner: time has passed, the fire has proved impossible to contain and the captain has been left with no option but to give the cry, *'Abandon ship!'* Fortunately, rescue vessels were already at the scene and the passengers, bedraggled and nearing exhaustion, are starting to come ashore.

The reporter is at the quayside with the instruction to get the *human angle*.

Closing in on the first of the passengers, a woman who is weary but obviously greatly relieved to be setting foot on terra firma, he asks:

- *How does it feel to be back on dry land?*
- *Were you able to save any of your possessions?*
- *When did you first realize the fire was out of control?*
- *How did the passengers react to the news? etc.*

Mercifully, the reporter has remembered that the hackneyed and crass *'How do you feel?'* should only be asked to let us share in someone's relief or happiness, never their tragedy or misfortune.

For emotional interviews the rule is to tread carefully when your foot is on somebody's heart, and then only walk where you have been given the right of way.

Entertainment

The entertainment factor often plays a part in attracting and keeping an audience. The *entertainment interview* looks at the lighter side of life, the things that make us smile. If, on board the liner, a troupe of dancing girls had kept people's spirits up when the flames were spreading amidships by doing the can-can, then that is entertainment and the reporter who sneers at that angle is likely to get a roasting when he or she returns.

Figure 32 The live TV interview – keep it crisp, penetrating and to time.
(*Top*) Livening up the studio interview – the composite screen displays the context of the story, while the studio set reveals the newsroom in the background. (*Courtesy Channel 4 News*)
(*Bottom*) Eye-contact is all an illusion. The politician stares at a camera lens while listening hard to the questions on a hidden earpiece, while Channel 4 News presenter Jon Snow engages with a bank of monitors. (*Courtesy Channel 4 News*)

Actuality only

The *actuality interview* is where the reporter's voice is removed from the recording, leaving only that of the interviewee. The technique is occasionally used to good effect in documentary or feature making, but is harder to master than it sounds.

The skill lies in building up a clear storyline, which needs no narration to prop it up and in asking questions that prompt the interviewee to give all the information that would normally arise as background in the question.

Wrong approach:
Interviewer: *'Where were you when the fire broke out?'*
Passenger: *'At the bar.'*
Interviewer: *'Who told you?'*
Passenger: *'The steward.'*
Interviewer: *'What was your reaction?'*
Passenger: *'I didn't take it seriously. I thought they'd manage to put it out.'*

Better:
Interviewer: *'Could you tell us where you were when the fire broke out, how you got to hear about it, and what your reaction was?'*
Passenger: *'I was at the bar with half a dozen others, when the steward came in and told us fire had broken out in the engine room. We didn't think much of it. We were sure they'd put it out. But we didn't know how wrong we were.'*

With this technique multiple questions are often required to get a good flow of answers. The interview will usually have to be worked out in advance with the interviewee, and several retakes might be necessary to get the important background while still sounding conversational and natural.

Telephone or remote

Interviews may be carried out on the phone or with a subject speaking from a remote studio. Remote studios are linked to the mother station by cables, microwave or satellite, offering studio quality sound for radio, and combining sound with vision for TV.

The scratchy quality of phone lines means phone interviews should be avoided where possible. Alternatives are conducting the interview along a studio-quality digital line, going out to record the interview in person, or, even better, getting the interviewee to do the hard work and come into the studio. Use a phone only if you have to, and then keep the recording as short as possible.

With our earlier telephone interview with the coastguard, a clip of that would be used for the bulletin, and, to produce a longer piece, this could be combined with narrative by the reporter to cut out as much phone quality material as possible. Few listeners will trouble to strain to hear what is being said.

Vox pop and multiple

Vox pop is an abbreviation of the Latin *vox populi*, or *'voice of the people'*. The vox is used in broadcasting to provide a cross-section of public opinion on a given subject. In the USA it is known as the *'person in the street'* interview.

The technique is to get a broad mix of opinion and different voices. Alternate between male and female, young and old. Begin and end with strong comments and make good use of humorous remarks.

Shopping precincts make a happy hunting ground, and one radio presenter was known for his regular vox about topical items recorded each week with the same crowd at a bus stop.

Vox pops work best where the reporter's voice is kept out as much as possible. A single question should be asked, which is introduced in the cue, and the reporter puts that question to people in turn with the recorder kept on pause during the questions.

Variations in background noise can make editing difficult, but recording and overlaying some of that background sound, known as *wildtrack*, can cover the edits.

Returning to our running seafaring story, if the holiday booking season is at its height, our reporter could catch people outside travel agents, and after making introductions, ask them:

> *'There's been another fire on a cruise liner, and passengers have had to abandon ship, so how does that make you feel about travelling by sea?'*

The *multiple interview* differs from the vox by taking a smaller number of selected extracts, often drawn from longer interviews and having the reporter link them together. This is known as a *package*.

Our ship saga is ideal for such treatment. Excerpts from the coastguard and the ship's owners could be mixed with comment by the shipping correspondent and glued together with narrative by the reporter.

Grabbed

Our final category concerns interviews that people don't want to give but which reporters are determined to take.

These are usually short and may comprise a few brief comments or a terse *'No comment!'*, which is often comment enough.

Grabbed interviews, also known as doorsteps, are obtained by pushing a camera or microphone under the nose of a subject and firing off questions.

Our reporter has caught sight of a smoke-stained uniform. It is the captain coming ashore. He seems in no mood to answer questions. Rushing over, our reporter pushes the microphone towards him and asks:

> *'How did the fire begin?'*
> (The captain ignores him and quickens his pace. The reporter pursues and repeats his question)
> Captain: *'It began in the engine room . . . overheating we think.'*
> Reporter: *'Why weren't you able to put it out?'*
> (No answer)
> Reporter: *'Could it be that there weren't enough crewmen on board?'*
> (Silence)
> *Reporter: 'Why did you set sail without a full crew?'*
> Captain: *'No comment!'*
> (He is hustled forward and swallowed up inside a big black car with official number-plates.)

The grabbed interview usually works best on camera, where, even if the subject says nothing, he or she can be watched by the audience and his or her reactions noted.

Frequently there are so many reporters that there is no chance to pursue a line of questioning. If you ask even one question at a free-for-all, you are doing well. Not that it matters a great deal; the melee and persistent refusals to answer add to the sense that here is Someone with Something to Hide.

Grabbed interviews are often intrusions of privacy. It would be unwarranted to grab an interview with a widow after a funeral or with anyone who is grieving or suffering. **Ethically, personal privacy should only be intruded upon where someone's understandable desire to be left alone runs counter to proper public interest**. That could be argued to be true of our captain.

Sometimes grabbing interviews can do more harm than good. Royalty will understandably take umbrage – they will usually speak to the media by appointment only. Similar rules apply to heads of state or anyone to whom the station would rather not risk giving offence. And as with the adversarial interview, there is always the risk of saying something libellous. Bear in mind that your unwilling subject may be only too happy to find occasion to sue you.

The disaster story continues . . .

Having concluded our foray into the jungle of the interview, let us return to hear how Mr Scargill and his hapless interviewer are getting on. They are still at it . . .

> **Interviewer**: *'Let's move on to something else . . . the meeting you're having tomorrow . . .'*
> **Scargill**: *'No, I'm sorry, we're not moving on to anything until you let me put the point of view across on behalf of those that I represent.'*
> **Interviewer**: *'I think you've put it over several times, Mr Scargill.'*
> **Scargill**: *'. . . all I've done so far is to be interrupted by an ignorant man like you, who ought to have more sense . . .'*
> **Interviewer**: *'Mr Scargill, we've . . .* (sigh). *Can we conduct this interview rather than having a slanging match?'*
> **Scargill**: *'Well you started it, not me! . . . All that you're doing so far is to present a question and then conveniently ignore the point that I want to give by way of response.'*
> **Interviewer**: (Struggling to get a word in) *'Let's move on to another question . . .'*

Perhaps it is not surprising the interview has turned out the way it has. If you can remember back to where we came in, it was with the statement that the miners were divided over following Mr Scargill, and a request that the fiery miners' leader *concede* that the strike was bitter and that *'like never before miner is pitched against miner'*.

You could hope for more success arm wrestling a gorilla than in asking a determined and embattled interviewee whose reputation is on the line to *concede*.

Another moral of this tale might be that if you plan to fight fire with fire, then don't pitch a match against a flame-thrower. If there is ever an occasion when interviewer and interviewee should be evenly pitted it is against one another in an adversarial interview.

There are signs that this interview may be just about to shudder to its conclusion . . .

Interviewer: *'It seems you're incapable of answering any questions, Mr Scargill.'*
Scargill: *'It seems as though you're the most ignorant person that I've ever discussed with on radio. Now either you're going to listen to answers even though you don't like them, or you're not. It's entirely up to you.'*
Interviewer: *'Mr Scargill, thank you for joining us and I'm afraid not answering any of our questions here in Sheffield this afternoon. This live interview with the miners' leader Arthur Scargill . . .'*
Scargill: *'This live interview has been absolutely appalling as a result of . . .'* (He is faded out)
Interviewer: *'Independent Radio News, it's 1.30!'*
REPRODUCED BY KIND PERMISSION OF INDEPENDENT RADIO NEWS

Fieldwork

1 Open a file marked 'interviewing'. Keep one page for each of the twelve categories of interview above and others for notes. Watch a variety of different TV news, current affairs and magazine programmes and see if you can identify all twelve types of interview in action.
2 See if you can come up with some new categories. Watch and listen to interviews critically. Each time ask yourself whether it worked or failed, whether it was good or bad, and why. File any tips on technique you pick up.
3 If you are in a class, break into pairs, preferably with someone you don't know too well, and without any preparation conduct personality interviews with one another. Attempt to discover what makes your partner tick and find out something new about him or her. Aim to spend between ten and fifteen minutes on each interview. Afterwards, sum up in a couple of paragraphs to the class what you have discovered about your partner. If you are not in a class, find a willing subject and see how you get on.
4 That interview was conducted off the top of your head. Discuss with your partner how you could best prepare yourself and your interviewee for similar interviews in future.
5 Log every interview you do in your file under the appropriate category. Over a period of time attempt to cover all twelve categories of interview. Make notes of any difficulties you experienced doing those interviews and any helpful tips. Share your problems and advice with others and pool your knowledge.

INTERVIEWING

9 Setting up the interview

> *'The interview is an intimate conversation between journalist and politician wherein the journalist seeks to take advantage of the garrulity of the politician and the politician of the credulity of the journalist.'* — EMERY KELEN

News is often too immediate to allow detailed research, and news items are frequently too brief to warrant an in-depth approach. The average length of a bulletin clip on British independent radio is around 20 seconds – just enough for one or two succinct points. Even a three-minute report (and many music-based stations keep interviews to half that length) can support only four or five questions.

Longer interviews are more frequently the province of speech-based stations and current affairs departments, though many regional TV newsrooms will produce a daily half-hour programme that takes longer items.

A common criticism of broadcast news is that it is shallow, tending to polarize issues into black and white for the sake of simplicity by removing all shades of grey. While broadcasters deal with the *what* of the story, they seldom trouble to explain the *why* or the *how*.

Background

But brevity driven by time constraints is no excuse for ignorance on the part of an interviewer. Reporters may not have much time to gather background to a story, but they are expected to carry much of that information in their heads.

Reporters should keep up to date with the stories their station is covering. Before beginning their shift, they should hear a number of bulletins, including those on rival stations, so they know what is happening that day and have a shrewd idea of the follow-ups they can expect to be given. They should also have read the local papers, which have more space to give to background.

Reporters are often expected to be their own researcher, constantly topping up their reservoir of knowledge about local news, so when they walk through the door and the editor says: *'Don't take your coat off . . .'* they know what to expect, and what to do next.

Figure 33   Journalists spend half their lives on the phone setting up interviews. Once the pre-chat is over, the presenter at the BBC World Service will switch a telephone balance unit so his questions can be put through a microphone and recorded in studio quality, while the answers are given down the phone line. (*Courtesy BBC World Service*)

A plan of campaign – the questions

Familiarizing yourself with the story is step one. Step two is getting a clear idea of what to ask, which depends on the type of interview involved and its duration.

One tip – if you are going out for a 20-second clip, there is no point coming back with 12 minutes of material. You would simply be laying up trouble for yourself; there will be 12 minutes to review and ten different answers to choose from. That takes time, and with hourly deadlines, time is one commodity the reporter never has to spare.

Five minutes beforehand spent thinking out the questions is worth an hour's editing back at the station.

Get your facts right

> Interviewer: *'Is this a plane that can run well on one engine?'*
> Interviewee: *'It runs best on one engine – that's all it has.'* – US TV

Before leaving the newsroom, make sure you have your facts right. There is nothing more embarrassing or more likely to undermine the reporter's reputation and that of the station than an ignorant and ill-informed line of questioning:

Reporter: *'Mr Smith, as hospital administrator, just how seriously do you view this typhoid epidemic?'*

Mr Smith: *'Hmmm. I'm actually the deputy administrator, and two isolated cases hardly constitute an epidemic. Oh yes . . . and the name is Smythe. Now what was the question?'*

What chance of a successful interview?

Sometimes the mind becomes clearer when its contents are spilled on to paper. So, working to your brief, set up a chain of thought – a plan of campaign – by jotting down a few questions and arranging them in logical order. Even if you never refer to your notes this can be a worthwhile exercise.

Fit the brief

Be mindful that whatever you ask has to fit the angle and length required by the brief and the result has to be relevant to your audience. Beware of leaping off at tangents that might interest you or a like-minded minority, but would be irrelevant to the majority. Keep to the point – and the point should be whatever has the greatest impact on your audience.

Let's take a bread and butter story and assume that the fire service has been called to a fire in an apartment block. It is serious and the flats have been evacuated. You go to the scene to talk to the chief fire officer. If your brief is to produce a 20-second clip then you have space for one line of questioning only. Human life is always more important than property, so your first question must be: *Has anyone been hurt?*

If the answer is yes, then the next question has to be *Who?* followed by *What happened to them?* and that should be enough.

Whatever you do, don't follow the lead of one local radio reporter who began every interview regardless of the story with the same question: *'Tell me about it . . .'* Leave that opener to doctors, psychiatrists and others who are paid by the hour.

Check arrangements

If time is of the essence, then no reporter can afford to waste it by heading the wrong way down a motorway or arriving at the wrong address. Arriving late for an interview only raises everybody's blood pressure. Check the arrangement before leaving and allow plenty of time to get there. Directions can be sorted out by telephone when the interview is being set up. At the same time you can get enough information to leave a brief story to tide the newsroom over until you return with your pictures or audio.

If you are working for radio, check your portable recorder before you leave. This is basic, yet often forgotten in the rush. One of my reporters interviewed a government minister then tried to play it back only to find there was no tape in the machine. Astonishingly, he agreed to wait while she returned to the station to get a tape and redo the interview. Another reporter grabbed a machine to cover a fire but found he could get no level on the meters. It wasn't that his batteries were flat – just that there were no batteries in the machine. **Check it out before you take it out**. A comprehensive test takes less than a minute and can save hours.

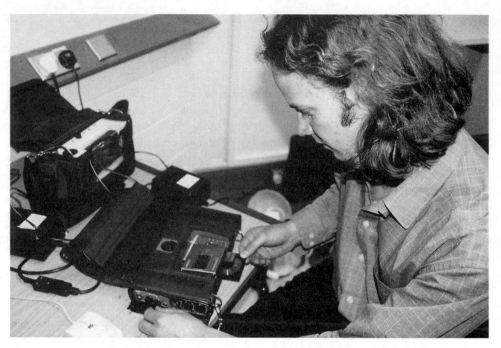

Figure 34   Check it out before you take it out. Always make sure your portable is fully charged, loaded with tape or a disc, and that it *works*. Do a full soundcheck before you leave the radio station. (*Andrew Boyd*)

Don't forget to take a spare tape, disc or whatever recording medium you use, and batteries.

Approach

Many young reporters, anxious to make a name for themselves, have to be reminded every now and again of the need not to promote their own careers at the expense of the station and its valuable contacts. Where the reporter comes face to face with the influential, want of a little wisdom can cause a great deal of damage.

It is old hat (but the hat fits too well to throw it away) to say that each reporter is an ambassador for his or her radio or TV station. How you look and conduct yourself can make or break a station's reputation.

Stations have different approaches to dress. Some permit an informal, even sloppy style, others insist on staff being suit-smart. First impressions matter. What your clothes and manner say about you in the first two seconds may affect the whole interview. A business suit might lose some interviews in a downtown area, where a casual style would be more credible, but if your news trade is with business people and politicians then dress to suit . . . in a suit.

How you deal with your contacts will have a lot to do with whether you keep them as contacts in the future. National reporters are often the bane of a local newsroom. Sometimes they don't seem to care whose toes they tread on as long as they get their story. As one local news editor put it: *'They don't have to live with their contacts . . . we do!'*

> *'I must say, I get rather nervous before these sort of interviews, my particular fear is that I'll dry up.'* – MARK TULLY, FORMER BBC BUREAU CHIEF INDIA, ON THE WAY TO INTERVIEW THE INDIAN PRIME MINISTER*
>
> *'If they're frightened it's a matter of just talking to them beforehand, joking with them and putting them at their ease. Usually I say how I keep making mistakes as well, and then I fluff a question, and say, "I'm sorry about that!" Although you go in as a professional, you can't be too aloof, because people won't talk to you. It's got to be a conversation, and you have to start it.'*
> – ROB McKENZIE, PRODUCER/PRESENTER CAPITAL

Almost as important as the interview itself is the pre-chat. This is when reporter and subject establish rapport, and the reporter sounds out the course he or she has charted for the interview.

Even if your deadline is only fifteen minutes away, your manner must be calm and relaxed, polite yet assertive but never aggressive. Approach is all-important. If the interviewee is inexperienced and nervous he or she will need to be relaxed and put at ease. Conversely, nothing is more unsettling than a nervous interviewer. Even if your adrenal gland is running riot, you must cover your trepidation with a polished performance.

A pleasant greeting, a firm handshake and a good deal of *eye-contact* is the best way to begin, with a clear statement about who you are and which radio or TV station you represent.

Eye-contact can work wonders for calming the other's nerves. A key contact at one radio station was the naval base's Port Admiral. Whenever it was necessary to interview him groans went up from the newsroom. He had an appalling s.s.s.s.stammer. Even a short bulletin clip would take an age to edit, and he could never be used for longer features. One day a reporter discovered the knack of stopping that stammer. He fixed him in the eye and smiled all the time the admiral was speaking and the stammer just melted away.

Never rehearse an interview, just discuss it. Repeats of interviews are like second-hand cars – they lose their pace and their sparkle. Even nervous interviewees usually perform better when the adrenalin is flowing. Agree to a run-through only if you think there is no other way to calm your interviewee's nerves, but make sure your recorder or camera is rolling. Then, if the 'rehearsal' goes well, you can ask the first few questions again when you sense they are into their stride and suggest dispensing with the retake. An alternative is to warm them up with some minor questions before getting down to the nitty-gritty.

Humour can effectively bring down the barriers; a joke or quip at the reporter's expense can often relax an interviewee and lower his or her defences, but obviously humour cannot be forced.

Beware also of putting up barriers. Even if you intend your interview to be adversarial, don't size up to your guest like a hungry lion to an antelope. To put it another way, every boxer knows the best punches are delivered when his opponent's guard is down.

* *See it for Yourself*, BBC, 1987.

Body language

Body language is also important. The way we sit, how we cross our legs and arms, reveals a lot about how we feel. If your interviewee is sitting legs crossed and arms folded, then you know he or she is on the defensive and needs to be relaxed. If the reporter is cowering in the corner, while the interviewee is leaning back exuding confidence, then something has gone badly wrong indeed!

Discussing the questions

Once you have established rapport, done your spadework and checked the important facts, you are ready to draw up your plan of action before beginning the recording.

Be careful. Some interviewees, particularly those who have been 'caught out' at some time, may want to take control of the interview. Don't let them. If they say they will only answer from a set list of questions, then politely but firmly tell them you don't work that way – you prefer to be free to respond to the answers. If they request not to be asked a certain question then try to steer around that without making any promises.

There is a trend among politicians and celebrities to refuse to give interviews unless all the questions are agreed in advance. Only cave in to that kind of blackmail if there is absolutely no other way to get them to talk. But make sure you get your boss's approval before you do.

Conversely, less media-savvy interviewees may want to answer from notes or a script. Don't let them. It will sound 'read' and artificial. Reassure them they will come across better without notes and that any mistakes can always be retaken. Discussing your first question may help to relax your guest and if the interview is more probing, that first question can be a dummy that you can edit out later.

If the interview is non-controversial and there are no conflicts of interest you can save editing time by outlining your questions and discussing the answers you are looking for. As Capital Radio's Rob McKenzie puts it: *'What I need is ninety seconds, so I will ask you these four questions, and your reply will be something like this . . . Yes?'*

This 'staged-managed' approach will only work where all the key facts of the story are evident beforehand and both parties agree on the angle. The biggest dangers here are the reporter showing his or her aces before the interview begins or putting words into the interviewee's mouth.

At all times beware of conflicts of interest and be assertive but always courteous. Remember, *you* are in charge. The BBC advises its fledgling reporters to adopt an attitude of 'informed naiveté' – in other words, be a wolf in sheep's clothing.

If you are unsure about the subject it can help to let your interviewee chat about it beforehand so you can be clear you are heading in the right direction.

Beware of letting the pre-chat drag on for so long that the adrenalin dies and the conversation gets stale. It should continue just long enough to explore the topic, establish a direction and relax the interviewee.

The questions

> Interviewer: *'Minister, why aren't you getting home to women?'*
> Minister: *'Could you please rephrase that?'*   – BRITISH TV

> *'If I said that, I was misquoted.'*
> – LORD HANSON ON *THE WORLD AT ONE*, RADIO

Our thoughts so far have been confined to the preparations for the match, the warm-up and the strategy. Now on to the tactics for the match itself – the questions.

There is more to the art of interviewing than developing the ability to engage complete strangers in intelligent conversation. **Good questions produce good answers**. The secret is to think ahead to the answers you are likely to get before asking your questions.

Using notes

Most interviewees would agree that preparing questions is constructive in planning the interview, but sticking closely to a list of written questions can be unhelpful during the course of the interview itself. The problems are:

- Eye contact is lost.
- When the interviewer is concentrating on the questions, he or she is unable to listen to the interviewee.
- Fixed questions make for an inflexible interview.

If you intend to use notes, use them sparingly. Write out the first question *only if you have to* to get the interview off to a good start. Complex questions are seldom a good idea, but if the form of words is critical then write the question down.

Write legibly. Preferably don't write at all – print. If you have to pause to decipher your handwriting you will lose the flow.

Perhaps the best compromise between maintaining rapport and keeping the interview on course is to make brief notes or headings of important points only. These should be sufficient to jog the memory without breaking concentration.

Ask the questions that will get answers

The *who*, *what*, *when*, *where*, *why* and *how* framework for writing copy applies equally to the news interview and the type of questions the interviewer should ask.

No reporter wants to be left with a series of monosyllabic grunts on the recording, so questions should be carefully structured to produce good useful quotes rather than single word comments.

- The question *who* calls for a name in response,
- *What* asks for a description,
- *When* pins down the timing of an event,
- *Where* locates it,
- *Why* asks for an interpretation or an explanation,
- *How* asks for an opinion or an interpretation.

Questions beginning with these words will propel the interview forward and yield solid facts:

- '*Who* was hurt in the crash?'
- '*What* caused the accident?'

- '*When* did it happen?'
- '*Where* did the accident occur?'
- '*Why* did it take so long to free the trapped passengers?'
- '*How* did you manage to get them out?'

Yes/no questions

Inexperienced reporters often fall into the trap of asking questions that produce *yes/no* answers. They may come away with some idea of the story, but will seldom have recorded anything worth using.

Sometimes though, a yes or a no answer is required to establish a fact that will open the way for a new line of questioning:

> Interviewer: *'In the light of today's street violence, do you plan to step up police patrols?'*
> Police chief: *'No, we think that would be unhelpful.'*
> Interviewer: *'Why?'*
> Police chief: *'It could be taken as provocation, etc.'*

Less artful interviewers are sometimes tempted to ask a yes/no question in the hope that it will prompt their guest to do the work for them and develop a new line of argument:

> Interviewer: *'Critics would say the plan to put a factory on the green land site is ill conceived. Would you agree?'*
> Developer: *'No, of course not. The design is modern and attractive and will bring many much-needed jobs to the area.'*

That time the technique worked. More often than not, it doesn't:

> Interviewer: *'Critics would say the plan to put a factory on the green land site is ill conceived. Would you agree?'*
> Developer: *'No.'*
> Interviewer: *'Why not?'*
> Developer: *'Well how could you expect me to agree to that . . . I'm the one who's building the darned thing!'*

Using the question this way encourages a non-answer, or worse still, permits the interviewee to pick on the 'yes' or 'no' in whatever way he or she wishes and head off on a tangent. The interviewer should always try to keep the whip hand.

Avoid questions that call for monologues

The opposite of the yes/no question, but which can have the same effect, is the question that is so wide its scope is almost unlimited:

> Interviewer: 'As a leading clean-up campaigner, what do you think is wrong with porn shops and peep shows anyway?'

Leave your recorder running and come back in an hour when she's finished! Pin the question to one clearly defined point:

> *'What's the **main** reason you're opposed to these porn shops?'*
> **Or**: *'Which peep shows in **particular** do you want cleaned up?'*

Question scope is important. Make it too narrow and your interview will keep on stalling. Open it up too wide and it can run away from you.

> Interviewer: *'Now obviously, er, Reverend, you don't like the idea of, em, these prep. schools being used as, em, fashionable schools for middle class parents, but, em, y . . . d-do you really think that i-i-it matters whether or not they believe – the parents themselves – in-in a Christian education as such. I mean, would you be happy if they particularly wanted and believed that the Christian, em, or th-the-the Anglic . . . the Anglican sort of education was right for their kids, would you like to see the church schools remain in that case, as long as you were convinced of their sincerity, rather than of the fact that they were doing it simply because it was a middle class fashionable thing to do?'*
> Reverend: *'That's a very good question. I don't know.'* — UK RADIO

Short, single idea questions

If a question is to be understood by both the audience and the interviewee it has to be kept clear, simple and straightforward, unlike this example:

> Interviewer: *'Coming back to your earlier point about owners who get rid of their pets, don't you think there should be some kind of sanction, I mean, some sort of measure or something, against owners who dump their unwanted pets, as happens so frequently after Christmas, when they get given them as presents and find they didn't really want a pet after all?'*
> Animal welfare spokesman: 'Em, well, er, I'm not exactly sure what you've in mind . . .'

Cotton wool, by the sound of it. Try:

> Interviewer: *'What penalty would you like to see against owners who dump their unwanted pets?'*

Keep the threads of the argument untangled and stick to one point at a time.

Progress from point to point

To maintain the logic of the interview each question should naturally succeed the previous one. If the interviewer needs to refer back to a point, this should be done neatly and followed through by another question that progresses the argument:

> Interviewer: *'Going back to owners who dump their pets after Christmas, would you like to see some form of penalty imposed against them?'*
> Animal welfare spokesman: *'We most certainly would.'*
> Interviewer: *'What have you got in mind?'*

Building bridges

Each question should arise naturally from the previous answer. If the two points are only distantly related the interviewer should use a bridge, as in the question above. Another example is this from interviewer Michael Parkinson, talking to Oscar-winning actor Ben Kingsley on Radio 4:

> Parkinson: *'Then I suppose after getting the academy award for best actor in **Ghandi** you must have been offered an enormous range of parts. What parts were you offered?'*

Avoid double questions

The interviewer should ask one question at a time, otherwise a wily subject would be able to choose which to answer, and which to ignore. Even the most willing of subjects may forget one half of the question.

> **Bad question**: *'What form will your demonstration take, and do you think County Hall will take any notice?'*
>
> **Better**: *'What kind of demonstration are you planning?'*

Following the answer with:

> What effect do you think it'll have on the views of county councillors?'

Keep the questions relevant

The news interview is not some esoteric exercise in analysing abstractions. But the trouble with experts in any field is that they are liable to lapse into jargon. If you let them, you will lose your audience. And the interview is for their benefit, not yours. So help your experts keep their feet on the ground. Keep them to the point. **And the only point that matters is the point of relevance to your audience**.

As with news writing, examples should be concrete and real. If you begin by asking how high inflation will rise, be sure to follow it up with a question about whether wages and salaries are likely to keep pace or what it will do to the price of bread.

If it is a question about inner-city poverty, don't just talk about living standards, ask about the food these people eat or get a description of their homes.

Get away from the abstract and relate ideas to everyday realities.

Avoid leading questions

A leading question is one designed to lead interviewees into a corner and trap them there. More often it has the effect of boxing-in the reporter with allegations of malice, bias and unfair play.

Take the example of an interview with an elderly farmer who was seriously burnt trying to save his photograph album from his blazing house:

> Interviewer: *'Why did you attempt such a foolhardy and dangerous stunt over a worthless photograph album. Surely that's taking sentimentality too far?'*

This question, like most leading questions, was based on assumptions:

- Saving the album was stupid.
- It was dangerous.

- The album was worthless.
- The farmer's motive was sentimental.
- And that a sentimental reason was not a valid one.

But assumptions can prove to be false:

> Farmer: *'My wife died three years ago. I kept all my most precious things together. The deeds to my house and all my land were inside that album with the only pictures I had of my wife. It was kept in the living room, which was away from the flames. I thought I had time to pull it out, but in my hurry I fell over and blacked out. Now I've lost everything.'*

The scorn of the audience would quickly shift from the farmer to the callous interviewer. If somebody is stupid or wrong or to blame, draw out the evidence through polite and sensitive interviewing and leave the audience to pass judgement.

> **Bad question**: *'You knew the car's brakes were faulty when you rented it to Mr Brown, didn't you? The car crashed, he's in hospital and it's your fault. How do you feel about that?'*
>
> **Better**:
> 1 *'When did you find out the car's brakes were faulty?'*
> 2 *'But later that morning, before the brakes could be repaired, didn't you rent it out to another customer?'*
> 3 *'Weren't you worried there could be an accident?'*
> 4 *'How do you feel now your car is written off and your customer, Mr Brown, is in hospital?'*

Expose the fallacy of an argument, not by putting words into a person's mouth, but by letting the evidence and his own words condemn him.

Leading questions are frowned on by the courts. The same should go for broadcasting.

Mixing statements with questions

Sometimes it is necessary to give some background information before coming to the question. The question and the information should be kept separate for the sake of clarity, and the question at the end should be brief:

> First commentator: *'So, for the fourth time in a row the Lions have romped home with a clear victory, and are now standing an astonishing eleven points clear at the top of the table. Manager Bill Fruford, tell us, what's the secret?'*

Avoid statements posing as questions:

> Second commentator: *'With me here is manager John Turnbull whose team's performance crumpled completely in the last five minutes, with the Lions making all the running over a dispirited side.'*
> Turnbull: (silence)
> Commentator: *'Mr Turnbull?'*
> Turnbull: *'Sorry, you talking to me? What was the question?'*

In passing the ball to the manager the commentator lost possession, but letting it go, especially after such a disparaging account of the team's performance, has left the commentator's own defences wide open. The manager could have said anything he wanted as no direct question had been asked of him. As it was, because of the phrasing of the question, the manager was completely unaware the ball had been passed to him.

Beware of questions that would be out of date

If the interview is being pre-recorded, remember to say nothing that would render the item out of date. If the piece is to go out next Wednesday, avoid:

'Well, Mrs Wilson, what's your reaction to today's events?'

Similarly, watch the changeovers from morning to afternoon, afternoon to evening, evening to night, night to morning. The safest position is to drop any time reference from a story or an interview. Broadcast news is about immediacy. Even an only slightly out of date time reference can make the news sound stale.

Avoid sounding ignorant

Always check your facts before you launch into an interview. Clear up details like the following during the pre-chat:

Interviewer: *'Mr Schaeffer, why have you decided to sack half your workforce?'*
Mr Schaeffer: *'They have not been sacked.'*

Figure 35 Setting up the interview at ITN . . . work your way through a list of contacts until you get a bite, this time on a story about AIDS; talk it through, then draw up a list of questions. (*Andrew Boyd*)

Interviewer: *'You deny it?'*
Mr Schaeffer: *'What has happened is that their contracts have expired and have not been renewed. And it's not half the workforce; it's 125 staff out of a total of 400.'*
Interviewer: *'Oh.'*

If you are not in the full picture, get filled in before the interview begins, but remember, as soon as you rely on your interviewees for background, you are putting them in a position where they can manipulate the interview to their advantage.

Winding up the interview

The words *'and finally'* are best avoided during an interview, as a point could arise which may beg a further question or clarification, and saying 'and finally' twice always sounds a little foolish.

A phrase such as *'Briefly . . .'* may also serve as a wind-up signal if necessary. Save your gestures and hand signals for experienced studio staff.

Finish strongly

An interview should go out with a bang and never a whimper. It should end in a way that gives the whole performance a bold and emphatic full stop.

Recorded interviews should not end with *'Thank you very much Miss Smith'*. Save your thank-yous for rounding off live interviews and handing back to a presenter.

If during a live interview a guest insists on going on over her time, then don't be afraid to butt in with a polite, *'Well, I'm afraid we must stop there'*, or *'That's all we've got time for, Miss Smith, thank you very much.'* And if she refuses to take the hint, it is the job of the producer to switch off the microphone and usher her out.

Being interviewed yourself: the Q & A

Often the tables get turned on reporters and they find themselves having to answer the questions. If they have been covering a major breaking story, such as an air crash or a gas explosion, they will have the latest information and the advantage of being available.

'Q & A' stands for *question and answer*. The reporters, hot foot from the air crash, may be invited to break into normal programming to give the audience a first-hand account of events. If they have been covering the story live the station can cross to them at the scene for description as well as background.

The reporter should script the questions. It would be pointless to leave the line of questioning to a music presenter or continuity announcer who has little idea what has been going on. Worse still, the presenter might ask questions the reporter couldn't answer.

The *answers* should not be scripted, though. The conversation would sound almost as artificial as an interviewee who insists on reading from a statement.

With unscripted pieces there is always a danger of repetition or hesitation. Beware of this. Under nerves, people often say too much or too little. Keep a check on yourself and say just enough to fill the allocated time with solid details and interesting information without resorting to filler, bulk, or repetition.

> *During a stormy budget interview the Chancellor accused the late BBC veteran Brian Redhead of being a life-long Labour supporter. Redhead promptly called for a minute's silence, 'while you compose an apology for daring to suggest you know how I exercise my vote, and I shall reflect upon the death of your monetary policy.'*

Introducing actuality

If the Q & A is with a radio reporter live at the scene, that reporter may want to introduce some actuality, such as an interview recorded earlier with a witness or an official. This should be edited on the machine, cued-up ready to go and introduced in the same way as any news interview. For a smooth production, it would be better to have that interviewee beside you when you go live.

Fieldwork

1 Listen to (and record if possible) a number of interviews on radio and TV and list the questions that were asked in each.

What proportion of the questions were of the *who*, *what*, *when*, *where*, *why* and *how* variety? Do all the questions follow on from one another? If not, why not? Does each interview follow a logical thread? Where do you think the interviewer has deviated from his or her planned list of questions to pick up on one of the interviewee's answers? Can you pick out any *bridging* questions or *double* questions? Are there any *leading* questions? If so, how do you react to them? Are there any badly phrased questions? How would you rephrase them? Do the interviews finish strongly? If not, how could they have been edited to give them a more definite conclusion?

2 Below are four scenarios. Draw up a list of five questions for each which would adequately cover those stories:

- A fire in a hotel where three people are trapped.
- The announcement of a major new contract at a steelworks.
- The launch of an outrageous fashion range by a local designer.
- A blind man who is planning to climb a mountain.

3 Interview simulation: taking control.

This is a power game requiring two players. One plays the reporter and the other the interviewee. The story is about a landlord who has bought houses that are due for demolition and is letting them to tenants and keeping them in squalor for profit.

The story concerns eight houses in Bridge Street split into single and double rooms, some are in need of repair and all are badly inadequate.

The landlord, Albert Smith, is leasing the houses cheaply from the local authority and charging high rents. The tenants are mainly poor immigrants. A shortage of rented accommodation means they have to stay there or become homeless. They have complained about the squalid conditions they say are to blame for the constant ill health of some of their children.

The reporter's brief is to interview the landlord to expose what is happening and, in a manner that is both fair and reasonable, call him to account. The landlord's aim is to defend his reputation and show himself in the best possible light. If the local authority accepts the case against him, he could lose his houses. The central plank of his defence is that the immigrants would be homeless without him, and he knows that if the local authority rules his houses uninhabitable, they would then have the responsibility of housing the immigrants.

The reporter has one constraint upon him – if the landlord disputes any facts that are not included in his brief, the reporter must not be dogmatic about them.

Both parties should finish reading this brief and then re-read it. The reporter should then spend up to five minutes privately thinking up questions, in which time the interviewee should anticipate the questions that would be asked and prepare a defence.

The exercise is one of control. Both parties want the interview to go ahead, though both are hoping for a different outcome. Each should try to take charge and to bend the interview to his own purposes – one to expose the facts, the other to gloss over them and turn them to his advantage by making them seem more acceptable.

If you have recording equipment, record the interview. Conduct it preferably in front of a small audience of classmates who can later offer constructive criticism. You have fifteen minutes to conduct the pre-chat and the interview.

4 Afterwards discuss the interview. Who came out on top and why? How did the reporter attempt to expose the facts and how did the landlord try to cover them up? How did each side feel about the attempts to manipulate him during the interview? Were the right questions asked? How did you resolve differences in opinion about the facts of the story? What did the audience think?

5 Interview simulation: Q & A.

There has been a serious accident on a main highway from town. Several cars are involved and some people have died. You are at the scene of the crash and your station wants to conduct a live interview with you about what you have seen. Imagine the scene and work out a scenario, then draw up a list of questions for the presenter. You should have enough material to stay on air for three minutes. If you are in a class, find someone to be the presenter and go ahead with the Q & A.

THE NEWS PROGRAMME

10 From 2-minute headlines to 24-hour news

News programmes come in almost as many shapes and sizes as the people who present them, from 2-minute headline summaries to 24 hours of non-stop news. As broadcasting develops new forms of expression and the choice of programmes continues to grow, news is having to be marketed in increasingly diverse ways to continue to win audiences accustomed to greater choice.

With the Internet has come global ubiquity. And with cable and satellite television has come greater specialization. Viewers can now stay tuned to one channel all day without glimpsing a headline, or watch wall-to-wall news if the fancy takes them. And as news programmes get longer, and become more consumer-oriented in the quest to cling to rating share in an ever-fragmenting market, the distinction between news and entertainment becomes more blurred. Keep-fit spots, recipe slots and even horoscopes now juggle for position amid the more usual news fare.

The bulletin

In the UK, the brief news summary is known as a *bulletin*. In the US, bulletin may refer to a one-item snap of breaking news, while in UK parlance that would be known as a *newsflash*. The UK definitions apply here.

The bulletin is a snapshot of the day's news at a point in time and is usually on air from three to five minutes. Individual items are kept deliberately short – at around 30 seconds – so a good number of stories can be packed in. TV bulletins are illustrated with video clips and stills, while radio bulletins use voice reports and extracts of interviews (*actualities*). Only shorter headline summaries are usually read straight through without illustration.

Figure 36 Keeping vigil outside the High Court. Every eye peeled, on the lookout for news. With 24-hour deadlines, getting the story fast and turning it around even quicker is the name of the game. (*Andrew Boyd*)

News programmes

News programmes aim to provide a broader view of the day's news, summarizing the best stories of the day instead of the hour. Length usually ranges from 20 to 60 minutes. Items are generally longer and more detailed than those in a bulletin and more sophisticated, using actualities or film footage, stills and graphics. Some shorter stories may also be incorporated to increase the breadth of coverage. If a programme is to gain audience loyalty, it will have to establish a clear identity and have a greater balance and variety of material than a bulletin.

Documentary

The *documentary* or *feature* deals with a topical issue or subject in greater depth, and is less dependent on a *news peg* – some immediate and newsworthy occurrence taking place before that subject can be aired. Features can be as short as seven minutes, while documentaries usually last between 20 minutes and an hour and will cover a single theme or a small number of issues.

Documentary styles vary from straightforward reportage to dramatized documentary and *vérité* techniques (also known as *direct* or *actuality* reporting). The *drama documentary* makes use of actors to reconstruct events and conversations. The use of reconstruction inevitably requires a degree of speculation and is a further smudging of the margins between fact and fiction, producing what is sometimes disparagingly referred to as *faction*.

Vérité

Vérité techniques try to get as close to the untainted truth as possible, by doing away with the narrator, chopping out all the questions and linking the various interviews and actualities so it seems as though no reporter was present. The intention is to produce a purer piece of journalism, closer to reality for being untainted by the presence and preconceptions of the reporter. But this is, of course, an illusion.

Figure 37 *'Standby for the 5 o'clock news'.* Stickers everywhere remind presenters to keep giving the station ident. (*Andrew Boyd*)

The reporter's influence, though unseen or unheard, is perhaps greater than ever, for a good deal of skilful setting-up and manipulation is required to get the interviewees to tell the story so it appears to be telling itself, without requiring linking narrative. Interviewees have to be primed to provide answers that effectively encapsulate the unheard questions so listeners can follow the drift.

Where it succeeds, vérité paints a picture that is closer to the subject and more intimate, giving the impression of looking in on somebody's life unobserved. Where it fails, it can be both contrived and confusing and a self-inflicted handicap to story telling. Vérité is best used where solid information is less important than atmosphere, such as a day in the life of an inmate at a prison, or this psychotherapy session below.

Psychotherapist: *'If you could place a flower at your mother's grave . . . what flower would you take?'*
Alan: *'A rose.'*
Psychotherapist: *'A rose. Well, let me give you a rose. Take it. What colour would it be?'*
Alan: *'Red.'*

Psychotherapist: *'Red. Take the rose in your hand. You're doing fine. Right? Come and place it. And if you could have been responsible for writing something on her tombstone, what would you have written?'*

Alan: *'I love and forgive you.'*

Psychotherapist: *'Just take this hand for a moment. I want you to be held in the way you were never held as a kid. No? You can't do that.'*

Alan: *'You're going to get all lovey dovey and then they're just gonna kick me in the teeth.'*

Psychotherapist: *'What's your fear of being held, Alan?'*

Alan: *'. . . being loved, and having that love and trust thrown back in my face. And to hold people. You know, it must be lovely that. You know, to comfort somebody. I'd like it. It must be nice.'*

Psychotherapist: *'One of the things that came over in your words is that you have a lot of anger and a lot of hatred from what happened in your family. Where do you think that anger and hatred went?'*

Alan: *'It went in myself. It's just filthy what I've done. I did worse by commitin' rape than what mum ever done to me. God knows what was goin' through my head that night. I don't know. I remember grabbing hold of her afterwards and cryin' and sayin' I don't know what's goin' on, what's happened? I'm sorry. There she is crying. I said, "I didn't hurt you, physically," did I? Mentally I've hurt her; it was degrading. Been standing there for about 10 minutes cryin'. I was doin' the more cryin'. I was goin' mental. I just walked along the town for about two weeks like a tramp. I wouldn't sleep in a bed, slept under bushes, in parks, just drinking. Bad news.'* – Actuality, Radio 4

This 'fly on the wall' method demands that highly intrusive equipment such as cameras become as inconspicuous as part of the furniture. The aim is to record an accurate 'slice of life', rather than the inflamed normality one might expect where the presence of crews and reporters must make interviewees feel like actors on a stage. To achieve this, crews will have to be present on location for long enough for their subjects to become acclimatized to them before filming can take place in earnest. Radio scores heavily over TV here, being dependent on nothing more obtrusive than a reporter with a microphone.

24-hour news

> *'See, we're gonna take the news and put it on the satellite, and then we're gonna beam it down to Russia and we're gonna bring world peace and we're all going to get rich in the process! Thank you very much.'*
>
> – CNN LAUNCH SPEECH, 1980
>
> *'CNN has become the most famous television station in the world . . . . a sort of intercom service for world leaders. Outside the United States its influence is out of all proportion to its audience. Enter any newspaper newsroom when important world news is breaking and its television sets will be tuned to CNN.'*
>
> – THE SUNDAY TIMES*

* Profile Cable News Network, 20 January 1991.

Figure 38   *'News on the hour, every hour – Independent Radio News.'* Bulletins are transmitted by satellite across a growing network. (*Courtesy IRN*)

Perhaps the ultimate news programme is the 24-hour news channel on satellite and cable TV. Ted Turner's Cable News Network (CNN) was the first in 1980. What was begun by the man dubbed the *'living embodiment of new media barbarism'**, has come of age. CNN International pumps out round-the-clock news via 15 satellites into 200 million households in upwards of 210 countries. CNN earned respect for its outstanding coverage of the massacre in Tiananmen Square and the Gulf War, when it was the only news network to cover the start of Operation Desert Storm.

Running hard to play the game of catch-up are BBC World and the British-based Sky TV News, which provides 24-hours pan-European coverage.

But 24-hour news was on radio years before television jumped on the bandwagon. All-news radio is credited with making its professional debut in Mexico in 1961, when the station XTRA in Tijuana began broadcasting a rip-and-read format that was later to spread to Chicago and be adopted and adapted by other networks.†

The 24-hour news format has since developed a number of distinct styles: the magazine approach, which presents a variety of programmes and personalities throughout the day; and the news cycle, which repeats and updates an extended news bulletin, and lasts usually between twenty minutes and an hour.

The US Westinghouse format adopted a news cycle, with a constantly updated sequence of hard news repeated throughout the day. *'Give us 22 minutes, we'll give you the world'* was the slogan. Repetition was not thought to matter, because Westinghouse stations catered for an audience that tuned in for the latest news and then tuned out.

---

* David Housham in 'CNN', *Broadcast* 4 October 1985.
† Philip O. Keirstead, *All-News Radio*, TAB Books, 1980.

Figure 39 Processing news 24 hours a day, seven days a week from more than 200 nations around the globe at the BBC World Service. (*Courtesy BBC World Service*)

CBS stations extended that cycle to an hour to try to hold an audience for longer. National news could be taken on the hour, followed by local news, with traffic, sport, weather reports and other items programmed into the cycle, moving away from the extended bulletin feel to become a news programme. Programmes became double-headed for variety, and the style aimed to be warmer and more relaxed than the Westinghouse model.

The other approach is the magazine style which builds programmes, such as phone-ins and discussions, on to a backbone of regular bulletins and summaries which run at intervals throughout.

> '*We have CBS news at the top of the hour for six minutes, then traffic and weather and a news summary – just local stuff – for about a minute or so, then we have a six or seven minute local package, some sport and a couple of features, and then we start all over again at the bottom – except at 30 the news package is seven or eight minutes long and involves both local and national news.*'
>
> – ANNETTE BOSWORTH, WEEI, BOSTON*

When the BBC took up the challenge of all-news radio, detractors claimed Radio 5 Live would mean squandering the licence fee on wall-to-wall speculation. But a healthy audience of more than five million silenced the critics.

* Ian Hyams, WEEI Video, 1986.

Who does what?

The bigger the news organization, the more specialists it is likely to employ. Job titles and descriptions vary across organizations and countries, but the news process in radio and TV is basically one of getting the stories in, and putting them out. These two jobs are called *input* and *output*.

Input	**Output**
Input editor	Programme editors/producers
Home/foreign editors	Anchors/presenters/newsreaders
Reporters and correspondents	Journalists/writers
Camera crews	Film/cutting librarians
Home/foreign assignments editors	Graphic artists
Operations organizer	Studio production staff
	Engineering staff

On the *input* side, stories come in from news agencies, with reports from international news services and material from freelances. Each is *copytasted* (scrutinized) by the relevant desk editor and potential stories are passed to the input (or intake) editor who will decide whether the station will commission them from correspondents or cover them itself. Assignments editors will detail reporters, correspondents and crews to those stories and the operations organizer will handle technical matters such as satellite booking and outside broadcast facilities.

Output is concerned with producing programmes from the material gathered. Editors and producers choose the items to go into their programmes. Journalists, writers or sub-editors write the stories and the presenters tailor them to suit their style of delivery. Reports are enhanced with graphics and archive shots, and put on air by studio production staff, led by the director, while engineers monitor the technical quality.

This is a simplification, and in most organizations there is a degree of overlap between input and output. The hierarchy in the local radio newsroom may run as follows:

Local radio news

News editor
Duty editor
Sports editor
Programme producers
Reporters
Programme assistants
Support staff

This pattern will also vary. The news editor will be responsible for the running of the newsroom and its staff. A duty editor may be delegated to take charge of day-to-day news coverage. The sports editor feeds items into programmes and bulletins. Producers organize particular programmes, from commissioning items to overseeing their presentation on air. Programme or technical assistants operate the studios. Newsreading and presentation may be divided among reporters and producers. Support staff include the newsroom secretary.

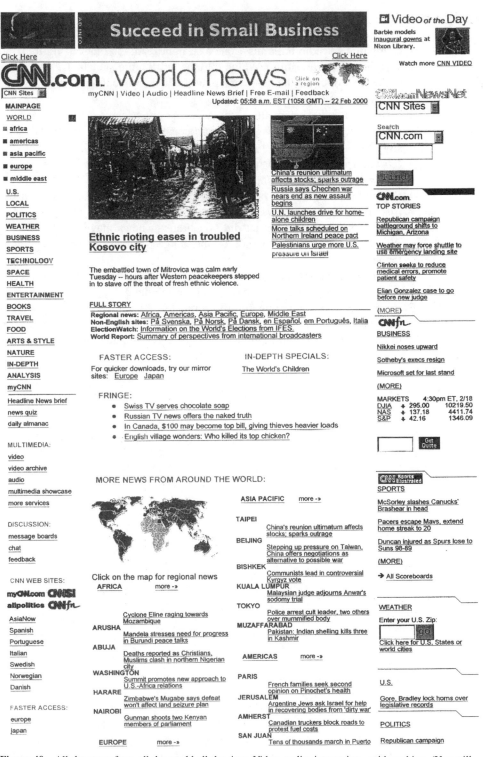

Figure 40 All the news from all the world all the time. Video, audio, interactive – with archive. (You still have to make your own coffee . . .) (*Courtesy CNN.com*)

Fieldwork

1 Compare two radio bulletins – one a straight read, the other using illustrations. Which was the more interesting? Which told the news more succinctly? Did the actuality add to the story or could the newsreader have said the same thing better? Which bulletin was the most memorable? Which did you prefer?

2 Listen to a radio documentary and a shorter radio feature. Apart from the length, what is the difference in the way they were constructed and the methods used to explain a story?

3 *'Dramatized documentaries cheapen the news by mixing fact with fiction and information with entertainment.'* Discuss.

4 If you can, compare the output of two 24-hour news stations using different formats. Listen or watch the news cycle run through twice. What changes were made in the second cycle? Which format did you prefer – news magazine or news cycle? Why? · Which format would (a) pull in the biggest audience? (b) keep an audience for longer?

   What are the advantages and disadvantages of a 24-hour news cycle over several short news programmes at fixed points in the day?

5 If you were given the opportunity to make a 30-minute fly-on-the-wall documentary, what subject would you choose, and why? Draw up a rough plan of coverage and think in detail how you would produce the first three minutes of the programme.

THE NEWS PROGRAMME

11 Item selection and order

In the world of the media the consumer is king, and today's audiences with remote control TV sets and radio tuners can pass judgement and verdict on a substandard programme or item in the time it takes to press a button. Greater choice and greater ease of making that choice have taken their toll on audience tolerance. Selection and comparison between broadcast news is now as easy as choosing a magazine at a news stand. More to the point, you can get the news you want, when you want it from the Internet. So more than ever the success of a programme depends on the producer's ability to select the stories the audience wants to see or hear – his or her news sense – and his or her skill in assembling those items into a popular programme.

The producer's first task is to match the coverage to the style and length of the programme. A two-minute headline summary may cover the current top eight stories, providing a sketched outline of events. A half-hour programme may go over substantially the same ground, but in more depth.

Researchers have found a surprising unanimity about what newsgatherers regard as news.* Importance, significance, relevance, immediacy, proximity, human interest and novelty, are all factors which go into the complex equation of news selection.

'A fair picture . . .'

From the million or more words a day that squirt into computers in newsrooms such as the BBC World Service, programme makers have to select and boil down just enough to fill their programmes. In the case of a three-minute bulletin, that may amount to little more than 500 words. But within these limitations the aim is to provide an objective picture of the day's main news.

'I hope it's a fair picture. A picture of light, dark and shade, but . . . it's a highly selective picture because we cannot be everywhere all of the time,' says Bob Wheaton, an editor of the BBC's *Six O'Clock News*.†

* See also Alastair Hetherington, *News, Newspapers and Television*, Macmillan, 1985, p. 4.
† *Inside Television*, BBC, 1986.

Figure 41 Going live at the BBC World Service . . . new items can come in even while the programme is on air. Stories may have to be cut or dropped to make room. (*Andrew Boyd*)

> *'In a sense we put a telephoto lens to the world. We only show in close-up the things that are newsworthy, and they tend to be sad things. It is a fact of life that a lot of what goes into the news is gloomy and disastrous and sad . . . News judgement . . . is not a very precise science but it is the way in which journalists are trained to say this is an interesting story, it is relevant, we ought to tell the audience this.'*
> – RON NEIL, CHIEF EXECUTIVE, BBC PRODUCTION*

Media feeds off media. Journalists as a breed are fiercely competitive. They scrutinize one another's output, grinding their teeth if someone's angle is better or their pictures are sharper, and if a rival comes up with a new story, then wolf-like (or lemming-like) they charge in packs towards it. As one editor puts it, news judgement *'is born of journalism, of reading papers every day, reading magazines, or watching other television programmes.'*†

ITN's *Channel 4 News* has different priorities to most other British news programmes. It aims to get into the *hows* and *whys* behind current issues. Its brief is also to look in more detail at neglected areas such as medicine, science and the arts and to extend British television coverage of foreign affairs to the oft-ignored and usually overlooked developing nations.

* *Ibid.*
† *Ibid.*

> *'Channel 4 News has a pace of its own in the sense that normally the first and second item can be quite long and there may be a third item, and then the "newsbelt" to pick up the pace. Then the idea is that you can settle down, feeling that you have been briefed on the stories of the day, and then, after the break, go into other subjects which are not part of the day's news.'*   – STEWART PURVIS, ITN*

Although *Channel 4 News* goes out at 7 o'clock it sees as its main competitor not the BBC's *Six O'Clock News* but the later and more analytical *Newsnight*.

On good days, where hard news abounds, media rivals will often run the same lead story. On quieter days, which produce fewer obvious headlines, it can look as though rival stations in the same city are reporting from different countries on different days of the week.

Second thoughts

After their programmes, most large news organizations hold a post-mortem to see what can be done to prevent mistakes recurring. Introspection can be useful in small doses, but too much criticism from above can stultify creativity, crush initiative, and instil a tendency to produce safe but predictable material.

The BBC, with its tiers of higher management and policy of 'referring-up' is renowned for its policy of rigorous self-examination. BBC news editors are still relatively small fish in a very large pond, ranking about fiftieth in the corporation's hierarchy and answerable to those above them for their decisions, and ultimately, their news judgements. ITN, which produces only news, has a smaller, and thereby less oppressive hierarchy and gives its executives a greater say in their own decision making.†

Item order

Harry Hardnose‡ is a typical (although mythical) news hack of the old order. He worked his way up to his position as a senior staffer in the newsroom by the sweat of his brow and does not plan to unveil the mysteries of his profession to every young upstart. If anyone asks about his news judgement, and few do, Harry simply points to his nose and sniffs, *'That's my secret.'*

But if the truth is known, Harry has neither the imagination nor the mental agility to explain the process of sniffing out and sorting out the news. For him it has long ceased to be the complex equation it once was. The myriad of baffling decisions and bewildering juxtapositions are now resolved in a moment, thanks to a mixture of pure instinct and neat whisky.

Harry is a 100 per cent proof hack. He does not *decide* what makes one story more important than the others, or which stories to run and in what order, he just *knows*.

Hard news is Harry's speciality. He calls it *information of importance to the listener*. Soft news is anything that is *interesting, entertaining* or just plain *juicy*. In the event, Harry

---

* Alastair Hetherington, *op. cit.*, p. 195.
† Alastair Hetherington, *op. cit.*, pp. 34–7.
‡ Creation of the cartoonist, Steve Bell.

Figure 42   How to cram the world's top news and the leading domestic stories into a half-hour programme . . . thrashing out news priorities in the editorial conference at ITN. (*Andrew Boyd*)

leaves the decision making to his glands. The more juices a story stirs up and the harder it hits him in the gut, the higher he slots it in the bulletin.

Thankfully, old soaks like Harry are a dying breed. But he does have a point. News selection does become a matter of instinct. Academics cannot resist the temptation to reduce the decision-making process to a formula, but formulae work best with subjects less complex than the human mind, and belong in the sterile conditions of the laboratory, rather than the creative chaos of the newsroom.

> *'Anyone who says you can make a journalistic judgement in a sort of sterile bath is talking bunkum, twaddle. You make a judgement because of your empirical knowledge store; you make it because of your family, because of the society in which we live.'*   – PETER SISSONS, BBC NEWSREADER*

The key factors in item selection are the story's significance, its impact on a given audience, its interest, topicality and immediacy. Most of these are related with a good deal of overlap between them.

1 The significance of the story

Harry Hardnose would tackle the issue of significance in its widest sense. *'Do we, or do we not, have a story?'* he would yell. *'This one'll rock 'em! Is there enough dirt here to*

*Alastair Hetherington, *op. cit.*, p. 195.

get that ***** out of office?' The academic would put the same questions, though couched in less colourful language: 'How important is this story in global or national terms? In what measure does it reflect our changing times, and to what degree does the story speak of political change or upheaval?'

2 The material impact of the story

'This'll hit 'em where it hurts!' drools Harry. The question is 'does the story materially affect *our* audience in terms of their earnings, spending power, standard of living or lifestyles?' Relevance is incorporated into this notion of significance and impact.

3 Audience reaction (the human interest factor)

When it comes to interest, Harry asks whether the story tugs at their hearts, causes them to suck in their breath, to swear or to smile. *'Blind nun on dope rescues dog from blazing orphanage'* is Harry's favourite story. He has already written it – now he is just waiting for it to happen.

More objectively, what strength of feeling is this story likely to provoke? It may not change the audience's way of life, but for it to be of human interest it should upset, anger, amuse intrigue or appal them, or be about people who have a similar effect.

The *Wow!* factor comes in here, with stories about the biggest, smallest, dearest, fastest, etc., which are intended to surprise or astound the hearer.

Figure 43   Juggling news selection for 24-hour rolling news and the main terrestrial flagship programmes – that's the task of ITN's editor in chief, Nigel Dacre. (*Andrew Boyd*)

4 The topicality of the story (the lemming factor)

As Harry would put it, *'Everyone else is flogging it, why the hell haven't we run it?'*

Has the story been in the public eye lately? If so, how largely has it figured? Linked to that is the immediacy factor.

5 The immediacy factor (the yawn factor)

Is it news just in? Is it a brand-new story that has broken, or a new angle on one that is still running? Conversely, has it been running for long enough to reach the point of boredom?

If a story is getting stale, then by definition, it is no longer news. On the other hand, a new item may breeze into the bulletin like a breath of fresh air. Its position may then be dictated by its freshness, especially when linked to topicality. In other words, if the bulletin is full of the latest hijacking, then news of a hostage release is fair bet for lead story.

Some news stations producing regular bulletins concentrate on providing a new-look programme every hour, in the hope that the variety will persuade the audience to tune-in for longer. Others argue that listeners don't stay tuned for long enough to get bored with the same bulletin. They prefer to let the lead story run and run, albeit freshened up and with a change of clothes, until it is replaced by something of equal significance. Again we see a mix of entertainment values and news values in operation.

Where bulletins are revised substantially every hour, there can be a loss of continuity, and stories of real substance are likely to be knocked down simply because they are regarded as old hat. Some stations attempt to strike a balance by running extended news summaries at key points in the day, such as 1 p.m. when the current stories are shelved and the day's major items are dusted off and re-run according to their significance that day.

6 Sport/specialisms

'Football results? – Bung 'em at the back of the bulletin.'

If the practice is to separate the sports news or other speciality like financial news into a section of its own, then each story within that section will be prioritized individually and run together in order of priority. The exception is speciality stories that are significant enough to earn a place in the general run of news.

7 Linking items

'Ah, return of the mini-skirt; record number of road accidents – I wonder?'

Frequently items have linked themes or offer different angles on the same story. Splitting them up would be a mistake. They should be rewritten to run together.

8 Actuality/pictures

'Strewth! Where'd you record this one, in a bathroom?'

Some stories are illustrated. The addition of actuality or footage and its length and quality may be extra factors in deciding where to place each item in the bulletin. It might be policy to spread illustrations throughout or to run no more than one phone-quality item.

9 'And finally . . .'

> *'Got a tickler here about some kid who tried to hold up a bank with a water pistol . . .'*

With items that are bright, frivolous, trivial and can guarantee a smirk if not a belly laugh, common practice would be to save them for the end of the bulletin.

Local considerations

> *'At Hallam, I aim for punchy stories that are not overdramatic with short cues and a mix of local and national stories. Delivery should be aggressive and confident, but not too speedy. Stories should be kept short, sweet and simple, and if a humorous item is included at the end of the bulletin, that's fine. I do not like to run gory stories at meal times, nor racy ones, such as sex court cases, when mothers and fathers may be sitting down listening to the radio with their children or even their grannies. We aim for a family audience.'*
> – JIM GREENSMITH, HALLAM FM, INDEPENDENT LOCAL RADIO STATION IN SHEFFIELD, ENGLAND

Local consideration could feature highly in positioning items in the bulletin. What might be of interest nationally is unlikely by itself to satisfy a local audience, so the relative weight given to national and local news has to be carefully considered.

Audiences and their needs can change throughout the day. First thing in the morning, all viewers or listeners might want to know is: *'Is the world the same as it was when I went to bed; will I get wet when I leave home, and will I be able to get to work on time?'*

Some of the most successful radio stations are based in big cities serving one clear community with a common identity. Others may serve regions with several small cities, a number of towns and many villages, so *'three people died today when a lorry went out of control in North Street'* would leave half the audience scratching their heads about *which* North Street the newsreader was referring to.

How local is local? News editors may find the strongest news coming regularly from one location, but may have to consciously drop good stories for weaker ones from elsewhere to try to give an even spread of coverage.

Foreign coverage

Central to the question of relevance is proximity. *'Is this story about me, about things happening on my doorstep, or is it about strangers 2000 miles away who I never knew existed?'*

Western news values are often insular and unfavourable to foreign stories unless they are about 'people like us,' as the BBC's Ron Neil explains: *'Our research shows that people in this country would far prefer a preponderance of British news to foreign news. The judgement can only be what are the most relevant stories around in Britain today.'*

All things considered, item selection and running orders will often be settled on nothing more objective than the gut reaction of journalists about the gut reactions they expect their stories to produce from their audience. In other words – impact.

* Speaking on Tuesday Call, BBC Radio 4, 30 September 1986.

HALLAM TODAY				
Guide time :	*Item*	:	*Running time* :	*Elapsed time* :
30" :	*Hallam Today Jingle*	:	30" :	30" :
:	Programme teasers (20 secs max > i.e. 3 teasers – 20 words each)	:	:	:
2' 30" :	NEWS DESK & WEATHER	:	2' 27" :	2' 57" :
2' 00" :	MUSIC	:	2' 10" :	5' 07" :
2' 30" :	Intro and Billboard 1	:	2' 42" :	7' 49" :
1' 30" :	<u>AD BREAK</u>	:	1' 10" :	8' 59" :
2' 00" :	Intro and Billboard 2	:	2' 15" :	11' 14" :
2' 00" :	MUSIC	:	2' 05" :	13' 19" :
2' 00" :	Intro and Billboard 3	:	2' 06" :	15' 25" :
30" :	Traffic	:	25" :	15' 50" :
1' 00" :	NEWS DESK	:	1' 00" :	16' 50" :
2' 00" :	Intro and Billboard 4	:	1' 46" :	18' 36" :
1' 30" :	<u>AD BREAK</u>	:	1' 30" :	20' 06" :
4' 00" :	SPORT AT 5.20 P.M.	:	3' 47" :	23' 53" :
2' 30" :	MUSIC	:	2' 35" :	26' 28" :
2' 30" :	Intro and Billboard 5	:	2' 30" :	28' 58" :
1' 00" :	Closing NEWS HEADLINES	:	1' 02" :	30' :
:	OUTRO	:	:	:

Figure 44 Programme running order. The **Item** column gives the standard programme format that the producer works towards when compiling the programme. The **Guide Time** column gives the recommended times of each item. When all the items are in, the producer puts their exact durations in the **Running Time** column. The **Elapsed Time** gives the cumulative time of all the items, which has to add up to 30 minutes – the duration of the programme. Music can be cut short or stretched out to make the programme fit to length. (*Courtesy Hallam FM*)

Story/Slug	Segment	Presenter	Graphic	Prod	Est	Actual	Event	Back	Time	Reporter
Package Details						1:26	18:30:00	18:29:37	1:26	Sarah Gilbert
Pre Record Sequence						:00	18:31:26	18:31:03	1:26	Munro Forbes
OPENING SEQUENCE	Opening		*			:15	18:31:26	18:31:03	1:41	Dominic Holland
	GLITTER					:00	18:31:41	18:31:18	1:41	Dominic Holland
	CRASH					:00	18:31:41	18:31:18	1:41	Chris Long.
	DOCTORS					:00	18:31:41	18:31:18	1:41	Chris Long.
	BIG MATCH					:00	18:31:41	18:31:18	1:41	Chris Long.
GLITTER	Lead in				:25	:28	18:31:41	18:31:18	2:09	James Wilson
	ROGERS VTR				2:00	2:13	18:32:09	18:31:46	4:22	Mike Rigby
MEDIA	Lead in		*		:20	:21	18:34:22	18:33:59	4:43	Dominic Holland
	DERHAM VTR				2:10	2:14	18:34:43	18:34:20	6:57	Kate Powling
ULSTER	VTR ULAY				:25	:30	18:36:57	18:36:34	7:27	James Wilson
CRASH	Lead in				:20	:18	18:37:27	18:37:04	7:45	David Stanley
	DAVIES VTR				1:15	1:18	18:37:45	18:37:22	9:03	Paul Davies
BIG MATCH	Lead in				:20	:16	18:39:03	18:38:40	9:19	James Wilson

Figure 45 Running order for the ITV *Evening News*. Note the estimated durations and the actual times of the items, as well as the cumulative running time. Producers can call up the story onto the screen by clicking on the document icons. (*Courtesy ITN*)

But impact without awareness has about as much educational value as being flattened by a runaway truck.

> '*Foreign news is mainly a series of unexplained and unconnected disasters. Most of these flit in and out of the news so quickly that we learn mainly to ignore them, in full confidence they will soon go away.*' — JAMES FALLOWS
>
> '*Our global coverage has become a comic book: ZAP! POW! BANG-BANG!*' — LARRY MARTZ*

If foreign coverage is to do anything more than leave us relieved that it's happening *there* and not *here*, it will need to be accompanied by analysis.

Producing a running order

> '*You never go into the programme at 6.30 am with a running order that stays the same throughout the show – ever. Always there are changes; sometimes the whole thing is rewritten. You're given a running order but you basically throw it away and just wing it throughout the morning.*' — JOHN HUMPHRYS, PRESENTER OF RADIO 4'S *TODAY* PROGRAMME.†

* 'News you can't use', James Fallows, *The Guardian*, 1 April 1996.
† *See it for Yourself*, BBC, 1987.

Many newcasters hold the bulletin running order in their heads – especially radio newsreaders who are operating their own studio equipment. Where a technical assistant drives the desk for the newsreader, he or she will usually want a running order listing the items and giving their durations, in-words and out-words.

Stations producing longer programmes sometimes combine running order with format. A pre-printed sheet shows what kind of stories should go where, and approximately how long each should be. Using this modular approach, features are plugged in and replaced where necessary, but for items to be fully interchangeable they will usually have to be of

Figure 46 Clipped to a camera in the studios at ITN, the programme running order. The operator of Cam 3 will listen through headphones for any last-minute changes. (*Andrew Boyd*)

a fixed length. The producer's job is to organize the coverage so suitable items of the right length are brought in, and then make sure the programme goes out to plan.

A completed running order can be an elaborate document, giving precise details of items, durations, ins and outs, or it could be a rough guide to what the producers and directors expect and hope for in the next half hour. TV news has more than one running order to work with. With the list of programme items, which may be constantly changing, will be a list of the visuals that go with those items. TV directors driving programmes which rely on sophisticated production techniques and make increasing use of live reports will frequently have to 'busk' the order, working with a schedule that changes so often, it may never be produced in final form on paper.

Fieldwork

1 What qualities do you think make a story big enough to run as a bulletin lead?
2 If you have access to a rip and read service take 10 stories from the printer and select seven to make up a bulletin. (If you cannot get any rip and read, cut the stories from a newspaper.) Then discuss how you chose the three to drop.
3 If the seven remaining stories are too long for broadcast or are written in a newspaper style, rewrite them for broadcast to a maximum of 60 words each.

Then working purely on instinct, rank those stories in order to compile a bulletin.
4 If you are in a class, switch your stories with those of a classmate and compare running orders. Now discuss your similarities and differences and see if you can agree an order between you.
5 Now listen to a five-minute radio bulletin and assess the running order. In what order would you have run the items and why?

THE NEWS PROGRAMME

12 Putting the show together

> *'Five years ago there were 50 stations in Paris, 40 in Marseilles. The owner of one had all his rivals on tape. He hit the buttons for me. "They all sound the same," he complained, "including us." He has since gone down the pan.'*
>
> – MICHAEL KAYE*

Every programme maker would be grateful for a guaranteed audience. Perhaps fortunately for the consumer there is no such thing. Where news stations and different news media compete, there can be no room for complacency. In the end, the best product should find the most takers – providing it gives the consumer what they want.

Audience loyalty is important. Even where rival news programmes are broadcast at the same time and there is little to choose between their coverage, sections of the audience will have their favourite and will probably stick with it. They might like the style, pace and rhythm of the programme, or the way the sport, traffic and weather are put over. Or it could be the special features that match their own interests, such as fishing or business news. It might be that one programme offers more audience participation – phone-ins, or discussions. Or the audience may simply feel more comfortable with the presenters of one channel, finding them warmer, more cheerful and more 'like folks' than the 'cold fish' on the other side. Meanwhile, the rival station could pick up viewers for precisely the opposite reason – the audience preferring their more formal, authoritative style.

To a family at home, the presenters are like friends or acquaintances that join them in their front room for half an hour or more each day – longer perhaps than most real friends. Small wonder the choice of presenters is viewed with such importance.

Every producer's aim is to find a winning format and stick with it, in the hope that the audience will do the same. But the familiarity factor can work against them. Even belated improvements to a programme that has been creaking with age will usually produce an audience backlash and – initially, at least – lose a number of viewers who were very happy with the product as it was. The art of maintaining audience loyalty is to find what the customers want, and give it to them – consistently.

* 'Waves of Protest', *UKPG*, 27 November 1995.

The BBC's latest revamp followed research that indicated viewers wanted the news to remain authoritative but to become more accessible. TV branding specialist Martin Lambie-Nairn was called in to do the makeover. Out went the austere blue virtual cut-glass coat of arms, and in came new sets, in a cosy shade of beige, new graphics, logos and music – less of an air-raid siren than a drum roll. *'It's part of a total editorial restructuring of the BBC news to make the ... bulletins clearer, warmer and more accessible,'* he told *The Guardian.**

Winning an audience – the openers

> *'What you decide to lead on is lent an enormous amount of importance. If you say [grave voice] "Good evening. The headlines at six o'clock, there's been a train crash in Scotland," then people will think, "this must be terrible, there must be lots of people dead." If, one or two stories in, you say [brighter, almost cheerful voice] "a train has crashed in Scotland," it's immediately a much lighter business.'*
> – BBC PRESENTER SUE LAWLEY†

The openers are designed to lure and capture the unsuspecting viewer. The first few seconds of a programme are all-important. During these moments the audience can be

Figure 47 Last-minute check before going live. Jon Snow (*centre*) is in the Channel 4 news studio. Cameras are operated by remote control from the gallery. (*Andrew Boyd*)

* 10 May 1999.
† *Inside Television*, BBC.

gained or lost. In television news, the openers are usually the most complicated and closely produced part of the programme. They will probably comprise a signature tune and title sequence, featuring sophisticated computer graphics and a tightly edited montage of still and moving pictures. This might be followed by headlines or teasers – tersely worded five-second phrases written to intrigue – perhaps each illustrated with a snatch of footage showing the most gripping moments of action to come.

The openers, demanding quick-fire operation and split-second timing, might be the only part of a news programme, barring the individual items, to be pre-recorded. This is likely to be done during the rehearsal shortly before transmission.

Radio news, which is spared the demanding dimension of pictures, has an easier task. The programme might begin with a signature tune, voiced-over by an announcer, which is faded down beneath the voice of the newsreader, who may give the headlines in turn, each supported by a colourful or intriguing snatch from an interview or report to be featured in the programme. This list of coming attractions is known as the *menu*.

Keeping an audience – headlines and promotions

> *'Television news is a marketable commodity, like peaches, computers, toothpaste and refrigerators.'*
> – CAROLYN DIANA LEWIS, AUTHOR, *REPORTING FOR TELEVISION*

Movie makers realized years ago that not even a blockbuster of a film can sell itself. For a movie to do well at the box office, it has to be promoted. Trailers have to be produced capturing the liveliest action and the snappiest dialogue to show the audience the thrills in store. News producers are not above using the same techniques.

Headlines achieve two important functions: at the middle and end of a programme they remind the audience of the main stories and help reinforce that information. Reinforcement aids recall, and an audience that can remember what it has heard is more likely to be satisfied. At the beginning, the headlines hook the audience in the same way as the cinema trailer, and later serve to encourage them to bear with an item that may be less appealing because they know something better is on the way. During the programme, forward trails, such as, *'Coming up, Spot the singing Dalmatian, but first news of the economic crisis'* do much the same job.

If a news programme is broken by a commercial break, the audience for the next part of the programme must never be taken for granted. Each segment is likely to end on what are known as *pre-commercials* – a cluster of headlines designed to keep the audience. ITN Producer Phil Moger:

> *'The pre-commercials are probably more important than the headlines at the beginning of the programme. My job during those three sentences before the break is to get them to come back. My ideal pre-commercial has something of weight, something for women and something of sport.'*

Good stories alone are no guarantee of an audience. Having the stories and persuading the audience to wait for them is the way to keep them.

Actuality

1936

'Members of your staff – they could be called BBC Reporters . . . should be held in readiness . . . to cover unexpected news of the day . . . a big fire, strikes, civil commotion, railway accidents . . . It would be his job . . . to secure an eye-witness . . . to give a short account of the part he or she played that day. In this way . . . the news could be presented in a gripping manner and, at the same time, remain authentic . . . Such a news bulletin would in itself be a type of actuality programme.'
– RICHARD DIMBLEBY, OUTLINING HIS PROPOSALS TO THE BBC'S
CHIEF NEWS EDITOR

'Actuality is what makes radio bulletins come alive – use as much as possible.'
– SIMON ELLIS, BBC LOCAL RADIO NEWS EDITOR

It took some sections of the BBC half a century to take up Dimbleby's proposals above for illustrating the news, but actuality – interview extracts and on-the-spot reports – has for decades been a central feature of TV and radio news reporting world-wide.

Actuality is used to transport the audience to the scene, to hear the words as they were said, and to see or hear the news as it is actually happening – hence the term *actuality*. This is where broadcasting scores heavily above newspapers. If a single picture is worth a thousand words, what must be the value of moving pictures – and sound?

Combine sound and pictures with text and rapid access to archive material and you have the new superbroadcasting system of tomorrow, today – the Internet.

Pictures

The supremacy of TV news suggests that moving pictures hold the greatest audience appeal, but the enduring attraction of radio must be due in no small part to the way in which radio stimulates the imagination of its audience. It makes radio listening a more active experience than the passive, attention-consuming pastime of watching TV.

Recent developments in TV news have had less to do with changing formats or presentation styles than the availability of faster and better pictures. Television is undergoing a continuing revolution. When TV news began, newsreel film, which could be weeks out of date, was superseded by film reports made the same day. Now the slow medium of film has given way to faster newsgathering using videotape, digital capture and live transmission of pictures. Access to the action has been made easier by long-distance relay techniques and more portable and less obtrusive equipment.

Good pictures don't just illustrate the news – they are the news. *'You don't want to look like a radio bulletin which just has a newscaster sitting there. You rely on the strength of the pictures,'* says the Chief Executive of BBC Production, Ron Neil.

The availability of pictures can determine whether a story is run or dropped, and the strength of those pictures will often settle a story's position in a bulletin. When mounted police charged pickets during one protracted and acrimonious strike, this significant escalation of police tactics was reported prominently by the BBC and mutedly by ITN. BBC cameras recorded the incident, but ITN missed the charge, having been misinformed about where the main picketing would take place. The BBC headlined the charge to a background of pictures, while ITN, with nothing more than a reporter's account of the incident, left it out of the headlines and ran a shorter version of the story in the programme.*

Graphics

> *'I put a tremendous emphasis on graphics. They are a marvellous asset in explaining things to people, so I always try to use a lot of them. You can spell out a story line by line: "Party policy is . . ." and use graphics to explain complicated points: "the meltdown pattern is . . ." and so on.'*   – ITN PRODUCER, PHIL MOGER

TV graphics can do much to overcome the broadcaster's bête noir – the difficulty most listeners have in absorbing and retaining background information while continuing to take in a steady stream of facts. The context of the story can be explained by displaying and holding key points or quotes on the screen. Without this advantage, radio news has to resort to the old adage of KISS – *keep it simple, stupid!*

Figure 48   In the production suite. Computer-controlled editing lays down pictures, soundtrack and graphics directly onto the Betacam videocassette. (*Andrew Boyd*)

* Alastair Hetherington, *News, Newspapers and Television*, Macmillan, 1985.

Radio producers will try to run an even spread of copy stories, illustrated items and voice reports, and may juggle the position of stories in the programme to try to achieve a pleasing variety. TV producers play the same game with taped reports, stills, graphics and to-camera pieces, working hard not to load the programme with too many static items or on-the-spot reports.

Programme balance – being all things to all people

Producers will never please all of the people all of the time, but they do their best to please some of them some of the time and leave everybody satisfied. The ITV *Evening News*, which is ITN's flagship, tries to cover all the important stories of the day, doing the job of a paper of record, and goes on to include human interest items to widen the appeal. The aim is to satisfy a broader audience than any newspaper, embracing readers of quality and popular press alike.

The formula has improved since the *News at Ten's* launch in 1967. Then editor, Geoffrey Cox, described the first two editions as having a *'jerky lack of rhythm . . . lumpy disproportion between items,'* and being *'ill shaped, broken apart rather than linked by the commercial break, and exuding . . . traces of lack of confidence.'**

Figure 49   On-air! Pamela Armstrong and Riz Khan presenting BBC World television news to Asia. (*Courtesy BBC*)

* Geoffrey Cox, *See it Happen*, Bodley Head, 1983, Chapter 41.

Groupings and variety

> '*Television viewers need relief from sorrow, suffering, pain and hate. A steady drumbeat of tragedy tends to leave the viewer weary and exhausted. Thus, in a series of waves, the program reaches a climax of shock and woe, then eases off for something light and unchallenging, and then later, it returns to stories that are murderous or scandalous or worse.*'
> – CAROLYN DIANA LEWIS, REPORTING FOR TELEVISION

'*Programme feel*' **is a key to the success or failure of a show. That feel is down to the rhythm, pace and variety of the programme as well as the substance of its reports, and that feel is enhanced by the way items are grouped together**. Sport and other special interest features are often segmented together, and even world news or local news, if these are thought to hold only a secondary appeal, may be grouped in segments short enough to hold those in the audience who have tuned in primarily to hear something else.

Story groupings may be broken down further by location or comparative weight. Some US radio stations operating an hourly cycle of news will divide the national and local news into major and secondary items and run the secondaries in slots of their own at fixed points in the cycle. These groupings of minor items will be kept short, with brief stories, and used almost as fillers to vary the pace between weightier or more interesting segments.

Segmenting can be counter-productive. Running all the crime stories together would lose impact. It might be better to group them at intervals in the programme. Likewise, film reports or actuality with a similar theme, such as coverage of a riot and a noisy demonstration, are often best kept apart. Too many talking heads (dry, expert opinion) may also bore the audience.

Research for the former British Independent Broadcasting Authority discovered that an audience is more likely to forget an item when stories are grouped together. Researchers also identified a 'meltdown' factor, when similar stories ran together in the audience's mind. They placed a Mafia trial story in the middle of four foreign news items and then among four from the UK. Recall among the British audience was 20 per cent higher when the Mafia story was placed in the unusual context of UK news – normally it would be kept separate.*

> '*To a great extent the news is produced. It is not simply gathered in, written up, put in a certain order, slapped on the air and punched out. It is produced by things like headlines, signature tunes, and stopgaps in the middle where we give the stories coming up next, little quotes at the end of the Six O'Clock News. We intend to make it both visual and entertaining and indeed to make you smile sometimes.*'
> – BBC PRESENTER SUE LAWLEY†

Beside all these considerations is one of taste. It may seem good for variety to follow a triple killing with Mimi the dancing dingbat, but the audience wouldn't thank you for it. It would make light of a serious and tragic story. Juxtaposition requires a good deal of

---

* As reported in *UK Press Gazette*, 21 July 1986.
† *Inside Television*, BBC, 1986.

care, and to keep the audience informed about where the programme is going, transitions should be clearly signposted:

> *'International news now . . .'*
> *'Meanwhile, back home . . .'*
> *'But there is some good news for residents of . . .'*
> *'Industrial news . . .'*
> *'On the stock market . . .'*

Transitions, timechecks, thoughtful linking and headlines, help to create programme feel and establish identity. They can be overdone, as *Times* humorist Miles Kington observes:

> *One example comes from a presenter who was linking a murder thriller to a programme about cheese making: 'And from something blood-curdling to something rather more milk-curdling . . .'*

In radio, it is best to separate phone reports of indifferent sound quality to avoid testing the patience of listeners straining to hear above the interference on their car radios. Indoor and outdoor reports can be mixed, and extra variety added by using male and female co-presenters. Alternating stories between the two can lift a programme, and research suggests it helps viewers remember the items. But on a short programme, too many voices can have a ping-pong effect if each presenter doesn't have enough time to establish an identity.

The idea is to give a spread of light and heavy, fast and slow, busy and static, to get the most variety and interest from the material.

'When you are planning an hour-long news programme you have to keep things strong right the way through, rather than do what happens in a news bulletin, where you start with the most important and finish with the most trivial. It's got to have a strong beginning, to hold itself up in the middle and have a good end. I want a piece that people can remember.'
— ROB MCKENZIE, PRODUCER/PRESENTER CAPITAL RADIO

Rhythm and pace

Rhythm and pace are as crucial to programme feel as the choice of items. The style of writing, speed of reading, pace of editing and length of each item determine whether the programme surges ahead or drags.

Individual reports should run to just the right length to hold interest, and leave the audience wanting more rather than wishing for less. Information also has to be presented at a pace that the slowest in the audience will be able to follow without frustrating the rest. The programme should be rhythmic, though with enough variety to stimulate interest. Aim for a standard length for items, with none cut so short as to feel truncated or abrupt, or allowed to run on to the point of boredom.

Where short news items are used, the overall rhythm of the programme can be maintained by grouping them in segments that are about the same length as a standard item, or by inserting them into the programme at regular intervals.

Where an item is less likely to be of prime interest to an audience, it will usually be trimmed shorter than the others, and positioned between stories which are thought to be popular and have been promoted as such. The aim is to tempt an audience to stay tuned for as long as possible and preferably longer than intended.

The importance of rhythm is even more closely observed in pop radio where news programmes belong in the context of a music show. The audience is conditioned to the rhythm of the three-minute disc, so any single news item of over three minutes would feel as though it were dragging. Many news bulletins on pop stations are three minutes long. Stations that pump out fast, beaty, music to a young audience will often want their news to be the same – bright, youthful and moving along at a cracking pace. Radio 1's Newsbeat and Capital Radio are followers of the fast and furious principle. The brisker the pace of the programme, the shorter the items should be, and interviews with people who are ponderous in their delivery should be cut even shorter to avoid dragging the pace. It's even been known for interviews to be speeded up electronically to give them a little more sparkle.

Nightly News

Let's pull all of this together with a closer look at ITN's *Nightly News*, an 11 pm roundup of news and sport which pulls in an audience of around three million – twice the size predicted by producer Phil Moger when the show began.

> *'The formula for the programme is very simple – a quick news digest before we go to bed. Hard news and pacey and slightly upmarket. You tend to get a lot of movers and shakers watching at that time of night, opinion formers and MPs who are just getting home.*
> *'We carry financial headlines and look at the newspapers, putting the front pages up on the screen and looking at as many as possible.*
> *'At the same time we pick up the bulk of the viewers from the preceding programme, which might not be an A/B [upmarket] type. To keep them we have got to keep the human interest. The aim has been to produce a digest of the important news of the day and to flag up any news that has broken during the evening.'*

ITN is prepared to revisit stories that have run earlier in the day, but will always give the package a new treatment. But reports from the *Nightly News* will never be repeated on the programmes the following day. Moger says the show is prepared to break midnight embargoes to get a story on air that day.

> *'If you can buy a copy of the paper on the streets of London at 11 o'clock with those embargoed stories in them, then there is no reason why the great British public in Leeds or Bradford should be banned from seeing them. We've had a couple of run-ins from organisations about this, but nothing serious.*
> *'What delights me is to hear the Today programme [on BBC Radio 4] at 8 o'clock to find their lead stories are the ones we covered at 11 o'clock. That makes me a happy bunny.'*

The *Today* programme is the politicians' favourite and universally considered to set the news agenda. That suits Moger: *'I see myself as prising open the agenda for the following day, rather than setting it. We just lift the lid off the sardine box.'*

The average length of a *Nightly News* item is 1 minute 20 seconds, though at a push a lead story could run to two minutes. Even so, that squeezes out any prospect of analysis, which is the province of the programme the *Nightly News* is up against – BBC 2's *Newsnight*. The formula seems to work, because ITN's offering trounces *Newsnight* in the audience stakes, pulling in almost three times the viewers.

A DAY IN THE LIFE OF A *NIGHTLY NEWS* PRODUCER

1.30 am	Read the first editions of the morning newspapers, then sleep!
8 am	Listen to the radio news, the BBC's *Today* programme or one of the stations fed by ITN.
9.30	Travel in to work on the train. Read all the morning papers.
11.30	Arrive at ITN. Get prospects from Home and Foreign Desks – for today and tomorrow. *'Normally there's at least one story slated for tomorrow which I'll say "Hey, why can't we be doing that tonight?" '*
12.30 pm	Watch the ITN *Lunchtime News*. Draw up a list of prospective stories.
2.15	Meeting with Nigel Dacre, Editor-in-Chief, or Editor of the day to discuss stories.
2.30	Staff of the *Nightly News* arrive. Go through the prospects for the programme.

Afternoon Talk to reporters, prepare stories, discuss with the Foreign desk. Consider how to make stories look different from the 6.30.

6	Look at the BBC 6 o'clock news headlines.
6.30	Watch ITN *Evening News*.
6.45	During the break draw up a more detailed list of prospects.
7.10	Meet the Editor, Nigel Dacre, attended by newscaster.
7.45	Team meeting with everyone – VTR, graphic and picture editors. Discuss pending 10 pm headlines.
8 onwards	Packages come in. Discuss with reporters.
9	Draw up running order.
9.50	Front pages of the nationals come in on the wire – sometimes before the papers themselves are off the presses. Check for legal problems. *'If I see something on the front page that I could be sued for I can't put it out. Also watch out that some of the front pages of the tabloids are not in bad taste or over raunchy, with boobs falling out all over the place.'*
10	Headlines with pictures go out, produced by the Chief Sub or APE – Assistant Programme Editor.
10.15	Write 10″ promo for 10.55. Check headlines, packages, papers.
10.30	Record the roundup of tomorrow's newspapers' front pages.
10.40	Programme rehearsal.
10.55	Promo slot before the commercial break.
11	On air.
11.15	Team debriefing.
11.30	Grab the morning papers and go home. *'Very long day!'*

– PHIL MOGER

And now the good news?

With tidings of global recession, war, ethnic cleansing and soaring crime swamping the airwaves even hardened news presenters are wondering whether the time has come to reconsider an agenda that equates doom and gloom with news values.

BBC presenter Martyn Lewis has accused TV of consigning viewers to 'a relentless culture of negativity'.

> *'We should be more prepared than we have been in the past to weigh the positive stories . . . The main criteria for including stories should not be the degree of violence, death, conflict, failure or disaster they encompass, but the extent to which those stories have the potential to shape or change the world in which we live . . . Pressure from the top traps large areas of journalism into a whirlpool of negativity.'*

Presenter Peter Sissons rebuked, *'it is not our job to go in for social engineering to make people feel better,'* adding for good measure that the BBC's job was to report the news *'the way it is, even if people slit their wrists.'*

Meanwhile those seeking solace in good news will have to tune into ITN's tailpiece, the light-hearted *'and finally'*, which Lewis dismisses as a 'sticking plaster' over the world's problems.*

Fieldwork

1 Watch closely several news programmes on TV and radio, and reconstruct the format used to compile them. Note the balance and length of the stories and the use of headlines and pre-commercials. See how stories are linked and whether back announcements are used. What gives these programmes their feel? Who are they aimed at and how could they be improved?

2 Set up a half-hour news programme from scratch. Choose a target audience (family, young people, business people, community cross-section, etc.) and consider the kind of programme you want to produce. Think about the contents, pace, length of items and programme feel and draw up a brief setting out your plans. If you are in a class, work on this in groups of four.

3 Using the Internet or copy from newspapers, find enough ideas for stories to fill your programme. Remember that length is a crucial factor. Decide the duration of your reports, then assemble those stories into a running order.

Write the cues to your stories in a style appropriate to the programme you have in mind. Decide whether your writing should be terse and emphatic, in a hard news style, or chatty and relaxed to suit a more discursive style of programme.

Think about the overall balance of your programme. Does it have a good blend of light and shade, serious and offbeat? Should you be running special interest items such as sport? Are the stories positioned to hold interest throughout? Is the first half overloaded with heavyweight items?

4 Now work on the headlines and linking. Set it up properly with headlines at the start and a summary at the end. Should you use full-length headlines or short teasers? Does your

---

* 'Uplifting experiences', Steve Busfield, *UKPG*, 10 May 1993; 'And now for the good news', Profile, *Observer*, 2 May 1993; *UKPG*, 6 November 1995.

programme have a commercial break? If so write some pre-comms. If not, produce a menu in the middle saying what is coming up. Revise the cues where necessary to provide better links between stories.

Consider whether back announcements would be beneficial.

If you are in a class, discuss your work with another group when you have finished preparing your programme and swap your ideas and criticisms.

5 If you have studio facilities, work in groups to produce actual programmes, using news from an agency feed or going out as reporters and getting your own.

THE NEWS PROGRAMME

13   Making the programme fit

> Emma and Jenni are working on timings with a stopwatch, cutting the length to split seconds. Emma has a complicated chart, adding and taking out seconds painstakingly from here and there. *'Witchcraft could lose 45 seconds ... cut the lead in to 40 seconds ... we're still five seconds over ... the music for the serial provides flexibility. You have to finish at 2.59.45 at the latest to make sure you don't crash the pips.'*
> – WOMAN'S HOUR*

Many programme makers will share the same bad dream – their show is either five minutes too short and grinds to a halt early, leaving a gaping hole before the next item, or it develops a will of its own, gathering momentum until it becomes an unstoppable juggernaut, overrunning hopelessly and throwing out the programme schedule for the entire network.

It's a nightmare that can be prevented with a little forethought. Few news or magazine programmes boast running orders that have every item buttoned up and timed to the second. Getting a programme to run to time is down to forward planning and flexibility.

Cutting

Where a programme is in danger of overrunning and has to be cut, the incision can be made in a number of ways. The most drastic is to drop an item completely. Another way of saving time is to replace a longer item with a shorter one. Where only a small saving is required, trimming an item on air usually does the job.

The easiest way to do this is to cut something that is live. If you are conducting a live interview, you will be told when to wind-up by your producer, who will also tell you the time you have remaining for the interview, and will count you down during the final moments. If you have 15 seconds left and still want to pursue another point you can put

* Penny Vincenzi, *GH*, May 1990.

Figure 50 Presenting a live news programme means making room for breaking news. Some stories will have to be cut and copy trimmed on the fly so the programme can end on time – to the second. (*Andrew Boyd*)

their question in a way that makes your interviewee aware time is running out, such as, *'Finally, and briefly . . .'*

Programme makers often include live material towards the end of a programme as a flexible buffer, which can be compressed or expanded to fill in time. Where all the items are recorded and all are to be run producers can be faced with the unenviable task of having to cut an item on air so it appears quite naturally to have come to an end.

This can be made far less fraught with a little help from the reporter. Before you finish editing an item, make a note of a place at which your story can be brought to an early end, along with the words that run up to that point and the duration of the item up to that point. This is known as *pot-point*, and it will give your producer the flexibility to run the item in either its shorter or longer version. Cutting early is known as *pot-cutting*, and is made by either switching out the picture and soundtracks or physically stopping the tape machine.

> *In India, four nuns have been raped by a 20-strong gang of Hindu militants in Madhya Pardesh. It's the latest in a wave of attacks against Christians. Mobs have burned and desecrated churches – often in full view of the police, according to witnesses. Until recently the Muslim community was the target of ultra-nationalists. But now the militants are turning their attention to India's Christian minority.*
> *From New Delhi, our correspondent Simon French reports . . .*

>> POT: 'turning a blind eye to the attacks'
>> DUR: (Duration) 56″
>> OUT: (Final words) 'nationalism has turned into a kind of idol worship.'
>> DUR: 1'06″

In radio the process of cutting or filling is perhaps the simplest of all. Assuming a five-minute bulletin has a sequence of sport, an 'and finally' and weather at the end, which should only be cut if essential, the newsreader works out the combined duration of those items and deducts this from the total length of the bulletin. If they come to a minute and a half, then the reader has three and a half minutes remaining for the 'meat' of the bulletin. If the programme started at 2 o'clock the newsreader knows that he or she has to begin the end sequence by three and a half minutes past 2. Watching the clock, the reader simply aims to come out of the main material as near to that time as possible, and any other stories that have not been read by then will have to be discarded. (See also Backtiming, below.)

Writing the weather or sport to flexible lengths, with paragraphs that can be kept in or cut, allows the newsreader to make final adjustments so the bulletin can come out exactly on time. This way, late news can be slotted in without throwing the programme timing.

Filling

Filling is a more serious problem than having to cut, because it implies the programme is short of good material and the producer has been failing in his or her job. Items should never be run simply as makeweights – every story should deserve its airtime. It is up to the news producer to make sure that on even the quietest news day there is enough good material to run, even if it means switching to softer stories.

Many newsrooms compensate for the ebb and flow of news by sending out reporters on slow days to produce timeless features that can be kept on the shelf and run whenever necessary. In theory, the day should never come when a gap appears in the programme, but if holes do appear, they should never be filled by running a story for longer than it deserves. Nor should they be plugged by second-rate items and limp ad-libs.

Where the programme is slightly short of material, say when a feature has been dropped to make way for a late item, the filling is best carried out in the same way as the cutting – with live material. More short stories may be inserted into the programme, but in TV, even this requires forward planning to line up the relevant stills or graphics to accompany them. The easiest place to pad is in the live to-camera items such as the weather or sport. Scripts for these should incorporate a number of *out-points* where the presenter can finish early, as well as extra paragraphs which give interesting additional information but which will not sound like padding on the air.

Another way to take up slack at the end of the programme is to promote items coming up in the next edition – but stand by for complaints if the station fails to deliver the goods the following night.

The last few seconds are usually filled with the goodbyes or *outs*. It is easy at this stage to be lulled into a false sense of security and to think the programme is over. Don't be fooled, many good programmes are ruined by ending badly. The most important 30 seconds of a show are at the beginning. Next come those at the end. The audience's lasting impressions will be gained in those moments. The start should persuade them to pay attention; the ending will persuade them to tune in tomorrow – or try the other channel.

For this reason, relying on inspiration to provide ad-libs to fill the final half minute is about as foolish as risking running out of fuel in the last half mile of a motorway. The art of the ad-lib is to make scripted comments sound spontaneous, and many broadcasters who may appear to be masters of spontaneity will probably have scripted every pause, stumble,

Figure 51 Monitoring transmission from the control room. A screen displays the programme running order while any necessary cuts or changes are marked by hand on hard copies of the scripts. (*Andrew Boyd*)

word and comma. Few things sound more forced and banal than the artificial exchange of unfelt pleasantries between presenters to pad out the final few seconds of a programme.

If desperate measures are called for, then the producer may use music as a flexible bridge before the next item. This obviously works better in radio, while television's equivalent is to linger for an uncomfortable length of time on the parting shot of the weather forecast. Music during a programme can often be lengthened or shortened without it showing – especially when there are no vocals – but the problem at the end of a programme is getting the music to end exactly on time and on a definite note.

Backtiming

The way to achieve a neat and definite ending is to backtime the music. Producers need to know the duration of the music – usually an instrumental signature tune – and they count back on the clock from the second the programme is due to end to find the exact time the music should begin. At that moment, regardless of whatever else is going on in the programme, the music is started, but with the volume off or the sound mixer on pre-fade.

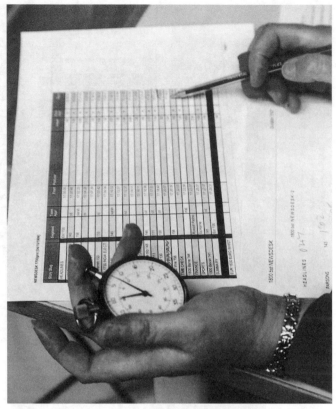

Figure 52 When a show is networked it has to begin and end bang on time. So the timing of every item is checked at every stage of the programme. (*Andrew Boyd*)

(This means the audience cannot hear the music but the technical operator can.) As the presenter winds up the programme, the music is faded up beneath his or her voice, and fills the gap from the moment he or she finishes speaking, to end exactly when the programme is scheduled to stop.

Whatever steps are taken to cut or fill a programme, it should never be necessary to resort to the practice once rife within the BBC of playing for time by using dull and irrelevant public service handouts.

The golden rule is that the audience should never be aware that the programme before them is anything but the polished and completely professional product the producer intends. Never pad with second-rate material, never cut raggedly, and plan ahead so you never have cause to panic.

Endquote – From the Newsroom of BBC Radio Ulster

'On Tuesday it was a quarter past five and we had 31 seconds for the entire programme. Everything else was still being edited.'
'What do you take for the ulcer?'
'Vodka – and lots of it.'

Fieldwork

1 Whenever you produce programmes get into the habit of providing standby reports and scripted material to use as padding. Give opt-out points on the filler material.
2 Next time you make a report, include pot-points, giving outcues and durations.
3 Even if you are not able to use a radio, you can practise pot-cutting by listening to news reports on the radio and hitting the off button when you think you can hear a suitable cut. With practice you will become reasonably competent at making clean cuts. The technique is to anticipate the end of a sentence.
4 Write up a weather report (taken from a newspaper, Internet or teletext) to run for exactly a minute. Script it so there are opt-outs at 30 seconds, 40 seconds and 50 seconds. The weather should be able to finish at any of those points and still make sense. Now try it with a sports report.

PRESENTING THE NEWS

14　News anchors and presenters

> *'Viewers want bimboys and bimbettes ... TV has always been a beauty contest.'*
> – BBC CORRESPONDENT JOHN SIMPSON*

The talent

In showbusiness, actors and performers are known as the 'talent' – a label that has been transferred to the newsreaders and anchors of TV and radio stations.

Despite the hard work of the reporters, producers and other talented members of the news team, a station's reputation will stand or fall on the performance of these few front-line people. A good anchor can boost a station's ratings while a bad one will send them crashing. Little wonder the Walter Cronkites of this world attract top salaries, and the headhunters are always out looking for the most talented and charismatic newscasters.

The appetite for information continues to grow, but the way it is served up has had to adapt to today's fast-food era. The old days of the announcer in his dinner jacket, proclaiming the news as one might announce the arrival of dignitaries at a state banquet, have long gone. The years have seen deliberate attempts to lighten the news with greater informality. The battle for ratings brought a babble of warm and winsome 'happy talk' to US and British TV, and breakfast presenters were schooled in the 'F' factor, to make them more fanciable.

Presentation styles differ between general programming and news. The more a programme aims to entertain, the warmer, friendlier and more relaxed its style will usually be, while news presenters tend to adopt a tone that is serious and more formal, in keeping with the weightier material of a bulletin.

Despite convention, the two approaches are moving closer together. Broadcast news is gradually becoming more personal and newsreaders more approachable and friendly. The authority is still there, but the mantle has been lifted from the schoolmaster and placed upon the shoulders of everybody's favourite uncle or wise friend.

* *1999 Media Guide*, Fourth Estate, p. 146.

> *'In a word, an anchor has to have **believability**. The viewer has to believe what he is saying and that he understands its significance. One gets the impression that some British newsreaders have less understanding of their stories. When one sees a leading newscaster working on a TV quiz show and others doing fluff things, it's the sort of thing most American TV journalists who have any ambition would never do. The good ones see themselves as journalists first.'*
> – PAUL CLEVELAND, ASSIGNMENT MANAGER, ABC NEWS, LONDON.

The term 'anchorman' originated in the USA with Walter Cronkite. In the UK 'newsreader' or 'newscaster' is preferred, showing something of the difference in presentation style either side of the Atlantic – styles which are emulated around the world.

Put simply, British newsreaders are seen as serious and slightly remote authority figures who would never allow their personalities to colour a news story, while US anchors are serious but friendly authority figures who comment on as well as present the news.

The term 'anchorman' suggests personal strength and authority, as though the bearer of that title, through a combination of experience, personality and charisma is holding the programme together and somehow grounding it in reality.

'Newsreader' has fewer personal connotations. The focus is off the individual and on to the news. 'Newscaster' suggests a benign oracle – an authority who has at his disposal privileged inside information, which he will graciously impart to all who will sit at his feet to receive it. In the personality stakes, the newscaster is a step ahead of the newsreader, but still several paces behind the anchorman.

BBC presenter John Humphrys, anchor of Radio 4's flagship news programme, *Today*, is a slim, silver-haired unassuming man who is against the whole idea of newsreaders being turned into stars:

> *'It's difficult for a news presenter who becomes such a celebrity that he or she becomes the news. There is a danger you become a less effective newsreader when people are watching you to see whether you arch your eyebrows. I don't like the whole personality cult. I'm just an ordinary, unexceptional guy who tries to read the news competently and not to allow my character to intrude on it.'**

Qualities of a newscaster

> *'On Radio 4 what we try to do is make sure that the professional voices . . . the announcers and the newsreaders . . . above all else speak with informed authority, and that means they must have credibility as far as the listener's concerned.'*
> – JIM BLACK, PRESENTATION EDITOR, RADIO 4

* 'Who's the Man in the News?' *Sunday Magazine*, 20 October, 1985.

The ideal qualities for a newscaster or anchor have been variously listed as:

- Authority
- Credibility
- Clarity
- Warmth
- Personality
- Professionalism
- Good voice
- Good looks

In America with its Hollywood tradition, film star features coupled with paternal credibility often seem top requirements for the TV anchor. The degree of warmth and personality will depend on how far station style has moved towards the 'friendly' approach. In the USA the policy seems to be *'Smile, smile, smile',* while in the UK credibility is everything – unless the presenter is a woman, when it seems that talent has to be combined with youthful good looks.

Women newscasters

When it comes to women presenters, though TV stations might be loath to admit it, the notion that sex appeal is paramount still seems universal.

ITN newscaster Julia Somerville sees no reason why middle-aged women should be kept away from the cameras:

'At the moment, the majority are moderately youthful – not too youthful, or they wouldn't be credible. But as we have craggy, seasoned, weathered, middle-aged men on TV, why can't we have some craggy, seasoned, weathered, middle-aged women? Television . . . doesn't want glamour reading the news. What is far more important to people in a newsreader is trust.'

Eventually, Somerville herself was traded in for a younger model.

The trend towards longer news programmes has resulted in the growing use of double-headed presentation, where newsreaders or anchors take it in turn to introduce the stories. Many programme makers believe a good combination is to put male and female presenters together.

More than just a newsreader . . .

'I'm not interested in newsreaders – actors reading the news – it debases the news. Many of them don't know what the hell they're reading. When they interview somebody they read questions somebody else has written. That's wrong. The news ought to be told by journalists – they have more credibility.'
— HARRY RADLIFFE, BUREAU CHIEF, CBS NEWS

A TV news presenter is usually more than just a pretty face, and the popular misconception that an anchor simply walks into the studio ten minutes before a programme, picks up a script and reads it into a camera could not be further from the truth.

TV newsreaders will usually be seasoned journalists, who have graduated from newspapers and radio and had their baptism of fire as a TV reporter. Their move to presentation will have been as much for their proven news sense as for their on-screen presence.

Like most journalists, newsreaders are expected to be news addicts, steeping themselves in stories throughout the day. They are required to be on top of the day's events and understand their background so live interviews on current issues will pose no problem.

As the day progresses newsreaders follow the material as it comes in and may offer their own suggestions for coverage.

> *'On big days you try to get in very early on the ground floor. You really need to be in the swim of things, in the full flow. It's important to be in on the discussions about who they plan to interview. Then people give all the reasons for the interview and that helps you about the line you should take.'* — ITN NEWSCASTER TREVOR MCDONALD

Where stations run several news programmes a day, newsreaders work with teams to update their show and help establish its own clear identity. Part of that process will involve rewriting stories to suit their individual style.

In radio, what scores is a clear resonant voice that conveys authority: in fact, the voice can often belie the looks. One British newsreader, who sounded broad-shouldered, seasoned and darkly handsome on air was in the flesh short and with a glass eye.

Radio news presenters can have a variety of different tasks, depending on the size and location of the station. In smaller outfits in Australia and the USA, radio news supplied by an agency is often read by disc jockeys, who have to undergo an instant personality change from purveyor of cosy banter to confident, well-informed bearer of tidings of significance. Their schizophrenia may then be made complete by having to read the commercials. To cap that, they may have to act as an engineer or technical assistant.

Figure 53 TV's most popular newscaster – ITN's Trevor McDonald: *'You have to aim for perfection – there's no other way.'* (*Courtesy ITN*)

Some bigger stations hire presenters simply for their news reading abilities; while others look for journalists who read well on air and can double as roving reporters after their show is over.

Most radio stations expect their news presenters to be able to rewrite agency copy and more besides. British radio usually insists that broadcasters are experienced journalists who can turn their hands to a variety of tasks, including live interviews. In the words of Jenni Murray, presenter of *Woman's Hour*: '*You're not a broadcaster if you don't write your own words.*'

Professionalism

'*I'm not particularly interested in pretty faces or pretty voices. I'm more interested in credibility. An anchor should have worked as a reporter and know what a story is about.*'   – JUDITH MELBY, NETWORK PRODUCER, CANADIAN BROADCASTING CORPORATION

'*Authority is not a sound. Authority is a state of knowing what you are talking about and being able to explain it convincingly and readily to somebody else.*'
– DAVID DUNHILL, BBC VOICE TRAINER AND FORMER NEWSREADER.

Figure 54 The radio technocrat at BBC Southern Counties Radio. Self-operated studios just get more complicated. (*Andrew Boyd*)

Credibility and authority – qualities every newsreader needs – are derived largely from personal confidence. That the newsreader knows what he or she is talking about should never be in question.

When cracks appear in the confidence and hesitation creeps into the delivery the newsreader's credibility can quickly go out the window – often closely followed by the newsreader. Such is the price of stardom in a business where consistent credibility and a flawless delivery are minimum requirements for a person whose performance has such a direct bearing on programme ratings – and profits.

Professionalism comes from having a cool head and plenty of experience. But it means more than remaining unruffled when all around you are performing their headless chicken impersonations.

Consistency in presentation is vital, irrespective of whether you got out of bed the wrong side, or whether you slept at all last night; whether your curry is giving you heartburn or your wife has just left you.

Professionals hang up their personal life with their coat when they arrive for work and only take it up again when their work is over and they head for home. Along with their troubles, professionals hang up their bias, their background, their politics and their prejudices.

No one can be truly free from bias, but a professional has a duty to see his or her work is as free from prejudice as is humanly possible. This can only be done by recognizing where personal preferences, opinions and prejudices lie and compensating for them by being scrupulously fair to the opposite viewpoints whenever they appear in the news.

Radio newsreaders have to purge any trace of bias from the voice. The TV newsreader's task is more difficult: the face, which could betray an opinion at the speed of thought, must remain objective throughout.

Voice

> *'Voice is music and I think we respond much more than we realize to the music of the human voice.'* — CHRISTINA SHEWALL, VOICE THERAPIST

Adverts for jobs in radio frequently call for a newsreader with a *'good microphone voice'*. This usually means a voice that is reasonably rich, crisp and resonant and free from obvious impediments, such as a hare lip, stammer or a lisp – what BBC voice trainer David Dunhill describes as, *'a voice with no pimples'*.

Voices that would not fit the description are those that are piping, reedy, nasal, sibilant, indistinct or very young sounding. Newsreaders with distinctive accents that are not local to a station might find it difficult to persuade a news editor to take them, on the grounds that their out-of-town intonations might not find favour with a local audience. One Radio 4 presenter's clear Scottish accent brought in an unrelenting stream of vitriolic hate mail.

Ideas about a 'suitable broadcast voice' differ, says David Dunhill: *'Obviously the voice should be comfortable to listen to, friendly and clear, but I don't think it should be a special kind of voice with a special vocal quality.'*

Minor speech impediments such as weak 'Rrs', or 'THs' that become 'Vs' could be barriers to an otherwise promising career. Professional voice training may sort these

Figure 55   Radio is all about intimacy. The human voice, reaching over the airwaves and engaging with a single listener. (*Andrew Boyd*)

problems out, and voices that are thick and nasal can be improved by teatment to the adenoids. With effort, voices can often be lowered to give a greater impression of authority: *'Mrs Thatcher very consciously pushed her voice down, which is the classic trick to indicate power,'* says voice trainer Patsy Rodenburg. In the long run, however, voices tend to sound richer and wiser as their owners get older.

Another essential quality in a newsreader is the ability to *sightread*. For some people, the seemingly simple task of reading out loud can prove impossible. Not everyone has the ability to read ahead, which is essential for a smooth delivery, and for them sightreading can mean a staccato stumbling from word to word, losing the flow and sense of the item. It can trouble people who are dyslexic or have to read in a foreign language. Some may have this problem without even realizing, as few people are frequently called on to read out loud. For many, their last public performance might well have been at kindergarten.

> *'What is it that makes the great newsreader? Certainly it is the voice . . . it also has something to do with timing, the way in which memorable or terrifying events are presented to the listener with diffusing normality. Indeed the greatest newsreaders have all given the listener a tremendous sense of reassurance, as war, disaster, royal divorce, scandal and sporting triumph rolled out over the airwaves.'*
>
> *– THE GUARDIAN**

*   'Voice of reason amid chaos', *Centipede*, 5 May 1992.

Fieldwork

1 Make a study of three different newsreaders. Award marks out of ten for *authority, credibility, clarity, warmth, personality, professionalism, good voice*, and for TV, *good looks*. Add the scores and see which newsreader comes top in your estimation. Was this the newsreader you preferred anyway? Do your scores agree with those of your classmates? Discuss any differences.

   What do *you* think are the most important qualities in a newsreader? Why?

2 How would you define *professionalism*, and how would you know if it was missing?

3 Do you think newsreaders should be more or less formal in their styles? How would this affect the credibility of their presentation?

   What do you think gives a newsreader his or her authority?

   What do you think would be the effect on the TV ratings of 'middle-aged, craggy-faced' women newsreaders?

4 Do you prefer single-headed or double-headed presentation? Why?

5 Record yourself reading a number of news stories from the wire, Internet, teletext or newspaper. How do you sound compared with a professional newsreader? What is the difference and how could you improve?

   If you are in a class, take turns to read a number of stories in front of your classmates and give your honest and constructive appraisals of one another's style. Discuss to what degree authority, credibility, clarity, warmth and personality are present, and how each of you could improve your styles.

PRESENTING THE NEWS

15 'On air!'

'Television is an invention that permits you to be entertained in your living room by people you wouldn't have in your home.'
— DAVID FROST

Performance

Newsreading is the point where the business of information and the game of showbusiness meet. How glitzy or glossy the presentation will depend on how far the TV station has travelled down the road to entertainment. But even among the 'heavy' set of newsreaders most outwardly disdainful of TV's gloss and glamour, the act of being oracle to more than a million viewers will always have something of the ego trip about it . . . however hard they may try to deny it.

TV presenters have to live with fame, but while being a public figure might massage the ego when the public is on your side, that same fickle audience will be as quick to complain as they are to compliment, not only if your performance begins to falter, but if they take offence at the cut of your suit or the shape of your tie.

TV presenters should never let their dress sense get in the way of their news sense. Says BBC presenter Sue Lawley: *'If you have a funny haircut or too low a blouse or something that's too dramatically fashionable people will say, "Look at her, what's she got on? Gosh!" Then they are looking at her and not listening to what she is saying.'**

Newsreader John Humphrys was once voted Britain's best-dressed man, although he says he is not interested in clothes. As though to make the point he turned up for the award at London's smartest hotel wearing a £50 suit. He later admitted to *Woman* magazine, *'Mind you, all the smartness on the News was only from the waist up – I was my typical scruffy self below the desk!'*

Conservative without being frowsty is probably the safest dress style to aim for.

Similarly, presenters' mannerisms can sometimes draw more attention than the stories they are reading. Leaning back or forward, swaying from side to side, scratching the nose, licking the lips, blinking hard or waving the hands about, are all tics which the budding anchor may have to iron out by patient practice in front of a mirror, or better still, a video camera, before risking his or her reputation before an audience.

---

* *Inside Television*, BBC.

Presence

In the hot seat of the TV studio, with flooding adrenalin and a wildly beating heart, the newsreader might find it difficult to remember that real people are sitting the other side of the screen anxious to hear what he or she has to say. The camera, lights and other paraphernalia can seem as impersonal and uninviting as a dentist's chair. But the newsreader has to screw down the lid on any panic and somehow dismiss all that hardware.

The camera must cease to be a single staring eye set in a metal face, and become an acquaintance or friend. You would not talk *at* a friend, so you should not talk at a camera. Speak *to* it. It *likes* you. It is on your side. But what you say and the way you say it will need charisma and the force of confidence to carry through the lens to the viewer the other side. This is the x-factor that marks out a good newsreader. It is called *presence*.

Figure 56   Going live in the middle of the newsroom. Note the autocue and the script – belt and braces. Before this study in cool, all the TV monitors are turned down and a hush descends on the ITN newsroom. (*Andrew Boyd*)

> '*Sometimes you are verging on hysteria. I always take a deep breath before the camera comes on to me. The first time I ever went into a TV studio to do a live broadcast my teeth were chattering. I said to the presenter, who'd been doing it for 15 years, "You must feel quite calm by now." He replied, "Dear boy, the day you come in here without any nerves is the day you'll stop doing it because you'll have lost your edge." I know he was right. You have to feel the adrenalin pumping.*'
> – BBC NEWSREADER, JOHN HUMPHRYS*

* 'Who's the man in the news?' *Sunday Magazine*, 20 October 1985.

Adrenalin can be a problem – either way. While the first-time presenter might have to fight to bring it under control, the older stager might have to fight to keep it going. One radio newsreader used to deliberately wait until the last moment before hurrying into the studio. Often the disc jockey would have fired the seven-second signature tune into the bulletin before the newsreader even sat down. All this was to keep the adrenalin going. Not recommended. Brinkmanship can, and does, lead to disasters on air. But a steady stream of adrenalin, always under control, could be the mystery ingredient behind that all-important and indefinable commodity – presence.

Getting through to the audience – rapport

> *'When I'm on air, I often imagine I'm talking to my own sister or a friend.'*
> – BBC *TODAY* PRESENTER, SUE MACGREGOR

BBC trainees are given the following pearl of wisdom:

Information + Presentation = Communication

Successful communication is largely a matter of presentation, and that depends on the way the copy is written, and the way it is read. Good newsreaders are ones that establish rapport with their audience.

Such rapport defies satisfactory definition. It is a kind of chemistry that exists between newsreaders and their audience. Where it is present, both presenter and audience are satisfied. Where it is absent, the information seems to fall short or fail to connect, and the presenter, cut off behind a barrier of electronic hardware, will usually be aware of the fact.

BBC trainer Robert McLeish says rapport is established by *'thinking outwards'*. Voice trainer David Dunhill calls this *'radio reaching out'*. Trainee newsreaders are encouraged to *'bring the script to life', to 'lift the words off the paper', to 'project their personalities', to 'establish a presence'* or to be *'up-front'*. What's needed is a kind of focused energy, a summoning up of your vitality and the projection of that energy towards your audience.

But rapport begins with never regarding a mass audience as simply that. Each listener is an individual who has invited you into his or her home. You are a guest; an acquaintance or even a friend, and you have been welcomed in because you have a story to tell.

Newsreaders, particularly in radio, can easily forget about the audience. Cocooned within the four walls of the studio, they can begin to sound as though they are talking to themselves. They are going through the motions, their concentration is elsewhere and their newsreading will begin to sound stilted, singsong, and insincere.

The solution to strident anonymity or mumbling into the microphone is to remember that you are not reeling off information or reading from a script, but *telling* someone a story.

Radio newsreaders have an added disadvantage. In normal conversation, the person you are talking to will be able to see your face. Your expressions will reflect your story. If it is sad, you will look sad, if it is happy, you will smile. Your hands may do the talking for you, gesticulating and adding emphasis. You may have a tendency to mumble but people will make up with their eyes what is missed by their ears by watching your lips.

Now imagine you are talking to someone who cannot see your lips, your eyes, or your hands. That vital part of your communication has gone. This is how it is in radio. This handicap is overcome by working to put into your voice all the expression that would normally go into your face and hands.

A word of warning – overdo the intonation and you will sound as though you are talking to a child, and talking down to the audience is something no newsreader will get away with for long.

Another handicap for the radio newsreader in particular is the unassuming nature of most radio sets. Not since the Second World War have western audiences sat and stared at the wireless. Most people regard radio as a background activity.

The news trickles out of a tiny speaker from a tinny tranny in the kitchen while the audience is up to its arms in soapsuds over the washing up. So to command attention for your news bulletin you have to reach out across the room with an energy and a tone, which cuts across the distractions and says, *'Listen to me!'*

What helps is that most radio bulletins begin with a fanfare of sorts – the urgent news jingle. But to reach out and grab your audience you should picture your single listener some distance from you, summon your energy and focus it on that point.

Know your material

> *'Liverpool . . . About 500 people, or 500 – I think that should be half a million people rather – were treated for broken arms and ribs . . . No, heh, sorry . . . 500 people were treated for broken arms and ribs, hysteria and bruising after half a million screaming fans gathered outside an official reception to see their FA cup winning heroes – Almost a disaster!'* – UK RADIO

Confidence comes from experience, from being in command of the bulletin and thoroughly familiar with the material. Inexperienced newsreaders should spend as much time as possible reading and re-reading the stories *aloud* so when they go on air they are on familiar ground. This will also highlight phrases which clash and jar, mistakes, unfamiliar names that need practice, poor punctuation and sentences that are impossibly long. All these problems are easily missed by the eye, but are likely to be picked up by the voice.

Many newsreaders rewrite their stories extensively to make certain the style suits their voice – the best way to be familiar with a story is to write it yourself.

> *'I read all the copy on every story so that I'm totally familiar with it. I think that affects the way you read it. I write several of the stories myself and I adapt others to my style.'* – CHANNEL 4 NEWSREADER ZEINAB BADAWI
>
> *The essence is to completely understand what you're reading before you open your mouth. Provided **you** understand it the listeners will understand it.'*
> – JOHN TOUHEY, BBC WORLD SERVICE NEWSREADER

Figure 57   Self-op radio – watch the levels, ride those faders and keep your mouth a handsbreadth from the mike. (*Andrew Boyd*)

Ad-libs

Few professionals rely on ad-libs to see them through a programme. Back-announcements, station identities, comments and seemingly casual links are usually scripted. When the programme is running against the clock, a live guest is settling down in the studio to be interviewed any moment *and* there is a constant stream of chatter in your ear from the control room, even the snappiest quips and witticisms thought up before the show tend to be driven from your mind. The best way to avoid embarrassment is to script *everything* barring the timechecks, and even these should be handled with care.

'*It's 13 minutes to two*' is the sort of phrase a presenter can take for granted, but trying to glance up at a clock yourself and try to give an immediate and accurate timecheck and you will see how difficult it can be to get right. From the half past onwards, the timecheck can involve some tricky mental arithmetic. Special presenters' clocks are available – at a cost – which display the time as it would be said: '*13 minutes to three*'. Even distinguished broadcasters who have fallen foul of the timecheck might consider this money well spent:

> *'The time is six o'clock. Good evening, this is Jon Snow with the news. I'm sorry, the time is half past six, and this is Jon Snow with the local news, but first, a look at the headlines . . . half past five! – I'm sorry; very confusing clock on the wall, here.'*
> – UK RADIO

Always engage your brain before putting your mouth into gear – *think before you speak.*

After newsreaders have rehearsed the bulletin, they should try to insist on a few minutes peace and quiet before the programme to read it through again, though in TV this can be a vain hope.

In the end, performance is everything. What would you prefer to hear – a newsreader stumbling through an unrehearsed bulletin bursting with up-to-the-minute stories and failing to make sense of it, or a smoothly polished delivery of material that may be as much as 10 minutes old but makes complete sense?

The gate

Some newsrooms operate a gate to give readers a chance to compose themselves. This is a bar on new copy being handed to the newsreader later than five or 10 minutes before a bulletin. Old hands might scoff at this – they can pick up a pile of scripts and deliver them sight unseen without batting an eyelid, but for the less experienced reader, a gate can make the difference between a smooth performance and wishing the studio floor would open up and swallow you.

Making a swift recovery

> *'The worst disaster that ever happened to me was when I was smoking during a news bulletin and set my script on fire. I tried waving it about but if only made it flame up more. We got it out somehow, but it was a bit distracting. I dare say anybody listening attentively will have realized something had gone a bit wrong. I don't think I said anything; just carried on in the British tradition.'*
> – DAVID DUNHILL

When things do go wrong, the anchor or newsreader is expected to stay cool and professional. Whatever the ferment beneath the surface, no cracks must appear in the calm exterior. The coolest recovery on record was probably that of a wartime BBC announcer who pressed on with his script after a bomb fell on Broadcasting House.

'I always think of a fluff as a kind of small microbe,' says David Dunhill, *'Once it gets in and gets you, you will go on fluffing the rest of the bulletin.'* The answer is to immediately and completely dismiss the mistake from your mind and focus your total concentration on the rest of the bulletin.

Most fluffs occur when newsreaders are expecting trouble, like a difficult foreign name, or when they have already fluffed and their mind is side-tracked. The irony is that the difficult name is usually pronounced flawlessly, while the reader stumbles over the simple words before and behind it in the sentence.

> 'A flash from Washington . . . the House of Representatives Jurish . . . Judiciary Committee, which is considering, em, a, the impeachment of President Nixon has voted umanimously . . . unanimously to call Mr Nixon as a witness. Of course, whether Mr Wick . . . Nick . . . Wixton . . . winwhether Mr Nixton . . . Ahh! (tut) Sorry about this! (laugh) whether Mr Nixon will agree is quite ano-nother matter.'
>
> – BRITISH RADIO

'When a programme has been tricky and you think you have done it reasonably well, that's a very exhilarating feeling,' says ITN newscaster Trevor McDonald. 'But there are times when you know you haven't done awfully well and you feel really bad about it and wish you could go home and forget it, only you can't. My own mistakes always loom much, much larger in my own mind. When I talk to people about them, they haven't noticed them sometimes, but even the little mistakes always loom. You have to aim for perfection. There's no other way.'

Perhaps it is this striving for perfection and quality for merciless self-criticism that turns a broadcaster into a top professional.

The art of the accomplished recovery is to prepare for every contingency.

The worst mistake any presenter can make is to swear on air – *don't even think it*; **otherwise you will probably say it.**

The commonest problem is the recorded report that fails to appear. The introduction has been read, the presenter is waiting, and – nothing. Next to swearing, the broadcaster's second deadliest sin is *dead air*. Silent airspace is worst on radio. On TV, viewers can watch the embarrassed expression on the presenter's face.

If an item fails to appear the radio presenter should apologize and move smartly on to the next. In TV, presenters will usually be directed what to do by the control room. Up to three seconds of silence is the most that should pass before the newsreader cuts in.

> 'Police are finding it difficult to come up with a solution to the murders . . . the commissioner says the victims are unwilling to co-operate.'   – US RADIO
>
> 'Well, the blaze is still fierce in many places, and as a result of this fire, two factories have been gutted and one homily left famless.'   – AUSTRALIAN RADIO
>
> Following the warning by the Basque Separatist organization ETA that it's preparing a bombing campaign in Spanish holiday resorts, British terrorists have been warned to keep on their guard . . . I'm sorry (chuckle) that should be British tourists . . .'
>
> – UK RADIO
>
> The . . . company is recalling a total of 14,000 cans of suspect salmon and fish cutlets. It's believed they're contaminated by poisonous orgasms.'
>
> – AUSTRALIAN RADIO

> *'The President is alive and well and kicking tonight, one day after the assassination attempt, just two and a half months into his pregnancy ...'* — US TV
>
> *'And now here's the latest on the Middle East crisis ... crisis ... Lesbian forces today attacked Israel. I beg your pardon, that should be Lesbanese ... Lebanese. (Laughter)'* — ANON

Novices often make the mistake of pausing for ten or more seconds in the hope that the technical operator will find the fault and cure it.

Confusing the audience with technical jargon can compound the problem, like: *'I'm sorry, but that insert seems to have gone down.'* Or, *'We don't seem to have that package.'* Practise what you are going to say when something goes wrong until it becomes almost a reflex action.

Figure 58 Like being interviewed through a serving hatch ... the presenter at County Sound Radio is stuck behind a high-tech barricade, firing questions, checking levels, making sure the next item is lined up – and he still finds time to fiddle with his headphones. (*Andrew Boyd*)

When that report does eventually arrive, the audience will have forgotten what it is about and the presenter should re-introduce it by re-reading or paraphrasing the cue.

Where you stumble over a word or phrase, you should judge quickly whether to repeat it. If the sense of the item has been lost, by saying, for instance, *'Beecham pleaded guilty to the murder,'* when he pleaded not guilty, then the sentence should be repeated. Avoid the cliché, *'I'm sorry, I'll read that again'* – *'I'm sorry'* will do. If the mistake is a minor one, let it go. Chances are the audience will quickly forget it, whereas drawing attention to it with an apology might only make it worse.

Corpsing

There are few threats greater to a newsreaders' credibility than that of corpsing on air. Corpsing is not be a literal occurrence but it can feel pretty much the same. It means to dry up, grind to a halt, or, worse, burst out laughing.

These are signs of nervousness and panic. Such laughter is seldom sparked off by genuine humour; it is the psyche's safety valve blowing to release a build up of tension. Anything incongruous or slightly amusing can trigger it off.

The audience doesn't always see the joke, especially when the laughter erupts through a serious or tragic news item. Where professional self-control is in danger of collapsing, the realization that untimely laughter can bring an equally untimely end to a career and that a substantial part of the audience may write you off as an idiot unless you pull yourself together, can often have the same salutary effect as a swift sousing with a bucket of icy water.

Self-inflicted pain is a reasonable second-line defence. Some presenters bring their mirth under control by resorting to personal torture, such as digging their nails into the palms of their hands or grinding the toes of one foot with the heel of the other. A less painful way to prevent corpsing is to not permit yourself to be panicked and pressurised in the first place.

> '*Finally, the weather forecast. Many areas will be dry and warm with some sunshine ... It actually says shoeshine on my script, so with any luck, you might get a nice light tan.*'
> – BBC RADIO

Relaxation

The key to the confidence that marks out the top-flight professional is the ability to be in command, and at the same time relaxed. This can be a tall order under deadline pressure and the spotlights of the studio.

Tension can manifest itself in a number of ways, especially in the novice newsreader. The muscles of your neck and throat can tighten to strangle the voice and put it up an octave. Your reading can also speed up. Try stretching the shoulders and arms like a cat before relaxing and breathing deeply. This should reduce this tension. (Note: Do this before you go on air!)

Another problem is that beginners can sometimes – literally – dry up. Tension removes the moisture in the throat and mouth and it can become impossible to articulate. Relaxation helps and a glass of water – sipped slowly to prevent the splutters – will usually be sufficient to moisten the lips, mouth and throat.

A word of warning – drink nothing containing sugar or milk. Hot, sweet coffee is out. Milk and sugar clog the palate and gum up the mouth. Alcohol should be avoided for obvioush reashonsh.

The same goes for eating food just before going on air. A bolted sandwich before a bulletin can undermine the coolest demeanour. Stray particles of bread and peanut-butter lodged in the molars are a sure way of turning on the waterworks and leaving the newscaster drooling with excess saliva – and there is always the risk of going into the bulletin with a bout of hiccups.

Tiredness can also ruin otherwise good newsreading. Broadcasters often work shifts and have to cope with irregular sleep patterns and, for early birds, semi-permanent fatigue. Weariness can drag down the muscles of the face, put a sigh in the voice and extinguish any sparkle. Gallons of black coffee – without sugar – may be one answer, limbering up the face by vigorously contorting the lips, cheeks and mouth may be another. But don't let anyone catch you doing that on camera, unless you want to end up on the Christmas collection of out-takes.

Fieldwork

1 Think back to your study of different newsreaders (Chapter 14). Which had the most presence? Is this the one who scored highest on your list? How do you define presence?

   How successful were those newsreaders in establishing rapport with their audience? Do you think rapport is conscious or unconscious? How would you go about establishing rapport?

   If you are in a class, prepare and read a bulletin out loud and get votes out of 10 for presence and rapport. Ask your colleagues to try to define why these factors were present or absent in your reading.

2 Practise reading bulletins on tape and listening back to find ways to improve your powers of communication. Remember that communication is not so much technique as a state of mind.

3 If you are in a class, swap a bulletin you have written with one of your neighbour's. Now read it out loud without checking it through or even glancing at it beforehand. Did you have any problems? What with? Why?

   Does the copy need rewriting to suit your reading style? Rewrite it then read it through once for practice and then out loud for real. What difference did being familiar with the copy make?

4 Plan what you would say if (a) a recorded item went down on air; (b) the wrong item was played after your cue; (c) the next item went missing.

   Practise some impromptu timechecks throughout the day. Glance up at the clock and immediately say the time out loud. Which is easier, before the hour or after the hour? How long does it take for the time to register accurately once you have glanced at the clock? Remember to always allow yourself that much time before starting to give a timecheck.

5 Practise the relaxation exercises outlined in the chapter and see if they help you. If not, develop your own that will.

PRESENTING THE NEWS

16 Newsreading mechanics

> *'Radio news is bearable. This is due to the fact that while the news is being broadcast the DJ is not allowed to talk.'*
> — FRAN LEBOWITZ

Speed

The acceptable pace of newsreading, like hemlines, seems to go up and down with fashion. My first attempt at newsreading was giving the headlines at the end of a half-hour radio programme. I was told to go at it as fast as I could and duly complied. That evening, still flushed with pride and wonder, I asked a friend what she had made of my debut as a newsreader. *'Couldn't understand a word of it,'* she said, with characteristic bluntness, *'you were gabbling.'*

The right reading pace is one which is comfortable for the reader, clear to the listener, and which suits the station's style. That could be anywhere between 140 to 220 words per minute. British radio usually favours three words per second, or 180 wpm, which is a natural and pleasing pace. TV can run a little slower.

Three words per second is also a handy formula for timing a script – a 20-second lead becomes 60 words, a 30-second story is 90 words, and so on.

The ultra-slow 150 wpm, which finds favour on and off in America and on foreign language stations, permits a delivery which is almost Churchillian in its portentousness, and highly persuasive. It is the pace popularized by broadcasting giants like Edward R. Murrow who critics used to say took 10 seconds to get through his wartime dateline: *'This . . . is . . . London.'*

Pace is less important than clarity, and one of the most helpful aids to clear reading is the pause. The pause is a cunning device with many uses. It divides the copy into sense groups and allows time for an important phrase to sink in. It permits a change of style between stories; can be used to indicate the beginning of a quote, and it gives newsreaders time to replenish their oxygen supply.

Breathing

Newsreaders, like swimmers, have to master the art of breath control. Good breathing brings out the richness and flavour of the voice.

First you have to sit correctly to give your lungs and diaphragm as much room as possible. The upper half of the body should be upright or inclined forward, with the back slightly arched. Your legs should not be crossed.

Air to the newsreader is like oil in an engine. Run out of it and you will seize up. The aim is open the lungs and throat as widely as possible, so breathing should be deep and from the belly instead of the usual shallow breathing from the top of the lungs. Never run into the studio. Breathless readers will find themselves gasping for air or getting dizzy and feeling faint.

Figure 59 *'One should sit in a reasonably upright way with one's face towards the microphone. A lot of people I've noticed tend to drop their heads over their scripts, so the soundwaves from the mouth are reflected rather than going directly into the microphone. Always address the microphone properly. Breathing should be from the diaphragm and one should not make a noise. You hear a lot of heavy breathing and that should be avoided. Instead, take a controlled intake of breath at the start of each item.'* John Toughey, BBC World Service newsreader. (*Andrew Boyd*)

> *'One of the golden rules is to never run before a news bulletin. I went downstairs – it was a very long way down – and I sat there with two minutes to go and suddenly realized to my horror that I had left all the national and international copy upstairs, and so I stupidly ran. I got into the news, and of course I couldn't breathe. Panic makes it worse and it was – GAAASP! – like this all the time. And I felt absolutely awful, I just wanted to die and I had to pull out after two minutes. It must have sounded dreadful. Fortunately none of my immediate bosses were listening or they would have rocketed me sky high and quite rightly.'*
> – PENNY YOUNG, BBC LOCAL RADIO NEWS EDITOR

A newsreader should take a couple of good breaths before starting and another deep breath between each story. You can top up at full stops (periods) and paragraphs, and, faced with a long sentence, can take shallow breaths where the commas should be. If you have time, rewrite the story and break down those sentences; but failing that, you can insert slash marks to indicate where you can safely pause while still making sense of the copy:

> *'UNICEF has criticised world governments / for waging an undeclared war on women, / children and adolescents. According to the UN Children's Fund, / more than 600 million children / are now living in poverty / – more than at the start of the decade. The world's poorest / survive on less than a dollar a day, / and around a quarter of a billion children / aged between 5 and 14 / are sent out to work. / Armed conflict has killed or injured eight million since 1990. / But the biggest child killer in the developing world is not warfare / but AIDS.'**

Breathing through the mouth permits faster refuelling than through the nose, but beware of snatching your breath. Avoid gasping by opening your mouth wider and taking the air in shallow draughts. The general idea is to avoid making a noise like a parched Australian swilling down a tube of his favourite amber nectar.

Projection

There are different schools of thought about whether newsreaders should project their voice or talk naturally. In television a conversational tone is more appropriate to the illusion of eye contact with the audience, and projection matters less because television audiences offer more of their undivided attention than do radio listeners.

Radio presenters have to work harder. They should project just enough to cut through distractions and get attention. Overprojected newsreading makes the listener want to back away from the set or turn down the volume. Under normal circumstances there is no need to bark out the story like a war correspondent under crossfire.

If you can picture yourself at one end of an average-sized room with a single person at the other whose attention is divided between chores and listening to what you have to say, then your projection will be about right.

The radio newsreaders' voice often has to cut through a lot of background noise before reaching the listener, especially if you are being heard on somebody's car radio or in a living room full of hyperactive two-year olds. **Yelling is not the way to make sure every syllable is heard – clear diction is**.

* BBC, 1999.

All too often newsreaders can be heard running words together, swallowing the ends of words and leaving sentences trailing in mid-air because their attention has already drifted on to the next story. Newsreaders' eyes can't move from the page so neither should their minds. There should be a kind of magnetism between your mind and the script if you are to have any feel for the copy and sound sincere about what you are reading.

Emphasis

Copy should be read aloud to establish which words should be given extra emphasis. These are usually the key words and descriptions. For example:

> *'Canada's FISHERMEN are preparing for the BIGGEST EVER SEAL CULL in their country's history. The government has declared OPEN SEASON on HARP Seals. Up to a QUARTER OF A MILLION are to be SHOT and CLUBBED TO DEATH as they BASK in the sun on the ice floes off NEWFOUNDLAND. The QUOTA for the annual HARVEST has just been INCREASED. Now ANY Canadian citizen, not just FISHERMEN, can JOIN IN the seal hunt.*

These words can be capitalized, as shown, or underlined. Some readers favour double underlining to highlight different degrees of emphasis.

Shifting the position of the emphasis in a sentence can completely alter its meaning and tone. This can have a dramatic effect on the story:

> *'**HE** said their action had made a walkout inevitable.'*

Stressing the word he might suggest there are others who would disagree with this statement.

> *'He **SAID** their action had made a walkout inevitable.'*

Emphasizing the word said casts doubt on the truth of the statement, implying there are grounds for disbelieving it.

> *'He said **THEIR** action had made a walkout inevitable.'*

The speaker now sounds as though he is pointing a finger in accusation at another group of people.

> *'He said their action **HAD** made a walkout inevitable.'*

This has an intriguing double-meaning. Does *had* suggest the possibility of a walkout was true earlier, but is no longer the case, or is the stress on *had* a rebuttal, as though denying a suggestion that the action would not lead to a walkout? Think about it. The answer would probably become obvious from the context, but it highlights the importance of having a clear understanding of the item before attempting to read it on air.

A common failing of untrained newsreaders is to imagine that due stress and emphasis means banging out every fifth word of a story and ramming the point home by pounding the last word of each sentence. This is about as elegant as tap-dancing in jackboots. Each sentence must establish its own rhythm without having a false one stamped upon it. Stress exists not to make the copy punchier, but to bring out its meaning.

Pitch

As well as having rhythm, the voice also goes up and down. This is called *modulation* or pitch, and some readers who are new at their business or have being doing it for too long can sound as though they are singing the news. The voice goes up and down a lot, but in all the wrong places. Voice trainer David Dunhill describes this as '*Redolent of an air hostess telling me to fasten my seat belt or extinguish my cigarette*'. Modulation can add interest to the voice and variety to an item, but random modulation coupled with universal stress can make an audience grateful for the commercial break.

> Sentences usually begin on an upward note, rise in the middle, and end on a downward note. These are known as uppers and downers. But what happens to the downers when the last word belongs to a question?

Read this sentence yourself to find out.

These uppers and downers are signposts to the listener. They subconsciously confirm and reinforce the way the sentence is developing and help convey its meaning.

Microphone technique

Next to swearing on air, the important things to avoid with microphones are *popping* and *paper rustle*. Popping occurs when the mouth is too close to the mike and plosive sounds, such as Ps in particular, produce distortion. The radio newsreader can tell this is happening by listening on headphones, and can prevent it by backing away or turning the mike slightly to one side.

Incidentally, the best way to tell your sound levels are set correctly is to always use headphones, and to have them turned up high enough to drown out your normal speaking voice. Anything too loud will cross the threshold of pain and soon have your reaching for the volume control.

Different microphone effects are possible. The closer the mike is to the mouth, the more of the voice's natural resonance it will pick up. Late-night radio presenters use the close-mike technique to make their voices sound as sexy and intimate as someone whispering sweet nothings into your ear. Where a voice is naturally lacking in richness, close mike work can sometimes help compensate.

Conversely, standing away from the mike and raising the voice can make it sound as though the presenter is speaking live on location – useful for giving a lift to studio commentary over outdoor scenes or sound effects.

Most directional mikes give their best results about 15 cm from the mouth.

The microphone, being closer to the script than the reader's ears, will pick up every rustle and scrape of the page, unless great care is taken in moving the paper. Use thick paper that does not crinkle, or small pages, which are less prone to bending.

The best way to avoid paper rustle is to carefully lift each sheet, holding it in tension to prevent it bending, and place it to one side. To cut any noise that even this might make, lift the page while it is still being read and place it down *after* you begin reading the next item. The sound of your voice will drown out any paper rustle.

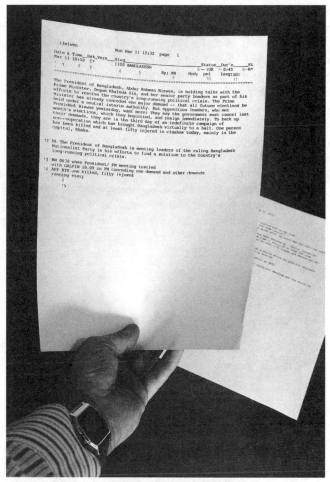

Figure 60 Preventing paper rustle. If you brace the script between your thumb and fingers the page will be held in tension. It won't be able to scrape along the table, or, worse still, flop out of sight. (*Andrew Boyd*)

Using the prompter

(Credits roll . . . Police 5 with Shaw Taylor.)
'Good evening. One of the most difficult crimes to detect is that . . . (pause) committed by a stuck Autocue.'
'Autocues can make or break you in a live programme'.
> – BRITISH NEWSREADER ANNA FORD

'The most important thing with an Autocue is to make sure that you check it. The operators are very good, but everybody's human. Words can be misspelt, words can be left out.'
> – ANDREW GARDNER, UK NEWSREADER*

* *It'll Be Alright on the Night*, London Weekend Television.

Most TV stations use devices to project the script on to glass in front of the camera so presenters can give the impression of eye contact with the viewer as they read the news.

The intention is to make it appear that they know their material off by heart and are simply telling the story to the audience. What frequently spoils the illusion is the way some newsreaders stare woodenly into the camera, as though trying to make out a spot on the end of the viewer's nose. Worse still is when they screw up their eyes to peer at some mistyped or corrected word on the prompter.

How often do you see junior newsreaders with their faces frozen in a permanent scowl of concentration, eyebrows never moving, as though permanently glued in an ingratiating arch across the forehead? If the camera is the newsreader's best friend, then the prompter has to be seen as the smile on your best friend's face, and responded to as such.

But newsreaders cannot afford to relax too much – they might destroy another of TV's illusions. TV stations often display computer pictures or stills in a box or window to one side of the newsreader. To the viewer the box appears to be behind the reader, but often

Figure 61 Half the battle in TV is learning to read the prompter without appearing to peer. Imagine it's your best friend's face – relax and smile. This handheld model is usually used on location. (*Courtesy EDS Portaprompt*)

the reverse is true and readers who are prone to fidget are liable to disappear behind the window.

As most scripts are now originated on computer, many radio stations are experimenting with the idea of reading them off a monitor. But the terror of a computer crash and the perennial need for back-up means paper copy is likely to be with us for some time to come.

'We tried reading off the screen but it just wasn't quick enough,' says BBC World Service newsreader Julie Candler. *'It would skip, jump and just couldn't do it. The technology then wasn't up to it. Even our new computer system has gone down – frozen – and there have been a couple of times when we've had to get out the old typewriters, so they're still in a cupboard somewhere.'*

Noise, noise, noise

One blight TV newsreaders have to live with is the constant babble of noise injected directly into their ear through the earpiece, which keeps them in touch with the control room. Into their ear comes not only their countdown but everything said to the cameracrews, videotape operators, graphics operators, caption operators, etc. Putting it mildly, it can be a distraction:

'You've got to develop a split brain to be able to read the news and listen at the same time,' says John Humphrys. *'When I say, "Here's a report from Beirut," they have to start the machine rolling with the report on it five seconds before it comes on, otherwise the picture doesn't stabilize and the sound's wonky. So I have a countdown going on in my ear, and I have to make sure my last word finishes on zero. Inevitably, things go wrong. I'm saying, "Here's a report from Beirut" and someone starts screaming in my ear, "It's not ready yet!" Once, something went wrong with the countdown three times in succession and I lost my cool and said on air, "I wish someone would tell me what is going on".'**

Bringing the story to life

Once a script has been written and handed to the newsreader it becomes his or hers alone. The reader must identify with the story and transform it from being mere words on a page. The copy has to be lifted off the paper, carried through the microphone, transported over the airwaves, and planted firmly in the listener's imagination. And that is done by *telling* a story.

The test of whether communication has taken place is audience reaction. A new story should produce a response of pleasure or pain. If you were to tell a friend about a family illness, you would expect her to react. If she listened to you with a deadpan expression and turned away unmoved, you would wonder whether she had heard you right.

News should be the same. The audience will respond to you as they would to an actor on stage. As actors strive to give life to their lines, your task is to bring your copy to life. Newsreaders' talents lie in perfectly matching their tone to the storyline. Skilfully done, this makes the story more accessible by signalling its meaning, significance, importance and relevance – the emotions in the voice reflecting in part the emotional response that the

* 'Who's the man in the news?' *Sunday Magazine*, 20 October 1985.

story should produce in the hearer. For most experienced newsreaders this process is automatic, but for many new to the business it is a skill that has to be learned.

The skill lies in the subtlety of the storytelling. If newsreaders were painters, they would use watercolours and washes, never lurid oils. Histrionics over the airwaves will result in the listener diving for the off-switch. Only a ham goes over the top and a poor actor fails to do justice to the script. So this is the task of the newsreader – to do justice to the script.

A simple tip – when you are happy, you smile, so when you smile, you sound happy. If a story is light-hearted, then crack your face and smile. But if the news is grave, then the newsreader could do little worse than to sound as though the unfortunate victim has just won the lottery. Hearing, *'Four people have died in a pit disaster'* read by someone with a broad grin is not only embarrassing, it is insulting. If you want to convey gravity, then frown. If the story is sad, then look sad.

One way to spare yourself from reading with a gleeful grin what turns out half-way through to be an obituary is to make some indication of the tone in which the copy should be read. It can be helpful to draw a suitable face at the top of the page. If the newsreader assumes that expression, then the tone should be just about right.

'Take care of the sense and the sounds will take care of themselves.'

– LEWIS CARROLL

Fieldwork

1 Practise sitting correctly to read some copy. Make sure you take plenty of air, but not so much that you have to strain to hold it. Now read the copy into a recorder and hear how you sound. Try different postures to see which gives you the most air and feels the most comfortable. Go through that copy again, marking it for breaths and then read it to see if that helps you.

2 Ask someone to time you reading an item of copy that is more than 230 words long. Get them to stop you after exactly a minute and work out your reading speed by counting how many words you have read.

3 Record yourself reading again and practise removing scripts that have been read without making a sound. Also try different amounts of projection to see which sounds best and underline difficult stories for emphasis to see if this helps you.

4 If you have access to a TV studio with a prompter, practise reading to camera. Avoid staring at it and animate your features while still keeping a natural expression.

5 Try reading out loud the stories below and bringing them to life by stressing the correct emphases and using the appropriate tone. Then, just for fun, try them again in a tone that is totally unsuitable, and see how ridiculous they sound.

'Three people have died in a highway pile up on the outskirts of Boston.'
'A Lancashire window cleaner has won more than five million pounds on the lottery.'
'Good news for industry . . . the latest figures show a major upswing in trade.'
'Unemployment is getting worse . . . the Government has just announced a sharp rise in the numbers out of work . . . and more job cuts could be on the way.'
'New Zealand's longest surviving heart transplant patient has just celebrated her golden wedding anniversary.'

'*But despite all efforts . . . there were no survivors.*'

'*The blaze tore right through the warehouse, exploding tins of paint and showering flaming debris into the air. The building was completely gutted.*'

'*Jonestown's new civic offices are due to be completed tomorrow . . . at a cost of 20 million dollars.*'

'*Council tax payers say they're disgusted at what they describe as a huge waste of public money.*'

'*The strike call went out and the members obeyed it . . . despite warnings the company would fold as a result.*'

'*Lucky, the black and white kitten's done it again . . . Determined not to live up to his name, he's got himself stuck up his owner's oak tree, and firemen have been called out to pull him down . . . for the fourth time this week.*'

DUTIES AND DILEMMAS

17 Power, freedom and responsibility

Power

> *'Television is credited . . . with almost superhuman powers. It can – they say – start wars, and it can sap the will to continue those wars. It can polarize society, and it can prevent society talking sensibly to itself. It can cause trouble on the streets.'*
> – FORMER BBC DIRECTOR OF PROGRAMMES, BRIAN WENHAM
>
> *'There is weird power in a spoken word . . .'*   – JOSEPH CONRAD
>
> *'I know that one is able to win people far more by the spoken than by the written word, and that every great movement on this globe owes its rise to the great speakers and not to the great writers.'*   – ADOLF HITLER IN *MEIN KAMPF*

Framed, and hanging in a prominent position on the wall of a commercial radio station is a poster depicting a wild-eyed, battle-dressed revolutionary clutching a microphone and shouting slogans across the airwaves. The caption informs: *'Any budding Che Guevara will tell you the most powerful means of communication.'*

Come the revolution, every radio and TV station becomes a strategic target. The poster might have been aimed at advertisers but its message is universal: even in peacetime, whoever controls the media has the whip hand in the war for people's hearts and minds.

> *'It's a frightening thing with television that we have this enormous power,'* says ITN producer Phil Moger, *'I don't think we should ever forget it.'*

No wonder that media control, its accountability, impartiality, and the vexed issue of censorship have featured so largely in debate – where such debate is permitted – in recent years.

At the heart of the issue is the question of who should hold the reins – the government or the broadcasters.

A free media is one that has its first responsibility not to politicians but to its audience. This is known as public trust. Whether the media uses or abuses its liberty and that trust

Figure 62

will determine the esteem in which the media is held by those it serves. That esteem could prove decisive in whether the balance eventually tips towards freedom or control. Currently, esteem is running at a pretty low ebb. As one prominent US reporter observed: *'Poll after poll shows journalists ranking lower than political dog meat.'**

> *'Over the last 20 years the esteem of reporters has slithered even further down the scale – from "hacks" to "reptiles" ... news organisations are now part of the "media industry" and a subdivision of showbusiness. The old distinctions between the serious and the frivolous ... have largely broken down. "Stories" are important because they sell ... therefore they will be bought, stolen, distorted, spun, sentimentalised, overdramatised, and – should all else fail – invented.'*
>
> – IAN JACK†

But if journalists have lost public trust, then how do we turn that around? The first step must be to recognize where the pitfalls lie, then to weigh them up against the duties – and dilemmas – of the reporter. Not easy. But if it were we wouldn't be in this mess. And if as journalists we fail, then the regulators will make absolutely sure they succeed. As it stands, the restrictions on broadcasters – in the UK at least – are already tougher than on their newspaper counterparts.

> *'Broadcasters should be encouraged to practise self-discipline and self-regulation in areas such as codes and standards, on the basis that increased responsibility is a concomitant of increased freedom.'* – FEDERATION OF AUSTRALIAN BROADCASTERS

The law

The biggest legal trap facing many journalists is the law of libel. This differs in detail from country to country but has its similarities. In Britain, a libel is defined as the publishing of anything that would:

> *'Expose a person to hatred, ridicule or contempt, cause him to be shunned and avoided, lower him in the estimation of right thinking members of society generally, or disparage him in his office, profession or trade.'*‡

British libel laws also hold a reporter responsible for broadcasting a libellous statement made by somebody else. So, if a council leader gave you some dirt on the leader of the opposition, *you* could be sued for libel, for putting those words on air.

Without some protection investigative journalism and court reporting would be impossible. In Britain, the main defences are complex and provide a lucrative field for lawyers. In essence they are that the report was true, or offered a reasonable opinion based on facts that were true, or that it was protected in law by *privilege*, which covers reporting of Parliament, courts and public meetings.

---

* Danny Schechter, *Global Vision*, USA.
† *The Granta Book of Reportage*, 1998.
‡ *McNae's Essential Law for Journalists*, Butterworth, 1992.

Figure 63 The power of the spoken word. Achala Sharma of the Hindi Service of the BBC World Service. (*Courtesy BBC*)

In addition to the mantraps of libel there are laws governing court reporting, confidentiality, copyright, race relations, official secrets and other areas, which make reporting a minefield for the ignorant.

Safe and successful reporting requires a thorough working knowledge of the law that allows journalists to push reporting to the brink of legality without falling into the chasm.

> *'Journalism is too small or too distant a word to cover it. It is theatre; there are no second takes. It is drama – it is improvisation, infiltration and psychological warfare. It is destructive. It is exhilarating, dangerous and stressful. It is the greatest job. It is my job . . . It also earned me three death threats and a £50,000 price on my head.*
>
> *'The golden rule is this: as an undercover reporter you must never encourage anyone to do or say anything they would not otherwise do if you had not been there.'*
> – INVESTIGATIVE REPORTER, DONAL MACINTYRE*

The regulators

In Britain, newspapers can back the political party of their choice, but broadcasters are required by law to be impartial and balanced. It's the job of the regulators to keep the broadcasters in check.

* I Spy, *The Guardian*, 6 December 1999.

The purpose laid down for the BBC was that it should inform, educate and entertain. A premium is placed on the breadth and quality of its programming. The BBC is governed by Royal Charter, and its funds are provided by a licence fee set by the Government.

The arrangement means the party in power effectively controls the purse strings, leaving the BBC exposed to political criticism and attempts at interference, especially from unpopular governments who blame the media for their troubles.

The Government has the authority to prevent a programme going to air. In 1987, the Government banned a documentary contending Parliament had been deceived over plans to produce a costly spy satellite. Other programmes featuring interviews with members of the security services were also banned.

Independent television is regulated by the Independent Television Commission, which also oversees cable, satellite and commercial teletext. In common with the BBC, board members are appointed by the Government.

The ITC licenses commercial television and can step in over lapses of impartiality and the portrayal of violence. It is also required to maintain standards of 'good taste and decency' and may prohibit programming which could 'incite crime, lead to disorder, or be offensive to public feelings'. The ITC can issue warnings and demand apologies, and has the power to revoke licences.

The Radio Authority oversees the rapidly expanding independent radio sector of more than 240 local radio stations and three national stations. It also awards licences for *digital multiplexes*, clusters of stations broadcast on digital frequencies. The gradual switch to digital paves the way for many more radio stations in the future. The Radio Authority also plans frequencies, issues licences, regulates programming, publishes Codes and punishes offenders.

Radio and TV broadcasting in the USA is regulated by the Federal Communications Commission. FCC commissioners are appointed by the President with the consent of the Senate. The FCC awards and revokes licences and investigates complaints. Despite the partial deregulation of broadcasting in the UK, the FCC continues to hold a looser rein than its British counterparts.

Canada, New Zealand and Australia operate public and private TV networks. Public broadcasting in Australia is run by the Australian Broadcasting Corporation, which is answerable to parliament. ABC runs ABC-TV, a national television service, four national radio networks, nine metropolitan radio stations, 39 regional stations and the international *Radio Australia*. Like the BBC, it is regulated by Charter. Its independence is guaranteed by law.

Complaints from listeners and viewers also play their part in shaping output. In Britain, the Broadcasting Standards Commission adjudicates on issues of fairness. It also monitors the portrayal of sex and violence over the airwaves and considers matters of taste and decency. Its code of guidance to broadcasters is aimed at preventing *unjust or unfair treatment and unwarranted infringement of privacy* by the media.

Beside Government guidelines, broadcasters in many countries subscribe to voluntary codes of conduct – which are often seen as a hedge against further legislation.

'Independence'

> *'There can be no higher law in journalism than to tell the truth and shame the devil … Remain detached from the great.'* – WALTER LIPMANN, US JOURNALIST

> *'Reporters are puppets; they simply respond to the pull of the most powerful strings.'*
> – LYNDON B. JOHNSON, US PRESIDENT
>
> *'There are honest journalists like there are honest politicians. When bought they stay bought.'*
> – BILL MOYERS
>
> *'If it wasn't for us, who would know what was happening? Governments would get away with blue murder.'*
> – JOURNALIST MIKE NICHOLSON, ITN

Figure 64 Calling public figures to account. One of the first duties of journalism is to ask the questions ordinary people would want to put to the rich and the powerful. (*Andrew Boyd*)

Where broadcasters are controlled – by the state or big business – they can have only limited independence. And all are controlled to some degree. Where the bottom line is profit, we call that control *commercial pressure*. Where the control is political, we call it *censorship*. Several major questions lie at the heart of the censorship issue:

- *By censoring what we see or hear, is the Government exercising commendable responsibility in sparing less well educated viewers from 'harmful' opinions they might not have the mental capacity to judge for themselves?*
- *Or is the Government displaying a paternalistic arrogance that underestimates and patronizes its citizens?*
- *Is it wise and responsible government to ensure that a tool as powerful as the media is used as a positive force for social control, national development and the common good?*
- *Or is political censorship simply a cynical way for the Government to preserve its power by silencing the more outspoken voices of opposition?*

These questions come down to the right or otherwise of a government to decide for us what we can or cannot hear.

Political pressure and direct interference in British broadcasting is well documented – and usually strenuously resisted. Recent examples include:

1991 Reporting of Gulf War subject to censorship. Coverage is controlled so only sanitized images of the conflict showing seemingly bloodless 'surgical strikes' reach the screens. *'It was such a bizarrely controlled environment,'* recalls Alex Thomson from *Channel 4 News*. *'You were asked to sit around and get your pictures from teams with the military. The pictures were all pooled and then assigned by the military to tell the story they wanted telling.'**

1993 The US-based *Human Rights Watch* reports 'a significant increase in restrictions on liberty' in the British media.† A Right-To-Know information bill is defeated.

1994 The Government finally lifts the ban on the spoken words of representatives of the political party Sinn Fein, which is regarded as the mouthpiece of the Irish Republican Army. Broadcasting their voices was outlawed for six years in a bid to deny terrorists 'the oxygen of publicity'. The ban was lifted after calls by the BBC Director General and ITV chiefs to scrap the restriction.

1995 The Government calls for greater impartiality from the BBC. Radio 4 presenter John Humphrys retorts that journalists have a responsibility to grill politicians.

1995 Investigative journalist Martyn Gregory wins a groundbreaking libel suit against the Department of Trade. The DoT attacked his programme about British sales of instruments of torture. Mr Gregory called it *'an important victory for investigative journalism over a government that seems to have lost its moral authority'*.

1996 There are fresh calls for a Freedom of Information Act. John Griffiths, President of the Guild of Editors: *'Britain is reputed to be the mother of democracy, yet people would be astonished how difficult it can be to elicit the most basic information.'*

1997 A BBC *Panorama* documentary is dropped to avoid giving offence to Saudi Arabia. The programme investigated the imprisonment in Saudi of two British nurses, jailed for murdering a colleague. It was the second documentary to be ditched to avoid upsetting the oil-rich Saudis. *Death of a Princess*, which investigated the judicial killing of a member of the Saudi royal family, was dumped in 1980.

1999 The duty of the journalist to protect his sources is vindicated by the Belfast High Court. The Court overturns an order that Ed Moloney should hand over notes of an interview with a suspected murderer. Moloney describes the ruling as *'a victory for journalism'*.

2000 Despite repeated Government promises, there is still no Freedom of Information Act.

But censorship and government interference is no more rife in Britain than in many other nations. Britain's 'half-free' media, as it has been called, has a good deal more freedom than its counterparts under some regimes where freedom of speech is something it would be wiser not to discuss.

Censorship in developing nations

'Freedom of information is a fundamental human right and is a touchstone of all the freedoms to which the United Nations is consecrated, and that freedom implies the right to gather, transmit and publish news anywhere and everywhere without fetters.'
– UNITED NATIONS RESOLUTION 59, PARAGRAPH 1

* 'The Media Goes Off to War', *The Times*, 20 February 1998.
† 'Pressed down in the wicked kingdom', Martin Walker, *The Guardian*, 29 March 1993; '*Sunday Times's* famous victory over free speech', Ian Birrell, *Sunday Times*, 21 February 1993.

> *'In developing countries we cannot have a freewheeling press. It might be too deceptive and people would get too excited. People here have not yet developed the critical sense to judge stories without being unduly influenced or distracted.'*
> – INDONESIAN GOVERNMENT OFFICIAL*

Many developing and totalitarian nations see the issue of media control in a different light from the West. Their governments often seek to use the media as an instrument of social control, education and national development.

In areas of political instability governments usually attempt to exercise control over the media, which could otherwise become a powerful rallying point for the opposition. Failure to do so, it is argued, could destabilize a country that could already be suffering from unrest, famine, political or religious strife. In such an environment, truth-tellers can be seen as seditious.

The burgeoning Internet, with its unfettered access to global news, information and opinion, has posed a new challenge to totalitarian regimes. According to *Reporters Sans Frontières*:

> *'No fewer than 75 countries maintain a state monopoly on television, and 45 are trying to slow down the communications revolution by limiting citizens' access to the Internet. In Asia, this is happening in Communist countries such as China or Vietnam, and under the military dictatorship in Burma and the authoritarian government of Malaysia.*
>
> *'Beijing sentenced a web surfer to two years' imprisonment for supplying email addresses to dissident publications based in the United States. Hanoi still refuses to allow private Internet service providers to operate, Rangoon passes jail sentences of several years on anyone who fails to declare ownership of a computer, and Kuala Lumpur has been trying desperately to censor web sites that oppose the prime minister.'†*

For journalists reporting from war zones or from nations under dictatorship, the task of providing an unbiased and factual account of events can be fraught with danger. In 1999 ten journalists were killed in the conflict in Sierra Leone and a further six in former Yugoslavia.

The previous year, 31 journalists were killed and 19 others went missing, according to the International Federation of Journalists. They commented: *'These killings are only the top of an iceberg of physical assaults, disappearances and jailings which affect journalists every year. When a journalist is killed it is an attack against the entire population, not simply an individual. Whoever can silence the journalist can silence everyone.'*

War reporting is only part of the problem. Journalists who set out to expose corruption or human rights abuses often become targets.

> *'Win Tin and Myo Myint Nyein, two well-known journalists, have been forced to sleep on the concrete floor, with no mattresses or blankets in tiny cells normally used as kennels for soldiers' dogs. Their guards accused them of giving information about the prison conditions to the United Nations special rapporteur on human rights.'*
> – REPORTERS SANS FRONTIÈRES

* 'Indonesia dangerously still the same', *UK Press Gazette*, 12 May 1986.
† *RSF Annual Report*, 1999.

> *'You are a journalist, we are going to kill you.'* – EAST TIMOR MILITIAMAN
>
> *'An underlying hostility to journalists is unmistakable. No army likes critical coverage of its operations and the Russian performance in Chechnya has been torn apart by the country's press – producing an angry shame among many of the soldiers . . . A story of horror is unfolding in Chechnya and the age-old Russian response is to try to keep the horror a secret behind closed doors. Press and TV are now the enemy, almost as much as the elusive Chechen rebel.'*
> – JULIAN MANYON, ITN MOSCOW CORRESPONDENT
>
> *'In the Ivory Coast two journalists were jailed for two years for suggesting in print that the presence of their President at the African soccer championship had brought their team bad luck.'* – PRESS GAZETTE

The myth of objectivity

> *'The BBC has no editorial opinions of its own. It has an obligation not to take sides; a duty to reflect all main views on a given issue.'* – BBC NEWS GUIDE
> *'The very selection of the news involves bias, there is some bias in every programme about public policy; the selection of the policy to be discussed and those to discuss it means bias.'*
> – FORMER *NEWS AT TEN* NEWSCASTER SIR ALASTAIR BURNET

Contrast the statement above of how the BBC believes things *ought* to be with the statement of how things probably *are* from one of Independent Television's veterans.

Complete impartiality is like perfection; an ideal for which many will strive but none will wholly attain. Even the most respected journalist can only be the sum of his or her beliefs, experience and attitudes, the product of society, culture and upbringing. No one can be free from bias, however hard they may try to compensate by applying professional standards of objectivity; for objectivity itself, subjectively appraised, must by nature be an unreliable yardstick.

The journalist's responsibility is to recognize bias and compensate for it.

The BBC World Service claims to deal with the problem of personal bias through a combination of professional integrity and an exhaustive system of checks and balances.

> *'People do have their politics, but they are very good at keeping them out of the news,'* says a former World Service assistant editor. *'They'd never get through anyway, because there are too many people asking questions. There is a dual personality that says, "I'm an observer, this is not me talking politics, just me talking about things from both sides. I'm not directly involved, I'm merely telling you what is happening".'*

The process of eradicating bias begins by recognizing that every argument has at least two sides and the truth probably lies somewhere between them. The journalist must stand back and view the argument from all sides, before scrupulously drawing out the key points to produce as full, balanced and impartial a picture as possible in the time available.

And here is another of the journalist's dilemmas: that there is never enough airtime to paint the masterpiece he or she would wish. Even the fullest report of an issue can be at best a sketch, and at worst a caricature, of events.

> *'It is possible to observe live tank shells belting into the midriff of the Russian White House before anyone in Moscow or anywhere else knows who's doing the firing, upon whose orders and why. But television is notoriously bad at admitting that we don't actually have a clue what is going on. And as these instant/now images flood into our media centres in ever increasing volume, the incentive to get out and find out diminishes.'* — CHANNEL 4 NEWSCASTER JON SNOW

Opinion and comment

'The first law of journalism – to confirm existing prejudices rather than to contradict them.'
— ALEXANDER COCKBURN

'Self-importance killed more journalists than booze.'
— JOURNALIST, CANADIAN BROADCASTING CORPORATION

American broadcasting has a tradition of fine commentators: seasoned journalists who tread the margins between factual information and reasoned opinion.

The path was established by men like Edward R. Murrow, who did much to haul America out of the destructive introspection of the McCarthy era, with its fanatical witch-hunts against public figures with real or imagined links with Communism.

The British news tradition tends to shy away from the projection of personality, preferring to aim for the factual approach that permits viewers and listeners to make up their own minds on an issue.

Times change and there are signs that the pendulum could be swinging towards a more personal style of *telling*, rather than announcing, the news. The line has become blurred between factual reporting and interpretation and analysis, which is often presented in a more personal way. At the same time news organisations like ITN are going down the road of what they call *correspondent presence* emphasizing the role played by the reporter in getting the story and boosting the correspondent's on-screen personality.

All this might seem to be in conflict with a basic tenet of broadcast journalism: that there should be a clear separation of fact from opinion. But the line gets smudgier still when it comes to reporting tragedy or exposing iniquity. Here is the dilemma: under those circumstances should reporters be expected to forsake their humanity for the sake of objectivity? How can one be objective about genocide?

Campaigning journalism

Campaigning or committed journalism, must by necessity be biased journalism, yet when that bias is in favour of humanity it has its place. A report by the BBC's Michael Buerk on the famine in Ethiopia was credited as opening the eyes of the world to the crisis and led to an unprecedented flood of relief for the stricken region.

Media Week magazine described the Buerk report as *'unashamedly emotive'*, and quoted from Edith Simmons, Press Officer of UNICEF (UK): *'It seems as though he was no longer merely reporting, but actually experiencing something.'*

It went on to quote Norman Rees, then ITN's chief assistant editor: *'In scenes of great tragedy and conflict a reporter has to be touched by what he's seeing. I don't think the reports would be as valuable if we didn't get a feeling of involvement and concern on behalf of the reporter.'*

* Quoted in 'It takes six minutes of TV to make something happen', *Media Week*, 8 March 1985.

Impartiality under fire

The strongest test of media impartiality comes at times of internal division or external conflict. Nothing nails colours to the mast more quickly than a good old-fashioned war.

Kosovo conflict 1: '*My driver and I were stopped by military police in the suburb of Batejnica. They split us up and held us for nine hours. They kept cocking their guns in my face and asking question after question. I think they were angry enough to take it out on us because we were part of the British establishment, but in the end they let us go.*'   – MIKE WILLIAMS, RADIO 4*

Kosovo conflict 2: '*Three men pushed into my room, two brandishing rifles, the third a torch which he trained on my eyes. "Face the wall and do not turn around," shouted the leader of the pack. He wore a police uniform and in Yugoslavia that makes the wearer a law unto himself . . . Before being forced out of Pristina, we asked Serb officials for an opportunity to film the results of the first night of air strikes. Even though it would have been in their interest to show us, they refused. Later, all remaining foreign journalists were driven out of Kosovo. The Serb authorities want no-one to see what is happening there now.*'   – ORLA GUERIN†

Gulf War: '*The greatest failure of reporting in the [Gulf] War was the impossibility of showing the reality of what the airforces were doing to Saddam Hussein's armed forces . . . The allied tapes that were released . . . were sanitized so that people obviously being killed were never shown, and the Iraqi restrictions ensured that only civilians who were killed by accident were ever shown by Western reporters.*'
                                      – MARK URBAN, BBC *NEWSNIGHT*‡

Falklands War: '*The most pressure I have ever been under was certainly during the Falklands war. Communications were controlled by the Ministry of Defence and this meant they effectively had us by the b***s because they could cut the line of communications with our correspondents unless we toed the line and agreed to delay stories. On some we delayed for as long as 24 hours.*'
                        – BBC WORLD SERVICE SENIOR DUTY EDITOR TONY DUNN

Live global news coverage has stepped up the pressure on the military, politicians and journalists alike. The first televised war was Vietnam. Unfettered coverage horrified the US public and put a stop to the war. Since then repeated attempts have been made to put a stop to unfettered coverage – not always successfully.

When US Marines stormed a beach in Somalia by night they were blinded not by enemy guns, but by an army of journalists wielding floodlights for their cameras. At that stage, the military thought they were in for an easy task. Later in Somalia, a single image of a dead Marine being dragged through the streets is said to have resulted in a U-turn by US foreign policy.

Instantaneous reporting has forged TV news into a new and potent diplomatic weapon.

As TV's influence grows enormous, the pressure to control that reporting has become immense. And with such great power comes an even greater need for accurate and responsible reporting.

* *Ariel*, 29 September 1999.
† 'A knock at the door', *The Guardian*, 29 March 1999.
‡ *The Late Show*, BBC 2, 6 June 1991.

Responsible reporting

Reporting disorder

> '*Freedom of communication is the guarantee of all our freedoms. One of the main functions in the media is to ensure that the facts are available first in as unadorned way as possible. Another is to let both sides of an argument be heard, and a third is to identify and expose abuses of power and position of all types, not just the narrowly political.*'
> — ITN NEWSCASTER, TREVOR MCDONALD*

It is possible for the very presence of reporters and camera crews to create news by making a tense situation worse. Another danger is that the presence of cameras might be seen to be legitimizing or endorsing what is happening and encouraging that to continue.

In times of war, executions have been staged for the camera and at least one TV crew has been invited to have the privilege of firing the artillery piece it is filming. Demonstrations have been known to liven up at the first sign of a camera, and there will always be those who see the presence of the media as an essential weapon in their particular propaganda war. It can be difficult to distinguish where coverage of an incident becomes incitement. Many reporters, including this one, must have been tempted to ginger up coverage of a demonstration by encouraging the crowd to start chanting as they begin their live report.

And as every cameraperson will know who has ever had a good shot lain to waste by kids cavorting and yelling, '*Hi mum!*' the mere presence of a lens can bring out the performer in most of us.

The media is not always welcome where there is disorder, especially when it is coupled with violence and crime. The presence of a camera or recorder on the streets may be seen as a threat by those who fear identification if the recording is turned over to the authorities.

Journalist David Hodge was beaten to death as he photographed rioters looting a shop; a BBC crew was set upon by a gang of youths as it attempted to get footage of riots in Brixton – the camera was smashed and the operator got a broken rib;[†] and photographers have been beaten up by the police. *Daily Express* photographer John Downing said there was a good reason for the violence against the media: '*rioters . . . see us as an arm of the police, because newspapers are giving away pictures taken at the riots to the police.*'[‡] Under the Police and Criminal Evidence Act British police have the right to requisition unpublished pictures which might be useful in evidence.

Camera bias

This spiral of distrust tightens if camera crews are forced to retreat to the safety of police lines to film disorder, as happened increasingly during a lengthy miners' dispute in Britain. One TV crew, which went into Markham Main colliery with the agreement of the miners' union, was '*set upon, punched, kicked, and told that if they didn't get out they'd have the living daylights beaten out of them.*'[§]

---

[*] 'Making English better', *Press Gazette*, 26 April 1996.
[†] *The Journalist*, January 1996.
[‡] 'Why journalists are targets for the rioters', *UK Press Gazette*, 9 December 1985.
[§] From *News, Newspapers and Television*, Alastair Hetherington, Macmillan, 1985, p. 265.

Unfair film editing

SIR – It is said that the camera cannot lie. It can and does.

There was an unfortunate example of this in Newsview on BBC Two on Saturday evening, October 4. As this was a clip from BBC TV programmes earlier in the week it had had even larger audiences.

We were shown Eric Hammond of the Electricians' Union making a cheap jibe at the expense of Arthur Scargill, who, he said, was trusted on the issue of nuclear energy as much as a £6 note. Then viewers saw and heard uproarious applause from the delegates. This was followed by Ron Todd of the Transport Workers calling for the phasing out of nuclear power.

The truth is that Hammond received hardly any applause at all. The massive cheers were during Ron Todd's speech. I know because I was in the conference hall.

FRANK ALLAUN

Figure 65   *UK Press Gazette*, 3 October 1986

Forcing the cameras to shelter behind police lines inevitably produces a distorted, one-sided view of the action that will see the other side as the aggressors, resulting in accusations of bias.

Camera bias can be present even in run-of-the-mill industrial relations. If striking workers are filmed as an unruly mass blocking the roadway and management are interviewed in the calm sanctuary of their offices, the impression will be that management represents the virtues of order and reason, while workers are seen as the forces of disorder.

The camera can also distort the news by highlighting the point of action: a three-hour demonstration by 100 000 passes peacefully until a group of 20 trouble-makers throw beer cans and stones at the police. The skirmish lasts eight minutes before police drag off the culprits into waiting vans. A 40-second video report on the evening bulletin includes 20 seconds on the disturbance. The impression is of a largely violent demonstration. The only way to compensate for the contextual distortion is to stress the relatively small scale of the incident.

Distortion

'Today . . . watching a news telecast can be like looking at the country's reflection in a fun-house mirror. The society we see presented is a warped place, often morbid and alarming. An information conveyor, heaped with deviance, death, moral decay, adulterous ministers and paedophilic priests feeds a gaping media maw that has proved to have an insatiable appetite for the violent, the sexy and the salacious. . . Instead of rational tempered stories that might help explain the vexing crime problem. . . we find raw dispatches about the crime of the moment, the frightening – and often false – "trend of the week", the prurient murder of the month, the sensational trial of the year. If local mayhem suffers a lull, our hometown media borrow violence from afar to flesh out the day's blood and gore. . . For news consumers the US must seem to be a hopelessly savage place that stands teetering on the lip of the Apocalypse.'

– DAVID J. KRAJICEK, IN THE WEEK AFTER US TV
BROADCAST A SUICIDE – LIVE

Does Krajicek have a point? In the USA, a survey of the three main news channels found 72 per cent of stories depicted violence, drugs, assaults and crime. Prevailing news values can sometimes hold up a distorting mirror on the world. Decisions about what to cover are made with one eye on the clock and the other on audience appeal. They can be made by news editors away from the scene or live-action cameramen in the heat of the moment. They are always made under pressure.

Krajicek's point reaches beyond the USA. In the UK, four common causes of media distortion were isolated in a British working paper.* Professor Denis McQuail gave them as:

- Emphasis on action, conflict and personalities.
- Selection of particular events and themes for coverage, especially disorder and upheaval.
- Labelling or stereotyping in the reporting of sections of the community such as minority groups and women.
- The snowball effect where the media covers a story because the media is covering the story.

The selection of only the most dramatic items can paint a warped picture of the world and debase the currency of journalism.

Keith Somerville of the BBC World Service says efforts are made to resist the pressure to produce news that is sensational for its own sake. *'We have to ensure we don't get sucked into a sensationalist style of news where events have to be dramatic and involve conflict in order to be news. Something can be important and of interest to people and can reach out to them without necessarily having to be dramatic or sensational.'*

The trouble is, radio needs lively audio and TV needs exciting pictures. The strongest shots are given prominence in any report, and the strongest reports are given prominence in any news programme. But if the thrill appeal of the action flick is allowed to dictate news values, then from our sets will scream only spectacle. Daily life becomes the Coliseum, a theatre of blood.

> *'Local TV news has for the last decade operated under marketing consultants who preach: "If it bleeds, it leads." The broadcast invariably begins with the rape or the car crash or the shooting of the day . . . [giving] the impression that life has turned into a Blade Runner-ish Hell.'*
> — JAMES FALLOWS†

> *'What gets on air is what is easily pre-processed and most dramatic. It's an old saw that television is picture-led: calamity and death and polarised conflict on film make good TV. So argument becomes shorter and more extreme to fit 15-second slots.'*
> — A.A. GILL, *SUNDAY TIMES*‡

Sensationalism

The reporter's hunger for a good story with dynamic actuality can lead down the road to sensationalism, especially on a thin news day when the editor is scouting for a strong lead. The easiest solution is the unethical one, which is to 'hype' a story and blow it

* Adapted from working paper No. 2, HMSO, 1976, p. 5.
† News you can't use', *The Guardian*, 1 April 1996.
‡ *Sunday Times*, 26 March 1996.

up out of proportion. Thus a suggestion that overtime might be cut at a local steelworks unless more orders can be found becomes, *'Jobs threat as steelworks grinds to a halt'*, and so on.

Unless the facts are permitted to speak for themselves without embellishment, fact gives way to fiction as the story is inflated until it can stand up as a headline.

And with the pressure on to produce ever-shorter soundbites stories are reduced to their lowest common denominator. All complexity and every shade of grey are removed. The various sides are polarised for the sake of clarity and all caveats are removed for the sake of simplicity. Then only the strongest, liveliest, most vivid and dramatic soundbites survive. Public debate is turned into a duel at sunrise – one shot each and aim for the heart.

Much the same thing can happen with pictures where a premium is placed on the spectacular. The pressure is on to get the best shots – at any price.

The Japanese TV company NHK was accused of faking up to sixty scenes in a documentary about the hazardous conditions of a remote Himalayan region. The crew were shown footslogging up the mountain when they were actually flown in by helicopter. They were said to have faked altitude sickness and to even have staged an avalanche.*

US TV network NBC resorted to using toy rocket engines to stage an explosion in a report exposing a 'dangerous' General Motors pick-up truck.†

In Germany, reporter Michael Born was jailed for faking more than 30 documentaries 'revealing' neo-Nazis, child labourers and Ku Klux Klan reunions. At one point he even got his mother to run up fake Klan robes on her sewing machine. Born's defence was that his commissioning editors knew his material was hoax, but in the clamour for sensational stories they colluded with the fakery.‡

British TV is not immune to dressing up a story. A crew investigating the rise of the far right in London is said to have daubed swastikas on walls to help prove their point. But all they proved was their cynicism.

Far more spectacular was the Carlton TV documentary *The Connection*, which purported to reveal drugs being smuggled into the UK from Colombia. A carrier was shown swallowing heroin as he set out on his dangerous journey to London. If he failed to make it, the drug would explode in his stomach and kill him. US viewers were told he 'waltzed into London and another pound of heroin was on the streets'.

But in fact the 'drugs mule' was turned away at customs and forced to fly home. And the drugs he devoured were later claimed to be peppermints. To cap it all, the 'drugs baron' from the Cali Cartel interviewed on tape turned out to have been a paid actor.

The most charitable thing that can be said about *The Connection* is that it used dramatic reconstructions without labelling them as such. Guidelines require an audience to be told whenever pictures are not what they appear to be – viewers understand we can't get shots of *everything*. But it seems without the fake pictures, *The Connection* would have had *nothing*. In the end the real spectacle was of Carlton TV handing back eight awards and refunding the international broadcasters that screened the programme – following an inquiry costing an equally spectacular £200 000.

When news is faked to feed an appetite for sensation, all it does is drive down the value of journalism and fuel public despair – not least of all about journalists.

* 'When the camera distorts', Nigel Ryan, *Daily Telegraph*, 5 February 1993.
† 'Television admits rigging GM exposé', *The Times*, 12 February 1993.
‡ 'Spoofer's double exposure', Victoria Mapplebeck, *The Guardian*, 1 September 1997.

Good taste – reporting violence and grief

> *'Good taste ... means having a decent respect for our listeners. We cannot, and should not, shield them from the realities of life. But we do our best not to cause any listener unnecessary anxiety, shock or mental suffering, any parent or young child needless embarrassment or offence.'*   – BBC NEWS GUIDE

The same radio and television programmes can reach a mass audience of young and old, educated and ignorant and can span widely differing cultures. It is inevitable that sooner or later an item that appeals to one section of an audience will offend another. As journalists we have to consider whether the significance of that item will outweigh the offence or embarrassment it may cause.

Clearly a news item which pokes fun at minority groups or deliberately shows them in a bad light would be in poor taste. So would graphically detailed accounts of violent or sexual crimes that could upset young children.

With newspapers and magazines, parents have a chance to veto what their children might read. But with daytime TV or radio news, by the time they realize the item is inappropriate, it is already too late and the damage is done. So the onus is on the broadcaster to use sensitivity in selection.

Reporters who, hour by hour, are soaking up the worst of life's excesses, can overlook the effect of their words on the feelings of their audience. **It is easy to forget that every tragedy has a person at its centre**. Inexperienced reporters may feel it is their mission to 'tell it like it is' and expose real life in the raw, but few audiences will thank you for constantly and gratuitously rubbing their noses in the gutter of life just to provoke a reaction.

So how much do you show?

> *'If somebody gets his head blown off, I personally would be quite happy to show it – because that's what happens when somebody gets his head blown off. I don't want to put gratuitous violence on television, but I think sometimes we err too much on the side of good taste.'*   – HARRY RADLIFFE, BUREAU CHIEF, CBS NEWS
>
> *'We would exercise restraint at the point of showing a mangled body. We would show bodies under sheets and bloody sheets covering the body, but we would not show the body. Violence is around us every day. You don't really need to show those pictures to get across the violent nature of a story.'*   – PAUL CLEVELAND, ASSIGNMENT MANAGER ABC NEWS
>
> *'You've got to tread this fine line of not bowdlerizing it to the extent that it's all so pleasant. It's a matter of degree, suggestion and hint. Don't dwell. The difference between getting it right and getting it wrong may be about a second.'*   – SIR DAVID NICHOLAS, ITN

But these sensitivities post a problem when it comes to war reporting. Freelance cameraman Sorious Samura risked his neck to cover the conflict in his home country, Sierra Leone. His footage revealed the full horror of war, showing executions, amputees displaying freshly severed limbs and vultures feeding on corpses. He hoped his pictures would mobilize the international community. But the world's media couldn't stomach what they saw:

'I put my life on the line to get those pictures shown,' said Samura. *'I took the risks to make sure that people and policy-makers in the West were able to see every detail of what was happening, so that nobody could turn around tomorrow and say it didn't happen.'* Samura won an award and was feted by his colleagues. But only a safe and sanitized version of his pictures was screened.

> *'If you just show the soldiers – we call it the bang bang – blazing away in the ruins, and do not show what is happening at the other end – the pain, the violence and the bloodshed – the effect is to glamorize and prettify war. War is a bad-taste business. People do not expire gracefully out of sight.'*   – MARTIN BELL, BBC CORRESPONDENT

Privacy and voyeurism

At times of tragedy the media is frequently accused of preying on distressed victims by subjecting them to a further ordeal by camera. That was the criticism levelled after coverage of the Zeebrugge ferry disaster in which 187 died.

> *'Many from the national media didn't give a damn. The story meant everything to them. They thought nothing of arguing, bribing, cajoling – even lying. There had already been a number of incidents with reporters and photographers scuffling with relatives in hospital wards. At the height of the disaster more than 1000 journalists were in Zeebrugge – most of them hunting in packs. They pounced on anyone who offered even the slightest hope of giving them a new angle. There are times when, like all decent, honest journalists, I felt ashamed to be counted among their number.'*   – JOHN HAMMOND, NEWS EDITOR*

There were signs that lessons had been learned when it came to Dunblane. This was the shooting in cold blood of a class of primary school children and their teacher by a former scout leader who went on to take his own life.

Richard Sambrook, editor of BBC TV newsgathering told *The Guardian*:

> *'When the news broke we briefed editors, film crews and reporters that there was to be no doorstepping and no close-ups of grieving families. We used restrained language and kept adjectives to a minimum. A tragedy of this magnitude speaks for itself, there's no need to interject between the audience and the event by crudely pushing emotional buttons.'†*

TV images of distress were mercifully fleeting, and then carefully explained as tears of relief by parents who had discovered their children had survived. The pictures that found their way to the screens were from cameras keeping a restrained and respectful distance. Shots of grief were limited to images of stunned townsfolk praying for their dead in a church service to which the media was invited.

* From 'Ashamed of the Press', *UK Press Gazette*, 23 March 1987.
† 'What should the message be?', *The Guardian*, 18 March 1996.

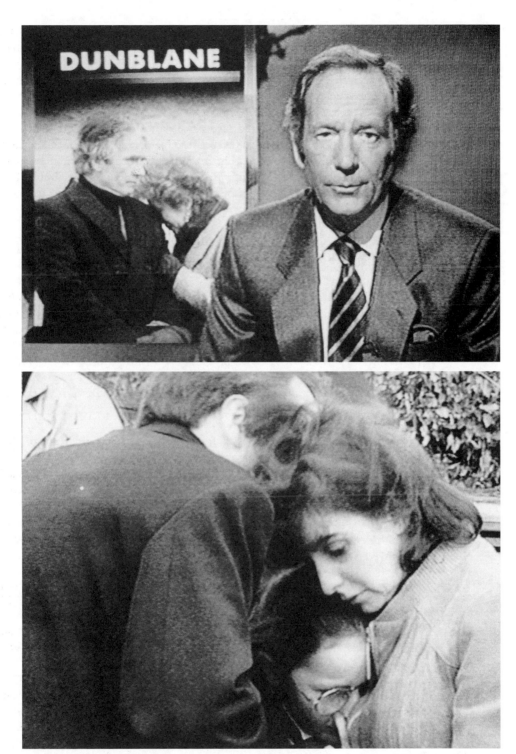

Figure 66   Should cameras intrude on personal grief? After schoolchildren were murdered at Dunblane news reports were anxious to point out that pictures showed tears of *relief*, as parents found their children were safe. (*Courtesy BBC*)

Yet sensitive editing and careful selection belies the immensity of the inevitable media invasion. One journalist described a town silent save for reporters and photographers roaming the streets searching for a new angle. Before long they had found it.

The story shifted from mass murder to pleas by residents for the media to end its intrusion. The spectacle of broadcasters reporting on the intrusion of broadcasters, thus compounding their own intrusion, seemed surreal.

When the funerals eventually did take place part of ITN's report was devoted to an explanation of why TV had no pictures: because the parents had demanded that the press be kept away. By now, many news organizations had begun to withdraw of their own volition, leaving the Press Association to provide pool coverage. But it took police intervention to persuade the more insistent among the media pack to back off and let Dunblane get on with its grieving.

URGENT NOTE TO NEWS EDITORS – DUNBLANE

THE MEDIA FACILITY BEING OFFERED THIS AFTERNOON WITH FAMILIES OF THE VICTIMS IS AN ATTEMPT TO HALT PRESS INTRUSION INTO THE LIVES OF ALL THE VICTIMS. I AM NOW BEING INFORMED PERSONALLY BY FAMILIES THAT THIS INTRUSION IS CONTINUING UNABATED. PLEASE BE ADVISED THAT IF CONTACT WITH THE VICTIMS' FAMILIES DOES NOT STOP FORTHWITH I WILL TAKE THE MATTER UP PERSONALLY AT THE HIGHEST LEVELS.

– SUPT LOUIS MUNN, STRATHCLYDE POLICE

Police high-handedness, or the need for authority to bring order out of chaos? One editor accused the police of running reporters out of town.

It is hard to imagine how tragedies of such epic and magnetic proportions could ever be handled with sensitivity when diverse news media from around the world inevitably flock to such scenes competing for the most dramatic images and soundbites – *right now.*

What is shown on page and screen is never the whole picture. The dilemma of how to get coverage while showing sensitivity extends to the methods used to get those images, multiplied by the number of journalists on the ground.

> *'As for all the instructions to the millions of us here, it only takes one idiot to knock on a door and we are all tarred with the same brush.'* – *PRESS GAZETTE**

To TV editors falls the task of weighing up the right to personal privacy against the legitimate demands of public interest – while avoiding the ever-present trap of voyeurism.

> *'Disasters are stories about human grief and it would be wrong in the coverage of any disaster, in fact it would be distortion, not to show the grief, but our rule is that one shows the grief and one doesn't dwell on it.'* – NORMAN REES, ITN†

---

* 22 March 1996.
† From *Network*, BBC 1, 21 April 1987.

The problem we face as journalists is that bad news is good news. And our lenses devour the best of the worst of it, like ravening, voyeuristic vultures. BBC correspondent Jane Standley summed it up when she recalled the words of a colleague covering a famine in Sudan: *'I usually run into the feeding centres shouting "show me your worst", but here they're all the worst. Great pictures.'**

Internal pressures on reporting

Resources

In a radio newsroom squeezed for staff, the only stories likely to be chased are those that will yield an acceptable result within the available time. News that is too far away or would need too much digging might be dropped by smaller newsrooms in favour of more accessible material. And even when the story gets back, there is no guarantee it will be ready in time to get the position it deserves in the bulletin.

Lack of space is a major constraint. A three-minute bulletin contains fewer than 550 words – a single page of a broadsheet newspaper will hold six times as many – yet the bulletin is supposed to cover *all* the important news stories.

A half-hour news programme probably comprises ten or fewer features with a sprinkling of short copy stories, yet is expected to offer information, comment and analysis on all the major events in the world that day.

Faced with a gallon of news to squeeze into a pint pot of a programme, many news editors might find themselves tempted to limit coverage to the bare facts which can be told quickly, and duck analysis and explanation, which requires context and takes longer.

> *'I get tired of trying to tell stories in 90 seconds. So much is left untold. It can be frustrating and repetitious.'*
> – MIKE NICHOLSON

> *'American television news demands immediacy, brevity, and, most pathetic of all, "soundbites" – words that are both tasty and meaningless, a five-second substitute for human thought, the journalistic equivalent of junk food.'*
> – ROBERT FISK

Selection

Lack of space forces the problem of selection. A highly visual item such as a spectacular carnival would look better on TV and so would be more assured of a place than a more significant story about increasing delays for elderly patients awaiting replacement hip joints. The more visual an item, the more likely it is to be covered on television.

The addition of good pictures or a snappy interview can lift a story in the running order – sometimes beyond its merits. The bulletin order will also be influenced by the need to spread the illustrations evenly throughout.

> *'People who defend pure journalism are operating in a world that's unrealistic.'*
> – NEWS CONSULTANT STEVEN MEACHAM†

* (Mis)reporting Sudan's famine, 17 July 1998.
† Anne Karpf, 'News with the miracle ingredient,' *The Guardian*, 22 July 1985.

Immediacy

> *'The pressure to be first, to beat the rivals with even more sensational pictures, puts a premium on voyeurism, while editors back at home require their correspondents on the ground to know it all as soon as they arrive and to stand and deliver in two minutes flat. Not easy when you are parachuted into a strange land without a compass.'* — JONATHAN DIMBLEBY*

Twenty-four-hour news equals 24-hour pressure. During the Kosovo conflict, while John Simpson was the only BBC correspondent in Serb capital, Belgrade, he often had to file 150 reports a day to feed the Corporation's ravenous news machine. What price analysis?

In the words of the BBC News chief executive, Tony Hall: *'We have moved from a world where journalists would have time to pull together a day's events to one, where, if we are not careful, every small nuance is seized upon to move the story on and gain advantage over the competition. It is a world, where, if we are not careful, we will spend more time asking what is going to happen next before we have described and assessed fully what has actually gone on.'*†

The BBC's Chief Correspondent Kate Adie goes further. She believes the instant techno-culture can kill. The satellite phone means journalists spend their time living constantly with the story, exposing them to constant danger, she told a British Film Institute conference: *'Instead of going back to a hotel to send your story, you can now set up a satellite dish on the back of a pigsty in Bosnia and be minutes from the story,'* she added.‡

And instant reporting winds up the pressure on editors, too. David Feingold of Reuters TV believes the combination of quick-fire technology and rolling news make it even harder to evaluate stories and to test them against the standards of accuracy and impartiality. He told the BFI: *'The very speed of gathering and the editing process . . . may go a long way to eroding some of our core values.'*

Pressures of ratings

> *'If TV were to do the Second Coming of Christ in full colour for an hour, there would be a considerable number of stations which would decline to carry it on the grounds that a Western or a quiz show would be more profitable.'* — ED MURROW
>
> *'We are more and more uncomfortable with challenging power. We're afraid of being unpopular, we are afraid of shrinking markets. We have forgotten to say the words "public trust". And the worst corruption of all is creeping commercialism.'* — CAROL MARIN, CBS

An uneasy alliance exists between the drive for profit and the quest for news on any commercial station that depends on ratings for its survival. When profit motive replaces news values there is pressure to pander to the lowest public taste for fear that audience and

---

* 'A poor show', *The Guardian*, 1 June 1998.
† *Press Gazette*, 1 November 1996.
‡ *Press Gazette*, 11 October 1996.

advertisers alike will desert unless the station delivers only the goods that the mass market will buy. And that pressure spills over into the newsroom.

A trend from America has been for commercial stations to employ news consultants to pep up the audience figures. Among their sweeping changes has been the introduction of 'happy talk' where the news is sugared with folksy chatter by presenters about their pets and kids. News stories have been squeezed to a 90-second maximum, and actualities cut back to around 10 seconds.

Outspoken critic of the consultants, Ron Powers, protests that news is being treated like any other commodity:

> 'The news ... can be restructured, improved, smoothed out, bolstered with miracle ingredients, and topped with a hearty rich flavour that the whole family will enjoy. Finger-lickin' good.'*

The dilemma for journalists is that at the same time as news consultants are pulling down the quality, they have been pushing up the ratings. The rise and rise of the commercial imperative dismays media watchers and media professionals alike:

> 'The new technologies have brought about a proliferation of the media. The main outcome has been the discovery that news is a commodity, whose sale and distribution can generate large profits. The value of news once moved within different parameters, in particular the search for truth. It was also the stuff of political struggle ... since its transformation into a commodity, news is no longer submitted to the traditional criteria of checking for authenticity or mistakes. It is now governed by the laws of the market.'   – RYSZARD KAPUSCINSKI†

One British MP has warned against the hazards of letting market forces rip:

> 'What I fear most is not political bias, but the steady growth of junk journalism – the trivialization and demeaning of everything that is important in our lives, and its consequent effect upon our culture.'   – CHRIS MULLIN MP‡

With the financial benefits of advertising come new pressures. It takes a strong-willed head of sales to let a business person storm out with a hefty advertising budget unspent because the station intended to carry an unfavourable news item about his or her company.

That will would have to be iron indeed if the amount at stake would make the difference between profit and loss or survival and shutdown for a struggling commercial station. Independence depends greatly on a news editor's ability to withstand pressure and maintain integrity.

Many commercial stations have a policy of not permitting news staff to read adverts on air. Their concern is that linking journalists, who are supposed to be impartial, with advertising, would compromise the authority of the station's news service.

---

* Anne Karpf, *op. cit.*
† *The Guardian*, 16 August 1999.
‡ 11 January 1995.

The advertiser's hope is that viewers will receive what is being said about the product with the same unquestioning trust they gave to the news – only now the scripts flow from the pen of the ad man whose sole concern is persuasion, not information.

An insidious development in the UK is that elements of the news, such as sport, weather, traffic – even the bulletin itself – are becoming wrapped around with a sponsor's message. This advertising slogan is often delivered by the newsreader in the same breath as delivering the news. So where does fact end and fantasy begin? What price impartiality when the news is linked with puffs for finance companies or other dubious claims and slogans?

But lest we get too self-important about our little business of story telling, let's consider the words of the journalistic giant, Ed Murrow:

> *'The fact that your voice is amplified to the degree where it reaches from one end of the country to the other does not confer upon you greater wisdom or understanding than you possessed when your voice reached only from one end of the bar to the other.'*

National Union of Journalists' Code of Professional Conduct

1 A journalist has a duty to maintain the highest professional and ethical standards.

2 A journalist shall at all times defend the principle of the freedom of the press and other media in relation to the collection of information and the expression of comment and criticism. He or she shall strive to eliminate distortion, news suppression and censorship.

3 A journalist shall strive to ensure that the information he or she disseminates is fair and accurate, avoid the expression of comment and conjecture as established fact and falsification by distortion, selection or misrepresentation.

4 A journalist shall rectify promptly any harmful inaccuracies, ensure that correction and apologies receive due prominence and afford the right of reply to persons criticized when the issue is of sufficient importance.

5 A journalist shall obtain information, photographs and illustrations only by straightforward means. The use of other means can be justified only by overriding consideration of the public interest. The journalist is entitled to exercise a personal conscientious objection to the use of such means.

6 Subject to justification by overriding considerations of the public interest, a journalist shall do nothing which entails intrusion into private grief and distress.

7 A journalist shall protect confidential sources of information.

8 A journalist shall not accept bribes, nor shall he or she allow other inducements to influence the performance of his or her professional duties.

9 A journalist shall not lend himself/herself to the distortion or the suppression of the truth because of advertising or other considerations.

10 A journalist shall only mention a person's race, colour, creed, illegitimacy, disability, marital status (or lack of it), gender or sexual orientation if this information is strictly relevant. A journalist shall neither originate nor process

material which encourages discrimination, ridicule, prejudice or hatred on any of the above-mentioned grounds.

11 No journalist shall knowingly cause or allow the publication or broadcast of a photograph that has been manipulated unless that photograph is clearly labelled as such. Manipulation does not include normal dodging, burning, colour balancing, spotting, contrast adjustment, cropping and obvious masking for legal or safety reasons.

12 A journalist shall not take private advantage of information gained in the course of his or her duties, before the information is public knowledge.

13 A journalist shall not by way of statement, voice, or appearance endorse by advertisement any commercial product or service, save for the promotion of his or her own work or of the medium by which he or she is employed.

Fieldwork

1 Who has the last word on what is broadcast in your country, the Government or the broadcasters? Is this healthy? Discuss.

Find out how the system of regulation works and what offences might cause broadcasters to lose their licences.

According to the Indonesian authorities *'the purpose of the media is to: "disseminate objective information, exert constructive social control, channel peoples' aspirations, permit communication between the Government and the public, and to mobilize the community in the process of nation building". Should the media be used in this way as an instrument of "positive propaganda?"'* Discuss.

2 *'The notion of an impartial and independent media is a myth.'* Discuss.

What personal biases and preferences are you aware of? Privately jot down your political position (left, right or centre), your religion, and the class, caste, or status of your parents. Now consider how those factors have influenced your thinking on a number of issues, for instance, whether you are for or against abortion, nuclear weapons, capital punishment, censorship.

Do you think it is necessary to attempt to be objective in the way you present issues that you hold strong personal convictions about?

Think of a subject you do feel strongly about. If you had to cover that issue how would you attempt to deal with your personal bias?

3 A passenger plane has crashed 30 miles away in a built-up area killing and injuring most of those on board and several on the ground. How would you cover the story for local radio while minimizing concern in the local community? Who would you talk to and what would you ask? What information would you need?

4 You are a news editor on a commercial radio station. Your bulletin includes a good story about a video rental chain that has been raided by the vice squad, who removed obscene videos. The company is owned by a major advertiser with the station who threatens to withdraw his account unless you drop the story. The sales director tells you not to run it. What would you do and how would you defend your actions? If you are in a class, role-play the discussion with another student playing the sales director.

Supposing you discover that your radio station is losing money and the loss of this account could mean redundancies or cuts in the news service? Does that make any difference to your actions? Justify your discussion.

5 Look through the NUJ code of conduct. Do you agree with everything it says? Do you think it leaves out anything? Could any of those rules be difficult to work out in practice? Why?

Part Two

RADIO

'The great syllabic storm of the age.'

– EDWIN JOHN PRATT

" I always listen to the BBC … I think the BBC's presentation is quite objective. Very marvellous. "

The Dalai Lama

Figure 67

18 The best of British

'I remember being in the port city of Matadi [in the Democratic Republic of the Congo], in what was then an exceedingly dangerous time. With a British cameraman, I was holed up in a hotel, feeling urgently the need to know the situation elsewhere in the country, where a revolution was going on. "The neat trick," he said, "would be to dial the Beeb." We located an ancient short-wave radio. The BBC told us that the Congolese armed forces had threatened to shell and destroy a hotel in Matadi. It was the one in which we were listening to the broadcast. We left. The hotel was promptly shelled and destroyed. Naturally, I have since had a certain affection for the BBC.'   – CHARLES KURAIT, CBS NEWS

'The BBC's World Service has achieved a reputation for political independence and reliability that gives it a stature no other national radio can match', enthuses The Washington Post. Wherever you live, the chances are you will be able to listen to the news of the BBC World Service. It is one of the slumbering giants of broadcasting, a rock of Gibraltar in a sea of change.

The newsroom

As you pass through the impressive portals of Bush House bearing the legend, 'To the Friendship of English Speaking Peoples' and step along the pale, travertine-clad corridors and up the wide and winding staircase, the effect is reminiscent of an art-deco hotel or once elegant gentleman's club. Only when you enter the doors of the newsroom on the fourth floor does the fin de siècle ambience give way to high-tech utility.

The cavernous World Service newsroom is one of the largest in the BBC. The editorial staff are at the hub of every international event of any consequence. Dominating proceedings is an elevated bank of clocks giving the current time in Beijing, Delhi, Moscow, Cairo, Buenos Aires, Washington and New York – a constant reminder that this is a 24-hour service reporting from and to every corner of the globe.

The task of this enormously productive news processing plant is to take the mass of raw material coming in and refine, reshape and rewrite it into the 100 or so hours of regular radio news programmes broadcast each week from the building.

The prime source of news is the BBC's global network of some 250 foreign correspondents: *'no news organization has more reporters,'* is the claim. Added to their input, an estimated million words a day stream directly into the newsroom computer from agencies such as Reuters, PA, AP, UPI and AFP. Meanwhile, BBC Monitoring in Caversham listens in to 3000 news sources in more than 150 countries, monitoring broadcasts, news agencies, the press and the Internet in some 70 different languages. It passes on all the world's most important stories to the newsroom. Finally, a steady flow of news about Britain is supplied by other newsrooms in the BBC.

Figure 68   The cavernous newsroom of the BBC World Service – *'you are at the centre of world events, you know everything that is going on.'* (*Andrew Boyd*)

Keeping up with the information is described by one insider as *'climbing a mountain that's terribly slippery. Even when you're close to the top, you just keep slipping back again.'*

Unusually, this is a newsroom with few reporters – it is staffed almost exclusively by sub-editors. The few specialists dealing with diplomatic, economic, political, defence and UK affairs work close to, but outside the newsroom. The journalists in the field are the stringers and correspondents who work out of 44 different bureaux and occupy key locations such as Moscow, Bangkok, Brussels, Delhi and Johannesburg.

Foreign correspondents

Correspondents daily file upwards of 75 voice dispatches from every international trouble spot and scene of upheaval.

The job is one of the most coveted positions in journalism and no easy option. One of the hardest tasks is to report from a country with a divided community – whatever is said about one side is likely to be regarded as unfair by the other. One correspondent's reports from Sri Lanka resulted in a row in Parliament, a Muslim MP threatening to knock his teeth out and a veiled threat of deportation, described as typical of the pressure on BBC correspondents who insist on their right to make independent assessments.

> *'Tuning into the BBC is like sharing a bit of its freedom as our own.'*
> – BURMESE LISTENER

> *'A skyful of lies.'* – BURMA GOVERNMENT DESCRIPTION OF BBC BROADCASTS*

There is no short cut to becoming a foreign correspondent. Would-be roving reporters are expected to join the BBC and work their way upward. Andrew Whitehead has reported for the BBC in Delhi:

> *'You need to have a sense of what is a good story and the ability to explain it to people who know nothing about the country. You also need to identify the stories that reflect something of the social tensions within a changing country. And you need to look for the sounds as well: how can I illustrate the story? What sort of ambient sounds and sound effects can I pick up round the streets? Who can I find who's going to talk in an interesting and arresting way about this story? And for television, what sort of shots do I need to illustrate this point?'*

Staff journalists are encouraged to take time out to work abroad as sponsored reporters. The BBC pays them a retainer and a fee for every item that is broadcast, and to supplement their incomes they are allowed to file to other news organizations as well. As an added incentive the BBC keeps their jobs open for when they return.

The system provides a useful safety valve. It satisfies journalistic wanderlust, the BBC holds on to and develops its talent, extends its eyes and ears abroad, and when the stringer comes back, swells the pool of knowledge and expertise available in the newsroom.

Bi-media reporting

Increasingly World Service journalists are being trained to work for both TV and radio, and many will go on to do a stint for TV. This bi-medial approach extends all the way to teaching radio reporters how to shoot their own TV reports on camcorders.

'It's nothing like as difficult as I thought it would be,' says former Delhi correspondent Andrew Whitehead, who is now a presenter for the Asia segment of *The World Today.* *'The hardest part is simply the logistics. Television forces you to go to the spot. In radio the temptation is simply to get the information fed to you and stay near a phone.*

'For example, there was a big car bomb explosion in the centre of Delhi. Eight people were killed and the target was a well-known politician from the ruling party, who escaped. It was obviously a big story. First of all, you file a piece for radio, then you try and liase with a camera crew and go to the spot, do a piece to camera, quickly wrap up the television [sound]track, record it at the television studio, then hot-foot it back to the office, but because you've actually been forced to report from the scene of the explosion, your reporting for radio is subsequently more vivid. So in some ways, working bi-medially actually strengthens your radio coverage.'

The voracious appetites of both TV and radio have persuaded the BBC to increase its number of correspondents, but the progress from one medium to two has not been entirely without hazard. Andrew Whitehead again:

* *A Skyful of Freedom*, Andrew Walker, Broadside Books, 1992.

'It's the cock-ups which cause the most embarrassment. When you're sending separate rushes [video footage] and [sound]track to London, from time to time completely inappropriate pictures are put over track. There have been occasions when I've said: "Outside this mosque," and we've had pictures of a temple. One dreadful occasion when I was talking about an election rally in Punjab pictures were being shown about a rally [by a different party] in Delhi, and that caused us a lot of innocent amusement.'

Less amusing was the accusation that TV coverage of disturbances at a temple in Ayodhya incited copycat rioting. There was also concern over pictures from Pakistan, which appeared to show the head of state being knocked down by security forces. The shots were actually of a bystander who resembled the premier.

Viewers in developing nations less steeped in the sophistry of television might be more inclined to take TV images at face value. What this illustrates is the importance of clear and appropriate commentary and sensitivity to a foreign audience.

'We sent a correspondent into Northern Iraq. He went in with his tape recorder and camera by foot and by donkey and got some wonderful pieces. He came back and did both radio and television versions of it. It's great fun. You produce your own film, see your own pictures and send it back. There's no one else to blame but yourself; you do the whole thing.'

– WORLD TV NEWS

Figure 69   Andrew Whitehead, BBC World Service *'Working bi-medially strengthens your radio coverage'*. (*Courtesy BBC*)

The news conference

The newsroom conference is a seismometer of world events. Every shift in policy, political upheaval or movement of troops is registered and analysed and its intensity measured on the newsroom's equivalent of the Richter scale. The severity of the crisis can also be gauged by the increase in the World Service audience, which rises dramatically wherever there is tension.

One commander in Afghanistan claimed he relied on the BBC to tell him how his battles were going: *'When the commanders hit a tank they didn't actually believe they'd done it until they heard it reported on the BBC,'* says correspondent Rahimullah Yusufzai. *'You hear plenty of Afghans joke that only the BBC can bring peace to Afghanistan – by not reporting on the fighting. If the mujahedin can't hear their exploits on the BBC, they'll soon stop. I only wish it were true.'**

The shape of each newsday is sketched out at the 0900 conference. This is shared between radio news, talks and features, the newsgathering departments and the regions. A further conference mops things up at 1630.

A computer-produced news diary provides a starting point for discussion and each representative offers his thoughts in turn:

'The UN are worried about the number of people still out in the hills in East Timor. There was a problem, because the UN official said that there were half a million people, but as Claire pointed out if you add up the figures for the number who are supposed to be in West Timor, Dili, elsewhere, and the people who are supposed to come back, it doesn't work out. But it's a figurative illustration that there's a lot of people out there who haven't come home. What have we got on that? Jonathan? Ingram?'

'Have you got the one about the pro-independence groups who are falling out with the Aussies? The pro-Independence groups are fed up with the Australians trying to disarm them when they're not ready to disarm. We've got an interview.'

'It might be worth seeing if you can work that up into a story. It wouldn't necessarily keep Timor as the lead but it would be an angle.'

'Just one slight thought of alarm. . . in Macedonia the aid agencies said they had lost some 20 000 refugees. We ran that quite strongly for a few days and it sounded tremendously alarmist and worrying and we dropped the story with some embarrassment when it turned out the aid agencies had made an accounting error.'

'Well, that's the problem with these figures . . .'

'Yes, you have to beware of nailing it down, but they say all the villages they have flown over are empty – where are all these people?'

'My concern is it sounds so dramatic, and it may well be true, but if we start this hare running and then drop the story . . .'

'Yes, there may not be half a million missing, but the basic fact is the villages and towns are empty . . .'

'The issue is that people aren't returning to their homes . . .'

'Exactly.'

'It points to a greater truth.'

Over at the World Service's sister operation, BBC World TV, the picture is much the same.

* 'A signal for truth', *The Independent*, 17 January 1996.

> *'10 am. Into BBC World where immediately I'm confronted by a lot of glassy-eyed people who have been up all night. Quick chat with the producer, then mug up on the top stories. Newspapers, cuttings, wires, edits. You're mining for the right angle. You're met with all these different sources of information and it can blow your mind. If there's one thing I've learnt it's that preparation is all. If you're ill-prepared, you'll be caught.'* — STEPHEN COLE, BBC WORLD TV PRESENTER*

From a purpose-built newsroom in BBC Television Centre in London, BBC World TV is delivering a complimentary service to radio that aims to take on and beat global rival CNN. BBC World reaches 230 million homes across the globe and has recently launched joint ventures with other broadcasters in the USA, Latin America and the UK.

The stories

> *'A good story is going to be of importance to the listener. Either they will feel that it will somehow change the world in which they live or be something that affects their immediate experience. We have an extremely broad agenda. At one stage world news was thought to be something like the Arab/Israeli conflict or the Cold War. Now it can be AIDS, a medical vaccine, GM foods, the war in Chechnya or refugees. It's something that has resonance for our audience.'* — KEITH SOMERVILLE, STRAND EDITOR, WORLD SERVICE NEWS PROGRAMMES

All news copy is entered directly into the BBC World Service Electronic News Production System (ENPS). The idea is that journalists across the BBC can trade stories, audio and even video. Once on terminal, the draft is revised by the sub or duty

---

The authorities in Pakistani-controlled Kashmir say they believe they've prevented supporters of a Kashmiri separatist party from reaching the line of control dividing the territory between Pakistan and India. Thousands of police have been deployed to hold up activists of the Jammu and Kashmir Liberation Front (JKLF), some of whom have got within three kilometres of the line. On two occasions police used teargas and fired warning shots to disperse large groups of protestors. Some activists are still trying to reach the line, but police say that if anyone does get that far, Indian forces are expected to open fire. The marchers say neither India nor Pakistan has the right to divide Kashmir. (The last time the JKLF tried to stage a similar symbolic crossing of the line of control in 1992, Pakistani forces opened fire and killed eight people.)

{NET HEADLINE: Police clash with pro-independence Kashmiris}

{RADIO HEADLINE: }

{SOURCES: RW 1000 when firing firmed up, 6 injured, Indian hostility with OBJ XN 1145 on police say prevented, details of clashes 0900 police firing new; 0030 police deployed ahead of march}

Figure 70 World Service copy story for radio transmission and the website. Details of sources are given so writers can check back. (*Courtesy BBC World Service*)

* 'Cole mining', Michaela Southby, *BBC World Television Guide*, April 1996.

editor. Revisions – 'mods' – can be printed to order. Stories can be adapted to suit different regions and whole bulletins can be rewritten in a matter of minutes.

News stories can be timed at the touch of a button. The pace of World Service newsreaders is no longer glacial. Improvements to the audibility of broadcasts means they now rip along at roughly the speed of their domestic counterparts – about 180 words per minute.

An elaborate system is employed for marking-up copy, to make sure every detail can be traced back to source.

Accuracy

> *'Accuracy is obviously of first importance. If we get things wrong, if we are careless or ignorant or naive, our credibility is damaged. That is why we have a Newsroom that puts every story through a process of briefing, scrutiny and revision at various levels of seniority. Accuracy is so vital that though we like to be fast, if possible first, with the news, if there is any conflict between accuracy and speed, accuracy must always come first.'* – BUSH HOUSE NEWSROOM GUIDE

World Service policy is to hold back a controversial agency story until it can be confirmed by an independent source. Even then the newsroom may be cautious. This is described as the *two-source rule*:

> *'We need reports from two agencies, or an agency and a freelance before we will run the story, and we actually watch to make sure the freelance hasn't filed to the agency as well to be certain we've got it right. The exception is correspondents' reports that are accepted as trustworthy. We also want to check we've got our names, facts, and figures right. Everything we write is checked by many people round the building who know far more about the subject than we do.'*

The exhaustive system of checks and balances is also intended to prevent hoaxers or propagandists pulling the wool over their eyes:

> *'Many years ago in the Portuguese section someone was monkeying around with the output and putting their own views in. It was picked up very quickly. All language sections undergo extremely rigorous checks of their output from time to time when the programming is backtranslated, discussed and pulled to pieces. If some sort of propagandist were inadvertently taken on they would be very quickly discovered.'* – ASSISTANT EDITOR IAN MILLER

The service

Bulletins go out on the hour 24 hours a day. The style is solid, factual information. More than 900 hours a week of news and programmes in English and 44 other languages are sent via the control room to transmitters around Britain and by satellite to relay stations across the surface of the planet. World Service literature spells out their aim:

> *The emphasis is on news as seen from a global perspective. Accuracy is the over-riding concern. Programmes are designed to give unbiased news and accurate reports of world events and to present a broad pattern of Britain's life and thought. News is the cornerstone of output.*

Story Slug	Status	Region	Creator	LastMod	Writer	Actual	Cume
CEN 1200 TOP	OK	Central	Maurice Walsh	1:34:4	Roy Haynes	:23	:23
CEN 1230 TIMOR MISSING	BUP	Central	Karen O'Brien	2:37:3	Roy Haynes	:39	1:02
CEN 1130 CROATIAN NAZI TRI	OK	Central	Peter Hiett	1:35:1	Roy Haynes	:42	1:44
CEN 1200 AUSTRIA ELECTION	OK	Central	Karen O'Brien	1:40:2	Roy Haynes	:43	2:27
CEN 0900 ZIMBABWE IMF	OK	Central	Julian Soar	8:51:0	Roy Haynes	:40	3:07
CEN 1300 SOUTH AFRICA BAS	BCOR	Central	Alan Johnston	2:34:1	Roy Haynes	:39	3:46
CEN 0900 INDIA ELECTION	OK	Central	Peter Miles	8:51:3	Roy Haynes	:34	4:20
CEN 1230 PAKISTAN KASHMIR	OK	Central	Peter Miles	2:58:5	Roy Haynes	:39	4:59
CEN 1100 CHECHNYA	OK	Central	Peter Hiett	0:41:0	Roy Haynes	:39	5:38
====ALSO AVAILABLE======	OK	Central	Kevin Hamilton	1:57:5	Kevin Hamilton	:00	5:38
CEN 1030 PALESTINIAN SAFE	OK	Central	Dennis Benton	0:42:1	Roy Haynes	:33	6:11
CEN 0730 JAPAN NUCLEAR	OK	Central	Muzafar Shakir	7:12:5	Steve Rowley	:32	6:43
CEN 0530 JAPAN TIMOR AID	OK	Central	Muzafar Shakir	5:19:5	Mike Fearn	:31	7:14
AFR 0330 NIGERIA CHOLERA	OK	African	Maggie Jonas	3:26:1	Mike Fearn	:28	7:42
EUR 1100 FRANCE TRAINS 20	OK	Europe	Magdi Abdelhadi	1:45:1	Roy Haynes	:20	8:02
EUR BRI 1130 CONSERVATIVE	OK	Europe	Magdi Abdelhadi	1:44:3	Roy Haynes	:28	8:30
CEN 1130 WORLD NEWS SUM	BUP	Central	Paulin Kola	1:27:5	Roy Haynes	1:02	9:32
====END OF CORE=========	OK	Central	Kevin Hamilton	6:11:3	Kevin Hamilton	:01	9:33

Figure 71   Central Core Bulletin running order. You can see at a glance what time the story was written. Other bulletins for the different language services are adapted from this. (*Courtesy BBC World Service*)

Major programmes include *The World Today*, *Newsdesk*, a roundup of correspondents' reports, and *Newshour* which offers analysis of major current topics plus interviews.

The backbone of the operation is the central news bulletin. All the news summaries in other languages are based on this. Incoming information is scanned by a *copytaster* who alerts editors to potential news stories. News for the foreign services passes through the six Regional Desks covering Europe, Africa and the Middle East, the Americas, Asia-Pacific, the former Soviet Union and South-West Asia, and South Asia. To keep the output pointed and relevant, bulletins are adapted for different audiences.

'If you are talking to an audience in China, their interests and concerns are going to be different from an audience in Europe,' explains Assistant Editor Ian Miller, *'so sometimes the lead stories and the emphasis will vary. But an important principle is that the main stories of the day will be there.'*

'There's a much greater willingness to devolve responsibility to programme makers to give them their heads. The language services, which for a long time felt somewhat oppressed, now have a much greater freedom to make the kind of programmes that they think will attract their kind of audience. They don't have to have an English person as a boss; they don't have to have a centralized agenda dictated by a bunch of white, middle-class blokes in the newsroom. They can look at what's on offer and select from it.'   – BOB JOBBINS, EDITOR NEWS AND CURRENT AFFAIRS, BBC WORLD SERVICE

The various news bulletins are then translated from English into 44 other languages. Each service employs academics, journalists and experts from many nations to translate, modify, adapt and scrutinize every word to be sure it satisfies the World Service standard of total accuracy. They don't always succeed. Sometimes the translation can go embarrassingly wrong. 'Public house' has been translated as 'brothel', 'taking stock', as 'raiding cattle'; and 'coaches telescoped' as 'coaches hurled so far away that one could see them only through a telescope'.

Newsdesk

The 20 minutes of *Newsdesk* allow the BBC's foreign correspondents to go into greater depth on the day's major stories than would be possible in a news bulletin.

The programme is put together by the English duty editor who draws up the running order, while responsibility for the getting it out on air passes to the producer.

The presenter for *Newsdesk* and other programmes sits in an adjoining studio separated by a glass panel. Watching his progress are the producer, the broadcast assistant responsible for timings and the panel studio manager who rides the faders. The editor listens in from another room.

At this point, a chuckle is likely to spring from any seasoned hand from commercial radio. In that lean, mean, pared-back world all those jobs, including the on-air presentation, would often be done by a single overstressed broadcaster – and probably sound like it, too.

Yet the BBC's belt, braces, Velcro and safety pin approach is still simplicity itself compared to anything on TV. The chains of communication are shorter and the atmosphere more relaxed. Instructions are infrequent and considerably less terse.

It's 1658 GMT. Two minutes from the next edition of *Newsdesk*. The only problem is they're set to overrun by almost 90 seconds and it's all good, strong material. Something will have to go.

The producer decides to do it the hard way, paring back the items as they go, a few seconds here, a few seconds there, live on air . . .

'So you should have headlines, and that cue is fine even though we've got the updated tape. I'll just check the in and outcue and then Norris . . .'

[Newsreader soundcheck] *'Chechnya says Russian forces have come within 20 km of the capital, Grozny, but Moscow has . . .'*

[A script is handed over] 'Oh great, thank you! Has it got some outs? Brilliant – thanks!'

[The computer printer bursts into life churning out updated scripts]

'This . . . is London.' [The theme tune rings out].

[Greenwich Time Signal – Peep, peep, peep, peep, peeeep!] *'It's 17 hrs Greenwich Mean Time. This is Newsdesk from the BBC World Service with Julie Candler. The news headlines . . .'*

'1 [minute] 24 [seconds] over . . .'

'. . . *Rob Norris reporting. You're listening to Newsdesk from the BBC World Service. The Zimbabwean government is denying reports that it misled the International Monetary Fund . . .'*

'We'll take a pot on this to save us ten [seconds], so the outwords will be '$3 million a month . . .'

'. . . *There's been violence in two constituencies in India . . . one civilian was killed and 12 security personnel were injured . . .'*

'We'll pot this at 1'06 at *'second bash and a third.'* [To newsreader:] 'It's not your speed, it's just we're very heavy (chuckle)'

'You're down to a minute, so it'll be OK.'

'United Nations officials who are supervising the aid effort in East Timor say they're still trying to establish the whereabouts of hundreds of thousands of people who fled their homes during the violence and disruption that followed the autonomy ballot . . .'

'53 [seconds] . . .'

'Right, I'll drop the Burundi copy . . .'

'Right, that's 32 . . .'

'. . . Making 21, so we might just read the heads at the end . . .'

'All right.'

'Sport now . . .'

'We'll pot it at 1'01 . . . oh, 1'19's better, we'll pot it at 1'19".'

'And that's the sport.'

'Excellent!'

[The phone rings] 'Hello, Newsdesk?'

'The headlines . . . a court in Croatia has sentenced the former commander of a Nazi concentration camp to 20 years in jail. And that's where we end this edition of Newsdesk.'

[And she might have added: 'Bang on time!']

'Thank you very much (chuckle).'

'Thank you – for the adding up!'

Newsreaders

World Service newsreaders are neither trained journalists nor simply actors chosen for the rich, resonant quality of their voices – though some do come from an acting background. High on the list of qualifications is a strong grasp of world events, as announcer Paul Jenkinson explains:

'You've got to have an understanding of the stories. It's no good just trying to recite words on a page unless you follow the story and make sense of it; it would just come out like a stream of consciousness.'

Figure 72 Seven minutes into an edition of *Newsdesk* at the BBC World Service. Julie Candler (*centre*) is the presenter. (*Andrew Boyd*)

The running order can change at any time while the programme is on air as breaking news comes in. (*Andrew Boyd*)

Checking the running order to make sure everything runs to time. (*Andrew Boyd*)

Figure 72 *Continued*

Paul Jenkinson began his career in the BBC as a studio manager and developed his abilities as an announcer by going on presentation attachments. Newsreader Julie Candler took a post-graduate diploma in broadcasting before joining the BBC. She agrees with Paul that understanding the story is paramount to making sense of it.

'You have to know a bit about the background, which is why we spend quite a lot of time reading through the stuff.' And she is in no doubt about what makes a top quality newsreader:

'Clarity. And lifting the story off the page. You need to be able to read ahead on the page. While I am reading one sentence out loud I'm reading ahead the following sentence. It's not something everyone can do straight away. You've got to be a very fast reader and it takes lots of practice.'

There has been gradual shift towards egalitarianism in the World Service style of delivery. The BBC claims a public school accent is not high on its list of priorities for presenters. But the tone is still well educated and decidedly middle-class; though educated, middle-class regional accents are beginning to creep in:

'We have about an equal number of male and female announcers,' says Paul Jenkinson. *'We have representation from all the regions of the UK: Northern Ireland, Scotland, Wales, England – all accents. You couldn't really say that is a World Service accent. The bottom line is: so long as it's clear and makes sense, that is all that is required. You don't have to turn up sounding like some retired Sergeant Major and speak with a plum in your mouth – that's definitely not what we're trying to achieve.'*

Strange-sounding names are a particular pitfall for World Service presenters, and the BBC's pronunciation unit offers advice on how to sound like a native. Real tongue twisters may be spelt phonetically.

Independence

World Service radio costs the British Foreign Office more than £160 million a year. That might sound high, but it works out at little more than £1 per listener per annum. Regular cutbacks keep whittling away at the service, otherwise government interference is limited to deciding the languages of the output:

'This piper [the Government] does not call the tune. If he did, people would not stop to listen.'
 – JOHN TUSA, FORMER MANAGING DIRECTOR, BBC WORLD SERVICE.

'I have never been in a position where I felt that any influence was being put on me as a journalist.'   – BOB JOBBINS, NEWS AND CURRENT AFFAIRS

'Impartiality means that in any conflict or dispute we always try to report the views of both sides . . . whether Britain is involved or not . . . and whether the Government is involved or not.'   – BBC PRESS OFFICE

The launch of BBC World TV represented the biggest expansion in BBC television since BBC2 in 1964. Yet repeated requests to secure government funding have all been turned down. So, unusually for the Corporation, BBC World has had to be paid for commercially.

The way ahead?

'Things have come full circle. The transmitters that the Soviet Union built in the 1960s and 1970s to jam World Service broadcasts are now being used by the World Service to rebroadcast into the Indian subcontinent and China – which is the biggest growth area of the moment.'
– WORLD SERVICE PRESS OFFICE

There seems to be some strange law governing the relationship between government spending cuts and World Service popularity. The more the British Government claws back into its coffers the higher the audience rises. The World Service is more popular than ever, pulling in a record 143 million listeners each week. No other radio broadcaster comes close.

A second 24-hour English language news channel is planned, and 20 dedicated FM stations have been deemed highly effective in reaching new audiences. Other key targets include expanding the listening audience in China and Central Asia, but tuning in can be a dangerous business. This listener from China was arrested for eavesdropping on the BBC:

'They accused me of listening to enemy radio, and I was forced to write a self-critical statement and guarantee that I would never tune to any foreign station. Because of the pressure from family and society, I dare not listen to BBC programmes openly.'
'There is a story', reports *The Guardian*, *'that in the clampdown following the Tiananmen Square slaughter, among those punished was a man put on public display in a cage and labelled: "This man is a BBC listener." '*

Another major growth area for the World Service is rebroadcasting. More than 1000 radio and cable stations take World Service programmes and £4 million has been invested in a new satellite digital distribution network to improve sound quality and increase availability. On the same lines, the World Service is pioneering global standards for Digital Radio (formerly DAB), which enables signals to be picked up direct from satellite on special portable radios.

Developments in digital communications allow more programmes to be made on location in the BBC's various news bureaux, making the output even more relevant. A new computer system enables copy, audio and video to flow digitally from location to location, allowing TV and radio to pool resources more effectively.

And having taken the plunge into all things digital, the World Service has also hooked up to the World Wide Web for transmission via the ubiquitous Internet. Chief Executive Mark Byford's aims are nothing if not ambitious:

'We want to be recognized as the world's reference point, a hub for global communications across the world. As the Internet is global it is going to be an important new interactive medium for us. It is not going to replace radio. Far from it. That will still be our dominant way of reaching our audiences.' *

The policy certainly seemed to pay off during the Kosovo conflict. The audience responded to the BBC's coverage with some 30 000 e-mails to Online.

* 'Brave new world', *The Guardian*, 25 January 1999.

But some suspect the Internet could be the World Service's swan song: *'In the public service sector, the Internet is a natural successor to the World Service'* says Carol Dukes, the managing director of Carlton Online. *'It's a fantastic way for Britain and the BBC to provide unbiased, first class public service information and news to a world-wide audience. In the long term it will be no surprise if it replaces the World Service.'*

Broadcast or webcast, for a journalist there is no bigger audience and no better stories. Whether it's World Service radio or BBC World TV, it's probably the best job in broadcasting: *'It's making sense of the chaos,'* explains presenter Stephen Cole, *'being on air when great events are happening, disseminating the news. A lot of people have their satisfaction through their hobbies – I have mine through my work.'**

HOSTAGE LIFELINE

'For four years . . . one had nothing, and then, out of the blue, a small radio set appeared. Just a cheap set, and I said, "Thank God I'm in the Middle East where the World Service can be received on medium wave for virtually 24-hours a day."'

'[For] 12 months, the World Service helped to keep us alive both spiritually, through the work of the religious department, and mentally, through the variety of cultural news programmes that are broadcast with such excellence.

'Thank you, World Service, Thank you very much.'

– RELEASED BRITISH HOSTAGE, TERRY WAITE

Fieldwork

1 Listen to the World Service news and compare its style and content with your domestic radio service and describe the difference.

2 There have been moves to make World Service bulletins more relevant to different national audiences. Have they gone far enough? What difference would it make if the news was coming from your country or nearest large city?

3 What system does your local radio newsroom use to review stories and check them for accuracy? How does it compare with the extensive checks and balance of the World Service?

   Do you believe that checks and balances in the newsroom can eliminate biased reporting? Give your reasons.

4 Compare, if you can, a major bulletin on World Service radio with another on BBC World TV. Do the pictures add to the stories or do they serve as a distraction? Which form of journalism is clearer, more effective, and more memorable?

5 Do you think BBC foreign correspondents are impartial or do you find their reporting biased? Give some examples and discuss.

   Suppose you were setting yourself up as a foreign correspondent in the country of your choice. How would you establish yourself and what contacts would you make?

---

* *BBC World Television Guide*, April 1996.

RADIO NEWS COVERAGE

19 Story treatment

> Crouching in the dust at the side of the road in Kosovo, radio journalist Huw Williams was up against a deadline. He had to finish his report about the Serb withdrawal in time for the evening edition of Radio 1's *Newsbeat* programme. He had interviews to edit, sound effects to mix in and he still hadn't recorded most of his script. Over Huw's shoulder, a small group of Kosovar children watched curiously as he seemed to move coloured blocks around the [computer] screen. He was using software called Cool Edit Pro. This allowed him to trim audio material and arrange it in the order he wanted to produce a report from a psychiatric hospital. *'There were babies tied into their cots and even one patient armed with a gun who fired it at us as we looked round.'* The challenge was to tell the world what was happening despite the nearest radio station being hundreds of miles away. *'I used a portable Sony MiniDisc machine to record the interviews and roughly edit them. They were loaded onto my laptop and mixed into a piece, which was sent back to London using a high-quality satellite phone. This was all powered from our car battery.'*
> – RADIO REVOLUTION, COMPUTER ACTIVE*

There are many different ways to present a news story for radio from the simple copy story to the full-blown documentary. Television and radio techniques differ because of the use of visuals, but in many respects are similar in the way they package information as news. This chapter explores the different treatments radio gives to news.

It is a quarter past two on a quiet summer afternoon in Surrey, England. The only news worth reporting is that it is hot. The Guildford newsroom is raking through the embers of the day's stories and wondering what to resurrect from the breakfast show to flesh out the 5 and 6 o'clock news programmes. The phone rings. Three hands grab for it but only the news editor's practised reaction connects. Relief is at hand. News has broken. News editor Ian Hinds is grilling the caller with all the zeal of the Spanish Inquisition:

*'When did this happen? Just **now**? **How** many dead!? Are you **sure? Where** ...? Outside Guildford station!!?'*

Fuelled by adrenalin, the news machine leaps into life. A story that develops quickly with new information coming in is known as *breaking news*, or a *running story*. Below are

* 23 March 2000.

Figure 73   Two approaches to radio news presentation – the self-operated news studio (here the training studio at Highbury College – top), and the World Service belt-and-braces approach where the programme is driven, leaving the presenter free to concentrate on his delivery. (*Andrew Boyd*)

the various treatments that a fictitious radio station might give to this equally fictitious – but feasible – story of a train crash at Guildford.

Newsflash (bulletin, US)

News editor Ian Hinds lingers on the phone for only as long as it takes to check the details, then bashes out a few lines on the newsroom computer. Next he strides across to the studio, moving quickly, but not so fast as to become breathless, and glancing to check the on-air light is off, he bursts through the soundproof double doors, informs the presenter he has a newsflash and parks himself in the chair in front of the guest microphone.

As soon as Hinds is in place, the presenter dips the music he is playing, and says, *'And now over to our newsroom for an important newsflash,'* before firing an urgent five-second jingle (sounder) and opening the microphone for Hinds:

'Two trains have collided just outside Guildford station, killing at least three people, injuring others, and leaving several more trapped in the wreckage. The accident, which happened in the past half-hour, involved the delayed 1.51 from Guildford and the 1.18 from Waterloo. The names of the casualties and the cause of the accident are not yet known. An emergency number for relatives is being set up. We'll be bringing you that number as soon as it's announced. 'That newsflash again . . . Two trains have collided outside Guildford station, killing three, and leaving others trapped and injured. More news on that crash as we get it.'

The presenter fires another jingle, thanks Hinds on air and puts on another CD, this time something more downbeat in keeping with the sombre news.

By now, Hinds is already back in the newsroom badgering the rail company for that emergency number, while the newsroom secretary is tasked with making sympathetic noises to clear the switchboard which is already getting calls from anxious friends and relatives of passengers.

Holding on for South West Trains, whose press office is permanently engaged, Hinds barks out instructions to his team of reporters, which has been galvanized into action. One is on to the police, another is alternating between the fire brigade and the hospital and a third has already filed the story to the network newsroom in London.

The opposition station output is being played through the newsroom loudspeakers and Hinds permits his team a moment's self-satisfaction when they hear their rival's newsflash go out on air – four minutes after their own.

Just then the South West Trains number comes through on the switchboard. Hinds holds the line to the press office in case they have more information, and toys with the idea of a second newsflash, but quickly drops that in favour of extending the headlines on the half-hour which is now less than three minutes away.

The newsflash is news at its most immediate, and highlights the task that radio does supremely well – getting news on air almost as quickly as it happens, and sometimes while it is still happening.

During the newsflash Hinds takes care to give the accurate departure times for the trains to limit needless worry from friends or relatives. At the end he repeats the information for those who may have missed or misheard it, at the same time seizing the opportunity to promote his station's news output. Listeners are left in no doubt that if they want to catch the latest on the crash first they should stay tuned to Surrey Radio.

Now Hinds has to make sure he and his team can deliver that promise.

Headline

The story makes the lead on the headline round-up on the half-hour. A headline is usually a brief summary of the main points of the story, and is seldom longer than four lines, or 48 words. In the case of the train crash, Hinds dispenses with convention and gives a fuller version. His second headline is more typical.

> '*A train crash at Guildford this afternoon has killed three passengers and injured four others. Several more are feared trapped in the wreckage. Rescue workers are now at the scene, about a mile north of Guildford station.*
> '*Both trains were travelling on the northbound line and collided head-on. They were the London-bound 1.51 from Guildford and the 1.18 from Waterloo. The names of the casualties are not yet known. An emergency phone number has been set up for relatives to call for details. The number is 023.0000.0000. That number again . . . 023.0000.0000.*
> '*Train services between Guildford and London are suspended until the track can be cleared. More news on the rail crash as it comes in.*'
> '*The rest of the headlines now:*
> '*Plans for a 20 million pound office block in Woking have come under fire . . . Opposition councillors say Woking is already full of empty offices and the fifteen storey building would be another white elephant and unnecessary eyesore in the town centre.*' *Etc.*

Headlines (or *highlights*) are often read at the start of a major bulletin or news programme to signpost the news and encourage the audience to keep listening. They may be given again at the end to recap on the major stories, or, as in the case above, be read on the half past or quarter hour in lieu of a longer bulletin.

Copy story

This is an amplified version of the four-line headline, giving the story in more detail, but without an accompanying interview (actuality). Copy stories are usually short – about 20–30 seconds, depending on house style. Hinds' first 'headline' on the train crash was really a copy story.

Normally on a major story a voice report or interview extract would be used, but the briefer copy-only form comes into its own when:

- The story is breaking and no interview or fuller account is yet available.
- There is not enough time in the bulletin for a more detailed report.
- A fuller account or interview has already been used, and a shorter version is required to keep the story running without it sounding stale.

Voicer or voice report

Reporter Julian Alleck is driving to the scene in the radio car, with a helper, known as a gopher, to lug the equipment and set up the interviews, but there is some doubt whether he will be there in time for the three o'clock news. The other reporters are on to the police, fire brigade and South West Trains to get information and try where possible to record interviews on the telephone.

With more information coming in, Hinds is not prepared to settle for a repeat of the copy story at 3 o'clock, so he asks a reporter to draw the facts together and turn it into a voice report.

GRINDLE/OWN   19.8   14.55   TRAIN SMASH

'The death toll in the Guildford crash has now risen to four, and rescue workers believe more people could still be trapped in the wreckage of the two commuter trains. Lesley Grindle has the details . . .

> INSERT: Rail smash
> DUR: 40″
> OUT: be to blame

'Less than an hour ago the 1.18 from London smashed head-on into the delayed 1.51 Guildford to Waterloo train just outside Guildford station. Four people died in the forward carriages, including the two drivers. Nine others are known to be injured, two seriously. Rescue workers say several more are still trapped in the wreckage and they're using cutting equipment to try to get them out.

'The names of the dead have not yet been released, but the police have set up a number for relatives to call for more details. It's 023.0000.0000 – that's 023.0000.0000.

'The cause of the crash is still uncertain, but South West Trains say early indications are that points failure may be to blame.'

As soon as the voicer is recorded, it is filed to network for inclusion in the national news on the hour. Some stations take this live, from a satellite feed. Others prefer to compile and present their own bulletins using a mixture of national and local news. This is a *newsmix*. As well as offering a live news service, the network newsroom sends out component stories of the bulletin individually – cues, copy stories, interviews and voicers – where they are re-recorded by the individual stations.

Voice reports offer an explanation of a story as well as additional details, and they permit a change of voice from the newsreader. They can also offer interpretation and analysis by a specialist, such as a sports editor or financial correspondent. In this way the voice report can express an authoritative opinion which would be less appropriate coming from the mouth of a newsreader.

Voicers are either recorded or read live, and are usually made at the stage where the information has outgrown a copy story, but where no actuality is yet available. They should be well researched, balanced, authoritative, crisply written and well read. They would usually run for about 20 seconds, excluding the cue, and longer in the case of a major breaking story.

The first paragraph of the voicer is known as the *cue* or *lead-in*, to the report. Most stories that use an illustrative interview or voice report require a cue.

Above and below the cue is a set of information about the story. This is the *marking-up*. Individual stations have their own ideas about how this should be done.

What Hinds wants most of all for the bulletin is the live report from the scene, but in case this is not produced in time, the voicer above has been recorded to provide *holding* material, which can be used as a fall-back or substitute.

Holding material can take the form of a copy story, voicer or interview. Good holding material has prevented many a last minute crisis and loss of face.

Teaser or taster

It is now five seconds to three and Hinds is seated in the *newsbooth* to read his five-minute bulletin, a mixture of local and national news. As the news jingle is playing, he is hoping that one of the other interviews planned will come up trumps in time for this bulletin.

He begins with a set of teasers:

'A train crash at Guildford claims four lives . . . passengers are still trapped,'
'Inflation is on the up again,'
'Councillors are gunning for Woking's white elephant,'
'And in sport, Big Bobby quits for first division soccer.'

Urgent, present tense and brief, the teaser is an enigmatic abbreviated headline used at the start of a bulletin or news programme to act as a lure by giving a taste of the story to come and teasing the audience into listening on to find out more.

A collection of three or four teasers is called a menu. It serves the same purpose as the menu in a restaurant – to whet the appetite.

Voice report from the scene

It is now 3.02. Less than five minutes ago, the radio car pulled up as close as it could to the crash, and reporter Julian Alleck spanned the last 50 metres by running a flying lead from the car with a microphone clipped to the end to bring him even closer to the action.

Alleck's brief is to go live into the news with a minute-long report. After snatching a few words with a South West Trains official and a fire officer, Alleck contacts the newsroom on the radio car's *talkback* and says he is in position. In as few words as possible, Lesley Grindle gives him the latest information gained over the telephone, and Alleck stands by to go live. Through his headphones he can hear the station output. Hinds has begun reading the bulletin, and the voicer by Grindle on the crash is going out on air.

Thirty seconds later he can hear Hinds finishing the story he is on and beginning the cue:

'As you heard just now, four people have died, and the number of injured is now up to twelve. More passengers are still believed to be trapped in the wreckage of the two trains, which collided head-on on the northbound line just outside Guildford station. Julian Alleck is there now and describes the scene . . .'

'The picture here a mile up the line from Guildford is one of devastation. The two trains are twisted together beside the track and firemen and rescue workers are cutting open the wreckage to free any passengers who are still trapped.

'For reasons that are not yet clear, both trains were on the northbound line when they hit head-on. Their front carriages were torn from the rails by the impact, and are now lying locked together. Both drivers were killed in the crash. It's known that two passengers have also died, both on the London train, where firemen with cutting equipment are now working.

'The remaining five carriages of that train have also overturned and are on their sides, while all four coaches of the Guildford train have concertinad together in a zigzag off the track, but are, remarkably, still on their wheels.

'Ambulance crews say they've taken twelve other passengers to hospital where they're being treated for injuries, and are now standing by while rescue workers continue to cut open the wrecked carriages, to search for any others who may still be on board.

'South West Trains officials are inspecting the damage, and though they won't say for sure, early indications suggest that points failure might be to blame.

'This is Julian Alleck returning you to the studio.'

Figure 74 The radio car with its tall pump-up aerial acts like a mobile studio for sending on-the-spot reports back to the station. The idea is to keep the operation as simple as possible so that even the most non-technical of reporters can cover a breaking story without having to bring an engineer along to press the buttons. (*Andrew Boyd*)

Back at the radio station Hinds picks up from him:

> *'And we'll be interrupting normal programming to bring you more news from the scene of that*
> *rail crash just outside Guildford as the information comes in. To repeat what we said earlier,*
> *all rail services between Guildford and London are suspended until the track is cleared.*
> *'Meanwhile, in the rest of the news . . .' Hinds continues the bulletin.*

Alleck's voice report, hastily set up with precious little time for preparation, concentrated on describing the scene for the listener. He has placed himself close enough to the action to pick up the sounds of the rescue operation, yet not so close as to interfere with the work of rescuers. His live report has stimulated the imagination by adding colour and description to the more factual studio voicer that was broadcast earlier in the bulletin.

On-the-spot reports can be made by mobile phone, radio telephone, regular phone, radio car or by a special studio quality line called a circuit.

The voicer from the scene gives more opportunity for descriptive, accurate and up-to-the-minute reports than is possible with a studio voicer. Given time, Alleck would have liked to include live or pre-recorded actuality, such as an interview with a survivor or rescue worker. His next task will be to gather more facts and get hold of the chief fire officer or a spokesperson for South West Trains. He could either interview them live, or record interviews to be played into his live report.

The main difficulty with location interviews is that it might not be possible to edit them, so there is little leeway for mistakes. Increasingly, journalists are going out into the field with notebook computers with sound-editing facilities. This allows them to edit on location and file the story by e-mail. Alleck's computer is informing him the programme has performed an illegal operation and politely inquires if that is OK? He barely restrains himself from hurling it onto the railway line.

He ended his report by handing back to the studio. Another common way to wrap up is to give a *standard outcue* (*payoff*) like this: *'Julian Alleck, Surrey Radio, at the scene of the rail crash, Guildford.'* The standard outcue (SOC) is more than simply a neat way to round off a report, it promotes the fact that the radio station has a reporter at the scene and heightens the impression of the station's news power.

In this case, the newsreader, Hinds, follows the live report with a *back announcement* (back anno). This is a further piece of signposting and promotion, letting the audience know that if they stay tuned they will hear more on the story.

If Alleck had had more time to take in the situation, Hinds could have conducted a *Q & A* (question and answer) session with him, interviewing him live about the story to get more details. To make sure he is not caught out by a question for which he does not have the answer, the reporter will usually provide the list of questions for the presenter to ask. This helps the flow without detracting from the impression of spontaneity.

Interview

Radio stations frequently interrupt their schedules to provide on-the-spot coverage of major breaking news, and Alleck is asked to give his next live report as soon as he has enough information.

By 3.15 his gopher, a student who is getting work experience in the newsroom and hoping to break into radio, has come up with a witness to the crash. The woman was out walking her dog along a footpath less than 300 metres from the collision. She is shaken, but seems almost relieved to be interviewed and unburden herself of the things she has seen.

Alleck weighs up whether she is too unsteady to be interviewed live, but she is intelligent and articulate, and he thinks with careful handling she will cope. He decides to take a chance. Raising the studio on the radio car's talkback he tells the producer of the afternoon programme to stand by. He bangs out a cue on his notebook PC and sends it back to the newsroom computer via the digital phone which is hooked to his modem. As soon as it is printed, the producer tells him to stand by to go live, and moments later, the presenter is reading the cue for his second report.

> *'More news on the Guildford train crash now. If you've been listening in, you'll know that two trains collided just outside Guildford station on the London line, killing four passengers and injuring others.*
>
> *'Our reporter Julian Alleck is at the trackside, and he's been joined by Mrs Petra Cavanagh from Guildford, who saw the crash when she was out walking her dog near the railway line . . .'*

J.A. *'Mrs Cavanagh, can you describe what happened?'*

Mrs C. *'Yes (County accent), I was walking Lucy, my Dalmatian, along the footpath, quite close to the track really, when I saw the London train coming, some way in the distance. At the same time I could hear another train behind me. I didn't think anything of it because the railway line has two tracks at this point, and . . . and one just assumes, of course, that the trains are on different lines.*

'Then the northbound train passed where I was standing and gave a terrific blast on its hooter; then there was a frantic squealing of brakes and I . . . I suppose I realized then, just . . . before they hit, that they were both on the same line. It was really quite appalling. One could do nothing to stop it.'

J.A. *'What happened when they collided?'*

Mrs C. *'Well, you understand, I . . . could only see the back of the Guildford train, but there was a simply dreadful noise, like a . . . like a shotgun going off by one's ear, then the train seemed to lift for a moment, and, very slowly it seemed, the carriages began to come off the track, one to the left and one to the right, until they came to rest. One was just rooted to the spot. I mean, one couldn't believe one's eyes.'*

J.A. *'What did you do next?'*

Mrs C. *'Well, I . . . I suppose one should have run to the nearest house and called for an ambulance, but, er, the extraordinary thing . . . that, er, that didn't enter my mind. I ran to the train, and when I got there I realized how much more badly damaged the other train . . . er, the southbound train, that is . . . was, if you follow me.'*

J.A. *'Can you describe what you saw?'*

Mrs C. *'It was really rather too horrible. The, er, the two front coaches were crushed together, very badly; I pity anyone who was inside. The other coaches were on their sides. From farther back passengers were opening the doors and starting to clamber out. The side of the train had become the roof, as it were. They were having to jump down on to the track from quite a height. Some of them were quite badly hurt. It's a wonder nobody was electrocuted.*

'I must confess, I'd been standing there feeling quite sick, and when the people started to come out, I remembered myself, tied Lucy up so she wouldn't wander on to the track, and set to helping the people down.'

J.A. *'How long was it before the ambulances arrived?'*

Mrs C. *'I really can't say. We were all so busy just helping people out. Others had come by then, from the homes nearby, and I sent one of them back to fetch blankets and another to get some ladders. I can't say I noticed the ambulances arrive.'*

J.A. *'Thank you. Mrs Petra Cavanagh who organized the rescue from the trains until the emergency services could arrive.*

'The death toll from the crash currently stands at four, but amazingly, only 12 people seem to have been seriously injured. If the same accident had happened in the evening rush hour when those carriages were more densely packed, the figures could have been far worse.

'As I speak, rescue workers are checking the wreckage of the forward coaches to see if anyone is still trapped. It looks as though the line will be out of action for quite some time.

'This is Julian Alleck at the scene of the train crash in Guildford.'

'Thank you Julian. And we'll be going back to the scene of that crash, I'm sure, later in the programme.'

Julian's next live report comes at twenty to four. By then two more passengers have been freed from the wreckage, both seriously injured, and rescue workers are satisfied no one else is trapped. Work is going on to clear the line.

The newsroom contacts Alleck to tell him the South West Trains press office in London is now investigating the possibility that a points failure was to blame for routing the southbound train on to the northbound line. But at this stage, SWT will not be interviewed about it. The news editor wants Alleck to get hold of a rail official at the scene and put the question to him live. This Alleck does, but the official is, understandably, not very forthcoming.

The interview adds more depth, permits a further exploration of a story and gives an opportunity for informed comment. Standard radio news interviews vary in length depending on house style. Between 90 seconds and about three minutes is almost standard, though those on extended news programmes may run a little longer. Live interviews, which are seldom as concise as edited ones, may also be longer.

Newsclip

The most newsworthy quote from an interview is usually edited from it to provide a short illustration to go with the story in a later bulletin. This would be about the same length as a voicer – some 20 seconds – and is known as a *clip, cut* or *insert*. Clip or cut because it is an extract cut from an interview, and insert, because it is inserted into the bulletin. The cue will give the facts of the story, and the insert will develop them with explanation or comment.

Surrey Radio's 4 o'clock news is due on air shortly, and Hinds, ever eager to keep one jump ahead of the opposition, is extending the bulletin to make way for another full report from the scene.

Alleck's report will incorporate clips from the interviews with the witness and railway official. These are being edited by journalists in the newsroom from recordings of the two live interviews. These are known as *ROTs* (recording of/off transmission). The edited clips will be played in from the studio.

In addition, Alleck is asked to do a short live interview with a rescue worker. The report is complicated by playing in items from two separate locations and the timing is crucial.

Package

The 4 o'clock programme begins with a menu headed by the following teaser:

'The Guildford train crash ... Four die, 12 are injured ... South West Trains say points failure is to blame ... a witness describes the crash ...'

After the rest of the menu, Hinds begins the lead story:

'South West Trains say a points failure may be to blame for the train crash outside Guildford this afternoon which killed four and injured 14 others. Four people were trapped in the wreckage and had to be freed by firemen with cutting equipment.

'The 1.18 from Waterloo collided head-on with the London-bound 12.55 from Portsmouth Harbour minutes after it left Guildford station. Both trains had been routed on to the same line.

'For the past hour and a half rescue teams have been working to free passengers trapped in the wreckage and efforts are now being made to clear the line. Our reporter Julian Alleck is at the scene of the crash . . .'

(Live)

'The combined speed of the two trains was thought to be in excess of 70 miles an hour. The impact twisted together the front carriages of each, killing the drivers instantly. Firemen with cutting tools are still trying to separate the trains. In all, six passengers were trapped in the front compartment of the London train. Two were killed in the crash and the other four were pulled out injured, but alive.

'Mrs Petra Cavanagh from Guildford saw the crash happen:'

(Recorded)

'The northbound train passed where I was standing and gave a terrific blast on its hooter; there was a frantic squealing of brakes and I . . . It was really quite appalling. One could do nothing to stop it. There was a simply dreadful noise, like a shotgun going off by one's ear, then the train seemed to lift for a moment, and, very slowly it seemed, the carriages began to come off the track, one to the left and one to the right, until they came to rest. One was just rooted to the spot. I mean, one couldn't believe one's eyes.

'It was really rather too horrible. The two front coaches were crushed together, very badly; I pity anyone who was inside. The other coaches were on their sides. From farther back passengers were opening the doors and starting to clamber out. The side of the train had become the roof, as it were. They were having to jump down on to the track from quite a height. Some of them were quite badly hurt. It's a wonder nobody was electrocuted.'

(Live)

'In charge of the rescue operation was chief fire officer Tony Stims, who's with me now. Tony, how badly injured were the trapped passengers?'

'Several of them were quite seriously hurt. Lucky to be alive I would say. I'm surprised only two passengers died in the impact and more weren't badly injured.'

'Was it a difficult operation, freeing them?'

'More delicate than difficult, OK, obviously we had to take a lot of care with the cutters that we didn't injure anyone further.'

'You're trying to separate the trains now and clear the track. How do you plan to do that?'

'Well, we've had lifting gear standing by for the past 40 minutes, but we couldn't use it until we were sure everybody was out of the train. The first thing we want to do his haul them off the track, so the railway boys can get the trains running again.'

'How long will that take?'

'Half an hour. Maybe more, maybe less. Difficult to say.'

'Thank you. Chief fire officer Tony Stims. South West Trains are launching an inquiry into this accident, but say their first indications are that points failure may be to blame. This was confirmed earlier by their spokesman here at the scene, John Turbot:'

(Recorded)

'Obviously we're investigating; it could only really be points failure, beyond that I can't say at this stage.'

'You mean a faulty points operation directed the London train on to the wrong track?'

Figure 75 In the mixing studio interviews, sound effects, links and music can be combined to produce a professional package. Even in the digital age, tape decks linger. (*Andrew Boyd*)

'It's still too soon to be sure but that appears to be correct, yes.'

'How could that happen?'

'Well that's what we've got to find out. It's really a matter for an inquiry and for Railtrack to determine.'

'Do you suspect an equipment failure or an operator error?'

'I'm sorry but as I've already said, that's a matter for an inquiry.'

'Has the problem now been rectified?'

'Yes.'

'Then you must know what caused it.'

'We've got a good idea, yes, but as I told you, it's for the inquiry to make the final decision.'

'Four people have lost their lives this afternoon. If you're planning to open the line again today, what assurances can you give commuters that the problem had been solved and won't happen again?'

'Well let me correct you. We intend to get the trains running but on adjacent tracks which were not damaged in the accident.'

(Live)

'South West Trains spokesman John Turbot. Services between Guildford and London are expected to resume within the next hour.

'This is Julian Alleck, Surrey Radio, at the scene of the Guildford train crash.'

(Back in the studio)

'And a phone line has opened for anyone who may have had a friend or relative on either of those trains. It is . . . etc.'

As soon as the bulletin is over, Alleck checks on the talkback that the package was successfully recorded back at the station, then files again his last paragraph substituting a network outcue for the Surrey Radio tag. The station will switch the outcues and then send the package via a circuit to the network newsroom. It will be Surrey Radio's fourth item on the crash to be sent 'down the line'. Alleck has given the train's correct origin as Portsmouth Harbour to broaden the information for a wider audience.

From its London base, the network newsroom will send the item back by satellite for distribution to the other local stations in the network.

Alleck's piece with its three inserts is more sophisticated than the basic package, which usually comprises a cue and a couple of short interviews. These are wrapped up in the reporter's own words, which are grouped before the first interview, between the interviews and usually after the last interview. These are known as *links*.

Packaging is useful for presenting a balanced account of two sides of an argument and for permitting the use of more elaborate production techniques to include sound effects or music.

Unlike the standard interview, where the focus is on the interviewee, the package sets up the reporter as raconteur and guide. The cue presents an overview of the story and the reporter's first link adds flesh to that and provides an introduction to the first interviewee.

The middle link allows the reporter to summarize any important points that have been left out, and to tie what has just been said to the second interview, which he then introduces.

The final link is used for summing up the two arguments, adding important details, and pointing the way forward for the story, in this case by referring to the time it will take to restore train services.

A strength of the package is that you can use extracts of interviews that have been boiled down to their essential information. Contrast the edited interview with Mrs Cavanagh with the original live version with her. The edits have been made to focus on the description of the collision and to eliminate unnecessary information and verbal tics.

Mini-wrap

While Alleck is filing his report, the network intake editor is on to the newsroom asking for an update on the story. He wants a shorter version for the bulletin, preferably wrapped (packaged) and with a maximum duration of 30 seconds, which coming from network with its appetite for news fast and furious, is quite a concession.

No sooner has Alleck finished filing his package than reporter Phil Needle is on the talkback passing on the network's request.

Alleck decides to give it the full treatment, and solicits the help of Needle to further edit down the interview clips to cram something of all three into the report. In vain, Needle protests about squeezing quarts into pint pots, but Alleck will have nothing of it.

Ten minutes later Needle is on the talkback again offering 50 seconds, and Alleck sends him away with a flea in his ear. After two more hatchet attempts, they manage between them to concoct the following report:

ALLECK/OWN   19.8   16.38   CRASH/NETWORK U.D.

'South West Trains say points failure may have been to blame for this afternoon's rail crash outside Guildford which claimed four lives and injured twelve.
    'This report from Julian Alleck at the scene of the crash . . .'

> TITLE: CRASH/NETWORK UD
> IN: 'The crash happened . . .'
> OUT: SOC
> DUR: 30″

'The crash happened after the Waterloo train was accidentally routed on to the same line as the train from Portsmouth Harbour. Mrs Petra Cavanagh saw it happen . . .'
    'There was a frantic squealing of brakes and a simply dreadful noise. The two front coaches were crushed together; I pity anyone inside.'
'Six passengers were trapped and had to be cut free, but two were already dead. Chief fire officer Tony Stims was in charge of the rescue:'
    'Several were quite seriously hurt. Lucky to be alive. I'm surprised only two died in the impact.'
'South West Trains are investigating. Their spokesman John Turbot:'
    'It could only really be points failure, but it's for the inquiry to make the final decision.'
'This is Julian Alleck, Network Radio, at the Guildford train crash.'

All reference to the track being cleared has deliberately been left out, as the position by 5 o'clock could well be different. Up-to-date facts can be added nearer the time and included in the form of a back announcement.

The wrap works out at nearer 35 seconds to 30, and to boil it down that far has required some 'creative' editing to cut the actuality while still making sense of the narrative. A further two seconds have been shaved off by digitally speeding it up. Any more and Mrs Cavanagh will sound like she's on narcotics.

The piece is already slightly breathless and disjointed, and with time creeping up towards the bulletin, they decide to call it a day and give the duration as 30 seconds, hoping nobody in network notices the deception.

Sometimes reporters can be too clever with mini-wraps, and when Needle plays the edited version down the talkback Alleck is forced to concede that perhaps it does sound a little garbled in places. But his satisfaction at having crammed three pieces of actuality into 30 seconds (or so) overrules his other sensibilities, and anyway, there's no time now to mess around with a remake.

Meanwhile, back in the newsroom, Hinds has just listened to a recording of the opposition 4.30 bulletin and is having convulsions. They have got actuality with one of the survivors from the hospital, and his own staff reporter, Lesley Grindle, whom he had sent there to do the same has just rung in to say she is terribly sorry, but she has forgotten to take out a minidisc with her recorder. After some choice remarks, Hinds slams down the phone and, clutching his head, finds some consolation in the thought that Alleck at least has done a decent day's work.

In the corner another phone is ringing. It is the network intake editor. His tone is sarcastic. *'About that mini-wrap. Great,* **if you can follow it**. *Any chance of a remake? And could you cut it down a bit?'*

Out on the railway line at Guildford, somebody's ears are burning . . .

> *'You can be working on three or four major stories a day with little research backup. You go in and you do your three and a half minute interview, pick out your 20 seconds of actuality, do a voice piece, and at the end of the day you've got to say well, actually, I've just skimmed over a number of issues.'*
> – PARLIAMENTARY CORRESPONDENT RICHARD BESTIC

Fieldwork

1 Open a file for each type of story treatment. Then listen to a news bulletin that uses illustrations and actuality clips and list the story treatment given to each item (*headline, copy, story, teaser,* etc).

   Then do the same with an extended news programme. Make notes on stories that fit the various categories and see if you can pick up tips about technique or learn anything about the pitfalls. Keep listening until every category is covered.

2 Go back to Alleck's live interview with Mrs Cavanagh. Without looking at the edited version, show how you would cut it to reduce it to a 35 second newsclip. Print out the quotes you would leave in.

   What good material do you feel you have had to cut out to get it down to length?
   Now do the same with the Turbot interview.

3 Take a news story from a newspaper and produce from it a *teaser, headline, copy story* and *voicer.*

   If you are in a class, all work on the same story and then compare your different versions. Have you all agreed about what to leave in and what to take out? Discuss your differences and see if you can come to some agreement.

4 Now take a newspaper story which quotes two sides of an argument and write it up as though you were doing the script for a package. Include cues and links, and extracts from the interviews. Keep the whole package down to 2 minutes 30 seconds (at 3 words per second).

   Now cut the package to 1 minute 30 seconds.
   Do you find it difficult working out what to leave out?
   Now turn it into a mini-wrap of just 30 seconds (90 words).
   What do you think of mini-wraps? Do you find them slick and professional or do you think they can sometimes be too clever? Why? Do they tell you more or less than you would find out from a voicer or newsclip?

5 *'Editing distorts what people say by focusing in on only what the journalist wants them to say. To be fair, people's comments should not be edited.'* Discuss.

   How can you avoid distorting what someone says when you edit their interview?

THE EQUIPMENT

20   Recording

The recording business has come a long way since 1898 when Valdemar Poulsen first captured sound on piano wire fixed to a hand-turned drum. Today, digital recordings of sparkling quality can be made and edited directly on computers of all shapes and sizes, be they dressed up as camcorders, minidisc machines or solid-state recorders.

Miniaturization has made it possible for today's reporters to move unhampered to the forefront of breaking stories and send back live, studio-quality reports via satellite link or mobile phone to be played straight to air or to a web site.

Computer editing packages allow you to access your recordings at any point, doing away with the need to spool recordings back and forth to find the part you want to edit. You can trim recordings to within thousandths of a second, time them automatically, speed them up or slow them down digitally, sweeten them by adding bass or treble, and even loop them to run endlessly, which is especially useful for sound effects. News actuality cuts can be stored directly in the station computer to be played on air at the touch of a button. Welcome to the future, today! But before we get carried away, let's get back to basics.

Principles of recording

Sound

Sound is created by vibrations in the air. The faster the air vibrates, the higher the sound will seem to the hearer. The speed of these vibrations is known as their *frequency*, and frequencies are measured in *hertz*. One thousand hertz is a *kilohertz*. Human speech spans a range between around 50 Hz to 6 kHz. The deeper the voice, the lower the frequency. The human ear can hear sounds from about 16 Hz to 18 kHz.

As well as being high or low, sounds are loud or quiet. Their loudness, or *sound pressure level* (SPL) is measured in decibels (dB). The higher the number of decibels, the louder the sound. Speech rises to about 70 dB. A gunshot would approach 130 db and would cross the listener's threshold of pain.

How recordings are made

Microphones convert sound into an electrical signal that varies in relation to the sounds picked up by the mike. The signal is then boosted by an amplifier and passed to the recorder.

Digital recording does not suffer from the hiss and distortion inherent in older analogue tape recorders. You no longer hear the tape, just the signal.

That signal is converted into pulses of binary code. Once encoded, the original sound is locked in and cannot deteriorate, even after playing many times. Unlike a conventional (*analogue*) recording, this code cannot become corrupted by hiss, hash, distortion or wow and flutter (alterations in tape speed).

On playback, the binary code is decoded and turned back into a signal. As long as the code can be read the playback will be as close to the original as the hi-fi will allow. Digital techniques mean the machinery, and not the recording medium, has become the limiting factor in the quest for audio perfection. Copy after copy can be made without any significant loss in quality.

Digital recordings can be stored on computer, compact disc or tape. Computers can hold a radio station's entire playlist of music or many hours of programming. Audio can be edited on computer and items programmed to be played on air in any order.

Types of microphones

There are three main types of microphones: *ribbon*, *moving coil* and *capacitor*.

The ribbon type, which is one of the most expensive, has a *diaphragm* of thin aluminium foil that is vibrated by the sounds around it like your eardrum. It moves within a magnetic field to create a signal.

The moving coil, or *dynamic* type, has a wire coil attached to a diaphragm that also vibrates in a magnetic field.

In the *capacitor*, or *condenser* type of microphone, the diaphragm is replaced with the plate of an electrically charged capacitor. These microphones require an electric current, supplied by a battery or the recorder itself.

Ribbon mikes are *bi-directional*. They respond in a figure of eight, picking up voices on both sides. They are often used to record studio interviews or discussions and are placed on a stand or suspended from the ceiling. Most varieties cannot be used out of doors, as any wind will blow against the ribbon creating a whooshing noise.

A specialized version of ribbon mike is the *lip mike* used by commentators. These respond to nearby sounds only and are held against the mouth.

There are two types of moving coil microphone. Some pick up sounds all round. These are *omni-directional*. Others pick up from in front of the microphone only. These are *uni-directional*. Their pick-up pattern is described as *cardioid* (heart shaped).

Radio reporters use hand-held microphones of either type. Some mikes are unsuitable because they pick up movements made by the hand. This *handling noise* is kept to a minimum in broadcast-standard mikes.

Stand-mounted uni-directional microphones are usually favoured by newsreaders.

Capacitor mikes vary in their response pattern. These are commonly used in television clipped to a tie or lapel.

By using two tie-clip mikes with a stereo recorder you can avoid having to wave a microphone under your subject's nose. This is useful for longer interviews or where the interviewee needs to be put at ease.

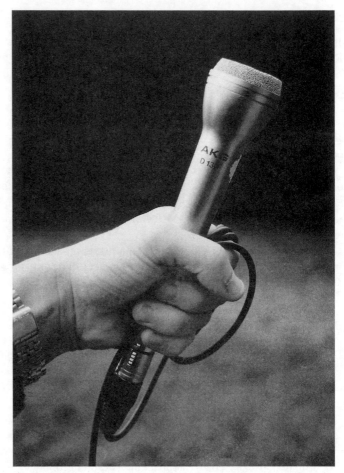

Figure 76 Where all it all begins – with the microphone. Take up the excess slack on the cable without tugging at the connection into the mike or into the recorder. Hold the mike firmly but lightly. Keeping your fingers still, tilt the mike towards whoever is speaking. (*Andrew Boyd*)

Using portable sound recorders

Digital recorders

Digital recorders transcend old-fashioned analogue tape machines in three important ways: they are smaller, the sound quality is better and they are also generally cheaper. It is possible to make CD-quality recordings on hardware that is a fraction of the price and the size of the excellent, but now-outmoded BBC workhorse, the UHER portable reel-to-reel machine.

Technology is making strides, and there are a number of competing ways of storing digital recordings, but the recorders most commonly used are of the DAT, MiniDisc or solid-state variety.

DAT

Digital audiocassettes are little larger than a postage stamp, yet allow up to two hours recording time – double, if you can put up with some loss of sound quality.

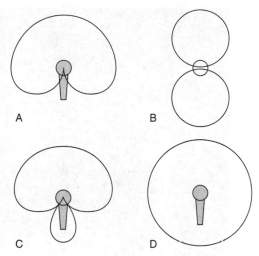

Figure 77 Microphones are sensitive to sounds coming from a specific area around them. This is known as their directivity pattern, which varies according to mike type:

A Cardiod
B Figure of eight (top view)
C Hyper-cardiod
D Omni-directional

Ribbon mikes with their figure-of-eight pattern are used for interviews conducted at a table either side of the mike. Omni-directional mikes suffer the least from handling noise, but because they pick up all round they can draw in unwanted background sounds.

Perfect copies can be made of each recording, so there is little appreciable drop in tone when tapes are dubbed for editing and then re-recorded. Most of the brightness and clarity of the original remains.

Analogue mike signals are converted into digital data streams and the signal is recorded onto the tape as digital code.

Each recording can be identified thanks to a separate track that adds inaudible subcodes. This makes it possible for the machine to skip from track to track to search out the band that you want to play. But the tape still has to be shuttled to and fro, so search times are not as fast as with a MiniDisc system or computer. Date and time can also be recorded.

Sony's TCD-D8 machine runs off standard batteries and weighs a mere 280 grams. Beefier variations on the DAT theme have been devised especially for radio stations with heftier budgets to spend on equipment. But there's a premium to pay for more durable microphone connectors. A professional DAT recorder costs three times the price of a domestic model.

MiniDisc

Sony broke new ground with the introduction of a miniature CD recorder, known as the MiniDisc. A single magneto-optical disc just 64-mm in diameter can carry 148 minutes of mono recording. This has been made possible by a compression system that cuts out sounds supposedly undetectable to the human ear.

Like CDs, MiniDiscs allow instant access to different tracks, and Sony have also managed to incorporate basic editing functions.

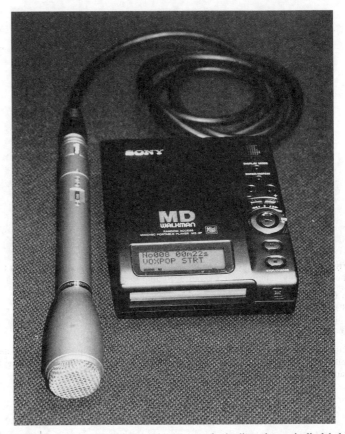

Figure 78 The MiniDisc recorder. You can store hours on a single disc, electronically label the recording, even carry out basic editing. All in a package small enough to lose down a drain. (*Andrew Boyd*)

Some thrifty radio stations have latched on to this and are even using MiniDiscs as inexpensive digital *cart* machines. These are machines which store actuality clips that are cued-up ready to be played on air to illustrate a news bulletin.

The MiniDisc system has been made shockproof by storing several seconds of recording in RAM memory. As a result the recorder can be thrown around without skipping or jarring. And it's claimed that discs can make up to a million recordings without any noticeable loss of quality.

One supplier to broadcasters has developed a sturdy case for this domestic machine with tough microphone connectors and a bigger battery to stand up to the rigours of day-to-day journalism.

Solid-state

Portable recorders are going the way of laptop computers, using microchip memory built into cards no bigger than a stick of gum or the sort you would use at a cashpoint machine.

The Nagra ARES-C can compress some two hours of mono audio onto a single computer PCMCIA card. An LCD screen allows you to edit in the field, saving valuable studio time, and a special interface permits reports to be transmitted directly to air in studio quality along a special digital phoneline.

A computer hook-up also allows text to be recorded into the memory so the cue and story details can be transmitted along with the audio back to the radio station.

Solid-state means no moving parts to wear out, no motors to add weight and no tape to deteriorate. Flash cards can be re-recorded up to 100 000 times. The trade-off for this sophistication is that the audio compression necessary to squeeze the recording into the memory reduces the sound quality.

Before the interview

The way you hold a microphone, even the way you sit or stand to conduct an interview, can have a crucial effect on the quality of your final recording. As can the background noise and ambience of your surroundings.

Setting up the room

Not all rooms are ideal for interviewing. Bare walls and wooden surfaces can produce a 'bathroom' effect. This can sound worse on tape than it did to you at the time, because the brain compensates for its surroundings. If the room is likely to echo, ask to do the interview somewhere else.

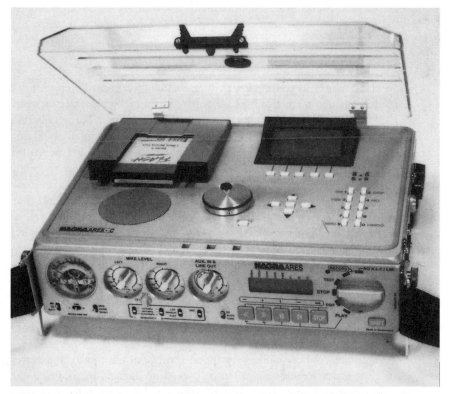

Figure 79 Getting more advanced – the solid-state recorder. This marvel from Nagra uses credit card-sized flash memory to store recordings. Interviews can be edited on the machine and downloaded directly onto a computer. No more moving parts. (*Courtesy Kudelski*)

Failing that, if you close the curtains and both stand to do the interview facing into them, that can help dampen down reflected sound.

If there are no curtains, standing and facing a corner of the room will cut the echo a little, and close mike operation will help some more. You could even drape coats over the backs of chairs to provide a screen to help to dampen reverberations.

Never record across a table. You will have to stretch too far with the microphone and risk one of you being off-mike; the polished surface will reflect sound back in the form of echo, and if your recorder is on the table the mike could pick up the noise of its motors. Perhaps just as important is the fact that if you are stretched out in supplication across your subject's executive desk you can hardly be seen to be in control of the interview! You will need to winkle your high-powered interviewee out from behind her desk and sit next to her.

Dealing with distractions

If there is a phone in the room, ask if it can be taken off the hook to prevent it ringing, and if there is noisy air conditioning, find out if that can be turned off during the interview.

The mike is more conscious of distracting noises than you will be. While you are concentrating on your interview, the mike will be getting on with its job, which is to pick up any sounds in the room.

If your interviewee has beads that rattle or a coat that rustles, ask her to take them off. The same goes for papers that flap or a clipboard that gets between the person and the mike. Few interviewees ever complain about being asked to disrobe (within reason!) if they are politely but clearly told why. Make a joke of it if it helps.

Lining up the victim

Next, arrange both you and your victim in a sensible recording position. One problem with the hand-held mike is that the user needs to invade the other person's physical space to get a decent signal. In body language terms, this invasion of space only takes place normally when people are fighting or being intimate, so expect some natural apprehension on the part of the interviewee and to feel uncomfortable yourself at first. At this point, plenty of confidence, a little charm, a ready smile, well-brushed teeth and a good deodorant are the reporter's most valuable assets.

A comfortable distance for normal conversation is with faces more than a metre apart. To record an interview without having to keep moving your mike arm, you will have to shorten that gap to half a metre or less. Arrange your chairs in an 'L' shaped pattern, so when you sit down your knees are almost touching. Other than standing up to conduct the interview, this is the most effective arrangement for the use of a hand-held microphone.

Mike handling

Seemingly inexplicable clicks and bumps on a recording can often be traced to handling noise from the microphone.

Hand-held mikes should be gripped firmly but not tightly and fingers should be kept still, as any movement can often be picked up as handling noise.

If you have a ring on your microphone hand, remove it before the interview, as mikes are particularly susceptible to the small scraping sounds that a ring might make. Also remove any bracelets.

Figure 80 Nostalgic about tape-hiss? Dismissive about all things digital? The good old cassette recorder to the rescue. The Marantz was, and still is, used in many newsrooms. (*Andrew Boyd*)

Take up any excess slack in the mike cable by looping it around your hand. This prevents loose cable bumping against the floor or furniture, which can cause clicks.

It is important *not* to stretch the cable so tightly that you tug at the connection into the recorder or the point where the cable enters the mike. These two electrical connections form the weakest part of the cable. It is easy to cause an electrical click on the recording or damage the connection by pulling at the lead.

Reporters' microphones typically work most effectively about 25 cm from the mouth. Don't worry, you don't have to lug a ruler around with you. If you spread your fingers and place your thumb on your lips, then the mike should be held just beyond your little finger. But mikes vary, and the only sure way to get the best performance is to experiment.

Beware of stuffing the microphone under the interviewee's nose. If it is that close she is likely to go cross-eyed, and an out of focus microphone windshield looks remarkably like a balled fist and has about the same effect on composure. Tuck the mike under her chin and out of direct line of vision.

The level check

Next, you need to take your levels. Make sure you are both sitting as you will be during the interview and that your interviewee is comfortable. Now check you are holding the mike at an equal distance between yourself and your interviewee, unless one of you has a louder voice. If so, you will need to move the mike until the levels are balanced.

Then get both your voices on tape. Ask your interviewee something about herself which is irrelevant to the interview to help her relax, like where is she going on her holiday, what does she think of the weather, or does she have any hobbies? Avoid stock questions like: *'What did you have for breakfast?'* An experienced interviewee will be bored stiff with that one.

Once you have taken the sound check and adjusted the levels make sure you listen back to it. A flickering meter is not always proof that a recording is being made. Then log the recording. This is a simple precaution in case it gets lost, mislaid or confused with another. Give the name of the interviewee and the time and date: *'Interview with John Smith, April Fool's Day, Whenever.'*

Having set your levels you shouldn't need to adjust them any more on your recorder. Instead, compensate for small changes in volume by moving your mike. This takes practice and it can help to wear discreet headphones while you are recording so you can monitor the sound.

If your interviewee leans backwards or forwards, feel free to break off the interview and politely explain that she must sit as she was when the level check was made, or volunteer to retake the level with her sitting in her new position. Never nod instructions or gesticulate at interviewees, it only confuses and worries them. Stop and explain the problem (unless you are live!).

Automatic level control versus manual

But why bother with level checks at all? Most recorders will set them for you automatically. It works like this: recordings made at too high a level (volume) can distort. Automatic systems keep signals below distortion point, and when they fall too low they cut in and boost the signal upwards.

Figure 81 Known as Dave, this machine has found its way into most newsrooms. It's used to record the newsfeeds from the network so actuality can be played on air. (*Andrew Boyd*)

Adjusting the recording levels manually gives you more control and creative freedom. You can use your professional judgement to choose settings to perfectly match different circumstances, instead of passing control to the machine, whose systems were designed to cope with ideal conditions.

Another drawback to some ALC systems is the problem of surge, or *pumping*, which can happen when there is a pause in speech and the ALC hunts for sound to boost the levels. If there is a lot of background noise, such as traffic, or clattering in a noisy canteen, the ALC will surge this forward whenever the person speaking into the microphone pauses for more than a moment.

Sometimes it is also possible to hear an ALC system stepping in to hold back the volume of a recording, because the level will dip momentarily.

None of these problems can occur with a manual recording that is correctly monitored, but having to monitor levels means your attention is divided between the recorder and your interviewee. Using ALC means you can save your concentration for the most critical element of the interview – the questions. If you must use ALC do so under perfectly quiet conditions. A better solution is to set the levels manually and monitor them by listening on headphones.

Maintain eye contact

While the recording is under way, don't keep glancing at the recorder or your notebook; this can be disconcerting for your subject and can break the rapport you have established.

A video of journalism students recording an interview revealed how little real communication there was once the all-important eye contact had been broken. One

Figure 82   A step up from Dave is Cool Edit Pro which will record and edit multi-track packages on a standard multi-media PC. Who needs a studio? (*Andrew Boyd*)

student divided his time between looking at the recorder, fiddling with the levels and trying to read his spidery hand-written questions. As soon as he looked away, his interviewee's eyes also wandered and before long the interview had drifted off the track as concentration was broken.

And finally . . .

After the interview, always remember to check the recording has come out before leaving your interviewee. A quick retake there and then can save a lot of embarrassing explanations later. Then, remove the recording and put a sticky label on it with your name, the date and the subject.

Fieldwork

1 Which kind of mike would you use for the following situations: reading the news; street interviews; interviewing one person in a talks studio; interviewing three people in a talks studio, or an in-depth interview in someone's home?

2 Practise using your portable recorder in different circumstances on manual and on automatic level control. Listen back and describe the differences.

3 Now use the portable first in a room with soft furnishings, such as a living room, and then in one without and compare the results. Have you picked up more echo from the unfurnished room?

   If there are curtains in that room, draw them and make your recording speaking into them. Does it make a difference?

4 Find a willing partner and practise your microphone technique. Move gradually towards your partner into your normal interviewing position and ask him or her to tell you exactly when you begin to get too close for normal comfort. Did you also start to feel uncomfortable at that point? Practise your technique and ask your partner to suggest ways you could make this invasion of privacy less intimidating.

   Then decide on a subject to interview your partner about and ask him or her to play the part of the inexperienced and awkward interviewee, by shuffling, moving around and coughing, etc. For your part, attempt to keep control in as pleasant a way as possible. Then, without comment, swap round and repeat the exercise.

   Discuss what you learnt and advise one another on how you could have best dealt with that situation. Did you keep up the eye contact?

5 If you can get your hands on a computer editing system, have a go.

   How intuitive is it? How fast can you edit? How would you go about mixing sounds together?

   Which would you rather use, a computer editing system or an analogue set-up using reel-to-reel tape? What are the advantages and disadvantages of each?

THE EQUIPMENT

21 Editing

> 'An editor should have a pimp for a brother so he'd have someone to look up to.'
> – GENE FOWLER

Few raw interviews appear on air without some form of editing – live interviews are the obvious exception. But where an interview has been pre-recorded, and time permits, the reporter will usually want to tighten it up and trim it to the required length.

Just as important is editing out irrelevant questions and statements to throw into focus comments that are newsworthy. You may also want to alter the sequence of questions and answers to point up a strong angle that emerged during the interview.

Finally, recordings are usually fine-edited to give them polish by removing hesitation, repetition and intrusive background noise, such as a passing lorry or a ringing phone.

Editing has four main functions:

- To reduce length;
- Remove unwanted material;
- Alter the sequence of recorded material;
- Permit creative treatment.

If your brief is to get a three-minute interview with a Maori leader about his claim to land rights and you return with seven minutes, then, unless the material is stunningly good, four minutes will just have to go.

The best part of the interview might be at the beginning, so the last four minutes can be chopped.

Or the best parts could be the answers to the first, third, fifth and seventh questions, so the others will need to be edited out.

On second thoughts, those answers might sound better in a different order, so the unwanted sections should be cut out and the rest edited into a different sequence.

Lastly, you may want to add a creative touch by beginning the item with a piece of Maori tribal music. This will have to be blended in afterwards to fade under the opening words of the tribesman. This is known as a *cross-fade*.

'You can't see the join'

The principle of editing is simple, but the practice takes longer to master. The art is to leave the finished recording sounding completely natural. A good edit should be like a good wig. The join should be invisible.

The first rule of editing is that the finished product must make sense. Hacking sentences in half and joining non-sequiturs is not so much editing as butchering.

Second, the editing must be in sympathy with the subject's speech patterns. A good edit will never leave the voice dangling on a rising note, as the sentence will sound unfinished and unnatural. Instead the edit should be made during a pause and following a natural downturn in the voice. Commas, full stops, and other punctuation points form natural pauses and are usually the best places to make the cut.

Where exactly the edit is made within that pause is also important. The pause will end with an intake of breath before the next sentence. The edit should be made *after* that breath, but in the split-second before the speaker starts to utter the next word.

That breath will then sound as though it belongs to the word after the edit. You won't be able to hear the join.

Obviously the final word on the recording should not be followed by a pause and a breath, as this would sound as though the speaker had been cut off in full flow!

The following shows how a reporter would edit a section to produce a clip for a news bulletin. The words in capitals are the ones the reporter will keep, while the rest are edited out. Read the whole passage through, then just read the words in capitals.

Figure 83 The virtual cart machine. Audio clips (actuality) are edited digitally and stored on computer for playback into news bulletins. The interface resembles an old-fashioned mechanical cart machine. (*Andrew Boyd*)

Editing a 30-second bulletin clip

Reporter: *'OK. So what we need now is for you to explain that again on tape, but we'll have to tighten it up a little, otherwise it'll be too long to get into the bulletin. So . . . we're recording – what will you be telling the council?'*

Councillor: *'Well, when we get together tonight, what I'll be wanting to know is / WHY WEREN'T RESIDENTS TOLD THEIR HOMES WERE LIKELY TO FLOOD AT HIGH TIDE? / I mean, nobody had any idea this would happen, / WHY DID THE PLANNERS LET THIS DEVELOPMENT GO AHEAD IN THE FIRST PLACE, FOR GOODNESS SAKE? / I mean, this is what we pay them for isn't it? / WHY WEREN'T THE NECESSARY CHECKS MADE – AND / who is going to pay for it? – That's the important one, / JUST WHO IS GOING TO PAY FOR THE DAMAGE? ONE THING'S FOR SURE, IT SHOULDN'T BE THE RESIDENTS, AND THEY'RE THE ONES WHO ARE HAVING TO PAY RIGHT NOW. / The . . .'*

Reporter: *'Have you . . .? Sorry . . .'*

Councillor: *'No, go on.'*

Reporter: *'What I wanted to ask was / HAVE YOU ANY IDEA HOW MUCH THE FLOOD DAMAGE WILL COST TO PUT RIGHT?'*

Councillor: *'THOUSANDS. HUNDREDS AND THOUSANDS OF POUNDS. CARPETS, WALLPAPER, FURNITURE, WHOLE HOMES ARE RUINED, AND ALL BECAUSE SOME FEATHERBRAIN DIDN'T STOP TO THINK ABOUT THE HIGH TIDES. IT'S NEGLI-GENCE, AND SOMEBODY SHOULD BE SACKED.' /*

Figure 84 At the BBC World Service they still don't trust reporters to carry out their own editing. Even in the computer age, packages are put together for them. *'The journalists get their levels all over the place.'* (*Andrew Boyd*)

Unethical editing

Care must be taken with editing not to distort the meaning of what has been said. Selective, careless or unscrupulous editing can make someone appear to be saying something completely different, and the easiest way to fall into that trap is to take a qualified statement and to harden it up into something stronger than the speaker said or meant.

> Reporter: *'Are you in favour of the death penalty?'*
>
> Interviewee: *'That's very difficult to say. / YES . . . / I suppose so, under certain circumstances, but it's an awful thing to take a life, whatever that person has done. When you're dealing with / MURDERERS AND RAPISTS WHO WILL PROBABLY KILL AND RAPE ALL OVER AGAIN AS SOON AS THEY'RE RELEASED . . . / I don't know, maybe / THEY SHOULD BE EXECUTED. / But there are always those who are genuinely sorry for what they've done and are serving their time – while there's life there's hope. They might change. But it's the others, / THE MANIACS AND FANATICS WHO CAN'T STOP KILLING – THEY'RE A MENACE TO US ALL, / but, on the other hand, that's what prisons are for, isn't it?'*

If you read only the words in capitals the statement becomes a strong and unqualified call for the death penalty. But taking the answer as a whole, it is apparent that is not what the interviewee was saying.

This kind of selective editing that distorts a person's arguments is never ethical, and could never be justified. But reporters are often faced with having to shed some of the context and qualifications to get the audio down to length, and the decisions about what to cut are usually made against the clock.

Where this happens, the story should be explained more fully in the cue or accompanying narrative. Your reporting skills will often mean your explanation will be more concise and economical than that of your interviewee, but the intention should always be to give a fair, accurate and complete picture of what has been said.

Digital audio editing

> *'The fastest cut and paste editing I have ever seen. Time with a razor blade can be slashed by 300% . . . an ideal replacement for quarter-inch tape editing. Affordable digital editing has finally arrived.'*
> – PAUL ROBBINS, TECHNICAL DIRECTOR THAMES VALLEY BROADCASTING

Radio without the razor blade has been a long while in coming, but cheap computer technology means digital editing is here to stay.

Think of it as word-processing – with the spoken word. Unwanted phrases can be cut out, pauses tightened, glitches removed, and the order of the interview can be turned on its head by a simple cut and paste process to point-up the strongest, most newsworthy sound-bites.

Next, background sound can be added – the hubbub of an airport terminal or engines revving up at the racetrack. Individual sound effects can be brought in – an airport announcement or a squeal of tyres. Then appropriate music can be introduced to illustrate the theme and faded down beneath the first interview.

So far, so conventional. There's nothing here that couldn't be carried out in a radio studio with a trio of tape decks.

But the *pièce de résistance* is to be able to turn around two different versions of the radio piece for different programmes, plus a couple of sound-bites for the news, all within a fraction of the time it would have taken with tape, while still retaining the same sparkling quality of the original, and then to shrink or stretch each item to exactly the desired length – to the second – without altering the pitch of the voice or music.

Digital sound editing offers all the functionality of a studio in a box at a fraction of the price and in a fraction of the space. It also saves on expensive studio time.

Many editing programs ape conventional radio studios by displaying the image of a mixing desk on screen. The mixing desk allows you to blend various sounds together. You can click on the sliding volume controls with your computer mouse and move them up and down. Familiar peak-level meters show you how loud or quiet your recording will be. Another window might display conventional tape controls: play, record, pause, fast-forward, rewind, cue and review.

Cut and paste

The sound is digitized – converted into computer code – by sampling each sound up to 48 000 times per second. Your recording is displayed in a band on the screen, which corresponds to a strip of audiotape. As well as displaying your 'virtual tape' the computer shows the pattern made on it by the recording. This is depicted as a waveform, a mirror image zigzag which looks like an inkblot test or a range of mountains reflected in water.

The peaks represent loud sounds and the troughs indicate silence. If all those fuzzy peaks threaten to give you eyestrain, then you can zoom in so that each peak can be picked out individually.

Moving the cursor back and forth will replay that section of 'tape', just like cueing and reviewing a conventional tape machine.

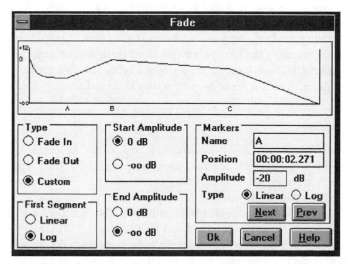

Figure 85 Using an editing programme audio fades can be carried out automatically or custom-made to suit. No more excuses for lousy levels or crashing the audio. Another bonus is edits are non-destructive. If you get an edit wrong, just undo and remake it. (*Courtesy Digital Audio Labs Inc.*)

To cut out a sentence, the cursor is clicked on to the breath space before that sentence begins and is then moved to the trough after it finishes. Then at the click of a computer mouse, the phrase is deleted. It's the digital equivalent of snipping out several inches of tape. If you want to keep that sentence but move it to another part of the recording, then the process is as simple as the cut and paste on your word-processor.

Unlike old-fashioned tape editing, if you find you have blundered by hacking out the wrong sentence you no longer have to fish around in the bin or on the floor to find the right strip of tape!

Digital editing is *non-destructive*. You need never edit your original, only a copy of it. The missing portion can be restored in a moment, just by pressing the undo key on your keyboard. If you make a slip you can cancel the offending edit and pick up where you left off. And if you make a complete pig's ear of the whole thing and need to start again, you can simply make a fresh copy of your original, which has been stored in all its pristine perfection on hard disk. Because each digital copy is a perfect clone of the original, the sound quality will never deteriorate, no matter how many times you reproduce it.

Multi-tracking

Overlaying sounds on top of one another to make a cross-fade is also simplicity itself.

Some sound editing software displays the recordings as tracks. Let's say the top track is your interview and you want to quietly fade up music under your interview to reach full volume as soon as the talking ends. You paste your recorded music onto the empty track below the interview and shuffle it around until it is in the right position. Then you draw in your fade with your mouse, pretty much like marking it in with a pencil. At any stage, you can listen back to the portion you are working on to hear how it sounds. When you are happy with the blend you save the result.

To construct an elaborate report, you can build it up section by section, layer by layer, or you can programme the overlay points into the computer and set it to compile the item automatically. Sophisticated edit programs use a timecode, like television, to guarantee the timing of each edit will be spot-on to the fraction of a second.

With digital editing you can be as multi-layered as you like. A single operator, who would normally have his or her hands full with several tape decks and a mixing desk, can combine multiple tracks from a single keyboard – though most news reports seldom call for more than four simultaneous tracks of sound.

Bells and whistles

An inevitable problem with multi-layered audio packages is one of variation in sound levels. With so many sources, some portions of the final report may be too loud while others are too quiet. The only way to even out the levels using reel-to-reel tape is to make another copy, while you ride the volume fader on the desk. But with digital recordings, a stroke of the *normalize* key will automatically even out your recording levels.

Similarly, you can adjust the tone of parts of your recording by tweaking the EQ (equalization). This will change the bass, treble or mid-range tone, or allow other filters to be used for more creative work, such as echo. A *pan* control allows you to send your sounds marching from the left speaker to the right, and making a *loop* will allow you to repeat endlessly background ambience such as hotel lounge hubbub.

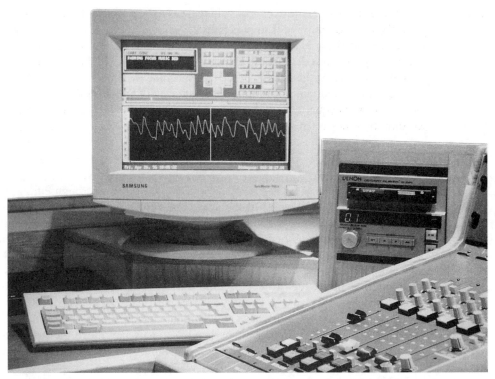

Figure 86 Revolution or evolution? Analogue faders, a cart machine and computer audio sit cheek by jowl. Sound is displayed on the monitor as a waveform. The 'tape' is shuttled back and forth by clicking on a button on the screen. Cutting and pasting is carried out electronically without a razor blade or chinagraph in sight. (*Andrew Boyd*)

The computer can be used to drive entire programmes or news bulletins, with all the interview clips stored on a playlist on the hard disk. The newsreader can choose whether to read the script from the screen or from paper and fires each clip at the click of a button.

Storing sounds in this way has been made possible by the ballooning size of computer hard disk drives. Each hungry minute of broadcast-quality stereo sound will gobble up 10.5 Mb of space on your hard drive.

When all this technology is crammed into a notebook computer digital editing can be carried out in the field. The journalist can produce a professionally mixed report and send it back to the radio station along a studio-quality ISDN (Integrated Services Digital Network) line or as an e-mail attachment.

Analogue editing

Some early defectors to the digital cause installed computer-controlled edit suites, like those in TV, only driving digital reel-to-reel audio decks.

Many broadcast newsrooms have yet to make the jump and still edit on conventional analogue machines. The reasoning goes: the technology is robust, uncomplicated, it works – and besides, it's already been paid for.

Tried and tested reel-to-reel decks allow tapes to be edited by hand. It's reasonably quick and it's far more intuitive than punching keys on a keyboard. Tape decks range from big trolley mounted machines such *as Studers, Otaris* and *Ferrographs*, to the smaller *Revox*. Allowing for various degrees of sophistication, the method of operation is usually similar.

Tapes are held on the spindle of the tape machine by a metal or plastic *hub*, which grips the reel. It is important not to mix different sizes of spool on the same machine, as this would create unequal tension on the motors that could slow down the playback. Studio editing machines often incorporate a timer, which is invaluable for editing.

Marking and cutting

A modern portable MiniDisc machine will allow you to do rough editing on location, including changing the order of the audio and discarding unwanted material. But with analogue tape machines, it's a different matter. Basic tape editing can be carried out on location using a specially equipped portable recorder, but this is a fiddly exercise and at best imprecise, so most editing is carried out back at the radio station. The wanted parts of your recording are either dubbed over onto another deck, or the tape is physically transferred to a large reel-to-reel machine where the *tape path* is exposed for easy editing with a razor blade.

Most studio tape machines have an *edit* mode, which allows you to stop the tape while it is still in play and turn the reels by hand. You can then move the tape backwards and forwards against the playback head while listening with headphones to find exactly the right place to make your edit.

Editing involves chopping out the unwanted passages from an interview, and joining together the rest. The cuts are made during pauses either side of the unwanted section.

The tape is then marked on the playback head with a *chinagraph pencil* and put on an editing block, where it is cut with a razor blade. The two ends of the tape are then joined together with splicing tape.

Where possible, master recordings should be preserved intact for reference and dubbed on another reel for editing.

Always think twice before discarding unwanted portions of tape. Your producer may ask for a longer version, which would mean reclaiming some of the edited sections. If in doubt, save all the out-takes. Number them with your chinagraph and hang them up out of the way with splicing tape with a brief note of what each numbered section contains, or simply save them on a separate reel. One length of tape looks remarkably like another and there are more productive ways to spend time than scavenging for a vital snippet in the mound of discarded tape across the newsroom floor.

The editing block

Most editing blocks have three cutting positions. The most acute angle produces the strongest edits. Joining the tape at an angle means the edit is unlikely to split open as the tape passes through the machine.

Sometimes the pause where the edit is to be made will be very brief, and there is little space between words to make the cut. In this case, use one of the more upright slots on the editing block.

The higher the speed of a recording the easier it is to edit, as the pauses take up more space.

1 The portion to be edited out is selected and marked with a chinagraph (grease) pencil.

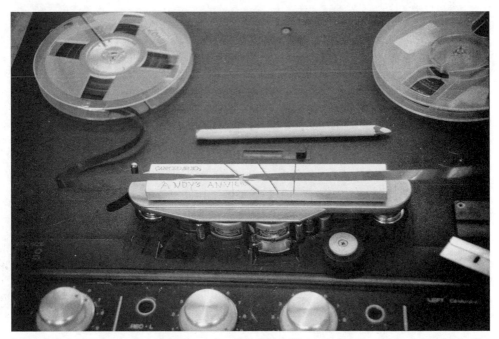

2 The mark is placed over the cutting slot on the editing block. The vertical cut is used for tight (close) edits.
Figure 87 Editing the old way, with reel-to-reel tape. (*Andrew Boyd*)

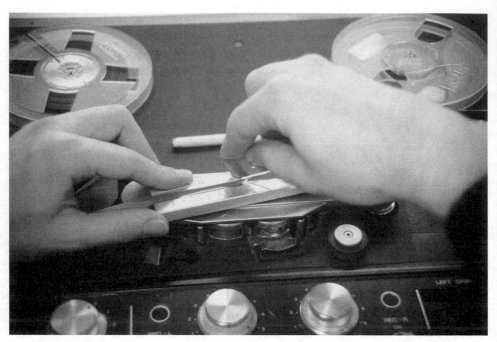

3 The unwanted section is cut out with an open razor blade (mind your fingers!) or a splicing machine.

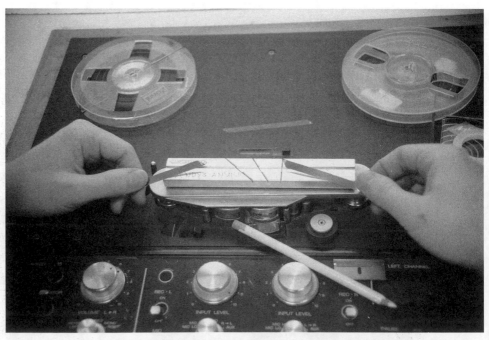

4 The two ends are butted together on the block to be joined. The unwanted portion – in this case a slight hesitation during an interview – can be seen above the editing block in the picture.

Figure 87 *Continued*

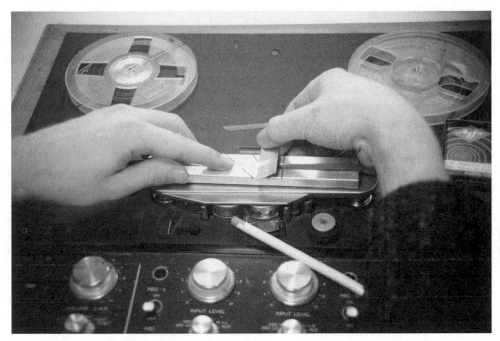

5 A short length of splicing tape joins the edited sections.

6 The final edit. The reel of splicing tape is on the right. (*Andrew Boyd*)

Figure 87 *Continued*

Leader tape

Different coloured plastic tape is used to mark the beginning and end of a recording. This is called leader tape. About 40 cm is joined to the start of a tape and used to lace it up on the studio machine for playback.

Coloured leader tapes give different information to the tape operator. Leader codes vary. In independent local radio in Britain, the leader code usually follows the traffic light pattern; green for go, red for stop. Green is placed at the start and red at the end. In the BBC, tapes usually begin with high-visibility yellow leader and go out with red. Stereo tapes begin with red and white striped leader.

Where several tapes are joined on a large reel this is known as *banding*, and three seconds (55 cm) of yellow or white leader is used to separate each band. Leader tape cannot be recorded over, so any leader *must* be removed before using the tape again otherwise there will be gaps in the recording. Many good interviews have been ruined by small strips of leader that went undetected because the reel was not examined. It is not always possible to see strips of leader by looking at the reel. If in doubt, check by spooling it through on the editing machine at high speed.

The edited tape is cued-up on the playback machine by hand, by positioning the join between the tape and the leader to the left of the playback head. The start of the recording should be about 4 cm to the left of the playback head, rather than actually on it. This compensates for any tape snatch when the machine is put into play.

Dub editing

Recordings made on cassette have to be dubbed on to reel before they can be edited. The cassette recorder should be rewound to the moment before the section begins and put on pause and play. To make the dub, the reel-to-reel machine is put into record and play and, at the same moment, the cassette is flipped off pause. The reel should be stopped the moment the chosen part of the recording has been dubbed across.

With precision equipment it is possible to dub edit a piece entirely without having to carry out fine editing with a razor blade, although great care and split-second timing are required to achieve a noiseless and natural sounding edit. This has been made easier by remote starts where one machine controls the other and computerized editing techniques.

Mixing

For more sophisticated productions, one sound source can be mixed with another to achieve a blend. Returning to our interview with the Maori, the tribal song may be blended to fade into the background as he begins to speak and dipped down until it eventually disappears.

To do this using analogue equipment you would need three tape recorders and a mixer. One tape deck would have the Maori interview, another the music (which could be on disc instead) and the third deck would record the combination of the two, which would be blended through the mixer.

Mixers range from small boxes with a few controls to contraptions with a mind-boggling array of switches, sliders and knobs that look as intimidating to the uninitiated as the flight deck of a jumbo jet. Don't be put off – the idea is basically simple.

A mixer takes two (or more) sounds and allows you to blend them together as you wish. To do this it needs *inputs* to receive the signals, and gain controls to adjust their volumes. Meters display the volume levels, and a main gain sets the final level of the combined signal. When you have balanced the result to your satisfaction the signal is sent through the outputs to another tape deck or on to air.

And that is basically it, although sophisticated mixers also have a variety of extra controls for fine adjustments. Larger versions are used as the main *control desks* in radio stations to put programmes on air. Other versions mix and edit television programmes or produce music master tapes.

The volume on a mixer is set by a circular dial (*pot*) or, more commonly, a slider (*fader*) which is easier to use. The fader is usually pushed up to turn the volume up, and pulled down to turn it down. Nothing could be more logical; except the BBC in its wisdom decided to install the faders the other way up on its control desks, so instead of up for up, it is down for up and up for down.

The most plausible explanation offered for this oddity is that the presenter or producer could inadvertently push a conventional fader up by catching it with a shirt cuff.

Setting levels

The operator of the mixer, control desk or panel, rides the levels to maintain a consistent output. The sound should not be allowed to rise so high that it distorts, nor dip too low, or to surge and fall. Some desks have automatic level controls or *compressors* built into them to keep the sound output at an optimum, but running the desk on auto pilot stifles any creativity. It can be a bit like holding every conversation at shouting pitch.

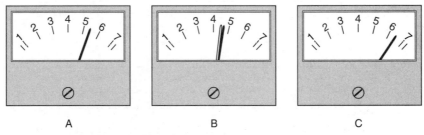

| A | B | C |

Figure 88 Setting the levels on the PPMs

A $5\frac{1}{2}$ is the usual peak for speech
B This stereo meter has two coloured needles to show the different peaks for the left and right channels. Music has a wider dynamic range than speech and sounds louder to the ear, so to avoid blasting the audience levels are usually turned down to peak at $4\frac{1}{2}$
C Speech over the telephone loses much of its dynamic range. It sounds quieter than normal speech and can be difficult to hear. Levels should be boosted to $6\frac{1}{2}$ to compensate.

Levels are often set on a *PPM meter* (peak programme meter), which registers the peaks of output but has a dampened action to stop it fluctuating wildly like a VU meter. This makes it easier to use. Alternatively, levels can be displayed as a sequence of green lights that rise and fall with the volume. When they rise beyond a certain point they go red, which means the volume is too high and is beginning to sound distorted.

Types of fade

Different fades are used to achieve a variety of effects.

Pre-fade

This is not really a fade as such, but a means of monitoring the sound source by listening to it without putting it on air. Pre-fade enables you to cue up the next item while the first is still being played.

An example would be when a local station is opting into the network news. The producer will pre-fade the network to make sure it is being received before crossing over on cue.

The pre-fade buttons on the mixing desk work by sending the sound from the source being monitored to one ear of your headphones, leaving you free to listen with your other ear to what is going out on air.

Cross-fade

The cross-fade is where one source is faded up as another is faded out, and is commonly used to mix music or sound effects with speech.

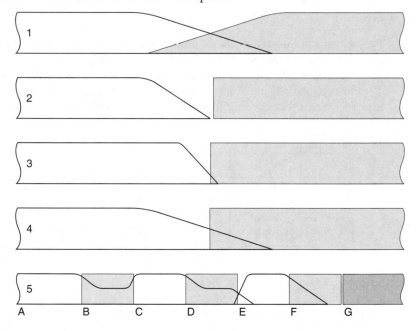

Figure 89

1 Cross-fade. Where one item is faded out and another is faded in at the same time. (For example, music giving way to sound effects)
2 Fade. The first item fades out completely before the other begins
3 The first item fades out quickly and the next begins sharply while the first is still dying away
4 The first item is faded out gradually, continuing to fade while the other begins. (For example, music under speech)
5 SIGNATURE TUNE: *'It's 4 o'clock and this is* Money Talks *with Andrew Barlow. Good afternoon.'*
(DIP)
SIG. (DIP) *'Today, new claims of insider dealing on the stock market and the companies that are cashing in on the Aids scare.'*
STAB (FADE) *'But first, the budget, and the question today that everyone is asking – will he, or won't he cut the tax? Etc.'*
'. . . could push share prices to an all-time high, as Peter Loyd has been finding out from the City.'
BUDGET/LOYD *'The market has been in a bullish mood today in anticipation of those tax cuts. Shares have risen, and look set to . . . etc.'*
The illustration represents the opening sequence to *Money Talks*. The signature tune (A) dips beneath Barlow's introduction (B) but does not disappear, bubbling underneath to re-emerge during a pause (C) and dipping again beneath the menu (D). It then cross-fades into a stab (E) which brings the signature sequence to an end. Barlow introduces the first item (F) which then begins (G).

Fading down and fading up

This is where the two sounds don't overlap but where one source is faded out and another faded in after a very short pause. This is useful where there are sounds that would jar together if cross-faded, such as two pieces of music in different keys.

Pot-cut

This means closing the fader rapidly to cut short an item. Care must be taken to 'pull the item out' very quickly and at a natural pause in the speech, otherwise the words will be clipped or trail off.

This is made easier by marking *pot-points* on your cue sheet that tell the technical operator where the item can be cut early, and what the last words are before that point.

Fading in and out

When a sound effect or piece of music is supposed to bubble under a recorded item before making its appearance it should be faded in gradually, or it will jar. Ideally, it should blend in so well that the listener will be unaware of its coming in or its going out. Judging the right length for a fade and the precise point at which the audio should be turned up to full volume takes practice. If you are using music, work with the rhythm or bring the song up at the start of a lyric. The fade down should also be smooth and gradual.

Fieldwork

1 If you have access to a reel-to-reel machine, record a song and try editing out one verse of it so you cannot hear the join. Try first with the angled cut on the editing block, and then with the vertical cut. Which was easier? Why?

   Now set the machine to a faster speed, re-record the song and edit it again. It should be much easier, but what makes the difference?

2 Record an interview or programme on cassette and choose a suitable clip for a bulletin. Now try dubbing that on to a reel-to-reel machine and making a clean edit without cutting the tape. Use the pause to control when to stop and start. Practise until you get it right.

   Then add a second clip to the end of the first by dubbing. Can you hear the join? Do you find it difficult to produce clean edits this way?

3 If you also have access to an edit computer as well as analogue tape decks, take two copies of an interview and edit one by hand before making the same edits to the other electronically. Compare the two techniques.

4 Take an interview you have made that could be improved by adding suitable music at the start. Practise using a mixing desk or digital editing programme to cross-fade that music beneath the interview. How long should the music run before being faded out? How loud should it be so it does not drown the interview or disappear too soon? What happens if you cross-fade singing under speech?

5 Go back to the heading 'unethical editing'. How would you produce a 15-second clip from the interview on the death penalty to give an accurate reflection of the interviewee's views? Write out your new version of the clip.

THE EQUIPMENT

22 The studio today and radio tomorrow

> *'The computer-driven system allows the presenter to switch microphones on and off; run audio for news inserts and commercials; switch in and out of network feeds, live traffic reports, business reports, sports forecasts, and even control building security after business hours ... The touch screen system eliminates the distractions of operating a sound mixing desk, allowing the presenter to provide a smooth presentation with no sacrifice of production quality ... The system goes one step further because it runs the station as a totally automated facility overnight.'*
> – INTERNATIONAL BROADCASTING*

While the smallest radio stations can be built into a shack or a shop with little more than a computer and some domestic hi-fi, most will boast a complex suite of studios, each equipped to perform a different function.

On-air studio

The main event is the main *on-air studio*. This is where the programmes are presented. A radio station worthy of the name would have at least two identical on-air studios in case one develops a fault.

On stations where technology has run rampant, gone is the mixing desk and in its place is the computer screen. Gone are the faders, buttons and controls. Now to turn on a microphone, fade down a recording, play a disc or fire a cart, all you have to do is touch the screen.

But the typical studio is likely to be a hybrid: a computer system coupled with a transmission desk with good old-fashioned faders. Combining manual controls that are pulled up and down with state of the art electronics might seem a strange compromise, but the hybrid system combines the tactile features and intuitive ease of control of a mixing desk with all the flexibility of digital technology.

* From 'At the touch of a screen', November, 1986.

Figure 90 Radio presenters still love mechanical faders. But for the next generation of technocrats here's the touchscreen studio. Jingles, adverts, music and reports are all fired by pressing the glass. It even flashes up the news for the newsreader. (*Courtesy Media Touch Systems Inc.*)

Standard equipment would include two or more compact disc players; cassette, DAT or MiniDisc machines; large monitor loudspeakers; telephone and mini-switchboard system; *talkback* (a form of intercom); presenter and guest mikes; a studio clock with on-air lights and some device for playing audio clips and jingles. And if the station is long in the tooth, it might even have some reel-to-reel decks.

The studio will be linked to the newsroom via a monitor to receive information such as headlines and the weather.

Commercial stations will also have a separate studio complex to make adverts. This will feature a comprehensive mixing desk and adjoining talks studio.

Talks studio

The talks studio is an acoustically treated room for interviews and discussions. Guests sit around a circular or hexagonal table facing individual microphones. There will be visual contact with the main studio through a large glass window.

The contributions studio

The news is typically read from a *newsbooth* or contributions studio. The control desk is simplified to allow presenters to operate their own audio equipment while they read the news. Audio inserts are fired off computer or from a bank of audio playback machines known as *carts*. The oldest of these use reel-to-reel tape. More modern cart machines play CDs, floppy disks or MiniDiscs or just access audio stored in the computer's hard disk. Sophisticated systems like the BBC's DCart (invented by the Australian Broadcasting Corporation) allow red-hot actuality to be edited on computer by anyone across the

Figure 91 Catering for every form of audio, old and new – computers, phone, CD, cart, record and tape decks all input through the mixing desk at BBC Southern Counties Radio. (*Andrew Boyd*)

network – simultaneously. It means producers for Radio 4 and 5 Live! can edit the same piece at the same time – even while it is still being recorded.

The contributions studio is also used to send out interviews and reports to other stations in the network along studio-quality lines or via a satellite distribution system.

Alternatively, the newsreader can present the bulletin or programme from an on-air studio. Stations with larger staffing budgets might employ technical operators to play in the audio inserts, allowing the newsreader to concentrate on the presentation.

Remote studios

Some radio stations serve large areas where reporters would struggle to cover a story and get back in time for the deadline. Likewise, because of the distance involved, guests might be unwilling or unable to travel to the station to record an interview.

Recording everything by phone is quick and cheap, but at the expense of quality. *Remote studios* are a better solution. These are usually small rooms rented in well-placed larger buildings such as city hall. They contain a microphone, mixer and possibly a recording deck. The remote studio is connected to the radio station by a broadcast-quality telephone line. Guests can go there to be interviewed and reporters can use them to send back reports.

That's how it works at Southern Counties Radio in Surrey, England. Reporters are based in bureaux dotted around the region. Each bureau contains a fully equipped studio that can be used to conduct interviews even when it is unmanned. Guests gain entry via a remote-controlled telephone link and the studio can be put to air automatically. It makes the prospect of being interviewed more attractive for busy newsmakers, who no longer have to drive all the way to the station HQ.

Radio car

Radio cars are essential news gathering tools for on-the-spot coverage of stories such as fires, demonstrations, or live events.

The car will contain everything you need to send back a studio quality recording from the scene. This includes microphones with hefty windshields and plenty of cable, often a sound mixer, a talkback system to base, and a UHF or VHF transmitter with a telescopic mast to beam the report back.

Outside broadcast vehicle

A development of the radio car is the outside broadcast (OB) vehicle, which has sophisticated equipment to mix complete programmes on location and send them out live. These are used for roadshows, large scale outside broadcasts, or live concerts.

Portable telephones

> *'We can record an interview from down a sewer pipe, in the middle of a field or up a mountain, and send it back from anywhere in the world. It's like having a mobile studio available to you.'*
>
> – PULSE RADIO NEWS EDITOR, GERRY RADCLIFFE

Battery-operated portable phones have paved the way for greater flexibility in news coverage. With a hand-held ISDN digital phone you can send broadcast quality reports from anywhere, doing away with the need for a radio car, outside broadcast vehicle, or even a studio. Britain's Classic FM took early advantage of ISDN to transmit an entire music programme live from the presenter's conservatory.

There are other advantages. More breaking news can be covered live; editors can keep in touch with journalists on the spot without waiting for them to call in; phones can be linked to recorders so interviews can be sent back from remote areas, and sports commentators are no longer rooted to the press box but can broadcast from around the ground.

Thanks to miniaturization and data compression techniques, satellite phones allow live audio and video reports to be transmitted from anywhere in the world.

Telephone reports

For the reporter out in the field without a radio link, the mobile phone and notebook computer have become tools of the trade.

Instead of dictating the story down the phone, the reporter hooks up the computer to the phone and speeds the report back almost instantly.

But you don't need a notebook computer to send a recording back by the phone. You can send recorded actuality back to base by connecting your recorder into the phone socket via a special lead. First you unplug the phone from the wall and clip a coupler unit into the socket to double the number of slots. Then you plug the phone lead into one socket and into the other plug the cable that runs from the line-out or telephone socket of the recorder.

Figure 92 Times past – broadcasting on the BBC local radio Mark I desk. Looks like something out of the back of an army Land Rover. (*Andrew Boyd*)

With a little practice it is possible to incorporate a recorded interview into a live report made on the phone. Interview extracts and linking narrative can be edited back at the station and played on air well before you have returned.

The telephone is a lifeline for foreign correspondents, and it is essential to use a phone line that is as free from crackles and interference as possible. Digital ISDN lines offer this clarity, but conventional telephones use a narrow waveband, so the voice sounds thin and reedy. To help compensate, a variety of devices can be coupled to the phone to boost the signal and make the voice sound fuller. These include the BBC's Scoop device.

> *'I went to East Anglia to cover a story about a missing teenager. I took a portable MiniDisc, a laptop and a Scoop. When I got there I did the interviews with the MiniDisc and downloaded them onto the laptop so I could edit them into short clips. Then I wrote my links and recorded them in the same way and put them onto the laptop as well. I mixed the piece together using Cool Edit and recorded it back on to MiniDisc. I needed a phone line to plug the Scoop into and eventually found one in a newsagent's shop.'* — NEWSBEAT REPORTER PHIL WILLIAMS*

Mobile phones can let you down, so always take a phone card with you for when you have to call back to base. If that runs out you can avoid constantly feeding a callbox with coins (embarrassing during a live broadcast) by reversing the charges (making a collect

* 'Radio revolution', *Computer Active*, 23 March 2000

call). Telephone systems differ, but often a reverse charge call will have a set of pips in the background and can be interrupted by the operator. You should politely ask the operator to remove the pips and not to interrupt the call.

If you are in a studio and your interviewee is on the end of a phone you need to find a way of recording your voice in studio quality. The answer is at hand in the form of a *telephone balance unit*, which allows you to use a microphone instead of the telephone handset and lets you adjust the levels to avoid sounding louder than your interviewee.

If things are desperate, you can even record your phone conversations by attaching an *induction microphone* to the phone and plugging it into a recorder. This provides a useful record of their answers, but your questions are likely to be barely audible. And here's a tip – if you use an induction mike anywhere near a working computer all you will record is hum and interference.

Ethically, an interviewee should always be told when their conversation is being recorded. In the USA, it has been a legal requirement to send a regular bleep along the line to show the interviewee that he or she is going on tape. The bleep, which was produced by a machine, could be turned off once the interviewee had been told the interview was being recorded.

Phone levels

Recording levels for telephone reports need to be boosted slightly to compensate for the poor quality telephone line.

The phone is unable to convey the full tonal range of the human voice so the ear will perceive the thin-sounding recording as being quieter than normal and listeners will have to strain to hear unless the levels are adjusted.

Another way to improve the quality is to filter the signal either in the edit program on a computer or through the mixer. Judicious use of equalization can eliminate some of the hiss and hash, and the range of the signal can be boosted to make the recording sound fuller and clearer.

Obscenity button

Telephones are used for *phone-in* discussions where listeners call in with their questions and comments to a panel of experts in the studio. Here there is an even greater hazard than the faint phone line – the probability that sooner or later a listener will swear, blaspheme, or utter a libel on the airwaves. The presenter's last line of defence is the *obscenity*, or *profanity*, *button*.

As soon as a caller says anything seriously offensive, the presenter presses the obscenity button, and the offending comment never reaches the airwaves – even on a live programme.

It works by putting the programme into *delay*. The show is recorded and played back seven seconds or so later. The delay is carried out electronically, by putting the programme through a *digital delay* unit which stores the programme in its memory before playing it back seven seconds later, or by recording the programme on a *tape-loop* which gives a seven-second pause before the recording reaches the playback head of the machine.

With a tape-loop, when the presenter presses the obscenity button, the programme is snatched out of delay and a seven-second jingle is fired automatically. When the jingle finishes, the programme reverts to being live, and the profanity has, hopefully, been bottled up in that seven-second segment which never went on air.

To put the programme back into delay, another jingle is fired and a fresh loop is set up. Or, if digital delay is being used, the unit gradually puts the programme back seven seconds by adding an extra tiny pause to the recording every time it detects a gap in the speech, until the programme is fully back into delay.

Tomorrow today

Audiotape is dead. Long live the digital revolution. What finally tipped the balance in favour of new technology was simple economics. Computers became cheaper than tape machines. Editing with a razor blade is about to pass into posterity – just as soon as the last remaining tape deck splutters to a standstill.

Modern meaty computer disks can hold a full day's output as well as thousands of adverts, jingles and announcements that would previously have been kept on tape cartridge. Record playlists, many of which are already being selected by a computer programmed to pander to the tastes of the target audience, can be stored in memory and revised in moments.

Computer operation can offer flawless playback quality, instant selection, editing accurate to a whisker of a second and fully automated programming. It is now possible to run a radio station from your back bedroom.

And in the newsroom, audio can be loaded onto hard disk and edited on screen. Newscuts can be played back in any given order, directly from the computer and cues can

Figure 93 A clean mixing desk and a clear line of visual communication through all the studios at BBC Radio Solent. (*Andrew Boyd*)

be read from the screen using an autocue system, though most newsreaders still prefer paper copy which is less prone to crashing.

Computer systems allow different stations in a network who are receiving the same programme to inject their own customized advertising, idents and local news – computer-timed to run exactly on cue. US systems even provide a legal printed record of programming for the Federal Communications Commission.

For the consumer, remote-controlled radio receivers with pre-tuned channels are making it easier to find specific programmes and are breaking the habit of staying tuned to one station. TV-style channel hopping is about to migrate to radio as competition for an ever-fragmenting audience grows fiercer. Wider use of the FM waveband has meant a big improvement in radio reception. Teletext can be picked up by radio, and car radios can scan the airways and home in on localized traffic reports. But the story doesn't stop at FM . . .

Digital Radio

Thanks to the devastating digit radio is converging closer to the Internet and television. Digital Radio, formerly known as DAB (digital audio broadcasting), offers the most unradio-like provision of pictures as well as sound.

The Digital Radio receiver looks more like a portable TV set, with a screen to receive text and graphics transmitted along with the programme. Obvious applications are stock market details and weather reports, with satellite shots showing exactly where the blizzard will hit next.

For the captive audience of motorists Digital Radio offers in-car navigation systems and local traffic reports complete with maps of the snarl-ups. Best of all, the signal is rock steady and never needs retuning.

'*Digital Radio offers interference-free reception, high quality sound, easy to use radios, automatic tuning and a wider choice of programmes,*' claims the BBC . . .

The Digital Radio specification was devised by a consortium of European broadcasters and manufacturers. Each *multiplex* transmission carries several services. Running alongside BBC Radios 1–5, which are all beamed out simultaneously, is the BBC Parliamentary Service and BBC Now, offering news, sport, traffic and weather on demand in a 10-minute rolling news format.

Digital means more radio of better sound quality than ever before. But a cautionary note from Sue MacGregor, one of the presenters of Radio 4's flagship *Today* programme:

> '*The pressure is on for quantity, not quality. We may even be the last generation to know and appreciate the excellence of good radio; to realize that the best of good radio produces unforgettable pictures in the head.*'*

There may be another disadvantage to all this 'progress'. As studio quality telephone technology becomes more widespread, radio reporters are finding themselves increasingly tied to the newsroom to conduct their interviews. Not only is this dull and hastens the slide towards smaller newsrooms, it has a terminal effect on reporters' expenses!

Even the newsreader, whose position must seem unassailable, could one day be a victim of the microchip. As technology becomes steadily more sophisticated tomorrow's audiences could be tuning in to hear the news read flawlessly with wit, warmth and urbanity in a pleasing regional accent – by a newsreader with no moving parts. It could be sooner than you think!

* 'Conjuring pictures on the radio', *The Guardian*, 7 October 1989.

> **'Voilà – the computer speaks'**
> The world's first computer newscast was broadcast by Ottawa radio station CKCU-FM. Students from the Carleton School of Journalism programmed the DEC computer to read the news in a voice that was 'remarkably close to that of a human', according to reports. The DEC can read the news in no fewer than seven different voices, each of them adjustable for pitch and resonance.
>
> Tutor George Frajkor said his talking computer could one day put newsreaders out of business, *'The newsreader can be replaced by anyone, putting the newscast back in the hands of the working journalists who write it . . . Voilà, the computer speaks.'**

Fieldwork

1 If you have access to a studio and a newsbooth, prepare a bulletin with inserts and present it first with a technical operator at the control desk, and then entirely by yourself in the booth. Do you prefer to drive the news yourself or be driven? What are the advantages and disadvantages of each type of operation?

2 As eye contact is so important in interviewing, what difficulties would you expect conducting an interview with a guest who is miles away in a remote studio?

   If you are in a class, simulate those difficulties by devising a scenario and conducting an interview with a classmate *back to back*. Don't forget, he or she will need advice on how to use the microphone, how to sit, and how to turn on the equipment.

3 If you have access to the necessary equipment, practise sending a recorded interview down the phone.

   Now try packaging that interview on location by writing a cue and links, and sending it back *in the correct order* along the phone line. Think how you would do it beforehand, then experiment. (Hint – use a microphone.)

4 Make a phone interview and balance the levels until they are equal. Now play it back and listen with your eyes shut. Whose voice sounds loudest, yours or theirs? Practise balancing the report so both voices *sound* as loud as each other.

5 Talk to a journalist and a presenter and ask them how they imagine the radio station of tomorrow will look. What are their views on new technology? Ask them which devices that have yet to be invented would make their jobs easier and more efficient.

   How do *you* see the radio station of tomorrow?

* Derived from 'Voiced by computer', *UK Press Gazette*, 6 June 1986.

Part Three

TELEVISION

'Television is the rampaging medium, dominating the life and rhythms of society, forcing all other media onto the defensive.'

– MARTIN JACQUES

Figure 94 On the set of the ITV *Evening News*. Don't believe everything you see. The pictures behind the newsreader just look like the newsroom. (*Andrew Boyd*)

Figure 95 The real McCoy – the ITN newsroom. Writing, subbing and editing are carried out directly on screen. The mainframe computer also gives access to thousands of agency reports from around the world. (*Andrew Boyd*)

INSIDE ITN

23   Independent Television News

> 'When I started at ITN as a TV journalist we used typewriters and made do without
> mobile phones. There were no satellites or electronic newsgathering. Now we have
> news on TV, radio and the Internet coming out of this building and we're going over
> to desktop editing. There is a considerable amount more multi-skilling.'
>
> – PHIL MOGER, ITN

Independent Television News (ITN) ranks beside the BBC in the UK's superleague for TV
news – despite having a third of the staff and a quarter of the Corporation's financial
resources. Each weekday some 20 million people tune in to ITN's terrestrial news
programmes in the UK. Since its first broadcast in 1955, ITN has had a history of
innovation, producing the nation's first half-hour and 50-minute news programmes and
home-produced satellite news. Its latest feature is the digital newsroom, where every
image, report, and scrap of information is stored on computer ready for instant recall.

No two organizations are identical. TV news is evolving as rapidly as new technologies
– and union rules in some cases – will allow. This chapter offers an insight into how ITN
works. Other TV stations will do things *their* way. Equipment, methods and terminology
will differ, but they will also have much in common. The following chapters attempt to
hold to that common ground without claiming to provide an exhaustive account of the
working practices of every TV news organization.

Getting the news

Every news organization performs two basic tasks: getting the news in, and putting it out
– *input* (*intake*) and *output*.

On the input side, the stories of the day are selected by the home and foreign desks,
which assign the reporters to cover them. ITN employs around 70 reporters among its
journalistic staff of almost 300 and can call on camera crews throughout the UK. There
are bureaux in Washington, Moscow, Brussels and Beijing, among others, including a
special bureau in Westminster for parliamentary coverage.

Once the stories have been chased up they are passed over to the relevant output desk which is compiling material for an ITN news programme or bulletin.

ITN seldom has to follow a cold trail for news, as agency wire services feed stories from around the world straight into the newsroom computer. These are scanned by *copytasters* who alert input and output to major items. The ITN computer is more than a bucket for news wires, though, as Head of Newsgathering, Jonathan Munro, explains: *'It can drive a programme from start to finish, roll tapes, play Astons [captions], reorder the running order, time it – do virtually anything apart from writing the script.'*

The work of staff reporters and crews is supplemented by specialists and a wide network of freelances. The basic ITN camera crew is known as the OMB – one-man band. A single operator works the camera and monitors the sound levels. But to further boost its coverage ITN has videojournalists standing by around the regions, with another in London dedicated to covering sport.

Freelance crews are retained abroad on contract to provide exclusive stories, but for long-running reports ITN will send its own crews. A major difficulty as the satellite age began is that if a government disapproved of reports being made about its country it could easily deny access to the satellite to prevent the story getting back.

To overcome this, ITN was the first British station to use its own portable satellite dish which could be transported to remote areas where it would otherwise be impossible to relay the story back. Today it owns ten mobile satellite uplink trucks, which are placed strategically around the country to offer a rapid response to breaking news.

Multiple deadlines have put an end to the old practice of bringing back reports by hand. Where satellite is not available, they can be sent by microwave link, or by cable from a nearby regional TV studio. Only if the report is made almost on the station's doorstep will it be taken back by the crew or despatch rider.

Figure 96 Setting the news agenda, *Evening News* producer Robin Elias (left). *'We pack a lot into the programme. We want to keep things bright and pacy.'* (*Andrew Boyd*)

More reports are now transmitted live from the scene by electronic news gathering (ENG) crews or outside broadcast vehicles, and portable editing equipment means items can be put together on location and sent back rapidly. It can be quite a job juggling scarce resources to make sure reporters don't waste their time chasing stories that never get on air, as ITN's Malcolm Munro explains:

'Juggling's a good word. If producers say they want the story, then my job is to make sure that they get it. Whether or not a story gets on air depends a lot on the resources you assign to it. If you put your best reporters on the story and send them all the "toys" – field editing, links or satellite dish – it makes it that much easier.'

Being a TV reporter is seldom as glamorous as some might believe. Newspaper journalists can draw on their imaginations to describe a scene, but TV reporters are tied to the camera, and that can mean doorstepping a VIP's house all day for one vital picture.

THE BEST AND WORST OF TV NEWS

'The worst of it is being stuck in London, shunted around from one silly story to another, standing outside somebody's door in the pouring rain, from four in the morning till eight at night with no return for it, or doorstepping the TUC while some big industrial debate is going on and doing absolutely nothing for most of the day. Then in 10 minutes you may suddenly get three or four people rushing out of the building and you have to try to grab them and interview them and they may just shake their heads and walk away, and you're left kicking your heels and thinking, that was a wasted day.

'The best of it is that you can go out on a story of national importance, spend all day on it, edit it, put your words to it and voice it up, and when it comes across as you wanted it to and people take notice of it, you have that feeling that some part of what you've put over in your minute and a half will stay in their minds and they'll have a better idea of what's going on.'   REPORTER KIM SABIDO

The good news for the egocentric is that ITN is placing greater emphasis on what it calls 'reporter involvement' – casting journalists in a larger role by showing them asking questions, not just doing a piece to camera. *'One of our distinctives is to built programmes around high-profile reporters,'* explains Editor in Chief, Nigel Dacre. *'We pioneered this and we're doing it increasingly. You get the best journalism from your most experienced reporters and the viewers like to know the people who are bringing them the news. Rather than just seeing the reporter pop up, you actually see them challenging somebody and asking the questions which are in the viewer's mind. It may mean having a studio graphic sequence involving the reporter, allowing the reporter to engage directly with the viewer and explain more clearly what's going on.'*

Stories can be made clearer by illustrating them with graphics. ITN pioneered their use with its VT80 – an ingenious adaptation of a knitting pattern machine. This could be programmed with graphics, such as maps of locations throughout the world, which could be recalled to order.

For researching facts or checking information, ITN's news information department keeps cuttings, reference books and background on a myriad subjects.

C4N PROSPECTS	C4N MONDAY 15TH NOVEMBER	STATUS TI READY 2:

PROG ED: WATKINS
PRES: SNOW. KRISHNAN
REPORTERS: RADO, RUSH, VEITCH, GLASS, HALLIGAN, RUGMAN, EASTON, GOODMAN, ISRA
ILL: MACDONALD, SHAH

Who/Where:
DSmith/Halfpenny – Washington
Hilsum – Moscow
Lang – to Paris

COMMISSIONED

ULSTER:
Parties return to Stormont for critical stage of talks process amid continued speculation over the republican offer, how far it goes towards decommissioning and whether it'll be enough to bring the Unionists on board. GIBBON/BANATVALA ex MPU or SIS Belfast

LIBEL:
Beginning of Neil Hamilton's libel case against Mohammed Al Fayed over the cash for questions allegations which deprived him of his seat. 4 weeks of court time have been set aside – today'll be mainly legal arguments. REPORTER/LLOYD

LIVINGSTONE:
On the eve of the declaration of the Labour party's mayoral short-list we profile 'Red' Ken Livingstone, looking back to his days on the GLC in the 1980s. IV with former ally, now staunch Blairite and minister Margaret Hodge. Bid for live. BECKETT

MENSON:
Trial of the two men accused of killing Michael Menson begins in proper. ISRA Watch

PRIVATE AMBULANCES:
Indy film on how virtually anyone can buy themselves an ambulance and set up a private ambulance operator, sometimes with disastrous results. INDY CREDIT

BRADLEY:
D Smith on Democrat Bill Bradley's apparently unstoppable presidential campaign and the concern it's causing VP Al Gore. Yesterday 5,000 people attended a fundraiser at Madison Square Garden basketball court. We look at the man behind the hype. D SMITH ex Washington

ARTS:
Glass vtr on the Arts Council's announcement of £70m of lottery funding. GLASS

OTHER NEWS

HOME

RAIL: Times reports 2 trains a day are passing red lights, and passenger delays are worsening.

WEMBLEY: 11h30 presser to unveil new plans for the stadium's rebuilding – what will replace the twin towers?

Figure 97 Prospects for *Channel 4 News*.

To back up those facts with pictures, the library keeps a store of thousands of agency photographs as well as original footage from camera crews. Each item is cross-referenced on computer so reporters can quickly draw on a wealth of previously recorded material to illustrate their reports. ITN's news archive is one of the largest of its kind.

Sixty news networks throughout Europe belong to the European Broadcasting Union and exchange their coverage throughout the day via the Eurovision link, chaired from Geneva. But to preserve competition, rival broadcasters in the same country are not permitted to filch one another's material. ITN has an agreement to use stories from America supplied by NBC and CNN, and can take stories from the Nine Network in Australia. It also has a reciprocal arrangement with ZDF in Germany.

The editors

The day begins for the duty news editor at the crack of dawn when he switches on his bedside radio to find out what has happened in the world while he has been sleeping. National newspapers and breakfast TV complete the picture before he turns up at ITN to begin a 13-hour day.

Planning for coverage begins the previous day with help from the forward planning desk. The editor will know how many reporters are on duty, the stories some have been assigned to, and how many crews are available. *'The news editor is the one person who knows what's going on any given day from all sides: producers, reporters, technicians and crews,'* says Malcolm Munro.

A list of prospects for the day features the news stories ITN knew about in advance, such as the announcement of unemployment figures or an election. Phone calls to foreign and regional bureaux swell that list further. The process has been likened to a fast-moving, never-ending, game of chess.

The mailbag is sifted by newsroom assistants and secretaries and the forward planning department is notified of details in the post about coming events. In the newsroom, every item of news entering the building can be monitored on computer or listened to discreetly through personal earpieces.

Once the news editor has allocated reporters to stories he then has to 'sell' his ideas to the producers of the different news programmes, each of which may have his or her own view about how to run the story.

Meanwhile the foreign editor is running up a large phone bill checking his reporters and contacts overseas. Later he will watch the early Eurovision link to see what stories are on offer.

Both editors need to have a clear idea of that day's coverage by the morning conference, which serves as the threshing floor for ideas. Suggestions are pooled and discussed, with the editor-in-chief acting as chairman and referee and checking that the stories fit ITN's style.

'What has served us well is hard news, unvarnished and attractively packaged offering good quality information. Tonight's news lead could be an interesting new translation of the Bible or a kidnapped girl in Surrey – as long as it's news.

'I always like to think we are in serious popular journalism, not popular serious journalism. There are Times [newspaper] households and Sun [newspaper]

> *households. We go into the Times and Sun households – into some extraordinary households. We know we are watched in the Palace and in parlours, so we have to be knowing and well informed to the considerable number of people who know more about a story than we do, and not condescending to those who know less.'*
> – SIR DAVID NICHOLAS, FORMER EDITOR IN CHIEF, ITN

The producers

After running through their prospects the home and foreign editors invite producers of different news programmes to tender their bids for items. There is no shortage of takers. ITN is the news provider for three commercial networks in Britain – ITV, Channel 4 and Channel 5 and runs the pan-European channel, EuroNews.

On ITV the *Lunchtime News* at 12.30 has to kick-start the newsday. This begins when the producer arrives at 6.30. It targets breaking stories and has little time to prepare elaborate packages. Unsurprisingly the live interview is a major feature.

The later programmes have the benefit of a rolling start. The *ITV Early Evening News* at 18.30 has replaced the now-defunct *News at Ten* as the ITN flagship. It offers a fast-paced 30-minute wrap of the day's main events, interweaving domestic hard news and human interest.

The programme was launched in 1999 following the decision to shift *News at Ten* to open up the evening schedule for bigger audience winners such as feature films. Many of the qualities of the old *NaT* have been retained in the ITN *Evening News*, including its editorial approach and many of its well-known features, such as the use of Big Ben in the titles and the clock's famous 'bongs' to introduce the opening headlines. The show also keeps the famous light-hearted *'And finally'* slot, which has featured skateboarding dogs and sunbathing bunnies. The average package still runs to less than 90 seconds, putting a premium on *what* is happening, rather than *why. 'It's the same approach – serious journalism told in a popular way,'* says editor Robin Elias.

Analysis takes time, and is the major strength of *Channel 4 News* at 19.00 which has 50 minutes to tease out the major issues. The brief is to be analytical, specialist and to give more weight to foreign affairs. A typical programme will cover five home and international stories, backed up with live interviews, and offer a summary of the rest of the news, *'We have time and space to bask in a whole day's activities,'* says presenter Jon Snow.*

Back on the more populist Channel 3, the new ITV *Nightly News* is broadcast Monday to Friday at 11 pm. It rounds up the top stories of the day and looks ahead to the events that tomorrow might bring, ending with a review of the next day's newspaper headlines and a pre-recorded montage of the day's most striking images.

ITN has ambitions to become a global player in the TV stakes. In 1997 ITN took over the pan-European broadcaster *EuroNews* and its *World News for Public Television* is specially produced for the continental market, featuring reports, features and investigations from around the globe. *World News* is broadcast each weekday night in more than 40 per cent of TV stations around the USA. It can also be seen globally, on demand, on the Internet on www.itn.co.uk.

---

* *ITN – The First 40 Years*, 1995.

With so many programmes to feed, reporters often have to cover the same story several different ways – as well as doing a piece for the ITN subsidiary, Independent Radio News. IRN is based in ITN headquarters and feeds some 230 stations in the independent network as well as the national stations, Classic FM and Atlantic 252. *'Reporters like doing it,'* says Head of Newsgathering, Jonathan Munro, *'They do phonos from abroad and can explain a story over seven or eight minutes, which is much longer than they would get on the* Lunchtime News.'

It's 9.30 – time to plan the day's news. It's a tight squeeze to cram everyone into the office of editor Robin Elias. And it will need even more shoehorning to jam all the breaking stories into the programme – new moves towards peace in Northern Ireland, brokered by the American George Mitchell, the war in Chechnya, and a celebrated libel case in London, to name but a few.

'Jim, will you kick off . . .'

'Ulster . . . George Mitchell will be leaving Stormont today for the last time and will be making a statement at 12 o'clock. He's expected to be upbeat. It seems both parties are finally likely to come to an agreement over the peace accord.'

'OK, we've asked Johnny and he's started to do a reflection on how the broader public are taking it . . . city centre scenes and vox pops.'

'Would it be a good idea to do a bit more about Mitchell, who he is and his family?'

'Personally?'

'He's got a very young wife . . .' [laughter]

'And that is *very* relevant, yes.' [drily]

'That could be classic briefing, a minute and 10, just a different reporter giving a bit of background on him. That could work quite well . . .'

'The libel thing will start today. There will be a statement by Desmond Brown, the QC [lawyer] for al-Fayed [who is being sued], although neither of the two main players will be in the box today. We've got cameras at both ends in case he does turn up.'

'Chechnya splits into two right now – we've seen the opening of the summit in Istanbul and it's really rather good. Yeltsin has turned up and is very vigorous. He makes this strong attack on the West defending Russia's right to pursue terrorists. Clinton answers him, conceding the point in principle that it is Russia's internal affair but warning them on violence. The language almost has a flavour of the 80s and the superpowers warring at each other with words. It's a good bit of television.'

'And Clinton stands up with Yeltsin sitting opposite him?'

'He faces Yeltsin – it's an effective speech. He says one of the most exciting moments of my life, Boris, was when you were standing on that tank and people said it was Russia's internal affair, but it wasn't, the West supported you and you've got to recognize the call for democracy in other countries.'

'Meanwhile [reporter] Mark Webster is going to go to the hospital where many of the victims have been brought and he'll see the head of the United Nations relief agency. She'll be the first foreigner to be allowed into Chechnya by the Russians.'

'Do cameras go with her?'

'Yes they will. I think the bit of her with the refugees will be particularly strong. At the moment we're going to wrap it all together with Paul Davies for lunchtime.'

[And so to sport. There's been a major international football match at Wembley – England verses Scotland in the qualifiers for a European competition. England get through – just – after a lacklustre game.]

'There'll be a massive inquest today. The big question now is what chance England against the Germans, Italians and the French?'

'We can throw forward some kind of graphic on the competition. The draw's on December 12, the 16 teams involved, that kind of stuff; we can do a briefing on it and look forward to this major event.'

'Best of the rest . . . Kevin has gone to the Foreign Office for a briefing on Kosovo war crimes. Hurricane looks pretty good, but it doesn't look like it's getting to America at the moment, it's in Puerto Rico. Another element that might go with this is the aftermath of the French floods.'

'This Arctic ice story. . . 40 per cent of the Arctic ice has disappeared – it was in *The Times*, I think. Let's get Lawrence to look at that.'

'Sounds good. Anything else, anybody?'

DAY IN THE LIFE OF ITV EVENING NEWS PRODUCER

'It's a fast programme,' says editor Robin Elias. *'We pack a lot into it. We want to keep things bright and pacy and are always looking for new devices for getting and grabbing attention. We use headlines and teasers before the break – verbal hooks to get people interested in the stories. It's finding that point of contact with the viewer that is a real hallmark of ITN.'*

6 am	Listen to the BBC news, catch the beginning of the *Today* programme [on Radio 4]. Travel into ITN, read serious and popular papers on the train.
8 am	Flick through the TV and radio channels, keep an eye on Breakfast Television.
9.30	Planning meeting. *'We bash around the stories of the day. You get a feeling for whether you've got too much material generally, or too much sport or domestic politics and make adjustments as you go. By the end you can draw up a rough running order and consider the treatment of the stories. You can't ever take your eye off the ball, because there are other stories that might not be on our agenda at all – what we call the watch list – which during the day push their way to the front of your mind.'*
2.30	Programme meeting chaired by editor of the day. *'You should have an idea then about the shape of the programme.'*
4 pm	Running order meeting. *'Should we move some items up or down? What are we going to headline – a much more detailed look at how the programme is going to work.'*
4.30	Check through the packages as they come in. *'The programme editor carries the can for the packages so he will certainly know before the programme what all the key ingredients will be – "The story we're telling is this, and these are the pictorial elements of it."'* Monitor the BBC and others through the day. *'I'm usually pretty pleased when they carry different stories to us. The BBC are moving closer to our agenda, but generally they have a more high-minded, po-faced view of what is the news than we do. I think our programmes are more balanced, accessible and watchable. But that doesn't mean we forget what is serious news and fill the programmes with showbiz and lighter stories. People wouldn't respect us for that or want it.'*

6.30	On air. Most days the programme begins with an incomplete running order. *'There is usually finishing off to be done while we are still on air. And you can never have enough back-up packages to cover every eventuality. We rarely fall off the clock – we are much more disciplined than we were 10 years ago. You'd wake up at night worrying if you thought too much about what could go wrong with the programme, but we're a very talented bunch of people, and if you are running a good team people feel as though they want to do the best for it.'*
7 pm	Review meeting with the editor of the day. *'This was good, this wasn't quite right . . . it's helpful to have an instant overview with an editor who's been watching the news throughout the day.'*
7.15	Meeting with the editor of the *Nightly News* as they begin to plan their running order.

It makes for a 13-hour day. Is it worth it?

'You have to go some to beat the job of editing a flagship programme on a very busy day with lots of different stories from different places in the world that you pull together to have a highly-polished well-produced, enjoyable, watchable, informative programme.'

– ROBIN ELIAS

Getting the programme on air

In the studio the newscaster can hear everything going on in the control room through the earpiece. This constant chattering into the ear can be a blessing or a curse. ITN newscaster, Trevor McDonald: *'One night I was interviewing an anti-apartheid spokesman and there was a great shout in the control room. For a moment I didn't know if I was interviewing the wrong guy so there was a long pause while I decided how to phrase the question. I have been reading the news for years and I still have a little jolt when somebody shouts.'*

On some TV stations the newscasters can hear only the director's comments, but despite the drawbacks, McDonald prefers to do it ITN's way and have all the voices coming into his ear: *'At times you can almost hear the genesis of decisions of change. You can sometimes hear the producer say softly to the director, through whom all instructions must come, "I'm thinking that we have to make a change in story 15," and you mentally gear for it. So the change when it comes is not sudden. Anything that gives you a few seconds warning is good. I'd be very worried if I couldn't hear what was happening. I'd feel cut off.'*

The task of making the programme happen on air falls to the director. He or she is responsible for blending the different camera shots, graphics and reports that go to make up the bulletin.

'Stand by ES1, CART A . . .'
'. . . three, two, one, zero.'
'On air.'

Electronic journalism and the satellite age have pushed deadlines back to the very last minute of the programme. Producers, presenters, reporters and directors have never been

Figure 98   Trevor times two. Inside the gallery at ITN where the *Evening News* is going out on air. (*Andrew Boyd*)

more tested than they are today, and more is to come. ITN offered Britain its first popular news service. It introduced the first on-screen newscaster; the first double-headed programme; computerized graphics, ENG and the electronic newsroom. *Channel 4 News* made room for analysis by extending the airtime to fifty minutes.

But that's small beer compared to the next milestone. After cutting its teeth on 24-hour radio, ITN has taken on its rivals BSkyB and the BBC with 24-hour TV news. The assault is via cable and satellite. Will it spell the end to the major news programmes on terrestrial ITV? Not according to ITN's Editor-in-Chief, Nigel Dacre:

> *'The big debate is whether when there are many more channels there will still be room for big flagship programmes alongside 24-hour news, or whether 24-hour news will supplant terrestrial. My view very strongly is there will be room for both. Viewers will want the choice of a big entertainment channel with well-packaged news programmes, or to pick up their news when they want, from a 24-hour TV channel, off their mobile phone or PC. Our job at ITN is to make sure we are in all those areas.'*

And the official line is, more news will mean more jobs. But this brave new world of ever-increasing competition is also driving down costs and forcing greater efficiencies. *'The basic philosophy of ITN news – the thrusting, assertive journalism – lives on,'* says Robin Elias. *'It's hard work, but it can be just as much fun as it was in the old days.'*

Figure 99 Meanwhile behind the scenes in mission control – a myriad monitors line the walls of the master control room (MCR) at ITN. (*Andrew Boyd*)

Fieldwork

1 Arrange to visit a TV station and watch a news programme being prepared and going out on air.
2 During your visit work out how news coverage is organized and who decides what to cover and what to run.
   Is there any arrangement for pooling reports with other stations?
   How are reports sent back to the newsroom from location?
3 Do you think it is a good idea for newsreaders to hear everything going on in the control room through their earpiece? What problems do you think it could cause?
4 Simulate wearing an earpiece by listening to a talk station on the radio through headphones and reading out a news story on tape at the same time. Listen to the result. Did your newsreading suffer at all? Did you find it difficult to concentrate?
5 What effect do you think expanding the length of news programmes has had on coverage? Is longer news necessarily better news? Discuss.

INSIDE ITN

24 A story is born

'It's a totally predatory business. You've got to have nerves of steel, because if you miss your slot or fail to get something everybody knows you've screwed up. It's a public humiliation. You can't carry someone who really doesn't know what they're doing, because it can go so horribly wrong. You rely on everyone, they all have to be good. And it's very competitive. It can be fraught sometimes – tempers flare because of the pressure, but everyone makes up afterwards.'
— ITN PRODUCER EMMA HOSKYNS

It's set to be an absolute blockbuster of a trial – a head-on libel clash between two outspoken egos, former MP Neil Hamilton and Harrods department store owner Mohamed al-Fayed.

Mr Hamilton is suing the charismatic Egyptian over his claims, made in a Channel 4 documentary, that the former MP had taken cash payments from the Harrods boss to ask questions in Parliament, giving rise to the allegation that MPs can be bought, given a plentiful supply of cash and brown envelopes.

The two characters are as colourful as they are controversial. Mr Hamilton lost his seat as an MP to a former television war correspondent standing on an anti-sleaze ticket. Mr al-Fayed notoriously blamed the British royal family for plotting the car crash which killed Princess Diana and her lover, al-Fayed's son, Dodi.

The exchanges in court are sure to be steamy. ITN and everyone else is running this one big. The trial is to take place at Court No. 13 in the High Court in London. If all goes well, whichever titan has the upper hand might stop and talk to reporters. If it goes badly, the loser will want to keep a low profile and duck the cameras.

To make that as hard as possible, ITN has all the doors covered. It has three cameramen placed strategically around the High Court, as well as sound recordists, reporters, producers, engineers. ITN alone has news programmes for Channel 3, Channel 4 and Channel 5 to satisfy. And that all adds up to a larger than usual media scrum.

8.30 am. An hour before even the court tea lady is likely to turn up. It's a foot-stampingly cold, grey day outside the High Court. And under British law, which bars cameras from court, outside is where the crews will remain. This poses a problem when it comes to coverage. TV thrives on movement and action. But the only colour in a court

Figure 100   Face the scrum – all eyes on the eminent libel lawyer George Carman as he heads for the High Court. ITN's sound recorder, Mike Parkin, keeps a steadying hand on cameraman Mike Inglis as he walks backwards to get his shot. (*Andrew Boyd*)

case is in the verbal slanging match going on inside. So there is one shot that's absolutely crucial – and that's the arrival of the main players at the court.

This case is going to go on all day, possibly all month, so updates will be needed for successive bulletins.

ITN's Home Affairs correspondent, Shiulie Ghosh, will cover the case, with back-up from producer Emma Hoskyns who will step into the court room while Shiulie dives out to do her piece to camera and file her report.

The report will be edited on location in an edit truck parked nearby and beamed back via an adjoining links vehicle for transmission. This arrangement means Shiulie can cut things fine and stay in court until the last possible moment.

'*You need to get used to working accurately and quickly,*' she says. '*Deadlines are all-important. There's no point waiting for that crucial bit of information if it means missing your slot on the programme. You have to learn to make do with what you have – even if it's not perfect – because there's always the next programme.*'

Outside the High Court, a gaggle of press photographers and cameramen have marked out their pitch and are checking their gear. Bags are slung over the railings and stepladders – to gain a vital height advantage – are set in place. Friendly rivalry exists between the TV crews and stills photographers. As the minutes tick by and more turn up there is some good-natured jockeying for position. '*Make way for the real press,*' quips a national newspaper photographer. Another peers both ways down the road in search of a car carrying either of the principal players. '*You never know which way these devious types are going to come in,*' he says.

Mike Inglis, the cameraman, has been at ITN for 26 years. '*These snappers are a good bunch of lads,*' he says. '*But it can sometimes turn into a bit of a fight. I've been pushed off my ladder before now with a £20 000 camera. The job's much more difficult with press corps like this, because you might fall arse over tit.'*

To make sure he doesn't, sound recordist Mike Parkin will cover his back – literally. *'I have to watch the back of the man I'm teamed up with,'* he explains. *'He's got to walk backwards, so we don't want him tripping up or falling over a pair of steps.'* There could be a fortune for the first genius to come up with a backward-facing camera.

Mike Inglis and the others could have just a matter of seconds to get those essential shots of al-Fayed and Hamilton arriving, their faces radiating confidence or betraying anxiety, depending on which way the winds of fortune are blowing.

'This job has changed radically,' Mike adds. *'We used to work in teams of three, now we're usually on our own.'*

Mike Parkin's not expecting any of today's newsmakers to give statements to the media, not at this stage in the proceedings, when they will want to keep their powder dry for the court. Parkin has travelled the world with ITN. He searches back in time for his most testing assignment, covering a conflict in Israel.

'When you're very young you come from the studio and join the crews and go straight to the war zone. It's bloody frightening. You go out with the crews at the start of the day and never know really whether you'll be coming back.' He grins. *'It's good fun.'*

Keeping the show on the road is Emma's job. *'It'll be an enormous story today,'* she explains, *'because al-Fayed is taking the stand. His own lawyer will be asking the questions, but in the afternoon the cross-examination will start and the lawyers will go for his throat.*

'My brief is to manage the cameras and make sure we're covered for every eventuality. There won't be many pictures, so it's absolutely vital to get good shots of al-Fayed

Figure 101 ITN correspondent Shiulie Ghosh braves the rain to do her piece to camera. *'The atmosphere in the court is electric'* (Andrew Boyd)

arriving, because he's the key witness today. I've also got to make sure we've got all the right library footage with it, that everything works and we do all the logistics right.

'When it starts, we both go inside and take notes, then when Shiulie has to pull out at a reasonable time to start editing her package for lunchtime, I'll stay in, and if there are any really good lines I'll come out and tell her.'

There are many more journalists in TV, like Emma, who work behind the scenes, than the few who appear on camera.

'If it's glamour you're after, it's worth remembering that for every journalist who appears on camera or in front of the microphone there might be eight or 10 working behind the scenes as writers, producers and subeditors.

'It's jobs in these categories which are available in the greatest numbers and which offer the most opportunities to new entrants to learn the basics of broadcast journalism. From there promotion can be swift – either to more senior positions on the editorial production ladder, or into the field as reporters or specialist correspondents.'   – IVOR YORKE, THE MOVING IMAGE SOCIETY*

Thirty-one-year-old Emma began her career working for ABC News in London as an intern – that's American for slave labourer. Fortunately, it worked out for Emma. ABC had a link with ITN. Her boss recommended her, so she started freelancing. *'It's all about being in the right place at the right time and meeting the right people.'*

Emma took a degree in politics and law but trained in journalism on the job. As a specialist in home affairs, she spends a lot of time outside the courts – hence the trapper cap with the furry earflaps. *'The hairiest moment is when someone arrives and you think you've missed something – you get crushed to death in the scrum and think you've lost your cameraman somewhere.*

'You keep learning all the time from other people's ideas. The trap is to become formulaic and relax into that. But you need to keep pushing.'

And this week, Emma has been pushing for some 60 hours – more than usual, she explains. Her job typically involves an early start or a late finish. Sometimes both.

Emma is grateful for the three cameras here today – a rare luxury. To make up a sequence of shots you need contrasting images. If you cut together similar shots from the same camera position it will look as though there has been a jump on the tape.

Suddenly, a luxury car pulls up and the media scrum surges forward. Al-Fayed arrives. He's is in a confident, effusive mood. Taking his time, he climbs out, beams, waves his arms and lets the camera crews take their fill, to calls of *'Mr al-Fayed!'* or *'Sir, look over here!'* But he's not giving any interviews.

From behind, it's a mass of photographers and cameramen, some with cameras in the air to shoot over the heads of the scrum, hoping to catch images they can't see. Others are teetering on ladders, forming an almost complete circle around al-Fayed, some spilling out into the oncoming traffic, everyone hoping for that elusive moment of eye contact with the lens. Looking on are a swivel-eyed posse of besuited minders. Whisper has it they are ex-SAS.

---

* www.bksts.com/training/journal.htm

As al-Fayed and his entourage start towards the court, the scrum oozes backwards ahead of him. Amazingly, nobody takes a tumble. In a moment, it's all over. The stocky grey-suited respondent is swallowed up by the High Court.

Emma pushes back a wisp of hair and looks satisfied. *'We had a camera to the side, so we got the only clear shot of him getting out of the car, walking towards us. Then we were able to follow behind him, which gives us a reverse shot of his back as he greets the press, with this whole mêlée in front of him. We've got a camera in the scrum, looking at him face on and another on a high shot, which gives us a bird's eye view of the whole thing. If we needed to do a very long sequence, we've got all the angles, so that's great.'*

'That's if I remembered to switch on,' says Mike with a grin.

'I hate it when you do that,' says Emma.

Now it's all eyes on the lookout for the plaintiff, Hamilton. Mike Inglis detaches himself from the pack and takes up position across the road on a halfway point marked by a traffic island. There he hopes to catch Hamilton and his wife, Christine, approaching the court via a zebra crossing – if they choose to come that way. It's a gamble, and Mike is the only cameraman to risk it. But Mike observed Hamilton coming that way yesterday, and hopes he's a creature of habit.

His guess holds good. Neil Hamilton and his wife roll up from the opposite direction and use the zebra crossing. Mike has a long, clear view. Hamilton is less effusive than Fayed, but he stops and smiles and waits outside the court until everyone is satisfied, before striding up the steps and through the main gate.

10 am. Emma takes the rushes to a waiting ITN links vehicle, which is illegally parked under sufferance and by dint of tradition on pavement 100 metres from the High Court. From there the rushes are relayed to a mast in line of sight at the London Weekend Television tower, and are piped out to ITN to serve the various programmes and bulletins that are following the case. The original tapes are kept in the adjoining edit truck to be compiled into a report for the *Lunchtime News*.

So ITN has the all-important arrivals in the bag. But the report would be dull if those were the only pictures. So Priscilla, the court artist, is busy inside Court No.13. She sits, she watches, she studies and she remembers. But heaven help her if she puts pencil to paper. British law again. No one is allowed to film, record or even draw on the premises, so she has to fix faces, expressions and positions into her memory. When she comes out she will have minutes to put together a small masterpiece.

The ideal thing would be to have a rostrum camera handy, so the picture could be well lit and shot from above. But ITN gets round this by using a statue of a war hero and a roll of masking tape. Priscilla, who supplements her income by selling her court portraits to pander to the vanity of barristers, tapes up the picture to the plinth of a statue of Bomber Harris. Mike Inglis mounts his camera on a tripod, points it at the picture, takes some static shots and close-ups of the key players, then pans around to give some movement.

There's one final visual element to come, and that's Shiulie Ghosh's piece to camera. This is the reporter's 20 seconds of fame, where the viewer can put a face to the report.

Shiulie emerges from the High Court, where she describes the atmosphere as *'electric'*. It's less than an hour to the *Lunchtime News*, but Shiulie has paced it well and seems in no hurry. *'A woman has to put on her lipstick,'* she says, smoothing her dark hair to stop it blowing in the wind. She stands close to the entrance, with the High Court behind her for visual impact and delivers her soundbite as the rain starts to fall.

PIECE TO CAMERA

The piece to camera is the reporter's in-vision personal address to millions of viewers. Health correspondent Anya Sitaram is doing a story about an Australian dentist who passed HIV on to one of his patients.

While Anya rehearses her lines, cameraman Roger Lorenzo sets up the tripod. Then it's take, retake, and retake again as shooting is interrupted by the wail of sirens. Anya does her piece five or six times until she's satisfied. Then she watches it back through the viewfinder: *'Yes, that's all right, apart from the hair. It's sticking up like a rooster.'*

Long-suffering Roger agrees to another retake.

'The State of New South Wales in Australia has said it will strike off doctors and dentists who fail to take proper precautions against spreading AIDS . . .'

Anya's piece is about 12 seconds long and comes out slightly different each time. Some reporters script their pieces and learn them off by heart, others, like Anya, opt for a more natural approach. She goes for a single concept expressed in two or three brief statements: *'I'm trying to get an idea across. I sort of remember thoughts and then I say them. It's more relaxed if you can do it like you're just talking.'*

With the soundbite on tape, it's off to the edit truck to put the report together, leaving Emma inside Court 13 to catch any new angles.

The edit truck is a heavily converted Volkswagen camper van laden with electronics. In charge of it is Dave McDonald, a multi-skilled technician, who can both shoot a camera and edit the footage.

These tapes are shot on DVC pro, a digital format using miniature tapes. Dave edits them on a device that looks like a James Bond briefcase with a couple of LCD monitors mounted into the lid.

The vehicle's engine is kept running to provide the power to run the hardware. Should the motor pack up the van can be plugged into the mains. *'You can take this anywhere in the country and edit a whole package for the bulletin,'* he says, *'then you can send it back via a satellite dish or the links vehicle.'*

Shiulie settles down in the seat next to him and begins to write her script. Oddly enough in this high-tech environment, there is no word processor on board, so she has to resort to the time-honoured method of scrawling her script in a notebook. Not that there's any shortage of good material – today, or in the days to come.

'It's a story of uncontrolled greed and unbridled extravagance.' – George Carman, QC

'What Mr al-Fayed has said repeatedly is that to prevent the forthcoming marriage of Dodi and the Princess of Wales they were murdered by British intelligence on the direction of Prince Philip.' – Desmond Browne, QC

'We shall say and prove in this court that Mr Hamilton was a greedy and somewhat unscrupulous politician at the time who was on the make and on the take.' – George Carman, QC

'Mr al-Fayed is a classic Jekyll and Hyde figure – a man with a jovial side, a man with a thoroughly evil side.' – Desmond Browne, QC

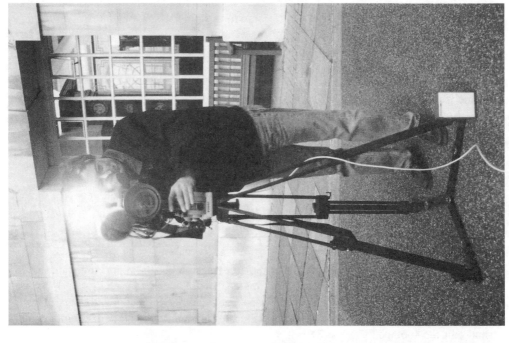

Figure 102 The piece to camera: 'Doctors say it's almost inconceivable that such a thing could happen here. What took place in a surgeon's private consulting room in Australia was clearly in breach of guidelines. Anya Sitaram, News at Ten, Central London.' 13″

(*Right*) Here's looking at you, kid . . . try not to be dazzled. Reporter's eye view of the light and the lens. (*Andrew Boyd*)

While Shiulie composes her script, Dave McDonald sets about editing the pictures. There is no time for shot logging and no need on a story like today's. There are only a few shots of the arrivals and the picture drawn by the court artist. Just as well:

> *'Sometimes a jury can come to a decision at 20 past 12 and ITN wants a package for the 12.30. If you know where all the pictures are and the journalist is quick at writing the script you can turn around a 1'30" package in 10 minutes,' says Dave. 'The journalist comes in and says, "Look, I just want 20 seconds of an arrival shot and 10 seconds of a soundbite." They go on writing their words and I can get on and choose the shots. It's easy.'*

Shiulie calls ITN for details of the lead they will use for the piece. This is the short cue the newsreader will read to set up the story. A journalist back at ITN has turned that around from agency material fed from the court.

(IN VISION)

The Harrods owner, Mohamed Al Fayed, today accused Neil Hamilton's lawyers of inhuman behaviour by raising the death of his son Dodi during the cash for questions trial.

   He was responding to accusations that he'd told lies about Dodo's relationship with Princess Diana.

   Our Home Affairs Correspondent, Shiulie Ghosh, was in court.

(TAKE VTR)

Next Shiulie lays down the narration using a lip mike to cut out the background noise of the van's engine and the London traffic.

Figure 103   Shiulie (*centre*) puts the final touches to the script in the edit van, with the help of producer Emma Hoskyns, while Dave McDonald edits the opening sequence. (*Andrew Boyd*)

The sound is split into two channels. Her narration goes onto channel one, while all the soundtrack of the arrival hubbub has been recorded on channel two.

Beside the DVC pro edit suite are two older Beta machines, which take analogue tape. Beta is tried, tested and of higher quality than DVC, which compresses the signal to fit onto a smaller tape. But the great advantage of the new digital format is its portability – permitting smaller cameras and a highly mobile edit suite.

'You can take this anywhere in the world, into a hotel room and start editing within two minutes,' says Dave. *'With the old Beta system, if you haven't got an edit van, you'd have to take two Beta machines, which weigh a ton, and plug them all up with their monitors, which would take half an hour.'*

The DVC editing may be digital, but the report is compiled the old-fashioned way. The shots are laid down one after the other to build up the report. This is called *linear editing*.

Non-linear editing, where all the shots are digitized on a computer and can be called up instantaneously and assembled and re-edited in any order, is touted as the way of the future. But Dave is not so sure. *'With a computer system, all the pictures have to be loaded in before you can edit them, which takes time. But if a news story breaks minutes before going on air, I can just stick a tape in a Beta system and edit it.'*

Dave also has his doubts about the move towards journalists doing their own editing. *'The dream was that a journalist would sit at an edit suite and put a package together, so you would have no editor. But the trouble is, they would have to get their story, write their script, and editing it as well would take more time. But an editor would find the tapes for you, get the pictures and lay them down. All the journalist has to worry about is writing the words.'*

It's well past 12 before Shiulie finishes her package and it's ready for transmission. Court has adjourned, so she stays in the edit truck to watch the report going out on air. It's been kicked out of the lead spot by the news that the Prime Minister's wife is going to have a baby. Ah, well. Time for a swift pub lunch before grinding back into gear for the evening news.

The story angle changes in the afternoon as the courtroom allegations start flying thick and fast. ITN's flagship news decides to go big on the story:

6.30 THE ITV EVENING NEWS WITH TREVOR McDONALD

Top shot al-Fayed arrival	The headlines: Drama in court as al-Fayed finally takes the stand . . .
TREVOR McDONALD IN VISION	Good evening. Mohamed al-Fayed took the stand in his High Court libel battle with Neil Hamilton today and launched into a tirade against the former Conservative MP. The Harrods boss was stopped several times by the judge and told not to make speeches. Mr Fayed denied he'd made up stories about giving Mr Hamilton cash. He said Mr Hamilton was a greedy man who thought he'd discovered the golden goose, and who would sell his mother for money. He said of Mr Hamilton, 'he puts his hand in my pocket and takes out £5,000, drinking vintage wine and champagne'. From the High Court, here's ITN's Shiulie Ghosh:

(TAKE VTR)

L/S al-Fayed	He arrived like the showman he is, ready to do battle.
M/S al-Fayed	Mohamed al-Fayed finally took the witness stand today in what's been billed as one of the biggest fights of the decade.
M/S al-Fayed	It was the first time he'd ever given evidence publicly, and the courtroom was packed.
3-shot Hamiltons	But if his opponent Neil Hamilton expected him to be embarrassed or nervous in the witness box he was sorely disappointed.
2-shot Hamiltons	Within minutes the former MP was under attack and being denounced as a man who would sell his own mother.
M/S Carman (rear)	Mr al-Fayed was first questioned by his lawyer, George Carman. He told him how he carried bundles of cash around in his briefcase,
M/S Carman (front)	ready to dole out to Mr Hamilton in return for political services.
	Dissolve to court drawing Mr Carman asked about the behaviour of the Hamiltons when they stayed at the Ritz Hotel
C/U al-Fayed drawing	as Mr al-Fayed's guests in 1987. With his heavy accent, Mr al-Fayed said:
Super	'You give him your hospitality and he go and get stamps on my bill.
Super	'All the tips to the doormen and the porters – on my bill.' He went on:
Super	'He puts his hand in my pocket and takes out £5000,
Super	'drinking vintage wine and champagne.'
Dissolve to Carman in drawing	Mr Carman asked if he was lying about events as an
Pan to al-Fayed in drawing	act of revenge against the former MP. Mr al Fayed became heated, replying:
Super	'Why I had to take revenge? To me he is nothing. He is not a human.
Super	'He is someone who would sell his mother for money.
Super	'No dignity, no honour, nothing.'
Dissolve to 2-shot	This afternoon Mr al-Fayed faced a tougher challenge – cross-examination by Neil Hamilton's lawyer Desmond Browne QC.
Top shot Hamilton	This was the moment Mr Hamilton had been waiting for – the chance to prove his one-time friend was a liar.
Dissolve to zoom in on drawing	Mr Browne began by asking whether he thought he had the integrity to be an MP himself.
Super	Mr al-Fayed replied, 'Yes, sir. 100 per cent, but I don't want to be a Member of Parliament.'
Super	He went on: 'I'm a leader, I'm important in business.
Super	I own the greatest department store in the world.
Super	Who has made it? I have made it.'
Dissolve to CU drawing	Mr Browne then went on to question Mr al-Fayed about the use of al in his name, suggesting he used it to make his name sound grander.

Dissolve to CU al-Fayed drawing	Mr al-Fayed said it was tradition, adding:
Super	'You can call me Al Capone if you like.'
Dissolve to wideshot drawing	Mr Browne continued to suggest he'd lied about his background, to which Mr al-Fayed replied:
Super	'You're just trying to discredit me
Super	'because you want to defend your crooked client.'
Shiulie in vision with super	There were frequent outbursts of laughter from the gallery, for example, when Mr al-Fayed forgot his date of birth and asked to check his passport. But the intention behind these questions is clear – Neil Hamilton's camp has to discredit this man as a liar in the eyes of the jury.
M/S al-Fayed	But when Mr al-Fayed left he appeared to enjoy the attention. The cross-examination continues on Monday. Shiulie Ghosh, ITN, at the High Court.*

Shiulie is assigned to cover the rest of the Hamilton/al-Fayed trial, which drags on for five weeks. As well as producing packages she has to do *live-spots* – live interviews with the newsreader, often at short-notice.

'It's easy to become flustered and nervous when you're on air,' she says. *'Live reporting can be very nerve-wracking, especially when there's a crowd around you or it's raining.*

'It's important to speak slowly and calmly – that way you sound authoritative. Don't gabble or raise the pitch of your voice. And, unless you've got a phenomenal memory, always keep crucial facts and figures on a notepad that you can glance at if you lose your way.

'The important thing is always keep going! The worst moment I ever had during a live-spot was forgetting my words – the stumbling to a halt in the middle of a sentence on national telly. It was the most embarrassing moment of my life, saved only by the quick thinking of the presenter who jumped in and asked another question.'

All good things must come to an end and, eventually, Mr Hamilton loses his case and declares himself penniless. As for Mr al-Fayed, after accusing the British royal family of killing Princess Diana and his son, his department store, Harrods, is deprived of its royal warrant. Meanwhile the media has a ball and the libel lawyers get a good deal richer. Looking back on the case, Shiulie Ghosh recalls:

'It was fascinating to watch a high-profile case like this from start to finish, but often difficult to cover on a daily basis, because I had to leave court frequently to file updates. Luckily, reporters from the different media got to know each other well during the five weeks the trial continued and I was able to catch up from my colleagues' notes.

'At the end of the trial, though, there were no such niceties – everyone was out for themselves! There was a mad scrum of newspaper reporters, TV and radio journalists on the day of the verdict. Then of course there are members of the public who stop for a look and police officers trying to control the crowd.

'It can be noisy and intimidating. You have to stay focused. In that situation it's vitally important to be at the front of the crowd with your camera and microphone in a position to catch any interviews. But I wasn't alone. I had the help of my excellent producer, who found people to interview and brought them to me.

'It's all mayhem, but there's a buzz when you get it right.'

---

* *Top shot*: Camera held high and looking down; *In Vision*: talking to the camera; *Take VTR*: play the tape; *L/S*: long shot (distant figure); *M/S*: mid-shot (down to waist); *3-shot and 2-shot*: number of people in the picture; *Dissolve*: where one picture fades into the next; *C/U*: close-up; *Super*: caption; *Pan*: camera swivels across the picture.

1 The ITV *Evening News* with Trevor McDonald . . .

2 Drama in court as al-Fayed finally takes the stand . . .

Figure 104

3 Mr Browne went on to question Mr al-Fayed . . .

4 . . . about the use of Al in his name . . .

Figure 104 *Continued*

5 There were frequent outbursts of laughter from the gallery . . .

Figure 104 *Continued*

Like Shiulie, Emma thrives on the sheer hectivity of it all. *'I'm an adrenalin junkie – you have to be in television news, it's so fast – constant updates. The logistics challenge everything. You don't just think, "What's the story?", but "How do I cover it? What's the angle? Where will I find the best shots?" And you have to get in there first.'*

Thirty-one-year-old Shiulie describes the highlight of her career as being stationed with the Royal Air Force during the NATO offensive against Serbian forces in Kosovo.

'I was based in Gioia del Colle in southern Italy at an airbase from which British Harriers launched their bombing runs. Over the weeks we reporters came to know the pilots and their commanding officers well. We watched as they took off and waited anxiously during the hours their mission was in progress. There was always relief when they all came home safely.

'I was lucky enough to be one of the few reporters allowed on a refuelling tanker – a plane responsible for the mid-air refuelling of American and British warplanes.

'During our 12-hour flight we flew close to enemy territory, from where we clearly saw the flashes of bombs exploding, dropped by NATO fighters. An unforgettable experience.

e-cortal
BNP-Paribas Group   At e-cortal

Fayed says Hamilton "would sell his own mother"

Harrods boss Mohamed Al Fayed has described Neil Hamilton, the former MP who brought a libel action against him, as the kind of person who would "sell his own own mother for money".

Mr Al Fayed said he had gone public with allegations that he'd paid Mr Hamilton to ask questions in Parliament because "The voter has to know, the ordinary people have to know what kind of people they have put in power,"

He told the jury."It's a very important decision ... I pay hundreds of millions in taxes and to see people like that in power, it's not acceptable. It's a duty."

Mr Al Fayed's counsel, George Carman QC, said that it had been suggested that he had made up the story about Mr Hamilton and lied about it for four years as some kind of act of revenge.

Mr Al Fayed became heated as he replied: "Why I had to take revenge? For me, he is nothing, he is not a human, he is someone who would sell his mother for money - no dignity, no honour, nothing".

Earlier he had accused Neil Hamilton's lawyers of "inhumanity" in capitalising on his grief over the death of his son Dodi.

Mr Al Fayed, wearing a grey suit and a black tie, repeatedly swallowed and licked his lips as he stood in the witness box at the High Court and haltingly told Mr Justice Morland and the jury how he felt about Desmond Browne QC's observations on the deaths of his son Dodi and Diana, Princess of Wales.

The pair died in a car crash in a Paris underpass two years ago.

Mr Al Fayed's lawyer, George Carman, had prompted him by saying that during his opening of Mr Hamilton's libel action Mr Browne had used words to the effect that Mr Al Fayed had "forfeited all sympathy" over the tragedy.

Mr Al Fayed said: "It's very hurting. It's inhumane. I think he's done it basically to upset me and upset the family ..."

He closed his eyes briefly as he went on: "... of the two beautiful kids who have lost their mother. And the grief that has hit me.

"To repeat such tragedy is completely inhumane and someone, if he is a father, he have children, and he understand what it means for a father to lose his son - he have to pursue every angle to find out if there is anything suspicious about the loss of my son.

Figure 105   Don't forget the web – on-line coverage of the libel trial from ITN. (*Courtesy www.itn.co.uk*)

> *'The best of the job is covering so many different world events. Journalism is a privileged seat from which to view history in the making.*
>
> *'The worst is the depressing realization that there's so much corruption, racism, violence, nastiness and poverty in the world. It's difficult not to let yourself become hardened, and journalists in general I think develop quite a cavalier attitude towards issues that would horrify most people.'*

Fieldwork

1 Record a TV news programme and scrutinize one particular report. Watch it again to see how it was constructed. Note every shot, giving its type, duration and subject. Note also the supers (caption superimposed on picture) and graphics and their duration.

Now transcribe the commentary and reconstruct the script in its entirety giving commentary, camera shots and visuals.

2 Discuss ways to improve that report. Could the script be tightened? Could it say more or should it say less? What do you think of the camera shots? Were they dramatic and interesting enough? Can you think of any better shots they could have taken? Why do you think they didn't?

3 Get together in teams of four if possible and imagine you are preparing the day's news from scratch. Your brief is to provide a 30-minute programme of national and international news. Using only the national newspapers as prompts draw up plans for enough items to fill your half-hour and to make a balanced programme. If you do follow the newspapers, make sure your ideas take the story a stage further than the press – don't resort to covering their old ground. Think about item length and the shape of the programme.

4 Now put together some proposals for graphics and visuals to provide extra illustrations for your reports.

5 Think up a scenario for an interview, based on one of your ideas for a news item. Find a willing volunteer to play the part of the interviewee and give him time to get briefed on the subject. There's a catch – he's to play the part of someone who's never been interviewed before and is very nervous. Conduct the interview, under lights in a TV studio if you have one, and record it if possible with a single camera. Do your best to reassure your interviewee and put him at ease. Discuss the interview afterwards and see if there are ways you could improve your 'bedside' manner.

TV NEWS COVERAGE

25   Gathering the news

> *'I don't think we're going to get the film. There are some difficulties. The cameraman has been eaten by a crocodile.'*
> – ASSISTANT FILM MANAGER FREDDIE PARTINGTON
> TO ITN EDITOR GEOFFREY COX*

ENG (electronic newsgathering)

In television, where the free flow of money leaves radio looking like a poor relation, technologists have had the incentive to come up with new ideas to satisfy the never ending demand for faster news.

Electronic news gathering (ENG) – also called *EJ* (*electronic journalism*), *ECC* (*electronic camera coverage*), *PSC* – (*portable single camera*), is the technocrat's solution.

ENG long ago overhauled film in news-gathering organizations around the world, with cameras that record sound as well as pictures and that are smaller, lighter, more robust and can be edged right up to the forefront of action to send back live reports. In the USA, where these were first used, they were dubbed 'creepy peepies'.

The latest generation of digital ENG cameras record directly on to digital videotape or computer disk.

There are big advantages to using the digital format over analogue videotape, which is still used widely. Picture quality is often higher and digital ENG cameras store the images in a form that cannot be corrupted, even after generations of copying.

Once the pictures have been downloaded into an edit computer, they can be compiled in any sequence, and that order can easily be changed. Extra shots can be inserted in the middle of a report without having to remake everything that follows. But with analogue recordings the report is built up shot by shot onto videotape. So if you want to make a change in the middle of a report you will have to redo all the sequences that follow.

* *ITN – The First 40 Years*, 1995.

Figure 106 Smaller, lighter, sharper. Digital equipment means the news can be gathered and edited on location. (*Courtesy Panasonic*)

The downside to this process, which is called *non-linear editing*, is that images recorded on digital videotape first have to be transferred to the computer, which takes as long to do as it took to shoot. This problem is avoided by using cameras that shoot the footage directly onto computer memory. Each shot can be accessed immediately without any spooling.

A battle for ascendancy between rival manufacturers backing different formats is being played out in the professional broadcast market: *'We are entering into the biggest format war you will ever see,'* says Panasonic Broadcast Europe.

Cameraperson

The cameraperson's stock in trade is likely to be an ENG camcorder equipped with a zoom lens operating on a ratio of up to 20:1. This allows the same camera to cover everything from wide-angle shots to close-ups without having to be relocated. The zoom can be operated by hand or by electric motor. Pictures and sound are recorded onto the same tape.

The standard camera kit will include a lens hood to cut out glare, rechargeable battery packs, spare videocassettes, a portable light and a tripod.

For location shooting in troublespots, where it is essential to be inconspicuous, some crews pass themselves off as tourists by using miniature digital camcorders.

The latest offerings from the likes of Sony and Canon shoot on an hour-long digital videocassette (DVC) little bigger than a box of matches. Their three CCD sensors offer 500+ line resolution, against the 700 lines of professional digital camcorders costing many times as much. As most domestic TVs display little more than 500 lines, the picture is embarrassingly good set against their costly professional cousins. And these domestic machines will even shoot in widescreen.

For filming in the dark, in circumstances like a battlefield where lights would be inappropriate or dangerous, the cameraperson may also pack an image intensifier to replace the normal lens and give the camera night vision. Some camcorders have a device built in which allows them to shoot in monochrome in almost total darkness.

Past form has been for camera operators to make a note of each different shot on a *dopesheet* which lists the subject and type of shot, stating whether it was a close-up or long shot, etc. The dopesheet is used to help select the best shots for editing. Videotapes are still labelled – it would cause chaos otherwise – but detailed shot-lists are rapidly becoming things of the past, or are confined to circumstances where the luxury of time permits.

What the editor needs from the cameraperson is a sensible selection of angles and sequences of long shot, medium shot and close-up. He or she wants well-composed, in focus, rock-steady pictures held for a minimum of 10 seconds, preferably 20.

The editor also wants a minimum of tape to look through. For a news report of about two minutes there can be no justification for filling up a couple of cassettes. **Use the camera like a sniper's rifle – not a machine gun**. Every unnecessary shot is a waste of two people's time – the camera operator's and the editor's – so even though tape is cheap every shot should count.

The cameraperson and reporter usually work as a team. In current affairs or documentary work, the crew include a director, but for news they will be on their own.

The reporter and cameraperson may both have ideas to contribute about which shots to use in the report. Some friendly rivalry usually exists, often accompanied by a degree of mutual leg pulling. Get them on their own and most camerapeople would say *they* call the shots, while most reporters would argue the credit goes to them.

Experienced camera operators have a well-developed news-sense of their own, and often take fledgling reporters under their wing. But in the end it falls to the reporter to act as director; he or she will have to pull the item together and write the script and so should

Figure 107 Shooting from the skies with the ITN helicopter. (*Courtesy ITN*)

have the last word about the story treatment. However, the shrewd reporter will quickly find that tact and diplomacy are better means of persuasion than dictatorship.

News camera operators are paid to be artisans rather than artists. Their filming is direct and to the point. Long, evocative zooms, sweeping pans, and shots filmed at artistic angles might go down well in the movies, but are guaranteed to give an editor apoplexy when it comes to assembling a news report. How do you cut into a pan or a zoom? How *do* you follow a shot looking up an interviewee's left nostril?

Recordist

Cameracrews comprise one, two or occasionally three people. Most of ITN's recordings are made by a one-person crew, who combines sound and pictures in a camcorder, occasionally aided by the reporter. But where sound is likely to be a problem or a media scrum is expected a sound recordist will join the team. As well as adjusting and monitoring the levels, he or she is traditionally the team's fixer, who makes the arrangements and gets the right doors open at the right times.

The recordist – and reporter – usually stick as close as possible to the cameraperson. There is more to this than mere chumminess. All three can be linked with cables, which can make the going difficult in a fast-moving situation such as a riot.

The recordist packs a wide selection of microphones. Most mikes are susceptible to wind noise, when even a slight gust across the top can be transformed into a roaring hurricane. Outdoor camera mikes will be protected by a windshield of acoustic foam covered by a fluffy fur-fabric muff.

A directional rifle mike is standard kit for location recordings. The recordist can stand or kneel out of vision and the mike will pick up sound from the direction it is pointed across a narrow angle. It can even isolate individuals within a group. The recordist's aim has to be good. A couple of degrees out and the gun mike will pick up the wrong person or background noise instead.

Another drawback with the gun mike is that with its cover off it can look a little too like its namesake, so it is best avoided in battle zones unless the recordist wants to become a target. The alternative for interviews out of doors is for the reporter to hold a stick mike with a foam windshield, similar to those used in radio.

Indoors, where wind noise will not be present, a pair of tie clip or clip-on mikes is usually favoured. The disadvantages are that they can pick up clothing rustle, and because they work on the condenser principle, they can draw in spurious background noise, such as the rumble of traffic or air-conditioning. An alternative is to use a couple of directional desk top mikes.

Another important part of the kit will be a radio mike. This frees the reporter from the leash and is useful for situations where lengths of microphone cable would be a handicap, such as in crowds where the reporter might get separated from the recordist, or where it is necessary to film the reporter walking alone without the unnatural accompaniment of 15 m or so of trailing cable.

There can be a personal price to pay for that freedom. Users of radio mikes have been described as walking radio stations. They have to carry a transmitter, which is a small box with a length of dangling wire. This is most conveniently clipped to the back of the belt, away from the camera, or put in a pocket.

Problems arise when the reporter or interviewee has neither a belt nor a pocket. To keep the mike out of sight, it may mean secreting it down a trouser leg or inside a dress. Women sometimes have to clip the mike to a bra strap, or if their dresses are tightly cut, tape the transmitter to the inside of a thigh.

Fortunately, radio mikes are usually small, being similar in appearance to tie-clip microphones, but they are seldom very robust and are prone to interference.

For documentary and current affairs work, where sound quality is at a greater premium than saving time, a boom mike, like those used in the studio, may be included in the recordist's kit.

Lighting technician

Not all news reports require the services of a lighting technician or assistant. Modern cameras can cope perfectly well with outdoor shots in bright daylight, and as technology develops, they might even be able to dispense with artificial lighting indoors.

What they will never do away with is the lighting assistant's artistic touch, which can render unflattering subjects attractive and work wonders with a poor complexion or indifferent bone structure.

The lighting technician's basic kit includes three or four lights for indoor use, each producing between 750 and 1000 watts, enough to light an average room. These lamps are powered from the mains, and will be fitted with moveable flaps, known as barn doors, to direct the stream of light.

The lights model the subject, pick it out from the background and eliminate unwanted shadows. Three tasks, for which at least three lights are required.

The first of these is the *key*. This is the main light, which is usually placed up to 5 m away from the subject at an angle of about 45 degrees to the camera. The light will be positioned to compensate for the brightness and colour of the room and the skin colour of the subject.

Figure 108   A news crew shoots an aircraft engine on a dull day. Extra lighting is brought in to compensate and a blue filter is placed over the lamp to blend the artificial light with the daylight. (*Andrew Boyd*)

Harsh shadows created by the key are softened and filled by the second lamp, the *fill*. This will be of lower power or have a diffuser to widen the beam and cast a softer glow. The fill is set up behind or beside the camera to the other side of the key to eliminate its shadows. Small extra lights can be brought in to remove maverick shadows and an eye-light may be used to give a little extra sparkle to the eyes.

The third of the trio is the *backlight*, which is placed out of vision, behind and to one side of the subject. This adds depth to the picture, creating an image that is more solidly three-dimensional, and helps separate the subject from the wall behind. It also fills in areas such as the top of the shoulders that the others might have missed.

If the subject is filmed against a window or natural daylight the backlight can be omitted. Where the predominant light is daylight but extra lighting is required, a clear sheet of blue plastic will be clipped over the lamp to act as a filter. This tones down the yellow artificial light to match the bluer balance of natural daylight. Camera-mounted lights incorporate built-in colour filters which the camera operator will adjust for different lighting conditions.

The camera's internal *white balance* should also be adjusted to compensate for daylight, twilight and artificial light. This is done by focusing the camera on a white sheet, such as the page of a notebook, and pressing the white balance control. Adjust the white balance every time the camera shoots in different lighting conditions.

Also in their equipment, lighting technicians will have one or two small hand-held battery-powered lamps, such as Sun Guns, for occasions where larger, tripod-mounted lights would be inappropriate, such as in a moving crowd.

For extra flexibility, an array of smaller lamps may be included, with spares, extension leads and sun reflectors for outdoor shooting.

Larger-scale lighting, to flood an entire hall, would usually be supplied by a contract lighting company.

Some TV stations do away with the lighting assistant by using cameras with a built-in light, though a single light source creates shadows and hot spots and the result can never be as satisfactory as with a full lighting rig.

Others opt for a one-person crew where the reporter is expected to be a multi-skilled jack-of-all-trades. A growing number of ITN and BBC correspondents are required to operate the camera *and* conduct the interview. To cap that, they're expected to report for radio as well!

MULTI-SKILLING AT WESTCOUNTRY TV

Each bureau typically employs a regional journalist, a reporter/presenter, a technical operator who can shoot tape, and a cameraperson who can edit. The news reporters are encouraged to come up with ideas for features and are given a couple of days off from their day job to make them. 'If someone's got a good idea, we'll do it,' says head of news Richard Myers. Recently, a reporter discovered that a Devon man was shipping out water containers to India, so he went to India to film for a week (unfortunately contracting dysentery at the same time). 'These programmes are very economical to make because the guys are all multi-skilled – only a cameraman/editor and the reporter go on shoots, so it's cheap,' Myers says. – PRESS GAZETTE*

---

* 31 May 1996.

The outside broadcast

The outside broadcast (OB) no longer requires an operation on the scale of a military manoeuvre to get live pictures on the screen. In times past, even the most basic OB would tie up crowds of highly paid professionals and tons of expensive equipment. Today, a two-person crew can send live pictures anywhere across the world.

But when it comes to televising set-piece events with multiple cameras – particularly in the world of sport – then it is back to the full-blown OB unit.

This is a complete mobile TV operation, minus only the studio set. Almost anything that can be done in a television studio indoors can be done on location.

The full-blown OB unit can comprise up to 30 people, several vehicles including a generator truck, and between three to five cameras.

At the heart of the unit is a large van, like a furniture removal van, called a *scanner*. This is a control room on wheels, with its own director/producer, engineers, vision mixers, bank of monitors for checking the action, and telephones for keeping in touch with the outside world and base.

The director has a talkback intercom providing spoken communications with all the camera operators. Their headphones have swing down microphones, so they can reply to his or her instructions.

Commentators take their cues through hidden earpieces, if they are to appear in vision, or through headphones. Their microphones also carry a talkback channel so they can reply to the director.

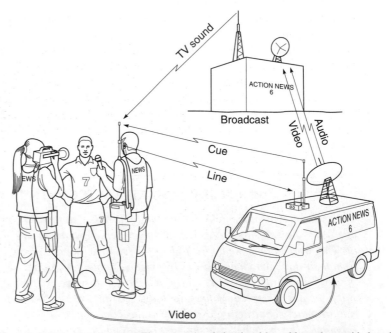

Figure 109 Live broadcasting in action. The camera sends its signal by cable to the outside broadcast (OB) van. The reporter's sound signals are sent via a transmitter carried by the reporter and an aerial strapped to his shoulder. Sound and vision signals are then beamed by microwave dish to a receiver at the TV station. The reporter can hear his report going out and receive his cues from the control room via another antenna on his shoulder. (*Courtesy Sony Broadcast Ltd*)

Outside broadcast commentators often work in crowded, noisy environments, so unless they are appearing on camera, they will use the same kind of close-work microphones as their colleagues in radio to cut out unwanted background noise.

Incoming pictures, plus commentary and graphics, are relayed back to the TV station's master control room along a cable, microwave or satellite link.

For really big set-piece events, such as a royal wedding or state occasion, requiring multiple camera and commentary positions, several outside broadcast units will be combined. At the other end of the scale are lean, lightweight portable production units that can quickly be assembled from boxes.

Getting the story back

Rushing camera crews to an event and producing good pictures is only half the job. Newsgathering isn't finished until those pictures are back at base being edited to go out on air. Every newsroom wants those pictures as soon as possible, and preferably half an hour ago.

On the rare occasions when there is time to spare and the story is breaking close to home, the crew will take their tape back with them for editing.

If a bulletin is approaching and the crew may have to stay at the scene, their videotape will be sent back by despatch rider. Some stations employ their own riders who form part of the camera crew's entourage, following them out and standing by until they are needed.

Figure 110 Portable ground-stations are used to beam news reports into space, where they are bounced off satellites and relayed to transmitters elsewhere in the world. (*Courtesy ITN*)

Figure 111   Even where a satellite ground station is not available, reports can be beamed back from inaccessible locations via a links vehicle. (*Courtesy ITN*)

Some despatch riders are even given cameras of their own – for the moment that big breaking story happens and extra shots are needed.

Raw videotapes can be turned into polished reports in as little as a quarter of an hour by an editor back at base. But if time is very short, recordings can be sent back by satellite or microwave link. Satellite time has to be booked by the minute and is expensive but, increasingly, TV companies are buying portable ground-stations that can transmit pictures from the scene of the news. This has opened the way for live coverage from previously inaccessible places.

Reporter Sandy Gall broke new ground after the Russians invaded Afghanistan. Undaunted by the terrain and lack of transport he loaded the satellite dish on a packhorse and went off in hot pursuit.

Where a microwave link is used, a *links vehicle* will be parked within line of sight of a receiving dish, which will be mounted as high as possible on a tall building or mast.

Links vehicles have masts stretching to 12 m or so to see over buildings. These can be adjusted by remote control from the vehicle. Microwaves transmit in a fine beam, like a penlight torch. The narrow beam means transmitting and receiving aerials have to be lined-up very carefully. An alternative to the microwave link is to send the signals along a cable but this is usually limited to short distances.

Master control room

Master control can be likened to a glorified automatic telephone exchange, only instead of dealing with calls, it handles every signal passing through the television station. MCR receives incoming reports from other television companies, both at home and abroad; it takes sound and vision from outside broadcast units, and receives feeds from remote cameras in key areas such as Parliament. It also maintains the quality of outgoing pictures.

The era of instant communications does have its drawbacks. The shrinking world has opened the way for more news, tighter deadlines and faster travel to ever more remote regions, but one piece of bad news is that foreign reporting is not the plum job it was. Spare time for reporters to relax and soak up the local ambience has been drastically reduced. With networks operating maybe four or five different news programmes a day, feeding radio outlets or providing 24-hour news – the pressure is constantly on for instant updates.

> *'Television – a medium. So-called because it is neither rare nor well-done.'*
> – ERNIE KOVACS

Fieldwork

1 If you can, practise using different format camcorders and compare the results. Which do you think offers the better quality pictures?

2 If you have access to lighting equipment, find a willing subject and practise using the three-light set-up. Experiment by adjusting the position of the lights to get the best results.

3 Now try recording an interview indoors with a single light mounted on the camera. What distance do you have to be away to avoid bleaching out the features? How can the light best be used to avoid hot spots and shadows?

4 Practise using a rifle mike on location. Don't forget to use headphones at the same time so you can monitor the results.

5 What kind of mikes would you use to record (a) an interview indoors with a single interviewee; (b) that same interview out of doors; (c) a discussion with a group of striking pickets; (d) an interview with someone on the big wheel at a fairground?

TV NEWS COVERAGE

26 Camera shots

> 'The camera is now the most powerful weapon in the world.'
> – DOCUMENTARY FILM MAKER PAUL BERRIFF

The shots

For aspiring videojournalists the following is essential reading. But even if you have no aspirations to shoot your own stories, you need to know the kind of shots your cameraperson will have to capture to compile your report.

The camera is only a clumsy impersonator of the human eye, but with one important advantage – it can zoom in and out of a scene. Three shots form the basis of all camerawork – the *long shot, medium shot* and *close-up*. These expand into at least six different shots in everyday use. The following shows how they would be used for screening a person:

- The long shot (*LS*) takes in the whole person from head to feet.
- The medium long shot (*MLS*) cuts in closer, revealing the head to just below the knees.
- The medium shot (*MS*) reveals the head to the hips.
- The medium close-up (*MCU*) gives head and shoulders.
- The close-up (*CU*) shows head only.
- The big close-up (*BCU*) fills the screen with the features of the face.

Different news organizations have their own names for these and may subdivide the categories further. Whatever you call them, the shots refer to the distance the subject is from the camera, and therefore how much of that subject fills the screen – long shots show the subject a long way off, while close ups draw them nearer the viewer.

On location, where the camera is also taking in the surroundings, the long shot would give a view of the whole picture: the tanks rolling over the hillside, the burning building with the firemen in front, or the angry mob advancing.

Figure 112 Pull back to get the big picture . . . Then get in close for the detail. (*Andrew Boyd*)

The medium shot reveals more detail: the tank commander perched in his turret snapping instructions into his radio; a jet of water swallowed up by flames billowing from a top-floor window; ringleaders urging on the mob.

The close-up focuses in on the action: the strain on the tank commander's face; the nozzle of the fire hose with spray bursting out; the wild eyes of the mob leader.

A shot commonly used for establishing locations is the *general view* (*GV*) or *very long shot* (*VLS*) which gives a panorama of the entire scene.

Local TV stations keep a stock of GVs showing important buildings such as hospitals which feature regularly in the news. You can choose your camera shots by running the sequence through in your mind's eye and deciding which shots would go best together.

Camera positions

Another set of shots describes the relative height of the camera to the scene:

● The *top shot* gives a bird's eye view.
● The *high shot* looks down on the scene from the front.
● The *level shot* is in line with the subject's eyes.
● The *low shot* has the camera looking up.
● The *low-level shot* takes a worm's-eye view of the world.

Single shots, *two-shots*, *three-shots* and *group shots* relate to the number of people in vision.

As well as zooming in and out the camera can crank up and down (*elevate* and *depress*). It can be moved backwards and forwards (*track*), sideways (*crab*), swivel (*pan*) and tilt (*cant*).

Zooming, tracking, panning and canting tend not to feature too largely in a single news report, which would prove impossible to edit and bear more than a passing resemblance to some obscure psychological 'B' movie from Eastern Europe.

Hold your shots

Shots should be held for far longer than you might think. Edited TV reports often cut from shot to shot every five seconds, but to give the editor five seconds of footage worth using the cameraperson will need to record at least twice that much. Every shot should be held for a count of 10 or even 20. Some documentary editors prefer to work with a minute per shot.

There's a good reason for this apparent over-production. From the raw footage an editor will want to find five perfectly framed, in-focus, correctly exposed, lively seconds that will begin and end on movement and add interest to the report. The cameraperson's job is to give the editor enough material to work with.

He or she should avoid pans and zooms unless absolutely necessary. For one thing, they often slow down the action. Cutting to a close-up is faster. For another, they can be difficult to edit. Cutting into a pan or zoom can make the audience nauseous. A pan or a zoom should be taken in three parts. It should establish itself, move, and then settle down. The shot should begin with the camera steady, then pan or zoom and rest at the end of the movement. The opening and closing shots should be held for 10 or more seconds, giving the camera operator three shots in one.

Figure 113   Throw a top-light on the scene and go for the over-the-shoulder two-shot. The camera looks over the reporter's shoulder to show the reporter and interviewee together, before zooming in on the interviewee. (*Andrew Boyd*)

Grab action shots first

In a four-bedroomed house in a well-heeled suburb of town, a cornered gunman is holding a wife and her five-year-old child hostage after they disturb him burgling their home. The TV crew gets there as a fresh wave of police reinforcements arrives at the scene.

This is no tidy, set-piece predictable story like a conference, where the crew will try to take pictures in the order in which they will appear in the final report. *Editing on camera*, as this is called, saves time and makes it easier to put together the item, but is often impossible with breaking news.

But at a shotgun siege or other fast-moving story the cameraperson becomes the hunter; his task is to *'shoot it quick before it moves'*, to capture the moment before it disappears.

After establishing with a glance that the gunman is out of sight and regrettably cannot be filmed, the cameraperson quickly grabs a long shot of armed police piling out of their vehicles and taking up positions behind parked cars.

Like the shots which come later of the gunman firing wildly from behind the curtain, and the police teargas driving him from the building, these pictures can never be repeated; they have to be grabbed while they are available.

The interview with the police chief, close-ups of his men and scenes of the house front can wait until a lull in the action. The temporary shots – shots that will go away – are filmed first.

Shoot for impact

News is about action and change, so the news camera should be looking for things that are moving or are in the process of change – a new printing press whirling into action, the ship going down the slipway, the plane taking off or landing.

Pictures which have the greatest impact are those that capture the action at its height. The sports photographer will try to snap the ball going through the posts or the batsman being caught; the news photographer will go for the champagne smashing against the side of the hull, or the ribbon parting the moment it is cut.

TV is the same, but the moving-picture sequence takes the viewer up to the point of action and follows it through.

Shoot in sequences

But there is a critical difference between the work of the cameraperson and the photojournalist who uses a stills camera. In news reportage both are looking for that crucial moment, but the photojournalist just has to freeze a fraction of a second in time. The cameraperson has to capture enough footage to show what is happening and to give the narrator time to explain.

In a news report, few shots are held for longer than several seconds. Yet a single element of the story could take 25 seconds to tell. This means that not one, but several shots are required, enough to give the editor plenty of choice. And those shots should represent a range of images from wide shots to close-up; from the big picture to points of detail.

The sequence could begin with a long shot taking in the entire scene of the siege, showing the street with the police crouching behind cars, and the gunman's rifle poking out of the window. Next comes a close-up on that window, showing the rifle firing, cutting to a reaction shot of a police officer as he ducks behind a car door. A close-up of the gunman's face could follow this as it appears momentarily behind the curtain. Next comes a long shot of several officers firing back, followed by a big close-up of spent cartridges clattering on the ground, and a final wide shot showing the stand-off. Seven shots, selected out of a possible 30, each running for around 20 seconds, which when edited will boil down to little more than 25 seconds.

Context

But there is more to most news stories than high drama and fast-moving action. Just as important are the reasons behind the drama; the consequences of it; its effect on people.

A major criticism of TV news is that by featuring the short scuffle with police or single ugly scene during a three-hour picket viewers are left with the distorted impression that the whole demonstration was violent or unruly.

1 Setting the scene. The newscaster reads the lead into the item. The window behind him signposts the story, by spelling it out in a word and displaying an image which is emblematic of what has taken place.

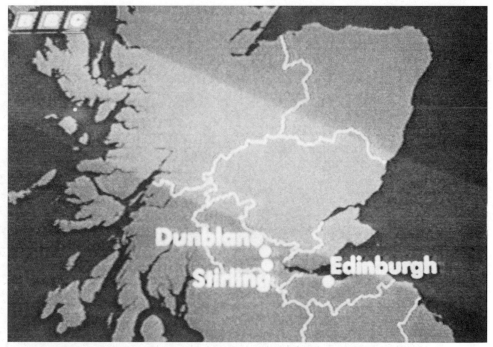

2 Schoolchildren were gunned down in their gym in a small Scottish city that few will have heard of. The map graphic pins down the location.

Figure 114 Telling the story. Shots are selected for a combination of narrative strength and variety. The aim of the sequence is to follow the story through in a clear and logical order. (*Pictures courtesy BBC and ITN*)

3 The *general view* of the school is the last of three scenes to specify the location and draw us into the report.

4 When events are not captured on camera, TV turns to reconstruction. This *top shot* graphic shows the gunman's approach.

Figure 114 *Continued*

5 The victims. This *group shot* is taken from a recent photo of the children and their teacher. TV news spares us close ups of the children.

6 Next a witness account is needed. This *mid-shot* of a boy who saw the gunman is featured on countless bulletins worldwide.

Figure 114 *Continued*

7 From the words of a witness to the gunman himself. Only a photograph is available at this stage in the coverage. It is shown as a still displayed against a *general view* with highlighted key points. Note the computer-generated 'shadow' behind the still to pick it out from the background. This is a *composite shot*.

8 Having seen the gunman, TV now shows the kind of gun that was used. This *big close up* is the opening image in a shot that zooms out to a row of similar weapons.

Figure 114 *Continued*

9 Following the description of what has taken place, the report moves into its second phase – the reaction. The journalist at the location describes the scene in his *piece to camera*. He stands at an angle so the viewer's eye will follow the line of his shoulder into the picture.

10 The human response to the tragedy. This *group shot* reveals the stunned reaction to the shooting. Townsfolk are shown in long shot from a respectful distance.

Figure 114 *Continued*

11 Now the camera moves in closer to a *two-shot* to talk to parents who have agreed to give their reaction. This is a *medium shot*.

12 A service is held in the cathedral and the cameras are invited in. This *long shot* is followed by a *group shot*, *mid-shots* and *close-ups* of people at prayer (not shown). The camera moves in progressively.

Figure 114 *Continued*

13 A *big close-up* is used of a church leader to highlight his emotional response. Such a shot would be considered intrusive had it been taken of someone more intimately connected with the tragedy, such as a grieving parent or schoolfriend. The report proceeds to open out to the wider community to gauge reaction from other key representatives.

14 On to a *group shot* of politicians at a hastily summoned news conference. The plethora of media hardware is indicative of the scale of the tragedy.

Figure 114 *Continued*

15 *Cutaway.* This extra shot allows two statements made at the conference to be edited together without creating an unsightly *jump cut.* The picture of assembled cameras further emphasizes the scale of events.

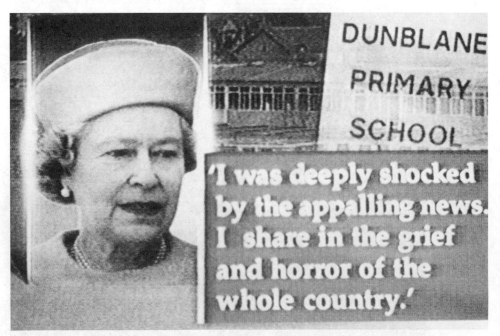

16 On to royal reaction. This elaborate composite graphic displays a videostill of the Queen against a *general view* of the school. The montage is overlaid further with a semi-transparent still of the school signpost and a quote. Every element of this shot has been carefully selected to be emblematic of what has taken place: the Queen, the school, the sign, and the quote.

Figure 114 *Continued*

17 Summing-up. Back to the journalist at the scene to update the report by adding live any fresh information. The presenter and reporter are displayed in windows that are tilted electronically to appear to face one another.

18 Lastly, the helpline for worried friends and relatives. Telephone numbers are displayed to give viewers time to write them down.

Figure 114 *Continued*

This is where it becomes vital for the reporter to explain the context of what has been shown and to screen other shots offering a clearer, more normal representation of the event.

The journalist has to bear in mind how to construct the report when he or she starts calling the shots to the cameraperson.

With the siege there are five phases: the build-up of police; attempts to negotiate; the gunman's violent response; police action to overpower him; his arrest and the release of the hostages.

Shots should be picked to tell the story, to illustrate each of its phases and the main points within each phase.

News is about events that affect people, and the most powerful way to bring home the impact of the story is to show its effect in human terms, and that means focusing on the people the item concerns.

Sound

The sound of the story adds to the viewer's sense of being there.

At the siege, sounds of gunshots, barked instructions, sirens approaching, warnings through the loudhailer, are all essential to the story, and the narrator should pause to let them come through.

Effects that are off-mike and fail to come out can be dubbed on later from the sound effects library, though the aim of this is to clarify rather than exaggerate the sounds that were there.

The microphone has an infuriating habit of amplifying stray sounds that the human ear would filter out. The trouble is, when those sounds are played back, the ear becomes almost perversely aware of them. It can be frustrating for the viewer, who can spend more time trying to work out where that mysterious *'chugga, chugga, chugga'* is coming from than in concentrating on the report.

There are three ways around this: turn off whatever is making the sound, do your shooting elsewhere or show us at the start where the noise is coming from. A little background noise, where relevant to the story (such as a shipyard), adds atmosphere.

Sound-bites

Even more important are the *sound-bites* (*grabs* – Australia) in the report. With TV's emphasis on pictures, these are likely to be shorter than those used in radio. The sound-bite should encapsulate the main point of the argument; the strongest opinion or reaction.

Again there is a danger of distortion by over-emphasizing the already emphatic and polarizing a point of view, and this danger can only be eliminated by carefully explaining the context in which the remarks were made.

To cover the siege story, the reporter will want to interview the police chief, the husband, and any witnesses – even get a statement from the gunman, but only if it were safe to do so.

The camera will usually be set up to feature the interviewee in three-quarters profile, looking to one side and slightly towards the camera, as he answers the reporter's questions. With several interviewees, get them to face in different directions to vary the pattern. The prerogative of addressing the camera directly is usually left to the reporter.

Cutaways

Back to the siege, and the reporter has just got the police chief to explain that he will use force if he has to, when the chief is interrupted by a call on his radio. After a brief conversation, he tells the reporter that police marksmen will shoot to kill if necessary.

The reporter wants to run both statements together, but decides to cut out the interruption on the radio, because it was garbled and largely irrelevant.

The difficulty here is that the police chief was standing in a different position when he made his second statement. If the two answers were edited together there would be an unsightly jump on the recording.

The reporter resolves to ask the chief to do the interview again, when another urgent message comes on the radio and he is called away.

The reporter has no choice. She has to go with what she's got. What she needs now is a *cutaway*.

In a radio interview the first and last sentences can be edited together, while the rest is discarded. Providing the editing is carried out professionally, no one will spot the join. But in TV, the join would be all too obvious. The sound might flow smoothly across the two sentences, but the picture would leap about the screen as the subject jerked in an instant from one position to another.

To cover the join, the original pictures either side of the edit have to be replaced with a different sequence. This is known as *intercutting*. The pictures shown should be of a related scene, such as the reporter nodding or an illustration of the speaker's remarks, which could be a shot of a police marksman with his rifle or the house under siege. The original soundtrack of the answers is retained, but the telltale jump in the film or tape is covered by the new pictures.

Cutaways are necessary where the shots of the subject are similar. However, it might be possible to do without them when the cut is from a medium shot to a close up, as the switch to a different type of shot could cover the jump.

The alternative to the cutaway is the *cut-in*, a close up that reveals a point of detail such as hands gesticulating or clutching a rifle.

Reverses

Cutaways of the reporter are known as **reverses**. These are used when the report is being made with only one camera, which is trained on the interviewee. Where two cameras are used they shoot across one another to film each person in three-quarters profile.

A common reverse is the *noddy* where the reporter is filmed after the interview appearing to be listening hard to the interviewee and nodding. Care has to be taken otherwise it can look as though the reporter is supporting the interviewee's point of view. On controversial issues, instead of nodding, the cutaway can be of the reporter listening intently.

Another common reverse is the *two-shot*, where the camera pulls out to show the reporter and her subject. This is often shot from behind the interviewer and over her shoulder where the camera cannot see the mouth moving, so the picture can be cut over the soundtrack of the interviewer's question without appearing to be out of sync.

Reporters can also re-voice their questions to camera after the interview, and use one of those as a cutaway. To help remember the exact wording it might help to record the original interview on a small recorder tucked out of sight of the camera.

Some news organizations see ethical problems with cutaways. By using them deviously, the reporter could reassemble the interview in any order she liked to produce whatever effect she desired.

> *'The aim of editing is to produce a clear and succinct statement which reflects fairly, honestly and without distortion what was seen and heard by our reporters, cameras and microphones.'*
> – CBS NEWS, USA

CBS lays down in its news standards that reverse shots are to be made in the presence of the interviewee if he or she requires, and the producer should compare the later questions with the originals to make sure there has been no distortion.

Some stations have a policy of not using cutaways at all, preferring to leave in the less slick, but more veracious jump cuts. A few take this further, insisting that edited answers are kept strictly in the order in which they were given in the interview.

The line

For cutaways the cameraperson will position the reporter so she seems to be looking at the interviewee. If they both appeared on screen looking say, to the left, it would seem as though they were talking to a third person and not to one another. TV people would say the camera had *crossed the line*.

The *line* is an imaginary border separating the two people. Providing the camera doesn't cross it, it can move anywhere and the two will appear to be facing each other in conversation. As soon as the line is crossed, the two will face the same way and the illusion will be broken.

The line has to be observed with action shots as well. Returning to our earlier example of the advancing tanks, if the cameraperson shoots them from one side, then crosses the column to shoot the other, the sequence will show the tanks advancing first in one direction and then turning tail and retreating. Crossing the line seems bizarre to the viewer because it is as though the observer of the scene has shifted rapidly from one viewpoint to another

Where you have to cross the line, the switch in direction can be disguised with a *buffer shot*. The camera can stand in front of the moving object and show it coming towards it, or pan to show the object approaching and then passing.

Continuity

Edited reports have a way of telescoping time that can play tricks on the unwary reporter. Someone might be filmed in a long shot wearing a hat and again three minutes later in close up without it. During that brief interlude he might also have loosened his tie, removed his jacket, put on his reading glasses, taken the nearby phone off the hook and closed the curtains behind him.

Cut those two shots together and the effect would be interesting, if not weird. At the very least it would distract from what he was saying. Always keep a weather eye open for good continuity.

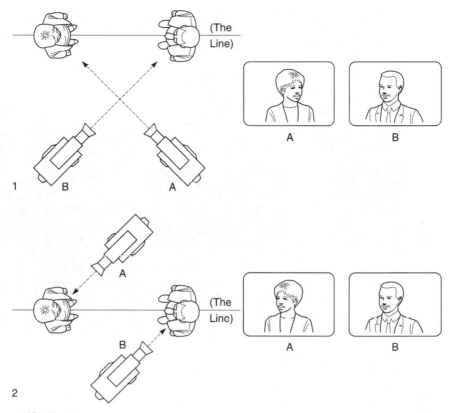

Figure 115 The line

1 Cameras are positioned to shoot across one another, showing each speaker in three-quarters profile. Providing neither camera crosses the line, when the speakers appear alternately on the TV screen they will be seen facing one another in conversation
2 If a camera does cross the line the speakers will be shown facing the same way, as though talking to someone else off-camera. The impression of conversation will be broken.

Pieces to camera

Most reporters like to enhance their reports – and their reputations – by appearing on camera from time to time.

These shots, known as *pieces to camera* (or *stand-ups* or *stand-uppers*) usually feature the reporter standing in front of the scene in question. If this is a carnival with lots of colour and movement, there is no excuse for the kind of stand-upper which has a blank wall in the background. This has been described as 'execution photography', where the reporter is put up against a wall and shot! The action should be used as the backdrop. It adds variety and shows audiences that the TV station goes where the news is – to the war zone, fire or factory opening – and that its reporters are out and about.

The piece to camera can be used at the beginning of an item to set the scene, in the middle to act as bridge linking two threads of the story or at the end as the reporter's way of signing-off; TV's equivalent of radio's standard out-cue.

Stand-uppers are usually short – their static nature can slow down the action and the reporter's memory might not be very good! Memory aids include a clip-board judiciously

Figure 116 Take one flak jacket and a bullet-ridden tram. Find a good background to heighten the sense of location for the piece to camera.

held out of camera, key words chalked on the ground, even a portable prompter set up beside the camera. None of these are recommended, because anything that could cause the reporter's eyes to flicker from the lens would break the illusion of eye contact with the audience and be more of a hindrance than a help.

A more useful trick for the retentively challenged is to write the commentary and speak it into a portable recorder. You can listen back through a concealed earpiece and take your prompt from that.

If none of these solutions is available and there is too much to remember in one take, the commentary can be split over two takes and joined by cutting from a long shot to a close-up.

At times the reporter might have to voice the entire script on location. This can happen when the deadline is close and film or tapes have to be rushed back to the studio by despatch rider.

Where *voice-overs (VO)* are to go over natural sound on film or tape, the VO should be made in a quiet location such as a hotel room or inside a car. If they are to go over a portion of silent footage, then the background sound in the VO should closely match the sounds behind the stand-upper or other items to prevent a stop–start effect in the background. This may mean recording the VO in the same location.

Planning – the full treatment

Full-scale planning is a luxury increasingly reserved for the world of TV current affairs. This differs from news in four respects: subjects are usually covered in more depth, larger crews are required to put the longer items together, there is more time at their disposal, and more detailed planning of coverage is necessary if television's expensive resources are to be allocated as efficiently as possible.

A documentary crew will include a field producer or director whose job it will be to plan and supervise filming. Camera crews will be given a scheme to work from and will rely less on shots taken 'on the hoof'.

A researcher will be despatched in advance to investigate the subject, explore locations, arrange interviews and gather background material. From the researcher's findings a draft script will be prepared listing the main shots that make up the programme. This is the *treatment*. Plans might change later, but the treatment offers a route map to show where the team is starting from, where it is heading, and how it intends to get there.

Producing a treatment gets your ideas out in the open where they can be examined instead of waiting until you start filming to find they don't work. Once they are on paper they can be knocked into shape. Anything left out can be added, sidetracks can be sidestepped and blind alleys avoided. You can also see if you've got enough good ideas to sustain a programme.

In *On Camera*, Harris Watts* draws up a simple formula for preparing a treatment. His advice is to decide what you want to say and what pictures you want to go with it. Jot down the headings the programme will follow, with visuals on the left and commentary on the right. Allow fifteen seconds for each point and a little longer for points made by interviewees. Add something for opening shots, scene-setters and pictures with no narration. Cutaways shown over existing narration will take no extra time. Work out the duration for each sequence of the programme and aim to run up to 25 per cent over length as the assembled programme will probably be tighter and more polished after it is trimmed down.

Once you have produced the treatment you will need to draw up a shooting schedule to minimize time wasted dashing to and fro.

Traditionally, every shot taken would be listed on a *dopesheet*. News crews usually dispense with these under pressure of deadlines; instead the reporter will return with the footage and talk the editor through it. Even then the cameraperson will make some record of his or her work, be it only a hastily scrawled note on the videotape box. For longer items, like a documentary, this information is vital if the team is to keep track of all the material.

Once the shooting is finished an *editing script* can be produced listing the takes that are to be included in the final programme.

Fieldwork

1 Record a TV news programme and look at an interesting location report. Study the camerawork and note the different shots that are used (LS, MS, CU, etc.). Do they follow a logical order? How could the sequence of shots be improved?

  Now identify the camera positions (from top shot to low-level shot) and note how the camera was used. Do you think the cameraperson could have been more adventurous? How? How do the shot changes relate to the structure and rhythm of the commentary?

  Which shots would you say had impact? Why?

2 How do the pictures and narrative complement one another? Is there any point where

---

* BBC, 1995.

the words simply repeat what the pictures were saying?

3 If there is a camera you can use, get out and about practising the different types of camera shot. Experiment with the camera positions as well.

4 Write up a 30-second court story and practise doing a piece to camera in the open air without reading from your notes. (If you haven't got a camera you can still try this – though I suggest using a microphone and recorder as props if you don't want the men in white coats to take you away!) Try memorizing the text first of all and recording it in two takes. Then try other improvised ways of prompting, including the cassette and earpiece method.

How difficult was it to remember your script? Which prompt technique did you find the most effective? Did you feel embarrassed about 'performing' in the open-air? How can you overcome that embarrassment?

5 If you are in a class and have access to equipment, find a news story to cover and then form a crew and produce a report. Do your planning in advance. Shoot in sequence and aim for a shot ratio of around 3:1. Don't forget your openers and cutaways. When you come to edit your report, work hard at getting shot lengths that suit the rhythm of the piece and keep interest. Write the commentary to complement the pictures.

Compare your work with that of other crews in the class. What can you learn from one another?

TV SCRIPTWRITING

27   Writing the script

> '*I was doing a story for the news at 5.45. I was so late back I had to do it live. You sit in a little booth behind the studios and as they broadcast the piece, when the pictures come you read into a microphone off your printed script.*
>
> '*Because it was such a last-minute thing I had to scribble my script in pencil on the back of a couple of envelopes. I had one minute before the bulletin and mine was the lead story. With 30 seconds to go, somebody came in to check my headphones were on and everything was OK, and they slammed the door and my two envelopes were blown out beneath it.*
>
> '*Then the newsreader went straight into my story, and I was sitting there thinking, "Oh, my God, I've got nothing, but I can't go out because they're starting the piece". So I started talking and my mind went into automatic. I was talking off the top of my head, trying to remember what I'd said, and it got to a stage where I almost repeated myself, but just managed to change the words around. When it was all over I signed off "Kim Sabido, ITN" and sat there gasping, with sweat pouring off me when this guy came in and said, "Why did you repeat yourself?" and I said, "because you blew my script under the door. Look, there it is . . . you're standing on it!" I just went to the bar and had a lot to drink.*'
>
>   – REPORTER KIM SABIDO

The cue (lead, or link)

The cue is the writer's way of preparing the viewer for what is to come. It grabs the attention and shouts, '*Hey you! Listen to this. This is important, this is interesting. Let me tell you what happened . . .*' The lead is the bait, but once the viewer is hooked, the writer still has to play him in. The bait can be made more appealing by dressing it up with a visual that illustrates the story.

The newsreader won't be expected to refer to that visual any more than he or she would be likely to say: '*in the piece of film coming up*', or, '*as you can see from these pictures*'. The newsreader will finish the cue before the report begins, or talk over the first few seconds of the establishing shot, taking care to stop before anyone speaks on the report.

Write the lead first, to make sure you don't repeat yourself when you begin the narration.

Complement the pictures with the narrative

Now you need to decide whether to write the script to suit the pictures, or to match the pictures to the script. Opinions differ. Some argue that as TV is a visual medium, the pictures must come first. Others will maintain the first job of a TV news report is to tell a story – the pictures merely serve to illustrate that story. Perhaps the truth lies somewhere in between. In practice, shot selection and script writing often take place together.

But where the script is to be written to the pictures, split-second timing is required to precisely complement the spoken words with the images on screen. A *shot list* is produced giving details of the camera shots (GV, LS, CU, etc.) the subject and the duration of the shots. This gives reporters a clearer idea of what they are writing to. Once again, in the hectic world of the newsroom, the shot list is often sacrificed for speed.

The shot list adds together the duration of all the pictures to give the cumulative time:

Shot		Time	Cumulative time
GV	Crowds at demonstration	4 seconds	4 seconds
MS	Police cordon	3 seconds	7 seconds
MS	Crowd faces and banners	4 seconds	11 seconds
CU	Leaders chanting	5 seconds	16 seconds
MS	Policeman in riot gear	4 seconds	20 seconds
MS	Crowd tries to break police lines, panning to	6 seconds	26 seconds
CU	Demonstrator falling	5 seconds	31 seconds
LS	Police vans appear with reinforcements	4 seconds	35 seconds
MS	Police charge	3 seconds	38 seconds
LS	Crowd retreats, police pursuing	4 seconds	42 seconds

Figure 117 Assembling the script to match the pictures in the edit suite. Every phrase has to run with the rhythm of the editing. It also has to complement the shot that has been chosen. Take care not to repeat what you see on the screen. (*Andrew Boyd*)

In 42 seconds the reporter could cram in around 130 words – and that would mean speaking solidly throughout – but for dramatic shots like these your script should be deliberately sparse, pausing to let the pictures tell the story. Less than half the sequence will be taken up with narration.

To say word for word what is blindingly obvious from the pictures would be wasteful as well as pointless. There are times when pictures should be left to speak for themselves. The reporter's script should never repeat what the viewer can clearly see, but should clarify, contextualize and explain what is shown on the screen.

As well as recounting the action at the demonstration the reporter will want to talk about the police presence and illustrate the build-up before the conflict began.

This could be done with close-ups showing the angry looks of the demonstrators and determined faces of the police.

Such images would tell the story more eloquently than any scripted reference to *'tension in the air'*. And to say, *'The atmosphere was tense while police awaited the onslaught'* becomes redundant and trite. *Show* the tension. *Show* the police waiting, and either say nothing or enhance the pictures with information that develops the story.

If footage of an accident on the highway shows a tailback of traffic receding into the distance, don't repeat the visuals by saying: *'The queue of trucks and cars stretched back as far as the eye can see.'* Add to the visual information. Tell us *'The tailback stretched for almost 8 km'*, or better still: *'The accident brought traffic to a standstill for almost two hours.'*

Writing to sound

Similarly, adjectives that describe what can clearly be heard on the screen are best avoided. Phrases like *'screeched to a halt'* and *'deafening blast'* are unnecessary. If the screech of tyres and roar of the blast can be heard on air, then viewers will already know about it. If the sounds are not there, they will feel cheated or suspect the reporter of sensationalism.

Where the commentary has to pause for a sound-bite or effect, the reader will need a clear indication of when to break the narrative and when to take it up again. The pause will be indicated by a break in the script or the word *cue*. The reader will know when to resume the story either from the duration and the last words of the sound-bite given in the script, or from a signal given by a *cue light* operated by the writer. The cue light should go on half a second before the commentary is due to begin to give the reader a moment to draw breath.

Effects which are to be played in live should be clearly noted in the script alongside the commentary with the precise times they should start and end, and copies of the script should be given to each member of the production team.

The line of script that leads into a sound-bite is known as the *throw-line*. A throw-line that requires an immediate response could be regretted when the script is narrated live. Even a moment's delay in the soundtrack will make it appear as though both the reporter and the speaker were lost for words:

> *'Turning to the Prime Minister, the opposition leader shouted . . .'* (silence)
> **Better to say**: *'The opposition leader turned to the Prime Minister, and launched an angry attack.'*

That sentence ends on a downturn in the voice and doesn't leave us poised in mid-air waiting for what ought to follow immediately.

Figure 118 Check it through before you go on air. Make sure what has been written can be comfortably read out loud. One trick is to read the script out as you write it. (*Andrew Boyd*)

The throw-line should never repeat what is about to be said:

not:
Reporter: *'The Home Secretary said the situation was dire . . .'*
Home Secretary: *'The situation is dire. It can't be permitted to continue . . .'*
but:
Reporter: *'The Home Secretary said he had no choice but to intervene . . .'*

Where names are given, the last-mentioned name should belong to the face that is about to appear on screen. If we are cutting from the cue to an interview with Peter Smith the cue should not be:

'Peter Smith believes a rise in bus fares is now inevitable, as he explained to Alison Bell.'

The sentence can be turned around or both names can be left out of the cue, unless one is newsworthy in its own right, or it is house style to give the reporter a name check. Names and titles can clutter and confuse, and are often better left to the caption generator. So our throw-line becomes the more streamlined and pointed:

'A rise in bus fares may now be inevitable . . .'

When Peter Smith has been on screen for about a second, his name will appear in the lower third of the picture, where it will linger for about four seconds and disappear. When the reporter appears on camera he or she will get the same treatment.

Where live commentary is to be added, care must be taken to avoid writing so many words that the film ends ahead of the commentary. Far better to have fewer words and be certain of pictures at the end of the report than to leave the newsreader mouthing a marvellous narration over a blank screen.

Keep detail to a minimum

Newspaper reporters tend to pack stories with as much detail as possible. Try that with the spoken word and you would lose your listeners before the end of the second paragraph. If the information is to sink in, the focus of the story has to be as tight as possible. Cut any unnecessary detail that would overload the listener. Titles, places and geographical relationships should be dealt with by captions and graphics.

This rule applies equally to pictures. Too many snippets of film or different shots in a report will force-feed the mind. Images can run through so quickly that it can be impossible to absorb the information. The viewer is left with the same sense of breathlessness that might come from listening to a presenter reading at 200 words per minute.

Visuals are to illustrate and clarify a report – not to add to the general clutter. A visual has to contain just enough information to get its message across in a few seconds. The fewer words, distractions and details, the better.

Television, like radio, is a medium of impression, not precision. Just enough should be said and shown to leave the viewer with a strong general impression of the story. Too much detail swamps the images and saturates the senses. Simplicity is the watchword if the audience is to retain what it sees.

Script layout

TV scripts are laid out differently from those in radio because they have to carry a lot more information. As well as the story, the TV script has to give details of camera shots, graphics and their durations.

TV stations lay out their scripts according to house style, but, for the sake of clarity, visual and narrative information is usually separated into two columns – visual on the left and script on the right.

The information in the left-hand column tells the director the visuals that will accompany the story. These are placed alongside the point in the narrative where the visuals begin.

For a *tell story* where only the newsreader appears in vision, his or her name will be given in the column at the start of the script:

ALASTAIR I/V:	The death toll in the Venezuela flood has now topped 10 000 – with fears that as many again could be buried beneath the mud. At least 150 000 have been made homeless in the worst disaster to hit Venezuela in living memory. In some areas homes and bodies are buried beneath seven metres of mud. Tens of thousands of people remain trapped by the floodwater.

I/V is short for *in vision* and tells the director that the presenter should appear on camera at that point. Where the presenter is out of vision, *OOV* is written. Visuals used to illustrate a story are marked alongside the script showing clearly where each begins and ends:

PAULA I/V	Fishermen in Mozambique have come up with a curious catch . . . a 100 kg prehistoric monster.
SLIDE_____/ (fisherman)	The massive coelacanth strained the nets of fishermen off the coast of Maputo.
SLIDE_____/ (fish) STILL (caption) (B&W first fish)	Only a dozen of these giants of the deep have ever been netted. Until the first was caught in the waters off South Africa in 1938, the coelacanth was thought to be extinct.
MIX TO GRAPHIC_____/ (bone structure)	This latest catch offers fascinating new clues into the life and times of this prehistoric throwback.
PAULA I/V	Mozambique's Natural History Museum said the coelacanth had 26 babies inside, offering the first insight into the way the dinosaur fish reproduced.

The term *caption* is BBC jargon for a still photograph. *B & W* means the photograph is black and white.

The use of stills and graphics make it just possible to use a story where video footage is conspicuous by its absence.

Where the cue goes into a pre-recorded report, basic details of that report are given in the video column at the foot of the script:

JACK I/V	A Hercules transport plane laden with food and medical supplies is now on its way to bring some much needed aid to Southern Sudan.
CAPTION_____/ (Map)	The plane, which has been chartered by relief organizations, is heading for the famine-stricken city of Malakal.

MIX TO ENG: 2

IN WORDS: 'Despite warnings that . . .'

SUPERS: TUNNY 35"
         MALAKAL 1'02"

OUT WORDS: Sign off

TIME: 1'22"

Mix to ENG: 2 tells the director the report will appear on ENG (videocassette) machine no. 2. Mix is an instruction to dissolve from the graphic of the map to the report, so one picture gradually gives way to the other.

The *in words* are the first words on the report, which can be checked to make sure the correct report is being played.

Supers are the captions and titles that are inserted live. The times given show the time from the start of the report when those supers should be displayed. These are usually left on screen for a few seconds and faded out.

Out words are the last words in the report so the director knows when to cut back to the newsreader; in this case it is a sign off, or standard out-cue, such as *'This is John Tunny, for the 6 O'clock News in Malakal.'*

The *time* gives the length of the report. Some stations prefer to give the *running time* (R/T) which indicates how long the programme should still have to run after the present report is completed. This gives the director an instant point of reference to see whether he or she is running ahead or behind and needs to pad or drop an item.

When a reporter is writing a script to fit visuals that have already been edited, such as when a live studio voice-over is required, the details of each shot may also be marked alongside the script. Cues show the time from the start of the report when the reader should commence reading that part of the script:

BANGLADESH/FILEY 6 O'CLOCK NEWS   MAY 5

CUE 02″
N/READER OOV   SUPER   / Up to 125 000 people are now feared dead
(GVs floods)   B/desh 2″   as the result of the cyclone and tidal wave
                                      that struck Bangladesh.

CUE 11″   / Bodies of the dead are still being washed
(GVs bodies)   back to shore five days after the disaster /
(GVs airshots)   and rescue planes report seeing many
                                      others scattered along the coastline.
CUE 21″   / Official estimates say up to a tenth of the
(GVs wreckage)   population may have been affected, and a
                                      million homes destroyed . . .

MS Minister/SOT 28″   SUPER
IN: This is the   Foreign.
      worst . . .'   Sec.
OT: 35″ '. . . this devastation.'

CUE 37″
N/READER OOV″   / And relief workers fear that thousands more
(MS survivors)   may face death from hunger, thirst and
                                      cholera.
                                     / Bangladesh has appealed for urgent inter-
(GVs islands)   national aid to reach the many survivors still
                                      marooned on islands around the Bay of
                                      Bengal.
                                     / But aid agency Care International says the
(GVs rescue workers)   Government may even now be underesti-
                                      mating the scale of the disaster . . .

MS Alan Smith/SOT 56″
In: 'Thousands of people . . .'
OUT: 1′ 06″ 'next few days.'
MS   PIECE TO CAMERA   SUPER: .
     SOT: 1′06″   Filey 1′09″
IN: 'But food and . . .'
OUT: Sign off
R/T: 1′35″

Cues are given after a pause to let the pictures or soundtrack speak for themselves.

The contents of the sound-bites or piece to camera would not be included in the script, as these would have been recorded beforehand. But the reporter's payoff is given below by way of illustration:

> Filey: *'But food and water supplies are of little value without the means to deliver them. Just as badly sought are the helicopters and flat-bottomed boats needed to reach the thousands still trapped on low-lying islands in the worst hit coastal regions. But even now, relief ships are hampered from entering the port of Chittagong by the wreckage of hundreds of boats tossed up by the storm.*
> *'This is Alison Filey for the 6 O'Clock News in Bangladesh.'*

Filey is reporting on location, so her piece to camera would show in the background the rescue ships struggling to negotiate their way into the port through the wreckage.

Balancing words with pictures

> *'Too much broadcast journalism tells me what I can already see, it doesn't tell me what it's about. The writing has to explain what you are seeing.'*
> – HARRY RADLIFFE, LONDON BUREAU CHIEF, CBS NEWS

Some reporters like to run the first and last scenes of their reports a little longer to give the opening pictures time to establish and to let the closing shots leave an impression.

Another good reason for leaving a couple of seconds at the start of the film before beginning the commentary is in case the report is put on air slightly late. If you look back to the Bangladesh story above, the opening shots last two seconds longer than the narrative.

When it comes to switching scenes, note that fresh shots usually appear at the beginning of a sentence, while one changes in the middle. If you read that sentence out loud, you will see that the new shot follows the rhythm of speech by coming in during a natural break.

The length of the shot may determine the number of facts that can be selected to accompany it. If all you have is a five-second shot of troops scrambling up a hill towards a fortress, then it would not be possible to write:

> Defying heavy machine gun and rifle fire from the troops inside the building, rebel forces laid down a curtain of smoke and edged towards its perimeter.
>
> 9 seconds

Too long. One way to retain all that information would be to add a three-second covering shot of the fortress at the beginning – if one were available. Failing that, the script would have to be rewritten to length:

> Under heavy fire, rebel forces laid down a curtain of smoke and edged towards the building.
>
> 5 seconds

Occasionally, a shot will be so good that it begs to run a little longer than the script might require. Such a shot should speak for itself, or be complemented with useful additional information:

LS seamen running up Jolly Roger on ferry 9 seconds	The men made it crystal clear they had no intention of handing back the ferry. 4 seconds
Better:	The crew's response to the company's demands came almost immediately – [pause] No mistaking the message of the skull and crossbones. 9 seconds

The rewritten version runs to time and lets the visual speak for itself by pausing to let the message of the Jolly Roger sink in.

A script keyed into a newsroom computer system can be displayed on screen in two columns: one for visuals and the other for text. The computer can also time the narrative.

Where such a facility is not available, some reporters produce their scripts in narrow strips of about three words per line. Each line represents roughly a second of speech, simplifying the process of timing.

Different coloured copies of completed script are handed out to all the staff involved in the programme.

Using the library

Most TV stations have their own libraries to provide a back-up service for reporters. The library will keep an archive of valuable footage and stills to illustrate and enhance reports, as well as reference material to help with research.

Newspaper stories provide valuable reference material. Database systems that can be accessed via the Internet offer access to millions of stories from newspapers and magazines. And many newspapers now market permanent archives of stories on CD-ROM.

Interrogating a database allows the reporter to retrieve every story on a given subject by entering a key word, such as 'euthanasia' or phrase such as 'nuclear weapons'.

The older method is to access cuttings via microfiche – transparent folios of miniaturized stories that can be read with the aid of a special magnifier.

Background information not found on database or in cuttings might be available in the library's reference section. Books will be on hand listing such information as the names and personal details of members of Parliament or Congress, background on companies and corporations, or census material showing changes in the population and social trends. Regional TV libraries also file and index their local newspapers.

Research aside, the library plays an important, though seldom appreciated, part in the final report. Archive footage, slides, useful graphics and agency photos are stored to provide a bank of extra illustrations.

> '*On one occasion we were looking for some lively material on the SALT talks [Strategic Arms Limitation Talks], and we went through our library and couldn't find it anywhere, and then someone uncovered it under the heading of Food and Drink.*'
> – UK NEWSREADER MARTYN LEWIS*

---

* *It'll Be Alright on the Night*, London Weekend Television.

Figure 119 Getting a sense of perspective. Broadcasters are often criticized for failing to put facts into context. But the news library offers access to background material, be it video, audio or stills, or in print, on-line or on a computer database. (*Andrew Boyd*)

Fieldwork

1 Rewrite the following TV throw-lines to tidy them up and give your reasons for any changes that you make:

'Our reporter George Frederick caught up with Peter Brown at the Opera House and first of all he asked him how much money the Opera House needed to keep going . . .'

'. . . the decision to expel them from the party was regrettable, but there was no alternative, as Mr Chadha explained to our reporter Gurinda Bhattacharaya . . .'

'In an angry outburst, Mrs Stellar said the voting had been rigged, the results were loaded, and her contempt for the judges was absolute. She called them all a . . .'

2 Working on the principle of keeping detail to a minimum, find a hard news story in a newspaper – the more complex the better (financial story, perhaps?) – and attempt to boil it down to its bare bones. Jot down headings of the crucial points. Then write up the story in just 90 words.

If you are in a class, call for two volunteers who are not familiar with the story. Get one to leave the room, while you read your version of the story out loud to the other. Without seeing your script he or she is to write up the main points of that story in 30 words or less.

Call the other in and give him or her the newspaper version of the story. Without conferring, he or she is then to boil that down to 30 words.

When they have both finished, compare versions. Do they sound like the same story? Do they differ in substance or detail? If so, why? Do both versions retain the important points of the story? If not, why have some been left out? Were some important points left out of the original 90-word rewrite? Discuss the differences.

3 Record and watch a TV news programme. Don't make notes, do not confer, or read the next paragraph until you have finished watching the programme and half an hour has passed.

Now, without discussing it with anyone, list all the stories in the order in which they appeared, and describe the main points in 30 words or less per story.

Then try to recall the pictures and graphics that accompanied those stories.

Now watch the programme again and see how good your memory was. Did you get the order of the items right? Were your summaries of the items accurate? What did you find easier to remember, the pictures or the commentary? Could you remember the graphics? Compare how you got on with other members of the class and discuss what made some items more memorable than others.

4 Now find another newspaper report of a strong news story and turn it into a TV script. Break it down into its component parts and decide what treatment to give the story – which pictures you would want to take and which of the interviews in the write up you would want to include. Think also about graphics and illustrations and any pieces to camera. Aim for a duration of one minute 20 seconds and produce a full two-column script for your report. Take care not to repeat in your narrative what you plan to show in your pictures.

5 Now do some research so you can find out what tools are available to you. Working on your own and using a library as your main source, find out the following (use the telephone only as a last resort):

(a) The population of your electoral boundary (both local and national government).
(b) The numbers of abortions that took place in your region during the past year.
(c) The phone numbers of any prisons in your area and the names of the governors.
(d) The name of the Bishop of your area (or other religious leader, if applicable) and how you would address him.
(e) The title of the company that employs the most people in your area, the number it employs and the name and phone number of the managing director.
(f) The name of the previous Mayor or Council Leader in your area and details of his or her history in active politics.
(g) The date and brief details of the last major air crash to happen anywhere in the world, and the cause of that crash.

When you have finished compare your answers with others in your class and swap notes about how you got that information.

COMPILING THE REPORT

28 Editing the image

> *'For the average programme-maker, contemplating life before non-linear editing is like asking Jeremy Paxman to abdicate and let News Bunny anchor "Newsnight" – in a word, unthinkable.'*
> – BROADCAST*

Writing the script is only half the story. Once the shots are back from location they have to be edited, library pictures sought and graphics and captions added. This section deals with editing the image and compiling the report using digital and analogue systems.

Sequence of shots

Editing is an extension of the shooting process. The editor is building on the work of the cameraperson who has compiled a collection of images that will tell the story and contribute to the report. But as we saw in the previous chapter, the camera shots will be longer than they would appear on air, to give the editor a choice, and will probably be out of sequence. The editor's job is simply to select the best shots, put them order and trim them to length.

Edited shots should cut from one to another smoothly and logically and follow a train of thought. If this rule is broken, the images that result are likely to be jerky, unrelated and confusing and detract from the story.

Every change of scene or sequence should be properly set up to register with the viewers. GVs or long shots are often used as *openers* or *establishing shots* to set the scene.

There's a riot going on . . . We see the angry mob advancing and get an idea of the scale of the disorder. As we begin to wonder who the troublemakers are, a medium shot cuts in to reveal the ringleaders striding ahead and urging on the crowd. They look wild and unstoppable. As though to confirm our fears, the close-up picks out the crazed expression on the face of the leader.

* *The Cutting Edge*, Hilary Curtis, 8 March 1996.

Figure 120 State of the digital art – edit suite at the Molinaire production house in Soho. (*Courtesy Sony Broadcast Ltd*)

Rearrange the sequence of these shots and you remove the context and offer the viewer more questions than answers.

Begin with the close-up and you have no idea of the scale of the disturbance; cut then to the long shot and the action appears to be moving backwards. Unless you cut progressively and smoothly – like the human eye – the logic of the sequence will be destroyed. It is easier to follow the action if you bridge the close-ups and long shots with medium shots.

Shot length

Every shot should say something and stir up interest. The moment a shot has delivered its message and its appeal begins to wane, it should be cut. Action and movement generally hold interest longer than static shots. The pace is kept up if the cuts are made on movement.

How long you should hold a shot depends on a number of different factors:

- The instinctive decision by the editor about what the shot is 'worth'. Four seconds could capture the action. Five seconds might linger too long. Three seconds may 'feel' right, slipping into the overall rhythm of the item, or the shot could be cut to deliberately vary that rhythm and change the pace.
- Shot length may be determined by the length of the soundbite. Here, a long quote need not dictate using the same visual of the speaker throughout. If visual interest wanes the editor can switch to another picture, while the soundtrack continues to run beneath. This could be a reversal, showing the reporter and interviewee together, or a visual chosen to illustrate the subject under discussion.
- Where visuals are being matched to the script, the shot will be cut to fit the section of narrative.
- Where the shot contains so much detail that it becomes impossible to take in at a glance, the editor may hold the picture for a while to let the scene register or give viewers time to read words on banners or placards.
- Shots can be held to allow them to be dissolved into one another, as the extra length creates space for the overlap.

The most obvious place for a change of shot is at the beginning of a new sentence or paragraph. This has a certain logic but can soon become stale and repetitious. You can provide welcome relief by illustrating a single sentence with a number of different shots.

Long sequences can be broken up with general views of related subjects. A longish commentary on the space programme could be relieved by adding shots of the space centre, technicians working and employees walking, over the soundtrack of the commentary.

The action can be brought closer to the viewer by using *insert shots*. These are the close-ups of the clenched fists, marching feet, spinning tyres, etc.

When it comes to editing, shots like these are called *overlays* because they are laid over the existing soundtrack. They should only be added once the soundtrack has been cut to its final length, otherwise they would have to be retrimmed to fit.

Telescoping the action

Real life can be grindingly tedious. But there's no room in news for the boredom of waiting around for something to happen. So to telescope time and drive the action forward you can use a technique known as *intercutting*.

A motorcade carrying a foreign head of state is approaching in the distance. The camera follows the arrival of the car and its motorcycle entourage for 45 seconds until it reaches the steps of the Parliament building, then continues shooting as the VIPs are escorted inside.

In all, the cameraperson has three minutes of footage. This is more than would be required for the report, so to telescope the action the editor decides to join the shot of the motorcade approaching in the distance to the last 12 seconds of the cars pulling up and the VIPs bundling into the building.

The editor links the two shots with a cutaway taken earlier of a clutch of armed guards scanning the crowds for the first sign of trouble. Another that would have worked is an earlier shot of the fenced-off crowds straining to catch sight of the approaching motorcade. These are related to the original scenes and tell us something new about them. The edited sequence telescopes three minutes of action into just 17 seconds – and even that is long-winded for news.

Figure 121 Digital images are edited on computer. The top screen shows thumbnail images of scenes that have been stored. They can be assembled in any order to produce an edited report. (*Courtesy Avid*)

Editing is usually done in conjunction with the scriptwriting, which is covered elsewhere in this book. Some reporters prefer to write words to pictures, others match pictures to words. But in practice, the process often takes place simultaneously.

The editing process could have been carried out by dubbing from one machine to another (*linear editing*) or on computer (*non-linear*), or by using a hybrid system that combines the two.

Digital editing

In just a few short years the world of video editing was turned upside down. And it wasn't the giants of the TV industry, Sony and Panasonic, who started the revolution.

A group of Apple Mac computer enthusiasts from Massachusetts might seem an unlikely band of revolutionaries, but the software company Avid upended an entire industry.

Avid took video away from tape and stuffed it into computer memory where it can be edited. Days of footage can be stored, cut, juggled and cross-faded on hard disk

with all the fancy transitions and special effects you could wish for. And because the system is digital, the quality stays sharp regardless of the number of copies made.

But the major benefit of computer editing is that it is non-linear. What that jargon means is you can edit out of sequence. With conventional video editing you build up the report on the tape shot by shot. If you want to add a fresh scene in the middle – too bad – either you drop it in over an existing shot, or you have to unstitch the rest of the report after the edit and make it all over again.

Unlike film, you can't cut and splice videotape – add a bit in the middle and shuffle everything else along to make space. But with non-linear editing you can do precisely that, far more effectively.

Systems differ, but the technique is basically the same. First the raw footage is loaded into the computer and digitized into clips. The computer can be programmed to swallow up a straight section of footage, or can capture clips individually or in batches.

A still frame from each captured clip is displayed on the screen. This is known as a *thumbnail*. The clip can be played simply by pointing the mouse over it and clicking. Then the editor selects the clips he or she wants and, using the drag and drop technique familiar to all computer users, assembles them in any order.

The clips, with their accompanying soundtracks are put together on a *timeline*. What looks like a filmstrip is laid out on the computer screen in a manner that mimics old-fashioned film editing. The editor can play the clip from any point on the timeline and can shuttle backwards and forwards to cue and review the sound and pictures.

Most news reports are compiled using straight cuts. As one image ends, the other begins without an overlap. But the point where one image gradually gives way to another is known as a *transition*. There are hundreds of types of transition, from dramatic page turns to explosions. Most of these have no place in news.

Figure 122   The Avid Camcutter rejoices under the title: *tapeless field acquisition system*. It's a digital camera that records directly onto hard disk. It means pictures can be accessed instantly. (*Courtesy Avid*)

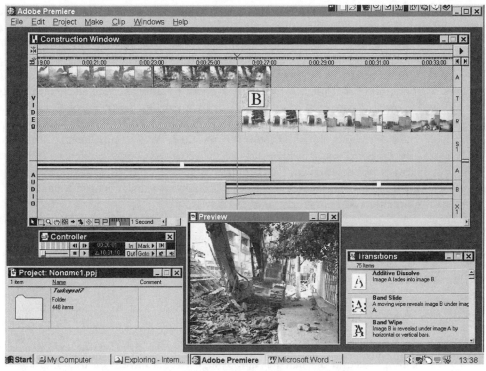

Figure 123 Editing a report on an earthquake in Turkey using Adobe Premiere.

The non-linear edit screen consists of a series of windows. The main construction window (*top*) displays the timeline. This is broadly equivalent to laying down strips of film or tape. The video sequences are displayed in strips in the top half of the window, with their accompanying audio beneath them.

Sequences are joined together by transitions. The large figure B (*centre*) shows that the pictures on track A give way to the pictures on track B beneath them. There are many different types of transition, from dissolves and cuts to special effects. The transitions widow (*bottom right*) offers 75 variations.

Audio levels can be altered, equalized and faded in and out. A fade-in has been drawn on audio track B on the timeline.

The preview window is bottom centre. This displays the image beneath the hairline marker, the vertical line in the construction window. The marker can be scrubbed backwards or forwards using the controller (*centre left*). Edit points can be marked with frame-accurate precision. All the images stored on the hard disk are kept in the project folder (*bottom left*).

The advantages of non-linear editing are that any shot can be accessed almost instantly, picture quality does not degrade with repeated dubbing and cuts or inserts can be made at any point without having to remake all the edits that follow. (*Andrew Boyd*)

The most common transition that sometimes does find its way into a news report is called a *dissolve* – as one image fades out the other fades in. To perform a dissolve using analogue equipment requires three edit machines – one for image A, another for image B and a third to record the images as they are combined. On a non-linear edit computer this is simplicity itself.

Two tracks are laid down on the timeline one above the other. These are known as A and B.

To dissolve between A and B so the image on track A gradually gives way to the image on track B you drag a transition onto the timeline and place it between them. You stretch the transition to the length you want and tell it to fade from track A to B or vice-versa. Then you *preview* your transition to check that it works.

Editing video sound is pretty much the same as in radio. You can adjust each element of the soundtrack for volume, equalize it to add bass, treble or a host of other effects, and crossfade one track beneath another. And if you don't like anything that you've done, then you don't have to bin it and start again from the beginning.

With non-linear editing you can start at any point and remake your work infinitely. And if you cut out a piece by mistake it doesn't matter, because non-linear editing is *non-destructive*. Any cuts you make are to a copy of the digitized footage, not to the footage itself, which remains intact in the computer memory. You can try, try and try again.

Editing can even be carried out in the field. Avid's CamCutter digital camera records directly onto computer hard disk, so the report can be assembled on location. That said, most news organizations still prefer to record onto tape. Undeterred, Panasonic has managed to combine a digital editor with two monitor screens in a single suitcase. Laptop computer systems are also available.

Inevitably, advances in technology will be measured in tumbling programme budgets and job cuts. According to ITN's director of technology, journalists are set to become 'journo-techs' and up to seven steps in the production process could be merged. And Central Television can even foresee the phasing out of dedicated picture editors.

Editing videotape

Many TV stations are in the process of switching from analogue to digital but few are willing to let go of analogue tape systems which have been tried and tested over many years and stood up to the punishment only news organizations can give them.

Many of the new digital systems, such as Panasonic's DVC Pro, still record digital images directly to tape. And while tape is still used, old-fashioned linear editing using two or three tape decks in an edit suite will often produce quicker results than non-linear systems which require the footage to be digitized before editing can begin. So videotape is likely to be around for some years yet.

Analogue videotape bears a family resemblance to its audio cousin, but has to work considerably harder. It carries a good deal of information besides the picture: it also stores the soundtrack, cue information for editing, and control information for the *videocassette recorder* (*VCR*) or *videotape recorder* (VTR). All this is stored on four different tracks.

The video signal is scanned by up to four heads mounted on a revolving drum, which flies rapidly past the tape, reading it at an angle. Editing machines can search for a picture at many times normal speed and can freeze a frame indefinitely.

Alongside the picture heads are audio heads which erase, record and play back the soundtrack. Another set of heads handles the cue and control information.

The tape editor

The job of assembling different video shots to make a report used to fall to a specialist editor, but increasingly camera operators or reporters are being required to do their own editing.

Unlike film, there is no actual cutting involved. Tape editing takes place by re-recording (*dubbing*) pictures from one tape to another until the final report is complete.

The original tape is viewed by the reporter and editor. The shots they decide to use are dubbed in sequence onto a master tape. Insert shots such as the reporter nodding can be added later by dubbing over the top of existing shots.

The editing suite

The action takes place in an *editing suite* (or *videotape booth*) which contains a lot of expensive hardware. Along with the VCRs will be an *edit controller* to make the edits, a *vision mixer* to blend scenes together, an *audio mixer* for handling the soundtrack, a *talkback system* for speaking to personnel around the building, and a bank of monitors, including one for each video machine and others for looking at graphics and watching station output.

The timer

Superimposed on the pictures is a *timecode*, which is a special clock for timing the edits. This counts the number of hours, minutes, seconds, and frames that have elapsed since the start of the report. British TV works on 25 frames per second; US and Canadian TV operates on 30.

The editing process is quick and clean and computer-assisted. The *rushes* – unedited tapes – are run through back and forward in fast and slow motion, freezing frames for closer scrutiny, until the editor decides the exact scene he or she wants to use in the report.

The chosen sequence might begin at 00.16.25.21 (zero hours, 16 minutes 25 seconds and 21 frames), and end just less than 11 seconds later at 00.16.36.09.

The edit controller

These timings are logged in the edit controller, which puts timecode reference points on the cue track of the videotape at the beginning and end of the sequence.

It then automatically dubs that sequence onto the master, starting the recording at the first timecode reference and ending it at the second.

The editor can then check that sequence through on the monitor. If he or she doesn't like it, they can take it again. The rushes are not recorded over, so the original scene is always there for a retake.

Video mixing

The above process describes a straight cut from one sequence to another. Dissolving one scene into another, by fading one out as the other fades in, or wiping one picture off the screen to reveal another, involves overlapping two separate images. This requires one VCR for each sequence and a third to dub them on to.

The tapes will be lined up, so the end of one scene overlaps the start of the other, and the vision mixer will be used to fade down the first image and fade up the other. A more sophisticated version of this, capable of a wide range of effects, is used in the control room for mixing live TV programmes.

Next comes the sound mixing. Editors can handle the sound separately or with the video. They have the same three choices as a non-linear editor: using the audio and video together; the audio without the video; or the video without the audio.

Recording the commentary

By now the reporter is probably ready to record the commentary, which is made in an adjoining *commentary booth*. There the reporter has eye contact with the editor through

Figure 124 Panasonic linear digital editing system, as used by ITN. A kit the size of a small suitcase can be up and running in minutes, using miniature DV tapes. (*Andrew Boyd*)

glass and verbal contact on the talkback. As the reporter watches the report going out on a monitor, he or she reads the commentary into a microphone, and this is dubbed by the editor on to the soundtrack.

If the timing is out, the reporter goes back to the start of the last shot and takes it again. The editor takes care to balance the reporter's voice over the natural sound on the tape (NAT SOF) so the commentary is never drowned out.

Audio mixing

As much care should be taken over the mixing of sounds as in the editing of the pictures. A cut from a busy street scene with roaring traffic to the near silence of a waving cornfield or the acoustically dead atmosphere of a studio would be abrupt to the ear, so the soundtrack of the traffic will probably be allowed to continue for a second into the next shot, with the editor fading out the traffic gradually, as the natural sounds of the countryside are faded in.

Using the audio mixer, the editor can keep the natural soundtrack if he or she wishes, fade it down beneath the reporter's narration, fade two soundtracks together so they overlap like a vision mix, or supplement the natural sound with special effects. These come in handy if the sounds of, say, a police van pulling up outside a court building are off-mike or too quiet on the original tape.

The soundtrack should be faded up slightly in advance of the pictures and never permitted to lag behind them. When sound emerges before pictures it makes for a smooth transition from one scene to another, but a moment of silence after the pictures have begun seems very odd indeed.

The TV station will keep a bank of hundreds of sound effects that can be added to a report. These will range from oil splashings to explosions – sounds which long-distance camerawork may fail to pick up. Effects are stored on computer hard disk or compact disc, and if time is short, can be played in live from the sound control room while the report is going out on air.

Graphics and other illustrations, such as captions, can be put in at the editing stage, or inserted live.

Playing the tape on air

The edit controller

The completed report can be played into the news programme live from VCR in the edit suite, or via a cartridge carousel offering instant playback.

Like so much of the equipment, the cart machines are computer controlled. Cartridges are loaded into a stack and can be fired at the touch of a button in a pre-programmed sequence, which can be altered at the last moment. The control room director will tell the

Figure 125 Desktop editing on a non-linear computer system. A setup like this costs a fraction of similar TV studio gear. Comprising (clockwise) sound-mixer, cassette deck, minidisc deck, monitor, NLE computer system running Adobe Premiere, second monitor/VHS deck, SVHS deck, DV input and edit deck, and laptop for writing the script. (*Andrew Boyd*)

operator over the talkback which report is required next, and the operator will key the name of that report into the computer. To put the report on air, all he or she has to do is press the play button at the director's command.

Fieldwork

1 Open a file on editing for TV. Get permission to visit video editors at work and watch them edit an item right the way through. Ask them to describe the process and say whether they prefer working with digital images or analogue tape – and why.

2 If you have access to the equipment, practise editing pictures on both analogue and digital equipment. Which process offers the most scope to be creative – and why? Which is faster?

3 Watch a TV news programme and note the fades and dissolves. Notice when they are used and how long they last. Listen for sound mixes as well. Describe the techniques used and comment on their effectiveness.

4 How does the editing technique used in a news report compare with those employed in a five-minute sequence from (a) a soap opera, and (b) a movie?

Would those techniques work if they were adopted for use in news reports?

5 *Cutaways are inherently dishonest. They conceal the fact that an edit has been made. The only ethical cut in a news interview is a jump-cut, so jump-cuts should be the only cuts used.* Discuss.

COMPILING THE REPORT

29 Visuals

> 'Television is chewing gum for the eyes.'   – FRED ALLEN

TV news is no longer the poor relation to newspapers and magazines when it comes to putting over information which cannot be easily stated in words. Facts can be displayed as three-dimensional and animated graphics, offering a depth and clarity of explanation once the preserve of the printed page.

The term 'visuals' covers a multitude of tricks, from stills, slides and captions, to computer-generated charts, graphs and stylish images that establish corporate identity and appear to fill the wall behind the newsreader. Virtual reality has come of age.

Stills

While most stations pride themselves on getting their TV camera crews first to a breaking story, they won't always succeed. News agencies with more troops on the ground will sometimes beat them to it.

Agencies send out hundreds of photographs daily that are input directly into an electronic *picture store*. This holds the pictures digitally as information in a computer.

Digital pictures can be reduced, enlarged or cropped on screen. Contrast and tone can be enhanced, and the final picture can be put to air electronically.

Most TV stations will have a stock of *freeze frames* or *video grabs* of leading politicians and personalities. A recent item about a prime ministerial address to a conference might throw up five new shots that can be updated from subsequent reports featuring the Prime Minister.

A variety of grabs are usually kept showing different moods and expressions. If the Prime Minister has just sacked a Cabinet colleague, it would hardly do to show a picture of either minister grinning, so a stern and determined looking shot of the PM would be chosen, accompanied by a suitably grim-looking picture of the hapless Cabinet minister. A big TV library could have up to half a million transparencies in store, indexed alphabetically.

Screening stills

The old-fashioned alternative is to take delivery of pictures on a photo-wire machine (like a fax). These can be screened in a variety of ways. The simplest method is to mount them on 30 by 23 cm cards, put them on a caption stand and point a camera at them.

Another method is to take a photographic slide of the still, and screen it on a *telecine* machine. The slides are loaded in a magazine and projected by remote control. Slides are usually 35 mm, although formats of 2 inches by 2 and $3\frac{1}{4}$ inches by 4 are also used.

Stills can be displayed together by mounting them side by side to form a *composite*. Care must be taken to balance the size and shape of the shots. Where the stills are of faces, they should be looking slightly towards each other to lead the viewer's eye into the picture. Another type of composite is a split screen with the face on one side and a quote on the other.

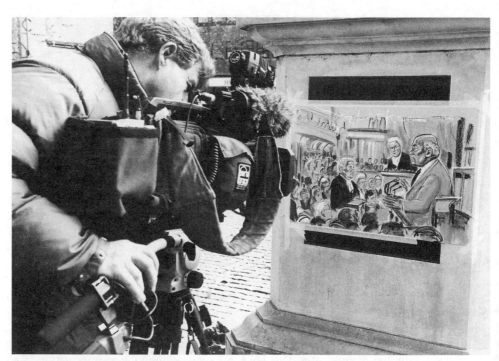

Figure 126 The low-tech approach to visuals. A drawing of a court scene is pasted to a convenient statue while the cameraman zooms and pans across it to convey the impression of movement. (*Andrew Boyd*)

Film library

Tapes of news programmes and reports are stored in the news library and indexed shot by shot. So if a riot breaks out in a city centre and the reporter wants to run footage of a previous disturbance to compare the scale, the film library should be able to come up with those pictures in a matter of moments. But beware of using the same old shots:

'We have breathalysed the same hapless man several times [and] shown another checking into Heathrow for countless holidays.'
                                                                    – BBC STYLE GUIDE

Electronic graphics

Computer technology is feeding TV's growing appetite for complex illustrations and special effects – all the better to explain a story.

Visual production effects machines (*VPEs*) have opened the floodgates to fast, polished, graphic design, where the only limits to creativity are the electronic memory of the machine and the designer's imagination. BBC news has featured a computer-generated three-dimensional cut-glass representation of the Corporation's coat of arms, complete with rotating glass globe that appeared to fill the studio beside and in front of the newsreader.

Graphic stills and animations

Graphics fall into one of two categories: still and animated. Still graphics include such items as the intertwined flags of two nations and maps with illustrated place names. Animated graphics include moving bar charts representing complex relationships such as the rise and fall of the economy, or three-dimensional images of solid objects such as rockets launching, which can be reproduced with photographic realism by computer graphics machines.

Video grabs can also be called up on screen and edited to change their colour, stretch them, rework them, combine them with a graphic or isolate a section of them and reproduce just part of the original.

Painting with light

Using an electronic graphics machine comes close to working with paints, but with no risk of getting your clothes dirty and with a greater variety of colours and brushes. Instead of oils, you are painting with light.

A light pen is moved across the screen, or a stylus is drawn across a touch tablet. Wherever it passes, corresponding lines appear. Their thickness can be varied by selecting different 'brush' sizes from a fine point to an airbrush.

Dots can be drawn and joined up to form a shape. That shape can be stretched or bent and moved round the screen at will, and filled in at the touch of a button with the artist's choice of colour, which is mixed on an electronic palette.

Pictures can be duplicated many times, and altered or moved a little each time to produce a very swift form of animation.

These machines work by dividing the screen into thousands of tiny dots known as pixels. Each has a precise location such as 340 pixels across by 235 down, and each can be painted whatever colour the artist desires, while the precise colour of each pixel is stored in the computer's memory, so any graphic can be instantly recalled at any time.

What might have taken weeks in the old days of cardboard and dry transfer lettering can now be done in a matter of hours.

Titles and captions

Supers or *captions* give the names of people and places, dates, sports scores and other statistics that can be flashed up on screen leaving the newscaster free to press on with the story.

Figure 127   A higher-tech approach – painting with light using a touch tablet and an Avid Media Spectrum. (*Courtesy Avid*)

Charts, maps and diagrams can clarify an item and show in a moment what might take minutes to explain – which makes for tighter scripting. Holding statistics on screen can also make it easier for the viewer to digest the information.

Through extensive use of subtitling, TV news has been opened up to a whole new audience – the deaf. Titles also do away with the problem that besets radio reporters of having to include a line of script to introduce each speaker.

For example, Professor Julius Hallenbach is invited to talk about his book on espionage that accuses the Government of setting up hit-squads in foreign countries. Hallenbach appears twice in the report, at the beginning, and later in reply to an official denial.

The first time Hallenbach is introduced by the reporter, but for his later reply the report cuts straight into his quote. After a second or two, when Hallenbach's picture has had time to register, his name is superimposed in the lower third of the screen. Supers are also referred to as *lower thirds*. They are usually kept in vision for up to five seconds and faded out.

Sophisticated special effects are known as *Digital Video Effects* (*DVEs*). Images can be shrunk, rotated or turned over like the leaves of a book. One shot can be wiped off the screen by another and many kinds of fades, dissolves and overlays can be used. These are produced by software in a non-linear computer editing system or by a stand-alone box of tricks like a vision mixer.

Captions and titles can also be created electronically by software or a *character generator*. These come with a wide range of typefaces and can be programmed to store captions or supers for recall at the touch of a button.

For election coverage, for example, the generator could be pre-programmed with the name of every candidate in every constituency with all the results from the previous election, so as the results begin to come in, all the relevant information can be flashed up on screen in an instant.

Electronic character generators have replaced paraphernalia such as title cards, slides and mechanical caption machines that operated like miniature printing presses.

Care must be taken to make sure captions and titles can be clearly read. Letter height should be kept above one twenty-fifth of the screen height, and the letters will need to be placed so they do not obliterate important parts of the picture beneath. To make allowances for badly adjusted sets, titles should be positioned within a part of the screen known as the *safe area* where there will be no danger of slipping off the bottom of the picture or falling off the side. Viewfinders of TV cameras are usually marked so the cameraperson can see when the picture is straying outside the safe area.

Caption information should be kept as brief as possible to avoid overloading the viewer or the screen, and should be displayed for long enough to allow even slow readers to take it all in.

Complete rehearsals of news programmes are seldom possible, but where complex opening sequences are used, featuring a mix of titles, graphics and animation, these are usually compiled in advance of transmission and recorded on videotape. This covers the embarrassment of the production team by giving them the chance to rehearse and correct mistakes off-air.

Overlays

Chromakey

Chromakey is an electronic means of displaying still or moving pictures behind the newsreader. Pictures can fill the entire screen behind the reader or occupy a rectangular box to one side. These are known as full-frame graphics or window graphics respectively. An onlooker in the studio will see only the newsreader at his or her desk sitting in front of the brightly coloured back wall of the set. Only the production team and viewers at home will see the newsreader and pictures combined.

Chromakey, or *colour separation overlay* (*CSO*) as it is sometimes called, works by eliminating one colour from the screen and replacing it with a picture or graphic.

Unseen by the viewer, the back of the set is a coloured backdrop of lurid blue, yellow or green. This colour is switched out automatically by the vision mixer and replaced with a picture or visual from a second camera, VTR or graphics machine. Green is commonly used for the backdrop because there are few shades of green in white human skin.

By using chromakey the studio set with its bright green drape can be transformed, for example, into an attractive backdrop of graduated Wedgewood blue created by a graphics machine.

This image can then be replaced with a full frame still or moving shot of a news story, or supplemented by a window in the top-right-or left-hand corner showing a picture.

The only problem is when the newsreader decides to wear the same colour as the one switched out by the chromakey. If the newsreader's tie, for example, is a matching shade, that too will disappear, leaving what appears to be a hole punched right through him to the photograph or scene behind. No self-respecting newsreader wants to be seen on air with

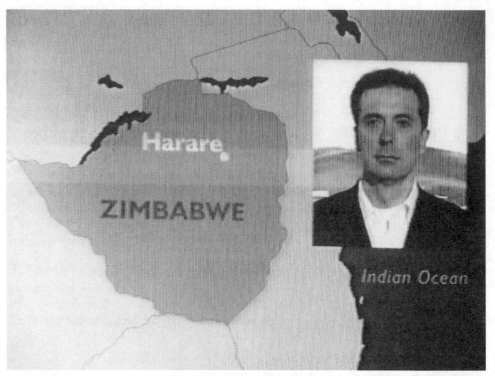

Solution A

Solution B

Figure 128 · How to avoid turning into radio when you've got no moving pictures.

Solution C

Figure 128 *Continued. Solution A* – screen a map of the location, overlay it with a still of the reporter and play his telephone report. (*Courtesy BBC*) *Solution B* – get a grab of the minister, pull out the key point of his statement and set it against a three visuals that illustrate the context . . . the car, cash and the ministry logo. (*Courtesy Channel 4 News*) *Solution C* – in this *composite shot* two complementary images are found – the leaders of South and North Korea, adjusted for size, and screened together so the two appear to be side by side. Their images are set against grabs of their national flags. (*Courtesy BBC*)

troops marching across his chest or politicians draped across his midriff, so care is taken to avoid clothing that matches the chromakey colour.

Bright blue eyes can also accidentally trigger the effect, but in practice the shade chosen is so unnaturally vivid that the problem of accidental switching seldom occurs.

A more common shortcoming is that the chromakey background can appear to sparkle at the edges where it gives way to the subject, particularly through the hair.

Back projection (rear projection, US)

Another alternative for inserting visuals on the set is to use a large TV screen beside the newsreader, or to display pictures on a monitor that is in vision, though this can cause problems with colour balance.

An older option that has been largely superseded by electronic picture insertion is *back projection*, where a slide or moving image is projected from behind the set onto a translucent screen. One scene can be replaced by another using a second projector.

This is less expensive but more inflexible than the electronic system and requires extra studio space for the projector. *Front projection* saves that space, but the image being projected into a well-lit studio might appear to be less bright. The lighting also has to be carefully set up to avoid the newsreader's shadow falling across the screen.

Fieldwork

1 Open a file on *visuals*. Watch, and record if possible, a number of news programmes. Note the types of visuals used. Is chromakey or back projection used? Are several types of visual on screen at the same time? For how long is a clip of an interviewee allowed to run before a caption appears? And for how long will that caption be displayed on the screen?

2 Visit a studio and see if you can work out which machines are producing all the different effects. Which effects are best and why?

3 Listen to a recording of an extended news programme on the radio. Imagine that same programme on TV. Story by story, what visuals and graphics would you commission to illustrate those items? If you are in a class, split into groups of four and draw up your proposals.

4 Make design sketches of one of the graphics you would use. Decide whether it should be still or animated, accompanied by words or figures, how long it should be kept on screen, and most importantly, whether it adds to the story and makes it clearer.

5 What are the advantages and disadvantages of chromakey over front or rear projection?

THE NEWS STUDIO

30   'Standby for transmission . . .'

> '. . . thick padded doors and walls, anything from two to five cameras looking hungrily for something to shoot, a flock of technicians waiting behind double-thickness glass (bullet-proof perhaps?) for the producer's every word (and mistake?) – all this could just as well be a torture chamber as a television studio.
>
> 'Once you know how to do it, directing a studio can become addictive, an exhilarating drug which can stimulate you to a "high" it takes hours to come down from.'
> — ON CAMERA*

The elevated backdrop of a city at night, presided over by a pair of benign oracles who dispense wisdom to the nation from behind the swish, uncluttered lines of a vast and authoritative newscasters' desk.

It's an illusion, of course. Walking into a news studio is like stepping into a cupboard or factory. It will either be a fraction of the size it appears to be on screen, or cavernously large. The impression can be one of confusion and overwhelming untidiness.

To the first-time visitor, the news studio is a bewildering array of lights and a snakes-nest of cables. Ceilings are high and incredibly cluttered with lamps of all shapes and sizes. The floor is a man-trap of wires and the cameras bristle with flex and look as brutal and uncompromising as ships' engines.

Even the set which appears so swish and urbane on the screen, looks uninviting in daylight. The illusion is all in the lights and the tricks of the camera.

And the tricks are getting more and more sophisticated. All hail the virtual studio. The plain blue background is switched out and replaced with a three dimensional computer-generated image. Sets and backdrops exist only in the minds of the computer programmers. They can be changed at the touch of a key, or tilted, rotated, zoomed into or panned across, all in perfect synch with the foreground.

Even the camera operator is being keyed out of existence, thanks to motion sensors that lock on to the presenter and follow him or her around. Illusion is piling on illusion.

* Harris Watts, BBC, 1995.

Figure 129 The news studio set at Scotland Today. (*Courtesy Scottish Television*)

The set

The news programme could have its own studio or share a set with the rest of the TV station.

Sets vary in sophistication. They may have elaborate desks with panelling behind giving the impression of an affluent sitting room, or be incorporated into the newsroom itself, presenting a backdrop of bustle. Alternatively, the background could be a picture window that appears to be looking out on a local scene but is in reality an image captured by a video camera.

Increasingly, set sophistication is giving way to electronic illusions created in the control room, offering full-screen graphics, windowing and computer-generated backgrounds. Behind the desk, the backdrop might be nothing more than a set of painted wooden panels or highly coloured cloth.

Where several programmes use the same studio, sets can be constructed to pull apart in moments; the boards behind, known as *flats*, may be turned around to reveal a surface of different colour and texture, or the whole studio may be transformed in an instant into some new computer-generated concept of reality.

On the desk in front of the newscaster, but out of view of the cameras, will be a pair of lights: one red, the other green. The red tells the newscaster he or she is on air, and the green is for rehearsals.

Built into the desk will usually be a microphone, clock, and a monitor to show what is going out on air. A second monitor off-camera may show a preview shot of the next item. Plenty of space is left on the desk for scripts.

Beside the newscaster could be a hotline for the sub-editor to give instructions live into the programme. This is used only in emergencies. Instead of a bell, which could interrupt broadcasts, it has a light that flashes when a caller is on the line.

A second telephone may be kept behind the desk in case the newscaster needs to contact the producer. This equipment is duplicated for each newscaster and the assorted clutter on the desktop is concealed from the cameras by a raised lip at the front.

Lighting

Each news programme requires its own particular array of lights to suit its style. When different programmes regularly use the same studio, permanent lighting rigs for each will be kept in place. This results in duplication, but saves having to reset all the lights for each change of programme.

Some lights are floor-mounted, but most are suspended by cables and poles from a framework of girders across the ceiling called a *lighting grid*. They range in power from a meagre 750 watts to a searing 10 kilowatts. The lighting director fades them up and down from a control panel.

In some studios the lights can be programmed to function automatically. Floodlights bring up the overall level of lighting to within the operating range of the cameras; large, square, matt fillers provide diffuse light to brighten up the studio, while spotlights act as the keys, lighting and modelling the subject. These have 'barn-door' flaps that can be adjusted to alter the spread of light.

Backlights pick out the newscaster from the background and add sparkle to the hair and areas that other lights might have missed, such as the tops of shoulders. Additional lamps may be used to illuminate the set and add sparkle to the newscaster's eyes.

Cameras

A typical TV studio will have between two and four cameras mounted on mobile pedestals. To cut costs and streamline the chain of command increasing use is being made of robot cameras that can be operated from the control room.

Each camera has a zoom lens that can shift the picture from long shot to big close-up without having to move closer to the scene. Another control adjusts the focus.

The pictures from remote cameras are displayed on monitors in the control room. Or if an operator is present, he or she will see the image through a viewfinder on top of the camera.

This displays a black and white picture, even on colour cameras, as a monochrome image is clearer and easier to focus.

The camera is mounted on a pedestal and the head can be raised, lowered, tilted or swivelled (*panned*). A *panning handle* is used to adjust its position. Fitted to this is the zoom control, similar to a motorcycle twistgrip.

The camera may be mounted on a lightweight tripod or heavyweight dolly, which can be remote-controlled. Between these two extremes is the pedestal, the camera mounting most commonly used in TV studios. It can be operated by one person and is adjustable for height. The studio floors are carefully levelled to allow the cameras to move smoothly across them without jumping or bumping on the screen.

Some cameras have pre-set controls that allow the operator to select the appropriate shots with the zoom lens and programme them into the camera's *shot-box*. Instead of adjusting the lens by hand, he or she can go straight to the shot at the touch of a button.

When the director puts a camera on air, an indicator will glow in the viewfinder, and a red *cue-light* on top of the camera lights up to let the presenter know the camera is live.

The cameraperson can line up the picture with another by superimposing the picture from the second camera into the viewfinder.

Each camera has its own intercom, so the operator can hear and reply to the director's instructions.

Pictures from the different cameras are selected and mixed in the control room. The vision mixer, or technical director, can cut directly from one camera to another, or can use a variety of *wipes*, *fades* and *dissolves* to gradually change between pictures.

Sound

The walls of the studio are acoustically treated to eliminate echo and provide a natural sound. Three different types of microphone are commonly used. Newsreaders are usually fitted with a personal mike that is clipped to the jacket. If the newsreader turns to one side to conduct a live interview the microphone will move with him or her and there will be no danger of going off-mike. A desktop mike will usually be in position as a back-up.

Where the presenter is likely to move around, a *boom microphone* will be operated by a sound engineer, or the presenter will be fitted with a radio mike. Both these solutions do away with the problem of trailing cables. The boom mike is either a microphone on the end of a pole, known as a *fishpole*, or a more sophisticated sound boom which can stretch up to 6 m and be adjusted for length, height and tilt.

The floor manager

At first glance, the *floor manager* looks a cross between a mime artist and racecourse tic-tac man (bookie). With a combination of hand signals and gestures he or she acts as the director's link person and makes sure everything runs smoothly on the studio floor. In the run-up to the programme the floor manager sees that all the props and equipment are in place, and during the programme guides the presenters and instructs the studio crew. He or she hears the director's instructions through an earpiece or headphones and passes them on by means of hand-signals. The floormanager is becoming a dying breed as remote control studios become more widespread.

Prompting

Newsreaders seldom work without the script on the table, though they may rarely refer to it. Few things look less professional than the top of a newsreader's head as he or she glances down to read the script. Most stations get round this problem by using a prompting device, such as an *Autocue* or *Teleprompt*.

The script is keyed into a computer and displayed back to front on a monitor screen slung below the camera. The words are reflected onto a glass sheet across the lens of the camera, which turns them the right way round. The glass is invisible to the camera, which looks right through it at the newsreader, who reads the script reflected on the glass, creating the impression that he or she has eye-contact with the audience.

The speed at which the script is run through the machine is regulated by the operator who matches it as closely as possible to the reading speed of the presenter.

Figure 130   The anchor's best friend, the prompter. An operator controls the speed at which the script runs across the screen. (*Courtesy EDS Portaprompt*)

Control room

> *'45 seconds to transmission.'*
> *'Stand by Cart 1, VT1, ES1, VT2, VT3, and ES2.'*
> *'20 to transmission.'*
> *'On air in 15, 14, 13 . . . three, two . . .'*
> *'Cart 1 roll.'*
> *'. . . zero. On air.'*

You have seen those submarine movies. The dim red lights, the atmosphere taut with expectancy. Each person at his post, every eye straining at a flickering dial or gauge. Reflexes that are nerve-end sharp, breathing that is shallow and rhythmic. The captain's instructions are terse and clipped, his utterances in a technical tongue. Not a word is wasted. Each cryptic command triggers a response from the crew as swiftly as tripping a relay. And when the crisis finally passes the atmosphere discharges like the night air after a thunderclap. To the uninitiated it is a little like that in the TV control room.

1 Inside the gallery at ITN. *'45 seconds to transmission . . . stand by Cart 1, CT1, ES1, VT2, VT3 and ES2 . . .'*

2 T-bars on the mixing desk dissolve from one input to another. The monitors are in black and white to give a crisper focus.

Figure 131

3 Cutting from picture to picture at the touch of a screen. *'Each cryptic command triggers a response from the crew as swiftly as tripping a relay.'* (*Andrew Boyd*)

Figure 131 *Continued*

The director

The control room captain is the TV *director*, who sits at the centre of the control desk, cueing the cameras and calling the shots from the studio. The red light for action stations is the red transmission warning. A bank of monitors dominates the wall in front of the director, displaying a more bewildering variety of pictures than most television showrooms. Each image and sound that makes up a programme; all the camera pictures, pre-recorded news reports, grabs, graphics and titles, are fed into the control room gallery where the director reigns supreme, deciding when each picture, report or caption should go to air.

The *transmission* monitor shows what is currently on air. Another displays the picture the control room is working on. Beside that the next shot is lined up ready to go. A fourth monitor displays a caption to be added to a report. Another has a graphic. Three more show what each camera is looking at in the studio. Several more display countdown sequences for each tape and machine that has a report standing by ready for transmission. On another is the picture called up from the electronic still store. A black and white monitor repeats the transmitted scene to provide a clearer image for checking the focus. Another shows what the network is seeing so the director can tell exactly when to opt in and out of network with the programme. And to make sure the station is keeping up with the opposition another monitor reveals what is currently going out on the rival station.

The director tells the videotape operators to stand by. They reply with a buzzer. One buzz for 'yes'; two means 'not ready'.

Located in a prominent position is a large and accurate clock. In the background the programme sound is being played over the speaker. On the long desk in front of the monitors are the rows and clusters of illuminated buttons and switches that make up the control panel.

Each picture on show can be switched to air. The director has to keep an eye on these and remain in constant verbal contact over the talkback with cameras and crew as well as acting on split-second decisions by the producer about the running order of the programme.

Presented with the need to have more heads than the Hydra, if only to keep watch on all those monitors, the director on a larger TV station farms out a number of responsibilities to other personnel.

Other personnel

The *production assistant* (*PA*) or *production secretary* keeps one step ahead of the programme. Some scripts are numbered shot by shot. He or she literally calls the shots and cues in items to be transmitted live on still store and videotape. The still store is used to hold still pictures that have been digitized, allowing them to be cropped and edited. Video cartridges can be played in from a variety of sources, including a central carousel (*Cart*) or from a player in an edit suite (*ES*). Machines that used to take five seconds to get up to speed now start instantly, eliminating the problem of awkward silences at the start of a report or the newsreader crashing in over the commentary.

The PA is responsible for copying and distributing scripts and for the timekeeping of the programme. He or she has timings for everything from stories to stills, knows exactly how long the programme should run and can tell from the stopwatch at any given time whether it is running over or under. If the times mismatch, items will have to be cut, dropped or added in. (On some stations the PA's task falls to the *assistant director*. On others, the production assistant directs, and the timekeeping is carried out by the production secretary.)

Where a script has to be altered, the *chief sub-editor* will whittle it down or pad it out with extra sentences or lines, carrying out a constant process of fine-tuning to make it fit. Prime targets for tinkering are the recaps at the end of the bulletin. The chief sub has a telephone link with the newscaster to pass on any emergency instructions.

At the director's command, *the vision mixer* (*switcher, technical director*, US) fades or cuts from one shot to another, punches up outside broadcast cameras, or plays tricks on the screen with special effects. Where effects are used extensively a second vision mixer may be on hand simply to operate those.

While all this is happening, a constant check is being made on the circuitry to make sure there are no technical hitches. This is carried out by the *technical manager* (*operations supervisor, senior engineer*). At the first hint of trouble, he or she will be on the hotline to the engineers in master control. Meanwhile the *vision controller* is checking and adjusting the quality of all the pictures.

At the end of the control desk, or in an adjoining room with visual contact through a plate glass window, is the *sound controller*, who regulates the sound levels of all the microphones in the studio. There may also be a grams operator who plays the jingles (sounders) and signature tune and adds any sound effects. These used to be kept on sound effects records, hence the *grams* in the title, but increasingly effects are being stored either on computer or compact disc.

From a panel in the control room or an adjoining room the *lighting director* and *console operator* work the studio lights. The lighting 'plot' can be keyed into a computer, which will operate the lights throughout the programme according to the pre-set plan.

If the programme is introduced by an announcer, he or she will sit in an adjoining *announcement booth* (*presentation area*).

Personnel and their roles differ from station to station.

Running order

With so much material to be coordinated from so many sources, the director and team could hardly be expected to rely on their memories to guide them through the programme.

As much as possible is scripted, though news programmes are fast moving and likely to change as stories come in. Every item will be on a separate page so pieces can be dropped or added as needs be. Each page of script will include details of camera shots and visuals such as stills and graphics, as well as a duration for the item.

Each item and lead is timed. Ad-libs are discouraged. The programme might opt out of the network to offer regional news or it could supply national news to the entire network. Either way, split-second timing is essential. On television an unscheduled two-second delay can feel like eternity.

Each programme will have a running order, but with instant updates a possibility, complete running orders are becoming something of a rarity. More often it will be unfinished and subject to corrections and additions. A new lead might arrive five minutes before the programme is due on air. Stories may be cut to make way for others, and extra items might have to be included to make up time. This is where a short copy story illustrated by a still can come in handy. Where a story has yet to arrive, a blank sheet known as a *skeleton* (or *blank*) is inserted into the script, to be replaced with the story as soon as it is finished.

The producer makes decisions about the content of the news programme and the director makes those decisions work on air. With news the problem is seldom one of having to fill: scripts might have to be edited and shortened even while the programme is going out.

The nearest the director may come to rehearsing the show is the pre-recording of the title sequences shortly before the programme begins. That a news programme ever gets on air without a mistake seems little short of miraculous to the onlooker.

> *'I have never known a programme that doesn't change. Sometimes we can go on air and not have the lead story, nor the second lead nor the third lead and start half way down the running order. We get into the VTR (taped report) and try and sort ourselves out to find out what we can go on to next. It can be an absolute mess!'*
> — MALCOLM JOHNSON, DIRECTOR, ITN

When mistakes do occur, there is always an inquest to find out how and why, to try to prevent them happening again but, with the shrinking world's news coming in thicker and faster, that uncomfortable sense of teetering even closer to the brink can only continue to grow. It is a tribute to the team's professionalism that, somehow, it never seems to show.

Fieldwork

1 If you have access to a TV studio construct a set that is suitable for a news programme and arrange the lighting for single-headed and then double-headed presentation.
2 Find a willing subject to act as a newsreader and practise using a TV camera. Concentrate on framing your subject well and keeping him or her in focus. Zoom in and out for best effect. Shoot some tape and see how well you have done.

How should the zoom be used during a news programme? Watch a bulletin and see if you can notice the cameras zooming or panning.

3 Make a recording of yourself reading the news from a teleprompter and criticize your performance. Is your expression natural or are you staring or peering at the camera? Are your eyebrows glued in position? Try again, taking care to relax and iron out any ticks or peculiar expressions.

4 Watch a number of news programmes and see which wipes, fades and dissolves they use. Do you think the producers could have been more creative? How?

Try your hand at vision mixing. Experiment with different types of wipes, fades and dissolves. Which work best for news?

5 Arrange to visit a TV control room to watch a live news programme going out. Find out exactly who is doing what and see if you can follow the action as the programme is broadcast.

ONLINE JOURNALISM AND NEW MEDIA

31   Videojournalism

> '"Just you?" It's a question thrown at every videojournalist at some point in their career and it's usually asked by people who have had experience of crews. Crews are impressive. They have huge cameras and large fluffy microphones. They carry lights and cables and ask where the power sockets are. They say things like "turning over" and "at speed". They have an assistant who rushes out to the van to get that vital filter and then stands just off camera holding an enormous circle of white that reflects natural light on the subject's face. They have a director who stands there pondering and asking them to reframe about a millimetre to the left. And they have a producer who set the whole thing up and wants to make sure everyone is happy because it's their neck that's on the line. You have, well, "just you".'
>
> – RICHARD GRIFFITHS, *VIDEOJOURNALISM**

There is a new breed of broadcast journalist. One who is not content just to write the words, but wants the excitement of shooting the pictures as well. Enter stage-left the videojournalist, the multi-talented, all-singing, all-dancing action-hero, whose very existence has been made possible by the rising quality and plunging prices of the new generation of camcorders.

The VJ is the ultimate one-man band. With all this talent and flexibility the VJ should be king of the heap, you'd think. You'd be wrong.

Employing videojournalists is the latest trick of the cost accountants who run the media. Why employ a crew of three – lights, sound, camera, plus reporter – if you can get away with just one? And why pay high rates when you can get your virtuoso fresh out of college for a song? The money goes where it has always gone – to the specialist. The VJ is the generalist *par extraordinaire*.

The term videojournalist was coined in the UK in 1994 when an ad was placed in *The Guardian* for 24 VJs for the London cable news station, Channel One. The station's contradictory brief was to make polished news at low cost. And its solution was to break down the barriers between job functions. TV neophytes drawn from backgrounds

* Focal Press 1998, p.89.

in newspapers, magazines and radio shouldered their camcorders and scoured the city for news.

The principle of multi-skilling (i.e. cost-cutting) was taken right into the studio where technicians worked lights, cameras, caption generators and even shifted sets. *'People have done things you'd never expect them to. They've discovered talents they didn't know they had,'* says Head of Operations, Tim Gates.

> *'Anyone working here for a year learns shooting, basic lighting, editing and how to run a studio. After that the world's your oyster. We are already losing people who learnt their skills here to conventional television.'*
> – CHANNEL ONE DIRECTOR OF PROGRAMMES, NICK POLLARD*

Channel One took its inspiration from cable TV in the USA and went on to break the mould in Britain. By the time it was forced to close, others were following suit. West Country television took on four videojournalists. *'A VJ can go off and do a special feature for two or three days without tying up the crew,'* output editor Jeremy Hibberd told the *Press Gazette*.

But big outfits like ITN were sniffy. One insider told an earlier edition of *Broadcast Journalism*: *'The quality of journalism can't be as good if you are carrying a camera round. If you're a reporter out on a story and you're worrying about how to get shots, whether interviewees are being framed the right way and planning cutaway shots, you're not doing the journalism.'*

And Live TV in Birmingham, which had experimented with videojournalists went back to its safe old ways, as reporter Sue Lloyd explained: *'One-man crews can work, but in my experience, journalists are better at being journalists and cameramen are better at being cameramen.'*

But where there's a wad, there's a way. Ask the head of news at Meridian TV: *'It's cheaper than having two people doing the job. No question.'* Today, ITN and even the BBC are recruiting videojournalists. ITN has eight based around the UK regions and a ninth in London, specializing in sport. More will follow.

They shoot on cameras that use tiny digital videotapes. ITN's machine of preference is a small Canon XL1, which costs around one tenth of the price of that seasoned old mainstay, the Betacam.

The picture quality isn't as good, but it's light years ahead of the ultra-portable standby it replaced, the Hi 8. DV was marketed originally by Sony as a consumer format, before broadcasters elevated it into the big league. It means anyone with a couple of thousand pounds can now afford a camera that will take pictures deemed by those who matter to be of broadcast quality. Something of an own goal by Sony?

ITN VJs are trained in editing, but usually feed their rushes back to London so they can get on with another assignment while a specialist editor sets about their pictures. Shots can be sent back from other network stations or one of ITN's ten satellite trucks standing by to go live from anywhere around the UK. VJs also send back their soundtrack for use by ITN radio.

> *'We wanted to increase our camera power around the country,'* says Head of Newsgathering, Jonathan Munro. *'We can see a network where we cover the entire country eventually – which we are far from doing at the moment.'*

* *Broadcast Magazine*, 1996.

Figure 132   The Canon XL1 DV camcorder is one of a new breed of lightweight machine that have made it possible for the journalist to work without a camera crew.

The lenses are interchangeable, but the built-in mike isn't considered up to the task. These machines eat batteries – note the large power pack on the back. (*Andrew Boyd*)

VJs are on the ITN staff. Some work from home and others from existing bureaux. They may be used to complement bureau coverage by staying on at a news conference to meet later deadlines.

Jonathan Munro describes the move as *'very successful. The VJs are on the whole journalists who have learned to use cameras. They're very enthusiastic and try to push the boundaries back all the time. They are making tremendous strides forward and are able to man a live-spot – to perform live pieces to camera. It gives us a lot more firepower.'*

Videojournalist Rachel McTavish (25), works from her home in Kidderminster, near Birmingham, and provides coverage for ITV, Channels 4 and 5 and ITN's radio stations,

Figure 133 Light, camera, action! – ITN videojournalist Rachel McTavish. *'VJs are faster and more efficient. It's great fun – and quite exhausting.'* (*Andrew Boyd*)

IRN and LBC. She shoots pictures and conducts interviews. Then, to get the footage back, she drives to Central Television in Birmingham or one of two other network feed points.

> *'It's great fun – and quite exhausting,'* she says. *'While VJs aren't suitable for some jobs, they're faster and more efficient. You can send them out where it wouldn't be practical to send a sound man, cameraman, reporter and producer. If it's a story that might break, it's much better to have one person waiting than to tie up four expensive members of staff.'*

Rachel's top scoop was to capture B52 bombers taking off on their first bombing run of the Kosovo crisis to drive the Serbs out of the region. *'I was the only person to get that,'* she says. *'The BBC had to borrow my shots from ITN and credit them. It was a great feeling to know my pictures were leading on ITN, the BBC 1 o'clock news, CNN and Bloomberg – everybody bought the shots.'*

Rachel admits that working by yourself has its downside. *'It can be exhausting at times – especially when you are in a scrum situation – but you get a sink or swim mentality. You know you've got to get the story and the pictures back and people are waiting on you and relying on you.'*

One consolation is that these new technocrats of the airwaves tend to stick together. Even VJs from rival organisations often help each other out, one filming while another gets in close enough to record the sound, then pooling their material.

Rachel took a hands-on media production course before beginning her career at Channel One stations in London and Liverpool. *'I've got a soft spot for them,'* she says. *'Where else would take someone fresh out of university and say, "You can read the news and present a programme." They really took risks and I'll always be grateful for that.'*

The Kit

Her standard kit is a Canon XL1, a tripod, a large Sennheiser rifle mike, two tie mikes, a hand-held light (handbasher) and top light for the camera. *'We do have a full lighting kit, but I don't even start to use mine, it's just too much to think about.'*

Along with these are wellies, walking boots, all-weather gear and a company car to carry it all in. It sounds a handful, but Rachel says it certainly beats lugging around a Betacam.

While the small cameras can't equal the quality of their bigger brothers – yet – they are very handy in terms of mobility and speed. *'You don't think anything of running across fields chasing protesters with a camcorder,'* says Rachel. *'It certainly doesn't take it out of you the same way.'*

As they say, size matters, and there are advantages in being small: *'You can get very close to interviewees or subjects and develop a relationship of mutual trust and produce better, more honest material. They are an absolute godsend if you are interested in observational type filming,'* enthused the *Press Gazette**.

The trade-off against miniaturization is that the cameras lack the robustness of their professional models. *'Some of these smaller digital cameras are a bit unreliable,'* says Rachel, *'and there are times when they let you down, which is incredibly frustrating.'* She keeps a spare Sony VX1000 – the first widely used digital camcorder – in her car. *'I swear by it. It doesn't like dust, damp or Mondays but I've had fewer problems than with the XL1. The Canon's got a better lens, though, and when the whole thing works it's fantastic.'*

---

* 'UK first for new generation TV cameras', 25 October 1996.

Another essential part of her kit is her combined mobile phone and fax machine. ITN VJs are issued with Nokia Communicators – phones which open up like a notepad computer and can receive faxes and e-mails. *'It makes it a lot easier,'* she explains, *'because we can be faxed the Press Association wire stories and copy, so we don't really need to be at base.'*

Drawbacks

The drawbacks are those you would expect where compiling an entire report is down to the efforts of a single person. Problems include recording sound at a news conference where the cameras are forced to remain at the back of the room. *'We learned early on that what VJs can do is limited by their kit,'* says ITN's Jonathan Munro, *'and the fact that they work on their own. For more complex assignments, VJs work conventionally, teamed up with a cameraman.'*

Richard Griffiths was one of Britain's first videojournalists working for the London cable outfit Channel One. He says videojournalism has gone through a learning curve:

> *'It's a superb method of production for story-led news, features and documentaries. The intimacy of one person and a small camcorder allows the videojournalist to get closer to the subject than an intrusive crew could ever manage. But it is really no good for live broadcasts (who changes the iris when the sun comes out from behind the clouds?); court reports (either you get the story inside or the pictures outside – you can't get both), or presenter-led productions.'**

[handwritten margin note: Implications on audience & quality]

Some of the old school at ITN still arch an eyebrow at the thought of videojournalists falling over their feet trying to do three or four jobs. One soundman said: *'You can't have your finger on the pulse if you are thinking about what you need to write in your story. You could lose your concentration for that crucial split-second. Some of the work I've seen has not been very good. The gear they're using isn't great. But they're on a learning curve and they'll get better.'* A cameraman added: *'We think the quality's going down – but you'd expect us to say that.'*

But Rachel McTavish handles the criticism with stoicism.

> *'Yes, there are days when things go wrong and people go "Oh, VJs!", but things can go wrong for full-time cameramen and journalists. With a VJ you are not going to get the same standard of lighting or inventive and creative camerawork when you are expected to interview a person as well. But we've been given enough training by ITN to know which shots will make it in a package and I think people are beginning to accept that VJs can be relied upon now.*
>
> *'Working on your own means that when things go wrong you've got nobody to share the stress with. There are always hairy moments when the weather's bad and you've got the newsdesk on the phone saying, "Where's this piece? – we needed it 15 minutes ago." Where the truck has moved to a new location and you are wrestling with the map in your car trying to speak on your hands-free telephone thinking, "Oh my God!" and it's driving with rain and you're thinking: "I can feel an ulcer developing!" but that's the same for any camera person or reporter.'*

And she says the ultimate accolade has been paid by the BBC, who are trying to poach some of ITN's VJs that they meet out on the road.

According to Rachel, ITN is currently paying its VJs around £25 000, plus a car and generous expenses. It's not bad, but it doesn't come close to the earnings potential of an

---

* *Videojournalism*, Focal Press, 1998.

on-screen network correspondent. The trouble is, no one has pioneered this career path before. Where does someone like Rachel go next?

'Some want to become full-time camera-people, but others like me have trained as journalists with the camera as an added skill, so want to move on within the journalistic role – more of a J, and less of a V.'

A DAY IN THE LIFE OF VJ RACHEL McTAVISH

7 am   Wake up, listen to *Today* programme on Radio 4.

7.36   Monitor Central TV's local TV news bulletin, then back to *Today* programme.

7.45   Switch to BBC local radio to catch their headlines.

8.15   Phone newsdesk. *'They'll either have a story for me or ask me what's happening here. If it's anything I have warned them about I'll go off and do that. Or I'll wait till after the morning meeting. Then they'll ask me to work on a package, produce, or find an ingredient for a story: "We need to talk to an estate agent about rocketing house prices."*

'There is no such thing as a typical day. I'll go out and film an interview with an estate agent, do the check calls to make sure there's been no big developments, or go out and do a story at 4.30 in the afternoon.

'It's impossible to say what the demands will be of ITV, Channel 4 and 5.'

6.30 – usually. Back home.

The VJ at work

All that multi-skilling breaks down into a number of elements: shooting, interviewing, scriptwriting and possibly editing. But for the VJ, first comes the preparation.

Preparing for the shoot

Preparation begins the day before the shoot, when you check the camera, the tapes, the lights and the batteries.

First clean the camera. Make sure the lens is spotless, using a proprietary lens cleaner and cloth, rather than a piece of scratchy old tissue or a shirt sleeve. Your lens should be protected by an ultraviolet light (*UV*) filter whose main purpose is to take any knocks and bashes. Remove the filter, clean it both sides and clean the lens beneath it.

Then make sure the camera body is free from dust and dirt before you open it up to insert a tape. Use a tape-cleaning head if you suspect dust might have entered the camera. Distortion on playback is a good indication. Cleaning tapes grind down the camera heads over time, so use sparingly – run for a few seconds only.

The videotape is the camera's food, so give it good-quality fodder, not cheap, discount stuff. And prepare it first.

Cameras record a timecode onto the videotape for editing, which you can turn off for playback. The timecode shows the number of hours, minutes, seconds and frames that have elapsed. In the UK, every second is broken down into 25 frames – 30 in the USA. This means that each image has a unique identification number, which is a great help when it comes to compiling the report. But if a gap appears in the recording, then the timecode will start again from the beginning. This is bad news. You could have several images sharing the same timecode. And that can confuse an editor no end. So it is important to make sure there can be no gap on the tape which would break the timecode.

Fortunately, gaps can't occur on a pre-recorded tape. The way to prevent them is to take each fresh tape, put it in the camera with the lens cap on and record all the way through it. This will stamp in a timecode from beginning to end that cannot be broken. The process is known as *blacking the tape*.

Always take more tapes than you think you will need. Unlike audio cassettes, these are specialist items and can be hard to come by. And always take more batteries than you imagine you will require, too. A DV camcorder can go through a fully charged battery in as little as 20 minutes, whatever the manufacturer's claim to the contrary. It isn't always possible to plug the camera into the mains, so the well-prepared VJ should charge up a good stock of batteries the day before and take a fully charged battery belt, which will supply enough juice to keep your camera turning away merrily for several hours.

Take a mains charger with you so you can run your camera off the mains when you get the chance. And take a car-charging unit so you can top up your batteries on the go.

And on the subject of batteries, like a computer, your camcorder will have a second internal battery to keep its microchip memory working. Take a spare. And take spares of any other batteries you are using, too.

Figure 134   The machine that started a revolution – the Sony VX1000. Smaller and lighter than the Canon, but without the benefit of being able to be shoulder mounted – which means you need a sturdy tripod. (*Andrew Boyd*)

If you are packing lights, check their batteries are also fully charged and that the bulbs are still working. Again, pack spares.

Cameras hate dust and damp. You wear a raincoat when it rains – your camera should as well. Always pack a camera rainjacket just in case the weather turns nasty.

And if you are likely to be shooting in dusty conditions you will need to seal the camera to prevent dust getting in. Specks of dust can play havoc with the picture, kicking up all kinds of digital distortion.

So if you plan to go out on Operation Desert Storm seal up the camera's tape door mechanism with waterproof tape.

Camera checks

Before you begin to shoot, adjust the camera's viewfinder to suit your eyesight. Like a pair of binoculars, twiddle the knurled adjuster on the viewfinder until the picture comes into perfect focus.

Now we need to get technical. You should adjust your camera's *white balance*. Different lighting conditions cast a different colour over the scene. Moonlight is blue; for example, while artificial light tends have an orange hue. Adjusting the camera for this is simple. Take the camera off automatic, hold out a sheet of white paper such as a notebook a little way from the lens, zoom in on it until it fills the viewfinder and then press your white balance button. As soon as the indicator stops blinking your white balance is set. That's all there is to it. Just make sure that whenever you move to a different lighting condition you remember to adjust the white balance all over again.

Tripod

Unless your camcorder is a large, shoulder-mounted model like a Betacam you are going to need to mount it on a tripod. Otherwise you will be filming in wobblevision.

Not even a bomb-disposal expert can hold a palmcorder rock-steady enough to shoot a broadcast-quality report. The more you zoom in, the more your wobbles will be magnified. If you must do hand-held shots, keep the zoom on wide-angle. And don't rely on the digital or optical image stabilizer built into your camera. It won't help. In fact, digital stabilizers degrade the picture quality and should be turned off.

The only kind of stabiliser worth having is twice the weight and four times the size of your camcorder and has three legs. Your tripod should be sturdy, self-levelling and have a fluid pan head. That means it won't flex with your camera on it, you can level it up against a built-in spirit level by turning a single screw beneath the head rather than fiddling around adjusting the legs, and you can swivel the camcorder from left to right using the panning handle without graunching, snagging or jerking.

Microphones

Camcorders usually have built-in microphones, but these are for ambient sound only and are not designed for recording interviews. They are omni-directional, which means they pick up all the background noise and lack the necessary range to record someone speaking several feet from the camera.

To overcome these limitations most VJs fit an additional rifle mike on top of the camera. This is highly directional and will pick up sound coming from several metres

Figure 135 Tripods come in two flavours – those with legs you have to adjust individually, and those with self-levelling heads. The latter are faster to set up for the bustling VJ against a deadline. Use the button spirit level to make sure the camera is on an even keel. (*Andrew Boyd*)

directly in front of it. But the pick-up angle is narrow and if the mike is shifted to one side, the sound will tail off.

If you use a wide-angle lens with your camera and shoot your interview close up, then your rifle mike should be adequate. But a preferred alternative for interviews is to fit a lapel mike to your interviewee's jacket. The mike should be run up inside the clothing so the cable itself is hidden and popped out over the top. Then the head of the mike should be clipped facing downwards to avoid any popping from words with ps and bs.

If you want to record your questions as well (and for news interviews you generally won't) you will need to clip a second lapel-mike to yourself and run them both into the camera via an adapter.

Always monitor your sound levels through headphones and always carry spare batteries for the microphones. If you don't you can guarantee one of two things: either you will forget to switch the mike on and will make a silent movie, or the mike will die on you mid-shoot and you will carry on filming regardless. Then don't forget to turn off the microphones after you've finished.

Set to manual

Most VJs use camcorders sold for the domestic market, with point and shoot facilities aimed at impressing Mums and Dads who want to grab instant pictures of their kiddies. But you are a VJ. You can't afford to be a technophobe. If you use a camcorder like a click and fling disposable stills camera you'll get the same kind of results.

Automatic settings control the focus, the light coming into the camera, and the sound levels. Ignore them. Put the camera on manual and set the levels yourself. Why? Because if you don't the autofocus will get distracted by something moving in the background and your subject will go blurry, the sun will come out and your subject will go dark, and a plane flying overhead will shut down the audio volume to the point where you can no longer hear what your hapless, blurry, benighted interviewee is saying.

Mount the camera on its tripod and set it at eye-level to your subject. That is, unless you want to make them look deeply intimidating, in which case mount the camera looking up at them so they loom above it. Or if you want them to look small and insignificant set the camera up above them and peer down on them.

Now set the camera back to auto. Use the zoom to close right up on your subject's eyes. Once you've got the eyes in sharp focus, you can turn the autofocus off.

Now you need to set the iris, the gizmo that decides how much light comes into the camera. If your subject's face is filling the screen the auto setting should give you a good light level. (See lighting, below for more details.)

Now put your headphones on (and keep them on) and get your subject to say a few words into the mike for five seconds – where they are planning to go for their holidays and why is a good one. And while they are still speaking, switch the camera to manual. You have now locked in the focus, iris and sound levels.

Next, zoom back out to a mid-shot (head and shoulders), frame your subject slightly to one side of the picture and your shot will be properly set up.

Lighting

If you don't have enough natural light you can either use lights of your own or turn up the gain on the camera. Adjusting the camera's gain (which works like a volume control for light) is the last resort, because more gain equals more grain, or coarseness in the picture.

In poor lighting conditions, your best bet is to set up lights. The simplest solution is to mount a light on top of the camera or hold one in your hand. These take their juice from their own battery or the camera's power supply. The trouble is they tend to make your subject look like a rabbit caught in headlights.

A better solution, if you have electricity on tap, is to set up an array of lights. Mount one on a tripod a metre or so away from the camera at 45° to your subject. This is called the *key*. Combine this with a second camera-mounted light and you will probably have enough to illuminate your interviewee and banish the shadows around the face.

If you want to go the whole hog, a third light, mounted on a stand behind your subject and set to one side can be used to pick out your interviewee from the background, light their hair and get rid of any remaining stray shadows. This is called the *backlight*.

On the other hand, you might have too much light. Some cameras have a zebra-stripe facility that puts a striped pattern over areas in the viewfinder that are overexposed. Mercifully, the stripes don't come out on tape. They are a useful guide to help you avoid hot-spots and burning out parts of the image.

If there is too much light you can click on the camera's built-in neutral density filter, if it has one. This just cuts down the light passing through the lens. A warning sign in the viewfinder will tell you if it is necessary.

If you are shooting a subject against a very bright background, you will need to adjust the iris of the camera accordingly, or the camera will set an average light level for the whole scene and your interviewee's face will appear too dark. So with the camera on manual, open up the iris until the face is correctly exposed. The background will get brighter at the same time, but providing it isn't dazzling that should be fine.

Now you are ready for the shoot.

The shoot

So how do you put together that news report?

Begin by imagining you are shooting a movie. What images would you need to tell the story, to give it all the breadth and the detail necessary to bring it to life? Watch the movie in your head, linger over it and take in every angle and image. Begin your report with your most dramatic shots that show us what the story is about. And save some good, strong pictures for the end. Show us what is happening, then bring on your interviewees to comment about it. You will need a good sequence of shots, from general views of the entire scene to close-up details. Avoid repeating the same shots in your piece because your audience will assume, rightly, that you've run out of images because you didn't shoot enough in the first place.

Start with a scene-setter; the endless queue of hungry, weary refugees, then go from a mid-shot of a mother waiting patiently, cradling her child, to a close-up of the baby's face. Then you will need to show where the refugees are going, to the Red Cross relief tent. Close up on the cross on the side of the tent. Then cut to the doctors inside, working overtime. Show us the needle going into an arm, then a big close-up of the look of concentration in the eyes of the doctor. And so on.

You will need to take more shots than you will use, but each should be well composed and serviceable, so your editor can discard the good for the best and assemble them in the right order. Go for the wide shots first, taking in the whole scene, then close in for the mid-shots and finally pick out the close-ups. These are the pictures that will draw the viewer right into the story. They will also allow you to cut from one scene to another, especially during an interview.

Forget about trying to shoot this in real time. Typically, shots that appear on screen will be held for around 4-seconds (talking heads aside). Each 4-second snippet will be the best part taken from a shot lasting for at least 20 seconds. When the adrenalin is flowing make sure you hold your shots by counting slowly in your head: *'One and two and three . . .'* up to 20 to be certain you've got enough.

For every shot that appears on screen, three or four also-rans will never leave the camcorder. At that rate, to shoot a 90-second report you will need to take around 90 original shots and fill up 30 minutes of tape. And that's a minimum.

Let's say your story is about a murder at a house in the country. Your report might have five elements to it. The first is a scene-setter of the location of the murder. The second is an interview with the Chief Inspector of police. Next comes a comment from a neighbour, followed by a tearful appeal at a news conference by one of the dead person's relatives appealing for help in finding the killer. And wrapping it all up is your piece to camera. That aside, each element when edited will need roughly five shots apiece. That means shooting some 20 shots for each element, in a variety of different ways, to make sure you have a good selection. Never leave yourself short of good pictures.

Think in sequences

Each story element is a sequence of wide shots and close-ups and variations on that theme. Don't stop shooting until you know you have enough to fully illustrate each sequence, including cutaways for editing. Once you've packed up your gear and have left the scene the opportunity is gone forever.

It would be great if you could record all the shots you need in the correct sequence, ready just to snip them into shape in the edit suite. Think again. The pace and excitement of the final report is down to the editing, not the shooting. Your job is to get all the pictures your editor is going to need. Go for the wide shots first then move in for the detailed close-ups that will draw the viewer right into the story. You will need to take roughly twice as many close-ups as wide shots in order to be able to edit.

These *cutaways* allow you to cut from one scene to another, especially during an interview, enabling you to cut from, say, the answer to your first question to the answer to your last question without the jump being noticeable. The cutaway could be a picture of what the person is talking about, or it might be a cut in, such as a close-up of their hands moving as they speak.

The art is to think in sequences. Get pictures that show us what is happening. Don't leave anything to the imagination. Let us see the story unfolding, take in its context and look at the people affected by it.

Remember you are shooting moving pictures. The best documentary stills photographs are ones that reveal the energy and dynamism of captured movement. This is even more important with video images.

Don't cut movements off in their prime. Make sure an object moving across the frame moves all the way out of the picture before you stop shooting. If a car enters your viewfinder from the right, wait till it exits on the left.

Zooms and pans can leave your audience feeling seasick, so use them sparingly. Moving the camera is no substitute for movement within the frame. If you do zoom or a pan, begin by holding a still shot for several seconds to let the image establish, make your pan or zoom, then hold the picture still at the end. This gives you three shots in one. Another problem with zooms is the time they take can slow down the rhythm of the piece.

A wide-angle lens is great for increasing the depth and perspective of the picture. If you shoot a general view with the camera held low a wide-angle lens will make the images seem more dramatic.

Make sure you fill the frame with your subject to avoid wasted space. But bear in mind that the border of the picture could be cut off by the television screen, so work within what is known as the *safe area* and keep important details away from the edges.

The interview

Sticking someone up against a brick wall and shooting them is best left to a firing-squad. We want a picture that is interesting. So you should set your subject against the *context* of the story. Place them against an interesting background, outside on location, if possible. Get the police inspector to stand in front of the striped tape roping off the house where the murder took place. Or have the factory owner on the shop floor with all the machines chugging behind him or her.

But before you conduct your interview you will need to shoot the sequence of shots that will lead up to it. These are to give the narrator time to link from the previous sequence into the new one: For example: *'Police and forensic experts have begun the painstaking task of searching the house and grounds for clues that could lead to the killer.'* For this you will need enough pictures to cover eight seconds of script – two or three shots. These could be a wide shot of the scene, followed by a group shot of police officers checking the ground beneath a shattered window. A third shot could be a close-up of hands placing soil samples in the bag – if they let you get close enough to take it.

For a talking head type interview – often a comment from a politician or spokesman for a pressure group – the standard shots to cover your lead-in would be your subject walking past the camera, talking on the phone or signing papers at their desk. Show them in their context, then cut to a mid-shot, followed by a close-up of the activity you have got them to do for the camera.

You don't need to name your interviewee in your link, as that can be done in the caption.

Photography has a *rule of thirds*. This means when you take a landscape shot, you should aim to place the horizon one third down, not slap in the middle. It makes for a more pleasing composition. Similarly, when you shoot a person, get them to stand slightly to one side rather than bang in the centre of the picture.

The camera also loves diagonal lines. They add depth to the picture and lead the viewer's eye into it. So if you get your subject to stand slightly on the diagonal, favouring the camera with one shoulder it looks even better.

Your interviewee should look at you, not at the camera. You are the one who is narrating and mediating this piece so it falls to you to address the audience directly, visually in your piece to camera and verbally in your narration. It would not do to have your interviewee usurping your position.

To conduct the interview you should position yourself close to the camera, but just back of the lens to keep out of vision. Stand if your interviewee is standing and sit if they are sitting to avoid shooting them looking up or down at you.

Your interviewee should be looking into the picture, not out of it. So if they are positioned to the left of the frame, you will need to stand to the right of the camera, and vice versa. Give them space to look into.

Before you begin your interview have a clear idea of how you intend to structure the report and what you would like your interviewee to say.

So talk through the facts of the story with your interviewee first to make sure you have got the story straight in your mind. This is known as the *pre-chat*. The purpose of your recorded interview is not to establish the facts – that's your job; you are the narrator. The aim of the interview is to extract some pithy *comments* on those facts. So home in on a couple of key questions that will produce dynamic and self-contained answers, such as questions that begin with *'Why . . .?'*

For a basic news report you are unlikely to use more than a single soundbite per interviewee, so letting them ramble on for ages will just give you an editing nightmare. Keep it short.

Now you are ready to roll. Flag the tape by getting your interviewee to say who they are and their job title. Check the picture through the viewfinder and monitor the sound through headphones.

Now stand slightly to one side of the lens and put your questions. If your camera has a pull-out LCD monitor screen you can glance at that occasionally to check the framing. If not, make sure your interviewee keeps still while the camera is rolling. If they wriggle out of shot, stop the interview and reframe the picture.

If you plan to ask several questions, pause between each and reframe the shot anyway, for variety. Go from a mid-shot (head and shoulders) to a close-up. For revealing or personal interviews, favour the close-up, which allows the viewer to concentrate on the interviewee's eyes so they can work out whether or not to believe them.

When you have finished, play the interview back and check the recording has come out – before you let your subject recede into the distance.

If you are going to interview several people for your report, alternate between whether they stand slightly to the left or to the right of the picture.

Piece to camera

Your piece to camera could appear in the middle of the story, to act as a bridge between different interviews or locations, or it could be the television equivalent of the radio journalist's payoff – the standard outcue: *'Peter Norris, BBC News, at the High Court in London.'*

Make sure the background you have chosen has a bearing on the story and shows its context. To check that you are standing in the right place you will need a camcorder with an LCD screen on the side which can be turned to face you, or an extra monitor. Take care to frame yourself well and avoid giving yourself too much headroom, chopping yourself off at the forehead or stepping out of the picture.

If you don't have a screen or a monitor, then pace out how far from the camera you intend to stand, find something to focus on that is the same distance away, and fix that focus by setting the camera to manual. If you shoot your piece to camera with the lens set to wide-angle you are less likely to go out of focus.

Record your sound on a tie-clip mike, if possible. Alternatives are a hand-held mike or the camera's rifle mike, providing you are standing within a couple of metres of the camcorder. Another option is to hold the rifle mike in your hand, out of shot and pointing up at you.

Most cameras have a remote control, which is ideal for occasions where you would otherwise need arms like a gorilla to turn it on. Set yourself up, look knowledgeable, press the button and go. Look directly at the lens and address the unblinking eye with all the confidence, credibility and warmth of a TV newsreader. Have a practice, play it back through the viewfinder, see how it looks and make any adjustments.

The piece to camera is your calling card and career-booster. So you want to get it right. Take it again and again until you do. To help you identify the best take, begin each attempt with: *'Take one [or whatever], coming in – three, two. . .'* But instead of saying *'one. . .'* at the end leave a gap so you look composed when you begin.

If your piece to camera is the final shot to appear in the report, then linger for a few seconds after you finish, in case there is any delay when they come to introducing the next item on air. It's better to close on an image of you gazing confidently into the camera than on dead air, or worse still, on you rolling your eyes, loosening your tie, unclipping your mike, lumbering towards the camera and turning it off.

Finally, before you do pack up, replay the recording of your piece to camera to make sure it has come out and that nasty small boys weren't doing obscene things in the background behind you.

Then don't forget to label your tape. It's amazing how easy it is to lose a single tape containing your precious footage in a pile of identical boxes. Label the tape and its box with your name, the title of the story, the date and the location. And remember to number the tape, if you are using several. A useful additional way of marking the tape is to write down details of interviewee names and the location in your notebook and to film the page at the beginning of the shot. Lastly, slide back the record tab so the tape is write-protected and cannot be recorded over again by accident.

When you have finished shooting you will need to log your tape, which means viewing all the rushes, and making notes of the timecode for each useable shot, with a brief description and evaluation of that shot. One method is to give one tick for a useable shot, two ticks for a good one and three for something exceptional.

Then you are ready to select which shots to use.

And finally, when you have finished with your camera, remove the batteries for charging, clean the lens and filter and wipe down the camera body. And don't forget to check the condition of any other batteries you have been using.

Editing?

> '*You might call it the "one pair of eyes" problem. If a reporter brings back the tape, then edits and scripts it, there has to be a danger – especially with "rolling news" as the jargon has it – that no other person will get to see the finished item before it hits the screen.*'
>
> – NICHOLAS OWEN, BRAVE NEW WORLD OF THE VJ,
> *THE JOURNALIST'S HANDBOOK*

They said VJs would never happen. They were wrong. Now they're saying VJs will never edit their own material. They're wrong again.

It makes sense in a news organization to leave editing to the specialists. A dedicated video editor will be faster and produce a higher-quality package. They will also be able to apply any necessary checks and balances. But desktop video editing has become a reality. It can be quick and it is certainly cheap. And at the end of the day, money rules.

Cheap video cameras and computer editing systems have empowered a new generation of freelance video-makers. For little more than the price of a PC you can now own a production suite capable of results that only a few years ago would have cost more than a family home.

These intrepid individuals are doing it all. Dreaming up the stories, researching, producing, directing, shooting, reporting, scripting and editing. And it has to be said; sometimes it looks like it, too. But the most successful VJs are marketing superb material to networks hungry for original news and current affairs material that goes beyond the mainstream.

Some have moved on to master the art of editing. And as the cost benefits of ever-cheaper technology become obvious, even the biggest news organizations are set to sit up and take notice.

More on editing and the other essential VJ skills of camera shots, scriptwriting and using visuals is covered elsewhere in this book. If you can master that lot, your future should be rosy!

Last words on the new and noble art of videojournalism to ITN's Rachel McTavish:

'*Compared with having to run round, check the sound, check the lighting and make sure I know exactly the questions I need to ask, after this, whatever I do will seem relatively easy!*'

Fieldwork

1 First familiarize yourself with your camcorder. Find out how to set the following controls to manual: focus, exposure and audio.

2 Now set your camera to automatic and shoot some footage indoors, before moving outside with your camera still running. Take a look at the results and watch out for the autoexposure kicking in when you move to a brighter location. Note also the colour cast over the two different locations. Now adjust the white balance for each location and reshoot. Compare the before and after pictures.

3 Practice doing a piece to camera. Try and deliver a 20-second soundbite from memory – don't learn it off by heart, just practise putting over the main points with confidence. Take and retake it until you get it right.

4 Shoot some raw footage of life in the city centre. It's a good exercise for getting rid of self-consciousness. Aim for a good balance of wide shots and close-ups. Practice holding your shots for 20 seconds. Count slowly in your mind.

5 Watch a news report and write down the number of sequences in the item and the number of shots in each sequence. Make a note of the type of shot – wide shot or close-up, and how long each one lasts. How would you improve on the images?

ONLINE JOURNALISM AND NEW MEDIA

32   Pushing back the frontiers

'The Dalai Lama drew his maroon and yellow robes around him and hastened over to a laptop computer we'd set up on a table. We were at his headquarters in exile at the foothills of the Himalayas in Northern India. We'd just been live on BBC News Online. *This was as novel an experience for me as it was for him. People had emailed questions from around the world. I put a selection to the Dalai Lama and, thanks to equipment we'd been pioneering in India, he could then be heard and seen answering them. It takes some time for the words and pictures to make their way to London and on to the computer screen, so he was able to see the last moments of the conversation on the laptop. He gave one of his irrepressible chuckles. It was the Dalai Lama's infectious enthusiasm for this latest gadgetry of ours that made me think how much our job has changed.'* – BBC CORRESPONDENT MIKE WOOLDRIDGE

'I see a future where there are millions and millions of reporters. You can cover the world with a modem. It scares the establishment. It doesn't scare me.'

– CYBERHACK MATT DRUDGE

It began with the judge's 16-page announcement on the Internet in the trial of Louise Woodward – the nanny accused of killing a baby. And it took off when dirt digger Matt Drudge scooped *Newsweek* magazine to reveal Monica Lewinsky's shenanigans with President Clinton. *'It hit me,'* said Drudge, *'the full impact hit me, on that January night when I hit the enter button. I said: "My life will never be the same . . . taking on the most powerful man in the free world from a Hollywood apartment using the Internet." '*

It was a public kick-start to what has been dubbed 'the fastest growing major new media in the history of news and information'.* Given time – not very much time – and the ubiquitous Internet will be as much a fixture in most Western homes as the telephone. It will be free, fast and an even more fantastic source of facts – as well as jobs in journalism. As TVs and computers merge and on-line services become cheaper and more efficient, the future no longer holds a mere 500 channels – take that to the power of 10. With the Internet, Sky is no longer the limit.

*Merril Brown, MSNBC.com, NetMedia 98.

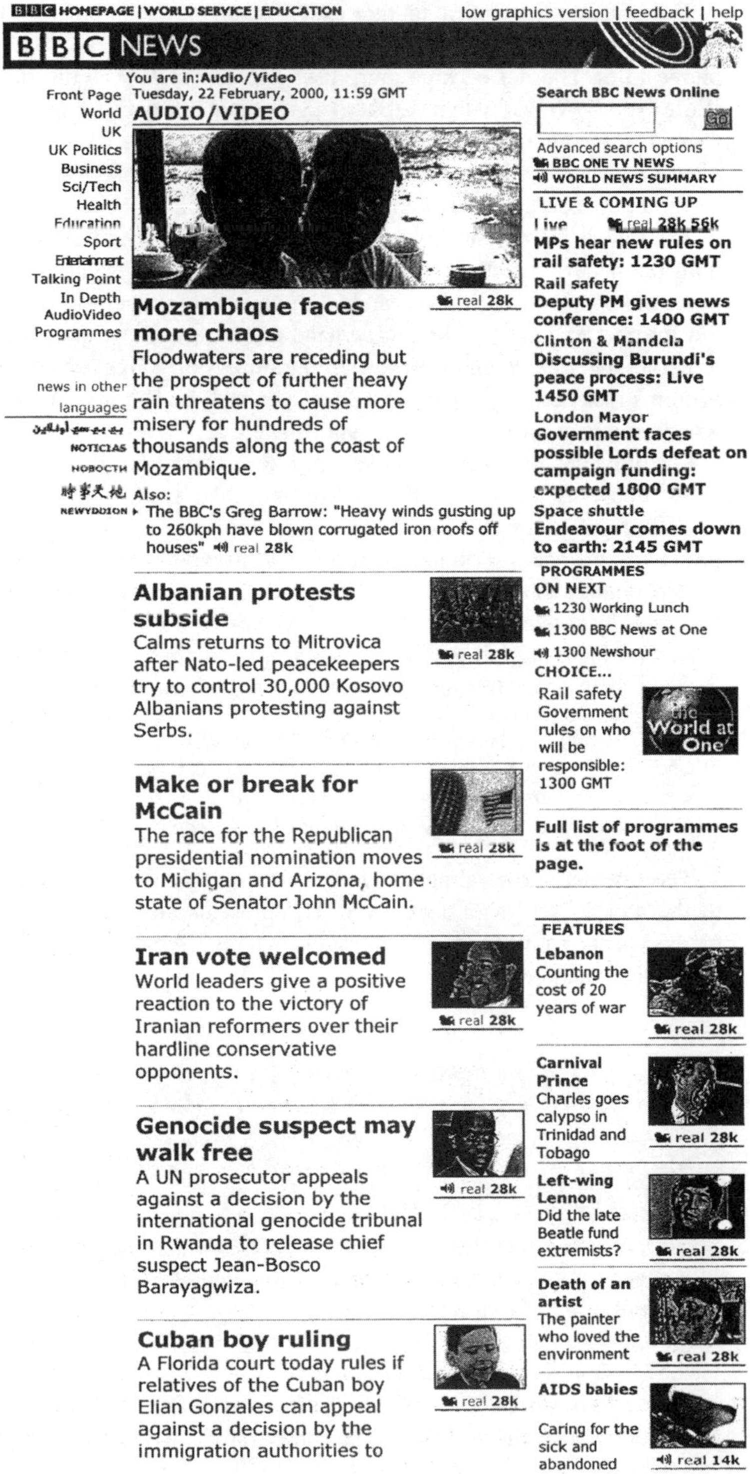

BBC HOMEPAGE | WORLD SERVICE | EDUCATION　　low graphics version | feedback | help

BBC NEWS

You are in: Audio/Video

Tuesday, 22 February, 2000, 11:59 GMT

Front Page
World
UK
UK Politics
Business
Sci/Tech
Health
Education
Sport
Entertainment
Talking Point
In Depth
AudioVideo
Programmes

news in other languages
NOTICIAS
НОВОСТИ
時事天地
NEWYDDION

AUDIO/VIDEO

real 28k

Mozambique faces more chaos

Floodwaters are receding but the prospect of further heavy rain threatens to cause more misery for hundreds of thousands along the coast of Mozambique.

Also:

- The BBC's Greg Barrow: "Heavy winds gusting up to 260kph have blown corrugated iron roofs off houses" real 28k

Albanian protests subside

Calms returns to Mitrovica after Nato-led peacekeepers try to control 30,000 Kosovo Albanians protesting against Serbs. real 28k

Make or break for McCain

The race for the Republican presidential nomination moves to Michigan and Arizona, home state of Senator John McCain. real 28k

Iran vote welcomed

World leaders give a positive reaction to the victory of Iranian reformers over their hardline conservative opponents. real 28k

Genocide suspect may walk free

A UN prosecutor appeals against a decision by the international genocide tribunal in Rwanda to release chief suspect Jean-Bosco Barayagwiza. real 28k

Cuban boy ruling

A Florida court today rules if relatives of the Cuban boy Elian Gonzales can appeal against a decision by the immigration authorities to real 28k

Search BBC News Online

Go

Advanced search options
BBC ONE TV NEWS
WORLD NEWS SUMMARY

LIVE & COMING UP

Live real 28k 56k

MPs hear new rules on rail safety: 1230 GMT

Rail safety

Deputy PM gives news conference: 1400 GMT

Clinton & Mandela

Discussing Burundi's peace process: Live 1450 GMT

London Mayor

Government faces possible Lords defeat on campaign funding: expected 1800 GMT

Space shuttle

Endeavour comes down to earth: 2145 GMT

PROGRAMMES ON NEXT

1230 Working Lunch
1300 BBC News at One
1300 Newshour

CHOICE...

Rail safety
Government rules on who will be responsible: 1300 GMT

the World at One

Full list of programmes is at the foot of the page.

FEATURES

Lebanon Counting the cost of 20 years of war real 28k

Carnival Prince Charles goes calypso in Trinidad and Tobago real 28k

Left-wing Lennon Did the late Beatle fund extremists? real 28k

Death of an artist The painter who loved the environment real 28k

AIDS babies Caring for the sick and abandoned real 14k

Figure 136 Video on demand from around the world (plus audio and a searchable archive). When Internet video gets as good as TV the revolution will be complete. (*Courtesy BBC*)

The Internet was born in the 1960s when the US Defense Department wanted a bombproof information exchange where computer could talk to computer along existing phone lines. The net became more user-friendly in 1990 with the creation of the World Wide Web (WWW), with its attractive graphical interface. Since then, developments have moved apace to enable individuals to send messages, documents, pictures, audio and video anywhere in the world for the price of a local phone call – albeit a long one. Faster methods of access include cable modem and satellite.

The Internet represents the convergence of TV and print with radio thrown in, combined with the depth, breadth and functionality of the largest database in the world.

As the problems of limited bandwidth constraining the flow of information are cracked the Internet will offer video on demand in full broadcast quality. You will be your own director, able to pick and mix news programmes of your choosing compiled from a menu of items matched to your interests, and you will be able to get the information you want when you want and where you want. Instantly.

For more details on a story, click on a longer version. For yesterday's take on the war or the economy, or the month's before that, then again, just click.

And if you want background, analysis and links to every manner of research, every shade and nuance of opinion, then given a little persistence and rudimentary skill with a search engine and they are yours. Search for an item by headline or phrase. Sift the selection by date or context; refine it and narrow it down – it's the greatest research tool ever. The Internet is to the Dewey Decimal System what Godzilla is to a gecko.

CNN allows you to specify the news you want, as Kaitlin Quistgaard explains:

> *'CNN Custom News sorts more than 2,000 articles a day. In addition to reports prepared by CNN itself, the service makes use of more than 100 other sources, like international wire services and dozens of magazines. There are some 2,200 categories to choose from in customizing your CNN page, with world news by country the most popular.'*

The Internet allows almost anyone with a phone, a PC and a story to tell to broadcast to the world from their back room. It represents an unheard of democratization of the media. At the same time it gives major players, like the BBC, CNN and ITN, access to even vaster audiences.

> *'The ability to broadcast with modest equipment has astonishing implications. If the entry requirements for global Internet audio broadcasting are in the mere thousands of dollars, we may see an explosion of broadcasting sites. We're talking about [thousands of] new broadcasters whose message is audible anywhere on the planet at any time. That's significant.'* — BYTE MAGAZINE*
>
> *'It is not hard to imagine a new Do-It-Yourself radio culture developing, with teenagers doing bedroom broadcasts and wannabe DJs setting up their own "pirate" stations.'* — THE INDEPENDENT†

That's the potential. The reality is the Internet can be creakingly slow, unreliable, teeming with the trivial, the irrelevant and the pornographic, with search engines incapable of sifting

---

* *Toss your TV*, February 1996.
† 14 October 1997.

the superficial from the profound and possessing all the discernment of a six-year-old in an ice cream factory. And as satellite, cable, and all manner of high-speed delivery systems roll out, the garbage will roll in even faster. Roll on tomorrow . . .

News online

As for today, Internet news has come from obscurity to ubiquity. BBC News Online (*www.news.bbc.co.uk*) is one of Britain's foremost web sites, providing text, radio and TV versions of news reports, grouped under headings such as UK, World and Sport.

The front page resembles the contents of a news magazine. Find the summary you want and click on it to jump to a full version of the story. Beneath that is a list of related items. And running alongside are links to some of the organizations mentioned in the text, such as government departments and pressure groups. These whisk you to websites beyond the control of the corporation and carry a health warning.

A few years ago bi-media was the buzzword at the BBC, with radio journalists expected to contribute to TV as well. Now there are three key areas for journalists: TV, radio and text. Text covers online, teletext and subtitling.

Damian Carrington is a science and technology reporter with BBC News Online. He researches story ideas from contacts, scientific journals, press releases and specialist websites, as well as groups who communicate globally via e-mail. He illustrates his stories with pictures, audio and video and provides links to other websites for further research.

'We operate 24-hours a day and we don't have to wait for broadcast times or presses to roll, so our deadlines come every minute of the day. For breaking stories, we have something on site in minutes, and then build it up. The pace is hectic, but we get a lot of positive feedback to keep us going.'*

Rebecca Woodward joined BBC local radio before moving to beeb.com, the BBC's commercial website, where she produces the pages for the listings magazine, *Radio Times*.

'We are frequently setting precedents and facing new problems. I need a technical awareness and work alongside our technology, design and commercial teams. I lead an editorial team and we are now moving into interactive TV.'†

Over at rival ITN (www.itn.co.uk), the website came second, is smaller and employs fewer journalists but has a large and enthusiastic following. Within two years of setting up, half a million users were logging on each month to view eight million pages. The website also provides headlines for digital TV and mobile phones, in line with ITN's aggressively expansionist policy. It aims to have its headlines on every possible platform.

'There's massive potential in it,' says editor Fergus Sheppard. *'There's nothing sacrosanct about the timing of a news bulletin. You have a younger audience who will not*

---

* www.bbc.co.uk/jobs/journal2.shtml
† www.bbc.co.uk/cgi-bin/education/betsie/parser.pl

sit and wait for the news, but who expect to log on and see it on their website, phone or personal organizer.'

Not everyone is a fan:

'It is a further shift in the direction of news being faster, shorter, simpler and a mere commodity. Never mind cutting pieces down to 800 words for the net – on a phone they need to go down to 80, at which point pretty much all personality goes out the window. It doesn't matter whether those words come from Reuters, the PA, ITN [or] the BBC . . . All that matters is who can deliver them quickest.' – SIMON WALDMAN*

So will webcast news eventually relegate broadcast bulletins to the media museum? Sheppard follows the party line: *'It's complementary to our armoury. In a world where everybody is chasing a fragmenting audience going to satellite, cable and the web, news channels will continue to generate millions of viewers for a long time to come, but there is a growing and significant audience who want the news to follow their lifestyles.'*

At CNN (www.cnn.com), Ken Tiven, Vice President of Television Systems, sings from the same hymnsheet. *'Each big news event generated increased use, but unlike TV, after the event the audience levels stayed up. Clearly television news helps drive people to our web site and what we are doing is keeping them.'*

CNN were stunned by their own success. More people logged on than they could ever have hoped for. Tiven spells out the guiding principles behind the US giant's web presence:

- Reliability – in journalistic and technical terms – is a must. Without this, everything else is useless.
- The Internet would use elements of television and newspapers, but become something new.
- Content is the big driver, not screen tricks.
- Dynamic content – news, especially breaking news – will build a steady clientele.
- The content must be deeper and wider than television because this is a new medium and not just repurposed television material.
- Screen speed is critical to keep users happy, because everyone wants to go faster.

And speed plays a central role in the turnaround of news stories. The CNN adage, *get it, check it, transmit it*, translates perfectly to the web. CNN is having to compete on its home territory with ITN. Each night ITN webcasts its World News programme, which is popular in the USA and can be seen on more than 50 public television services. Viewers of the web version can watch the whole programme or choose the segments that interest them, and view them in any order they wish. A third of the audience comes from the USA. The job of the webmaster is to hold on to that audience and keep them on site.

'We try to make our output sticky so we can retain people, otherwise they would flick through headlines, look at a piece of video and be on their way,' says Sheppard.

But the website does more than repeat mainstream TV output. The web has freed broadcasters from the straitjacket of the programme schedule and allows extended coverage of major events to be offered at the drop of a hat. So the website will host live coverage of the opening of Parliament, budgets or sieges. If there's an ITN camera at the scene, it will be hooked up to the site.

* 'And now the news at platform 10,' *The Guardian*, 22 November 1999.

L1 search

Fancy a head transplant?

Inside ▼

home   search   messages   help   assistant   log out

LineOne Search
Internet Search
FAQs
Search Help
LineOne Help

Quick Search

To search the internet simply type what you want to search for and click 'GO'.

Search for Broadcast Journalism GO

BUY A BOOK!

Advanced Search gives you more options that you can use to refine your search. Click here for the Advanced Internet Search

f∂st ∷ Advanced Search   "All the Web, All the Time^tm"

FAST SEARCH	**FTP SEARCH**	**MP3 SEARCH**	**PICTURE SEARCH**	**LISTENING ROOM**	**FA PREMIER**	**CONTACT US**
300M Pages	100M Files	1,000,000 MP3s	17M Pics & Sounds	Hot New Band Site	Largest Soccer Site	FAST Info

Search for   any of the words ▣   [   ]   FAST Search

LANGUAGE
Help
Filter results for any of our 25 supported languages
English ▣

WORD FILTERS
Help
Add filter words you wish to include / exclude from your results. One phrase per entry box.

Should include ▣   [   ]   in the text ▣

Must include ▣   [   ]   in the title ▣

Must not include ▣   [   ]   in the link name ▣

more / fewer terms ⊞ ⊟

DOMAIN FILTERS
Help
Filter results by including / excluding domains e.g. com, gov, dell.com, etc

Only Include [   ]   Exclude [   ]

10 ▣ results per page   FAST Search

Submit Your Site | Add FAST Search to Your Page | Join the FAST Team!
FAST, Dell Press Release | All the Web (Pictures)
Frequently Asked Questions (FAQs)

PowerEdge
Servers

Figure 137 Navigating the web – search engines, simple and advanced. (*Courtesy www.lineone.net and www.alltheweb.com*)

Two sentence teasers describe a news story and entice surfers to read on. *'These are the "roll up, roll up, read all about it" paragraphs, the chance to entice people in,'* says Sheppard. *'They have to be racy, cryptic and a come-on.'* Text stories run for around 12 paragraphs, often longer than they would on air. Initial fears that websurfers would have MTV-type attention spans proved groundless. Big stories warrant big coverage and pull in big audiences.

The style conforms to the usual ITN rubrics: *'authoritative and popular without being tabloid'* as well as some new ones: *'Could you hear the story coming from Trevor McDonald's mouth?'* McDonald is ITN's senior anchor and pitched as Britain's most popular broadcaster.

The ITN website is put together using a standard and relatively simple piece of software – Microsoft Front Page. Bright newcomers can get to grips with it in a week, but still have to learn other software skills, such as editing audio and video and still images.

Audio is edited using Cool Edit, a package familiar to most BBC radio reporters, while video is trimmed with Real Tools, though editing is usually confined to cutting down versions of stories that have already appeared on air.

While technophobes need not apply *'it's not like flying a fighter,'* reassures Sheppard. *'Nobody yet has given up the ghost or stormed out, unable to take any more.'*

In the future online journalism will be even easier. Reporters will be presented with a template and required to fill in the boxes with headlines and copy.

Research

Want to find the names of 116 alleged British secret service agents? How to build an atom bomb? Click on the net. Want to find impartial political analysis on the world's trouble spots? Then click on the net, but take care.

The problem with the net is how to pick sound information from the mass of hearsay and propaganda. The net is a sounding board for the insane, the profound and the profane. Key the word 'Truth' into a search engine and you will be offered two and a half million hits on websites ranging from conspiracy theorists to new age gurus. But for facts you can trust you will need to pick your sources more carefully. With the Internet it becomes more important than ever to check out who is saying what, and why and to run their assertions against reliable sources. The best propaganda is always the most undetectable.

Respected news providers like CNN and the BBC will give their mediated versions of the truth. No two opinions will ever be the same, but where even the facts are disputed, and they almost always are, try searching the websites of all the warring factions to hear their take on events. Why settle for the government line when you can check out the opposition? Just don't expect unanimity. Young Internet junkies like Bonnie Burton are bypassing the news corporations:

> *'I hate the news. I think it's pathetic, 'cos now I get my serious news on the Internet. Now I can talk to someone that's in Bosnia right now. I think older people don't understand that they can get real news . . . they'd rather have it pre-censored, pre-fed and pre-thought out, so they don't have to think about it.'**

But despite being a propagandist's idea of Paradise, the Internet has – so far – shown itself immune to censorship. Close down one contentious site and enterprising individuals will mirror the information on 50 others in different countries around the world. No surprise some 45 nations, including China, are trying to restrict Internet access. During the pro-democracy protests they tried to control fax machines in the same way for the same reason. Knowledge is power. As the old saying goes, news is something someone, somewhere, doesn't want published.

* *TV is Dead, Long Live TV*, Horizon, BBC.

> *'The net's an indispensable tool. At first it was more trouble than it was worth, and it can still be frightening and unwieldy, but from a research point of view it's revolutionized the way I work. For example, we go big on things like Cannes [film festival] and the Oscars. Before you go out there, you can check Variety.com and the hundreds of fan sites first. It's much easier than wading through old cuttings. What's more you can e-mail people for info and get a reply in minutes.'*
> *– KATIE DERHAM, ITN**

And Internet research is no longer confined to text-based material. The Internet provides audio and video broadcasting something it never had before – permanence:

> *'Today's radio programme is ephemeral: heard once then gone forever. Making radio archives changes the state of the art completely. Soon all radio programmes will have an on-line component, and that will allow every programme to be archived, cross-referenced and retrieved. A revolution in radio is on the way.'*
> *– NEW SCIENTIST†*

Qualities of an online journalist

So what qualities are top broadcasters looking for in an online journalist? This from the BBC:

BBC SPORT ONLINE, BROADCAST ASSISTANT

Duties include:
Capturing and gathering audio and video material and graphics . . . using desk-top editing . . . find contributors to support and illustrate site content. . . assist broadcast journalists in writing stories, background and analysis.

Skills required include:
Able to generate original ideas. . . a good understanding of sources of sports material. . . previous experience of working in a live newsroom. . . broad knowledge of a range of sports . . . ideas on how the Internet can be used to present sports material. . . ability to acquire technical skills and to operate technical equipment. . . flair and imagination to craft multi-media material. . . ability to work well in a team and enjoy the pressure of a 24-hour format where constant deadlines are the norm.

At ITN journalists are recruited from radio and newspaper backgrounds or are graduates from training courses. The aim is for a healthy mix of older and wiser heads with talented young people. Fergus Sheppard explains:

> *'I look first and foremost for evidence of mainstream conventional writing skills. For that reason people from newspaper backgrounds are always good, because you know they have been taught*

---

* *'Tips from ITN's net news pros', The Net*, September 1999.
† *Don't touch that dial'*, 17 February 1996.

to spell, to write crisply and to deadlines, and don't regard the apostrophe as a decoration. Also it's good for people to have been round the block and have some experience. If we get experienced writers in, then we will get a good product out. We need the old-fashioned skills of accuracy in assembling the story and the ability to sell it to the viewers.'

Salary potential?

'A few years ago online was seen as a retread operation where you could get in a teenager to press a button. That view no longer holds. It's becoming as professional as any other area. So salaries are rising accordingly. You have to pay to get good people.' Expect a starting salary of around £25 000.

Satellite and cable TV

In the quest for speed, electronic news gathering has brought instant images into the home, and the explosion in satellite communications has meant live pictures – and many more of them – now enter our living rooms from around the globe.

The world's battlefields are becoming increasingly pockmarked with the portable satellite transmitters of the news networks, defying censorship and raising issues about media responsibility. Pictures from low-orbiting 'spy in the sky' satellites are available to TV companies, revealing in remarkable detail events unfolding on the earth thousands of kilometres below.

While military satellites are able to photograph objects as small as your hand from space, pictures from commercial 'birds' such as The Spot can reveal your house quite clearly. Images of missile sites in Libya, flooding in Iowa or war damage in Iraq are typical of the shots being made available to television.

It all began as the dream of science fiction writer Arthur C. Clarke, whose imagination was fired by the wartime rockets used by the Germans. He figured that a spacecraft in orbit 36 000 km (22 000 miles) above the equator would keep pace with the earth's rotation and appear to be hanging stationary above the planet's surface. These could be used as mirrors to bounce communications signals half-way round the world. If this could be achieved, the technology would revolutionize broadcasting.

In 1960 his dream came true when the first communications satellite was launched – a giant reflective balloon known as ECHO. Two years later Telstar was relaying black and white TV pictures across the globe, heralding the communications explosion. By 1989, Rupert Murdoch's Sky TV began beaming its transmissions.

The speed is phenomenal. A signal can cover the 5000 miles between India and London (via space) in a quarter of a second. And as satellites become more powerful, digital replaces analogue and data-compression techniques improve, thousands of channels will be clamouring for the content to fill them.

Digital technology has been described as 'probably the biggest step forward for television since its invention by John Logie Baird'.* But it's movies and sport, rather than news, that are the big attractions. Multi-channels allow broadcasters to screen multiple camera angles on the same sports action simultaneously. In Britain, 36 new digital TV channels are on the way and 40 digital radio stations – and that's just for starters.

Hot on the heels of satellite TV has come cable. Using fibre-optic technology, cable has the capacity to pipe in an even wider variety of services, including local, satellite and terrestrial TV, as well as telecommunications.

* Stephen Grabiner, Chief Executive of Ondigital.

Cable TV took off in North America, and US investment funded the cable boom in Britain. The UK's first cable service began in Swindon in 1984. The industry's target is to reach 17 million homes in the UK. All the major players expressed their confidence in the cable system by announcing plans for 24-hour news channels. Once again, it means more jobs for journalists.

Before long TV and the web will look pretty much the same. As TV becomes digital and interactive, broadcast programmes will become like websites, with hotlinks to hurry the viewer to other sources of information, including the web itself.

> *'[TV is] an obsolete technology and there are two ways you can respond to its obsolescence. One is to apply cosmetics to the corpse. You have HDTV, you have interactive TV, you have games on TV, but they can't face the fundamental limitations of the medium ... There is a new medium that encompasses existing TV and multiplies it by a factor of millions in possibilities, and that is computer and Internet technology ... indeed the replacement for TV.'* – GEORGE GILDER*

Teletext

There is another dimension to television news that can offer considerably more information than could be packed into any conventional news programme – Teletext. David Klein, teletext editorial director, described it as *'The world's biggest and most widely distributed free newspaper'*.†

Competition is growing. The BBC's massive news operation keeps its CEEFAX system fed with news, providing summaries in brief on BBC1, and in greater depth on BBC2.

Teletext, which provides the service for the ITV companies, supplies national and international news from the Press Association and makes pages available for each of the ITV regions to provide local news. And Teletext now has a global following.

Teletext has the capacity to get news on air even faster than radio. While the radio reporter is still typing the script, that same story can be displayed directly on the viewer's TV screen.

'It's not only quick, it's continuous,' says Teletext manager Peter Hall. *'When we get a story we can have it on air within a minute of hearing about it. And the viewer can get information at any time without having to wait for a specific bulletin.'*

More than a thousand editorial changes are made each day to the news, sport and business sections alone. The copy style – concise and to the point – is closer to that of broadcast news than newspapers.

Other features include regional information, music, theatre reviews and business news. Teletext subtitles have been a boon to the hard of hearing, who no longer have to lip read or turn up the volume to catch the latest news. Subtitles in different languages are also a possibility.

The system looks set for steady expansion, believes David Klein: *'The potential in teletext is tremendous and as more open up there will be more jobs for journalists.'*

---

* TV is Dead, Long Live TV, Horizon, BBC.†
† 'World's biggest free ...' *UK Press Gazette*, 8 September 1996.

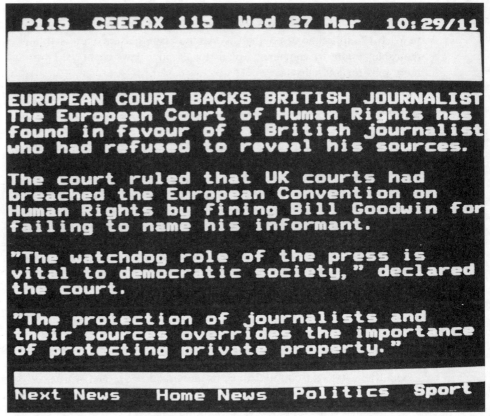

Figure 138 Good news for media freedom. Teletext stories can appear on screen the instant they have been written. (*Courtesy BBC Ceefax*)

Teletext works by using some of the extra lines on a television screen not taken up with picture information. These carry codes instead, which are translated into letters, numbers, graphics, and colour by a special teletext receiver.

Individual characters are transmitted one after another. Viewers select their chosen page with a remote control keypad that draws the information into the TV set's microprocessor.

Every page is given a number, so if the viewer keys in page 101 carrying the headlines, the teletext receiver will count through all the incoming pages until 101 is reached. The chip will store that page in its memory and then display that information on the screen.

In recent years Teletext has been eclipsed by the Internet. It's slow, hard to access and its graphics are crude and boxy. Plans are in hand to upgrade the system, with an end to delays and pages that resemble the web, displaying still video images, more colours and better graphics. But whether Teletext will survive the convergence of TV and the Internet remains to be seen.

The computerized newsroom

The digital revolution is today transforming the way we receive broadcast material, but for many years it has been transforming the way broadcasters work. The news business is about getting information rapidly and turning it around fast. And in newsrooms wordprocessors have given way to powerful computer systems that can speed up that process. The move is towards greater and greater integration – loading ever more tasks into the computer.

At a growing number of TV stations journalists not only key in and edit their copy on screen, but can edit their video reports on the same PC terminal functions. The version adopted by both the BBC and ITN is the Electronic News Production System (ENPS), which combines text, audio and video with a powerful search engine. Functions include script-writing, programme timing, prompting, planning, contact management, messaging, news wires, archiving, on-air control and remote access to staff in the field.

> '*Our journalism is split between three separate directorates: news and current affairs, the World Service and the regions. This system will allow them to talk to each other, to exchange information, eventually to exchange audio, to exchange video. Once you do that you have a powerhouse of journalism that is second to none.*'
> – TONY HALL, CHIEF EXECUTIVE, BBC NEWS

Newsroom computers can be used to time copy by calculating the presenter's reading speed. News items can be assembled into a programme and the computer will calculate the total running time. If any changes need to be made, the duration can be instantly recalculated and a new running order drawn up on screen.

For TV, scripts can be made to appear with text on the right and video and graphic instructions on the left. And every word of the bulletin can be archived electronically for as long as the station requires.

On location, portable PCs allow reporters to compose their stories and feed them back to the newsroom computer via a digital mobile phone even from abroad, providing the region is covered by a digital network.

For those reporting from far-flung regions as yet untouched by civilization the alternative is the satellite phone. The globetrotting journalist equipped with the latest model can file a report using a pocket handset with an aerial no thicker than a pencil. Hook that up to a laptop computer and you can file stories/radio reports/TV features from anywhere in the world.

And next?

The future is digital. By turning sound and pictures into computer code, they can be squeezed into ever smaller signals. For every conventional analogue channel you can fit up to twelve digital channels – with clearer sound and sharper pictures. We are facing what the Royal Television Society has called: 'the biggest changes in the history of the TV industry.'*

But while digital TV promises more for less, a major drive is taking place to improve the quality as well as the quantity of our broadcasting. The first high definition TV sets (HDTV) went on sale in Japan in 1991. HDTV crams more lines onto the screen to

* 20 March 1995.

provide a more photo-realistic image. Craggy-faced newsreaders will look even older, wiser and uglier than before.

As well as sharpening its image, TV is taking on a wider aspect. The old width to height ratio of 4:3 is giving way to widescreen 16:9 for a more cinematic experience. Alternatively, you can split the screen in two and immerse yourself in live coverage of different wars fought simultaneously over two continents with the bang-bangs brought to you in Dolby surround sound stereo – all from the safety and comfort of your armchair. Home cinema meets the 6 o'clock News.

Thanks to giant gas-plasma displays, before long we'll be hanging up the screen of our multi-channelled interactive PC-TV just like a picture. Projectors paint an even bigger picture, and some predict your entire living room wall could be turned into a giant TV screen – in three dimensions.

In the quest for speed, electronic news gathering has brought instant images into the home, and the explosion in satellite communications has meant live pictures – and many more of them – from around the globe. Twenty-hour news is here to stay, along with more sports journalism than ever before.

Many more channels means a greater degree of specialization and consumer choice. Instead of a few stations trying to please all the people all of the time, audiences are choosing the channels that suit their tastes, dipping in and out at whim and timeshifting the programmes on their VCRs to watch at their convenience.

The downside for broadcasters is that increased choice equals increased competition, and more than ever, programme makers will need to chase ratings. Entertainment will be

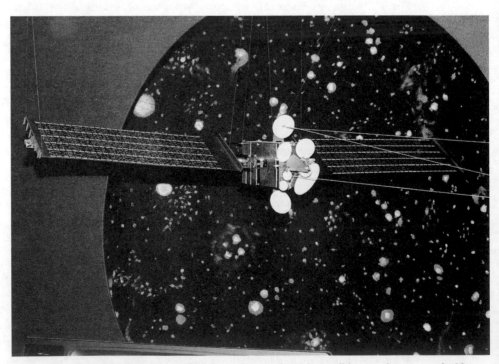

Figure 139 *'Some time during the working lives of many of you there will be news bureaux on the Moon and on Mars.'* Meanwhile, satellites in stationery orbit 36 000 km above the earth beam back their reports across the globe. (*Andrew Boyd*)

placed at a premium to information to satisfy audiences accustomed to viewing what they *want*, rather than what broadcasters tell them they *need*. News and information will have to become more sugar-coated than ever to keep impatient fingers from drumming on the remote control.

Narrowcasting has become the buzzword, with services becoming more and more closely targeted to specialized interests. Add the Internet to that picture and we see the atomization of journalism, as well as audiences. A fragmented audience means a smaller cost base, so inevitably more reporting will be carried out on the cheap. And the process of reporting will be linked as never before with technology. Even the most junior wordsmith will have to turn technocrat. At the other end of the scale, credible specialist correspondents who can command audience share will be able to demand salaries to match.

There has already been criticism that the all-news media has become all-speculation media, as the drive to report events as they happen nudges journalists into commenting on events before they take place. Either we are conducting the greatest experiment in the democratization of news or we are creating a CyberBabel.

Fantasies can become dreams, as Arthur C. Clarke found out. While shots from unmanned satellites were once science fiction, the stuff of today's daydreamers may just be around the corner:

> '*Some time during the working lives of many of you, there will be news bureaux on the Moon and on Mars. Some of you may even be competing to become their bureau chiefs, and others may be using the tag line . . . "reporting from outer space".*'
> – DR JAMES FLETCHER,
> DIRECTOR OF THE US SPACE ASSOCIATION NASA*

Cyberspace or outerspace, the scope for ever more news coverage seems unlimited. Whether the software – journalists included – can keep up with the hardware has yet to be seen.

Fieldwork

1 Log onto the Internet and track down BBC, ITN and CNN news websites.

How does the picture quality of their video reports compare with what you can see on TV? And on the audio reports, how does the sound quality stand up to what you can hear on your radio?

Can you call up programmes on demand? And is it possible to search for audio and video information by topic or keyword?

2 *Until technology changes the Internet will never become more popular than TV.* Discuss.

3 Find out how effective the Internet is as a research tool. See if you can find answers to the following questions:

● What is the gross domestic product of your country for last year?
● What is the current majority of the ruling party in government?
● How would you make an atom bomb?

* Jim Wilson, 'Reporting from outer space', *Broadcast*, 26 September 1986.

4 What limitations should there be to the information available on the Internet – and who should set them?

5 If there is a teletext set you can look at, compare the news headlines with news bulletins on radio and TV. Describe the similarities and the differences. How up to date is the teletext news compared with the others? Is the sports service more or less comprehensive?

Find out about the job opportunities for journalists in teletext and online journalism in your country.

APPENDIX: Courses in journalism

The broadcasting networks are hungry, nay, ravenous for trained journalists.

The UK alone has upwards of 200 local commercial radio stations pulling in more listeners and revenue from advertising than ever before. These are competing with regional and national independent services, new digital multiplexes, with stations broadcasting in near CD-quality, a growing legion of small community stations, and – in a single year alone – more than 900 temporary stations.

And that's before we get on to the BBC, with its five national radio services, some forty local stations and a further seven serving Wales, Scotland and Northern Ireland. Despite cutbacks, BBC local radio puts out some 200 000 bulletins a year.

But Britain's output of broadcast news is small beer compared to the newsbabble produced in the USA by thousands of radio stations and the world's highest concentration of TV channels. And there is no end in sight to the background noise now filling the ether.

Technology now exists to stretch the number of stations towards infinity. And don't forget the news services springing up on the Internet . . .

What they have in common is an inexhaustible appetite for talented broadcasters. Amazingly, there are still thought to be fewer than 10 000 full-time and freelance broadcast journalists in the UK.

A comprehensive list of course opportunities in the USA alone would probably fill a book, but budding Dan Rathers and Trevor McDonalds could do worse than begin here . . .

Australia

Australian Media Facilities Directory

The website of the Australian Media Facilities Directory contains a searchable database of media training and education opportunities.

www.amfd.com.au

Federation of Australian Broadcasters Limited

Unit 10/82–86 Pacific Highway, St Leonards,
PO Box 299 St Leonards, NSW 2065
Phone: 02 9906 5944
Fax: 02 9906 5128

Canada

Association of Canadian Community Colleges

200–1223 Michael Street North, Ottawa,
Canada K1J 7T2
Phone: 613 746 2222.
Fax: 613 746 6721
www.accc.ca

Association of Universities and Colleges of Canada

The national voice of Canada's universities, representing universities and university-level colleges.

Association of Universities and Colleges of Canada,
350 Albert Street, Suite 600, Ottawa,
Canada, K1R 1B1

The Canadian Bureau for International Education

220 Laurier Avenue West, Suite 1100, Ottowa,
Canada, K1P 5Z9
Phone: 613 237 4820
Fax: 613 237 1073
www.cbie.ca

Commonwealth

Commonwealth Journalists Association

A forum for the training and interchange of journalists between Commonwealth countries. Courses take place throughout the Commonwealth. The aim is to establish a branch in every Commonwealth nation.

Commonwealth Journalists Association,
Head Office, 17 Nottingham Street,
London W1M 3RD, UK.
Phone: +44 (0) 207 486 3844
Fax: +44 (0) 207 486 3822
www.oneworld.org/cba/

Links to CBA members' websites.

www.ozemail.com.au/~pwessels/cja

UK

BBC

The BBC runs training schemes for journalists.

Contact:

BBC Corporate Recruitment Services,
5 Portland Place, London W1A 1AA
Phone: +44 (0) 207 927 5799

BJTC

The Broadcast Journalism Training Council validates
and sets guidelines for undergraduate and post-graduate
broadcasting courses. Recognized courses encompass
theory and practice, and teach newswriting, bulletin
editing and interviewing techniques, as well as law,
public administration and ethics.

BJTC, The Coach House, North Road,
West Bridgeford, Nottingham NG2 7NH
www.bjtc.org.uk

BJTC-recognized courses:

Undergraduate:

Surrey Institute of Art and Design, Farnham
University of Bournemouth, Poole
University of Central Lancashire, Preston
The Institute of Communication Studies, Leeds
Nottingham Trent University, Nottingham

Postgraduate:

Bell College of Technology, Hamilton
Cardiff University
City University, London
Falmouth College of Arts
Highbury College, Portsmouth
London College of Printing and Distributive Trades
University of Central England, Birmingham
University of Leeds, Trinity All Saints
University of Central Lancashire, Preston
Sheffield Hallam University, Sheffield
University of London, Goldsmiths College
University of Westminster

Links to these courses are provided on the BJTC
website.

BKSTS

The British Kinematograph Sound and Television
Society (BKSTS) runs courses on production, specializing in technical areas, such as sound, editing and
camerawork. It also accredits college courses deemed
relevant to the needs of the industry, which offer a
realistic training and demonstrate industry involvement.

British Kinematograph Sound and Television Society
(BKSTS), 6–14 Victoria House, Vernon Place,
London WC1B 4DF
www.bksts.com/training

The BKSTS adds courses at the following colleges to
those on the BCTJ list:

Bournemouth and Poole College of Art and Design
Southampton Institute
Plymouth College of Art and Design
Salisbury College of Art and Design
West Herts College

For further details, go to:

www.meridiantv.com/about/careers_c.html

ITV

Information about ITV journalism training courses is
available from:

The Training Advisor, BACC, 200 Gray's Inn Road,
London WC1X 8HF

Radio Authority

The Radio Authority licences and regulates Independent Radio in the UK. Its TV and Radio Training Unit
provides a range of short courses.

Phone: 01332 296684
www.radioauthority.org.uk

Skillset

Skillset, the Industry Training Organisation for Broadcast, Film and Video, was launched in January 1993 to
ensure quality standards and training. Skillset publishes two guides to media courses: *Media Courses UK*
and *A Listing of Short Courses in Film, Television,
Video and Radio*. These are available, at a charge, from
Plymbridge Distributors Ltd, Estover Road, Plymouth,
PL6 7PZ. Phone: 01752 695745.

With such a range of different courses available,
standards will be variable. So Skillset suggests potential
candidates should inquire about the following areas:

- Ask what validation or accreditation a course
  currently has.
- Ask tutors about the employment track record of
  previous students or trainees. Visit the course while
  it is in progress and talk to current trainees.
- Is the equipment up to scratch, and is there enough of
  it? How much hands-on work is there on the course?
- Do the lecturers and trainers have broadcasting
  experience? Conversely, how much experience have
  they had as lecturers?
- Does the course offer placements in industry for
  each of its students?

- And will the course require you to make a demonstration tape or showreel of your work, to serve as a calling card when you begin job-hunting?

Skillset National Training Organization (NTO),
2nd Floor, 103 Dean Street, London W1V 5RA
Phone: +44 020 7534 5300
Fax: +44 020 7534 5333
www.skillset.org

Other contacts:

City and Guilds

C&G offer courses in Journalism and Radio Competencies, and Television and Video Competencies.

City and Guilds of London Institute, Division 24,
46 Britannia Street, London WC1X 9RG
www.city-and-guilds.co.uk

Commercial Radio Companies Association

Commercial Radio Companies Association (CRCA),
77 Shaftesbury Avenue, London W1V 7AD
www.crca.co.uk

USA

Broadcast Education Association

'Educating tomorrow's media professionals.' The BEA website offers extensive links to more than 250 member institutions and broadcast/media departments.

Broadcast Education Association,
1771 North Street, NW, Washington DC 20036
Phone: (202) 429 5354
www.beaweb.org

National Association of Broadcasters

The NAB's webcentre offers careers advice, including a list of publications, a how-to guide for job hunting, suggestions for audition tapes, and job descriptions in radio and television. It also provides information on fellowships and grants, and a list of current job vacancies.

National Association of Broadcasters,
1771 North Street, NW, Washington DC 20036
Phone: (202) 429 5300
Fax: (202) 775 3520
www.nab.org

South Carolina Broadcasters Association

Website with links to broadcast education resources and State Broadcasters Associations.

www.scba.net/links.htm

Other contacts:

American Film Institute

Primarily for filmmakers, but its website has links to training programmes for video-makers.

www.afionline.org

Broadcast Executive Directors Association

Describes itself as a national job bank for broadcasters and those seeking employment in the industry. Its web site links job seekers with employment opportunities in the USA and Puerto Rico.

www.careerpage.org

GLOSSARY

Actuality Interviews or sounds recorded on location.

Agency copy Story received from a news agency.

Analogue recording Where sound and/or pictures are recorded directly onto a recording medium (without being digitally encoded).

Anchor (US) Newscaster fronting a major news programme.

And finally *See* Tailpiece.

Angle An item of information in a news story that a journalist chooses to emphasize. It may be a *new angle*, giving the latest development in a story, or a *local angle*, emphasizing the point of relevance of that story to a local audience.

Archive File in which previously broadcast material is stored, possibly with clippings and background material.

Aston Brand name for a type of electronic caption generator.

Audio mixer (control panel) Control desk for mixing sound sources such as grams and mike.

Autocue, Teleprompter, Portaprompt Mechanical or electrical prompting devices which allow presenters to read a script while looking at or towards the camera.

Automatic cartridge recorder (ACR) Machine for recording video news reports on to cartridge for instant reply on air. Carts are stored on a carousel.

Automatic level control (ALC) Electronic device to reduce or boost the incoming signal to a tape recorder.

Avid Manufacturer of computer-based digital editing equipment.

Back announcement (B/A, back anno) A final sentence giving extra information to be read by the anchor or presenter at the end of a recorded item or report.

Backlight Lamp shone behind interviewee to pick him or her out from background, eliminate shadows and highlight hair. *See also* Key, Fill.

Back projection Where pictures are projected on to a screen behind the newsreader. *See also* Front projection.

Barn door Adjustable flaps around a studio light used to direct the beam.

Bi-directional mike A microphone which will pick up sound in front and behind it.

Bi-medial Reporters who cover news for TV as well as radio.

Blank *See* Skeleton.

Boom mike Microphone held on a long telescopic boom manoeuvred by a sound technician.

Breaking news (spot story, US) A story that is happening right now.

Brief Instructions given to a reporter about how to cover a story.

Bulk eraser Powerful electromagnet used for erasing reels or cassettes holding magnetic data.

Cable News Network International Atlanta-based global leader in cable television. Its 24-hour news service has become the benchmark for others.

Camcorder Hand-held camera and videocassette recorder combined.

Capacitor mike Battery-operated mike, often of the tie-clip variety.

Carrier wave Frequency wave which is modulated to carry a video or audio signal.

Cartridge (cart) Device used for recording and playing inserts into bulletins or items into programmes. May be audio or video. In analogue systems it is a self-cueing loop of tape in a plastic case. With digital systems the recording can be stored on disk.

Catchline A one- or two-word name used to identify a story, for example: world record. Also known as a *slug*.

Character generator Electronic caption machine.

Charge-coupled device (CCD) Solid-state sensor comprising light-sensitive diodes. Used in place of conventional tubes in some modern cameras.

Check calls Regular newsroom calls to the emergency services and hospitals to find out whether news is breaking.

Chromakey (colour separation overlay, CSO) Method of electronically replacing a single colour with a second picture of image.

Clip *See* Newsclip.

Commentary booth Small booth in which the reporter records the narrative for a news item.

Contact Source of news information.

Contribution circuit Network of landlines linking member stations of a network, along which news material is sent and received.

Contributions studio Small studio for sending reports 'up the line' to the network station.

Control panel *See* Audio mixer.

Cool Edit Pro Software for editing digital audio, as used by the BBC.

Copy story News story with no accompanying audio or visuals.

Copytaster Senior journalist who sifts incoming mail and agency copy to select items that are considered to be worth running.

Cross-fade The overlapping of one sound with another.

Cue 1 Introduction to a report. 2 Instruction to a presenter to start and stop speaking. This may be given verbally, by gestures or in writing. *See also* In-cue, Out-cue.

Cue-light Light on top of camera to tell presenter the camera is live. Also used in a commentary box to cue live narration.

Cut *See* Newsclip.

Cutaway The insertion of a shot in a picture sequence which is used to mask an edit.

DAT (digital audio tape) Matchbox-sized digital recording medium.

Decibel (DB) Unit of loudness.

Delay A recorded delay of several seconds in playing back a 'live' phone-in programme to trap obscene calls. *See also* Obscenity button.

Digital Radio (formerly DAB) Radio transmission system offering compact disc quality audio and requiring a special receiver.

Digital recording The storage of sound and/or pictures which have been encoded as a series of numbers. Playback translates those numbers back without the noise or distortion of conventional (analogue) recording.

Directivity pattern (pickup) Area over which a microphone will pick up sound.

Dissolve Where one picture is faded out and another is faded in simultaneously.

DOA Dead on arrival. Emergency services jargon for a victim who has died either before help could arrive or before the ambulance could reach the hospital.

Dolby System For reducing audio noise and improving high-frequency response.

Dope sheet (camera report) Camera operator's written record of each camera take.

Drive-time The period during radio listening when a substantial part of the audience is travelling in cars – early morning, lunchtime, early evening.

Dubbing Duplication of a recording from one recorder to another. System of electronic editing.

Earpiece Device used by presenter to listen to instructions from the studio control room.

Edit controller The heart of a computerized tape editing system which is programmed to control the precise location of each edit.

Embargo 'Not to be released until' date on a news release. Device intended to control the publication date of an item of information.

ENG (EJ, ECC, PSC) Electronic news gathering (electronic journalism; electronic camera coverage; portable single camera) with portable video cameras. *See* Camcorder.

ENPS Electronic News Production System. Powerful computer network developed by AP and used worldwide (including by the BBC and ITN) to allow any journalist in a news organization to call up story material on demand.

Equalization Improving audio quality by altering the frequency characteristics.

Fade out 1 Where a picture fades out, usually to black or to white. 2 Gradually bringing down the volume of an audio signal until it disappears.

Feature opener Informally written introduction to a soft news story designed more to arouse curiosity and to entertain than to inform.

Federal Communications Commission (FCC) The US governing body for broadcasting.

Fibre-optic Cable system composed of hollow fibres which carry light. Pulses of light are converted into information. Fibre-optic cables are used to carry telephone calls, computer data and TV signals.

Fill Lamp casting a soft light to fill in shadows. *See also* Backlight, Key.

Fillers (or pad) Second-string items used as make-weights to bring a bulletin or programme up to length.

Fishpole Hand-held sound boom. *See* Boom mike.

Flats Boards used as a backdrop to the set.

Fly-on-the-wall (Vérité) Documentary style unmediated by reporter or narrator. The camera watches the action unnoticed, like a fly on the wall.

Frequency Rate at which a sound or light wave or an electronic impulse passes a given point over a specific time. *See* Hertz.

Front projection Where pictures are projected from in front of the newsreader onto a screen alongside.

Futures file File in which stories and news events which are known to be happening on a certain date are placed, so that coverage may be planned in advance.

FX Shorthand for sound effects.

General view (GV) Camera shot showing an entire scene to establish location.

Gobbledygook   Jargon-laden and often garbled officialese intended to confuse rather than communicate.

Gopher (anorak)   Radio enthusiast, usually on work experience, who fetches, carries and generally 'goes for' on a radio station.

Handling noise   Unwanted clicks and sounds picked up by a microphone as a result of handling and moving it.

Hard news   Information of importance about events of significance.

Hard news formula   A hard news story will cover most of the basic facts by asking the questions, who? what? where? when? why? and how?

Headline   Short summary of a news story given at the start or end of a bulletin or grouped with other headlines in lieu of a longer bulletin. Also known as *highlights* or *summaries*. *See also* Teaser.

Headline sentence   *See* Intro.

Hertz (Hz)   Frequency of sound measured in cycles per second, for example 800 hertz is 800 cycles per second. 1000 hertz is a kilohertz (kHz).

High definition television (HDTV)   TV system of more than a thousand lines resulting in improved quality.

Highlight   *See* Headline.

Holding copy   The first version of a story left by a reporter to be run in his/her absence while he/she is out of the newsroom getting further information on that story.

Human interest story   Soft news item. Of interest to the audience, but of no great significance or importance. Typically showbiz, animals, lottery winners, etc.

Ident   Piece of recorded music played to introduce or identify a particular programme, feature or presenter. Also known as *stab, jingle, sounder.*

In-cue and out-cue   These are written instructions to say when a report begins and ends. The in-cue is the first few words of that report, and the out-cue the last few words. The in-cue is a useful check that the right report is being played, and the out-cue tells presenters, directors and technical operators when the report is finishing.

Independent Radio News (IRN)   Company which supplies hourly bulletins of national and international news to most independent radio stations in the UK.

Independent Television Commission (ITC)   British regulatory body for independent television.

Input   The newsgathering operation of a newsroom. *See* Output.

Insert   *See* Newsclip.

Internet   Global network of computers linked by modems. Set up in the 1960s as a bomb-proof information exchange by the US Defense Department. Now mushroomed into a new and personalized media, allowing individual access, via a modem, to uncensored pictures, sound and text from around the world.

Intro (Introduction)   1 The first, audience-winning, and most important paragraph of a news story, giving the main angle of the story and the central facts. 2 The introduction (cue or lead) to a report or recorded item. Also known as the *headline sentence*.

Independent Television News (ITN)   Company which supplies programmes of national and international news to the UK's other independent TV companies.

In vision (IV)   Instruction on script to indicate presenter should be on camera at that point.

Jingle   *See* Ident.

Jump cut   An edit in a sequence of shots which has the subject jerking from one position to another.

Key   Main lamp providing a hard light for modelling a subject. *See also* Backlight, Fill.

Key words   One or two words which sum up the most important point of a news story.

Kicker   *See* Tailpiece.

Kilohertz   *See* Hertz.

Land line   Cable transmission for audio and/or video.

Lead   First item in a news programme or the written cue to a news item or report.

LED   Light emitting diode. Low powered light used for electronic displays (on/off indicators, level meters, etc.).

Lighting grid   Construction suspended from the ceiling of a studio to support the lights.

Links   Narrative linking or bridging interviews in a report, summarizing or giving additional information. *See also* Package.

Links vehicle   Mobile vehicle used as a platform for a microwave transmitter. *See also* Microwave.

Live Real Audio   Internet radio system, making it possible to download radio programmes onto a computer via a modem.

Local angle   *See* Angle.

Lower third   Caption or super in the lower third of the picture.

Marking-up Marking a story with important details, such as who wrote it and when and the catchline.

Menu Collection of tasters at the start of a programme giving forthcoming attractions.

MD (Mini-Disc) Digital recording medium using miniature compact disc.

Microwave System for relaying audio and video signals on very short wavelengths.

Mini-wrap Brief package, often used in the news.

Multi-angled story One which carries a number of different angles on the same story. *See also* Umbrella story.

Multi-track Recording technique normally used in a music studio to record separately a combination of different sounds.

Newsbooth Small studio where bulletins are presented on air.

Newsclip (cut, insert) Short extract of an interview to illustrate a story.

Newsflash (bulletin US) Interruption of normal programming to give brief details of an urgent breaking story.

Newsmix A news summary comprising a mixture of local and national news.

News release Publicity handout from an organization or public relations company informing the newsroom about a possible news item. *See also* WPB.

Newsroom conference Discussion between producers and the news editor about what stories to run in the news and how they should be covered.

Newsroom diary (prospects) A diary or sheet in which is listed all the known stories and news events that are taking place that day and require coverage.

Noddies Shots of the reporter nodding or listening intently recorded after an interview to be cut in later to mask edits.

Noise reduction The electronic reduction of interference induced by the transmission system.

Non-linear editing Editing out of sequence, afforded by digital storage of audio and video data. Segments of sound or pictures can be cut and pasted like words in a word-processor. This offers greater flexibility than linear editing, where sounds or pictures have to be assembled in order.

OB Outside broadcast.

Obscenity button (profanity button) Switch used for taking a programme instantly out of delay to prevent an obscene caller from being heard on the air. *See also* Delay.

OMB (one-man band) Title given to ITN camera crews where a single operator works the camera and monitors the sound levels.

Omni-directional mike Microphone with circular pickup pattern.

Opt-in and opt-out 1 The process of switching between local and network transmissions. Opting-in occurs when a local station goes over to a live network programme and opting-out takes place when it returns to its own programmes. 2 Opt-out is an early point at which a report may be brought to an end.

Outcue Prearranged verbal cue to show that a tape or a bulletin has come to an end. A standard outcue is the regular ending to a voice report, such as 'John Smith, Independent Radio News, Nottingham.'

Out of vision (OOV) Instruction on TV script to show the narrator is not to appear in vision while reading the script.

Output The programme-making operation of a newsroom. *See* Input.

Out-takes Discarded pictures edited from a report.

Package Report comprising edited interviews separated by narrative links.

Padding *See* Fillers.

Paintbox Electronic graphics machine.

Panning handle Handle used to turn the head of a camera.

Peak programme meter (PPM) Meter for measuring peak signal level. Its specially damped action prevents flickering and produces a steady reading. *See also* VU meter.

Phono Report or interview made by telephone. Also a type of lead used to connect one piece of equipment to another.

Picture store Device for electronically storing wire pictures.

Piece to camera (stand-upper; stand-up) Information given by a reporter on location facing the camera.

Pixel Single dot of information on a video screen. Pixels are combined to form the pictures.

Planning board Large board used in some news rooms to show the stories that are being covered and which reporters have been assigned to them.

Portaprompt *See* Autocue.

Pre-fade Listening to an item without playing it on air. Used to check levels, cue records and check the network signal before opting-in to the network news.

Profanity button *See* Obscenity button.

Promo *See* Trail.

Prospects *See* Newsroom diary.

Question and answer (Q&A) When a reporter is interviewed on air about a story he or she has been covering.

Reading-in   This is when a reporter, coming on shift, reads all the copy and items produced by the previous shift to familiarize himself with the stories the newsroom has been following.

Recordist   Member of camera crew who operates sound and/or video recording equipment.

Remote studio   Small, often unmanned, studio some distance from the radio or TV station where guests who cannot make it in to the station can be interviewed. It can be linked to the main station by satellite or cable, permitting studio quality sound and pictures for TV.

Ribbon mike   Sensitive directional microphone, frequently used in recording studios.

Rifle mike (gun mike)   Directional mike for picking up sound at a distance.

Recording of (off) transmission (ROT)   Tape of the output.

Running story   One that is developing and constantly changing, throwing up new information that requires frequent revision and updates.

Rushes   Raw shots that are ready for editing.

Safe area   Central area of the screen where pictures and captions are unlikely to be cut off by poorly adjusted TV sets.

Scanner   1 Radio which automatically tunes in to broadcasts by the police and emergency services. 2 Outside broadcast vehicle. 3 Telecine machine. 4 Caption scanner.

Scrambler   Device for scrambling satellite TV signals so only authorized viewers equipped with an unscrambler can receive them.

Self-opping   When a presenter operates his/her own control desk without technical assistance.

Sexy story   A story that has instant audience appeal. Usually light and amusing. Very occasionally sexy in the usual sense.

Shot box   Switches used to preset the zoom of a studio camera.

Signposting   In a news programme, this means comprehensively headlining and forward trailing the programme to keep up audience interest. During a story, it means highlighting the central theme of the story at the start, amplifying that theme in a logical manner, repeating key points where necessary, and pointing the story forward at the end.

Skeleton (blank)   Programme script which has gaps between the pages for insertion of new and late items.

Slug   *See* Catchline.

Sound-bite (Grab – Australia)   Portion of an interview or snatch of actuality selected for screening.

Sounder (jingle, stab)   *See* Ident.

Spike   Newsroom anachronism. A metal prong on to which incoming copy and background material which is not required immediately is impaled.

Splicer   Device for joining manually edited film or tape.

Splicing tape   Sticky tape used to join physical edits made by cutting the recording tape or film.

Spot story (US)   An item of breaking news, such as a fire or an air crash.

Stab   Short, emphatic jingle. *See* Ident.

Standard outcue (payoff)   *See* Outcue.

Stand-upper (stand up)   *See* Piece to camera.

Stereo   A recording made using left and right channels to separate and spread the sound.

Stringer   Freelance correspondent.

Summary   1 *See* Headline. 2 News programme or bulletin rounding up the most important news events.

Super (caption)   Title or caption mechanically superimposed or electronically generated on the picture.

Switching pause   Short pause in transmission before and after the network bulletin to permit local stations to opt in and out cleanly.

Syndicated material   Recordings sent out to radio stations by PR and advertising agencies to promote a company or product.

Tailpiece (kicker, and finally)   Light-hearted story at end of bulletin or newscast.

Talkback   Intercom device for talking to station staff on location or in other parts of the building.

Talking head   Disparaging term used for a story which features dry expert opinion rather than the views of 'real' or ordinary people.

Teaser, taster   Snappy, one-line headline, usually at start of programme (*see* Menu), designed to tease the audience into wanting to find out more. May include a snatch of actuality.

Telephone balance unit (TBU)   Device used in the making of recorded telephone interviews. Permits interviewer to use a studio microphone and balances the levels of the two voices.

Teleprompt   *See* Autocue.

Teletext   Process for transmitting written and graphic information on to TV using the spare lines of a TV signal.

Ten code   Spoken communication code used by the emergency services, where the word 'ten' indicates that the code is being used, and the number spoken after it carries the message, i.e. '10–31' means crime in progress. The code numbers used will vary.

Tip-off   Call from a stringer, tipster or member of the audience to let the station know that a story is breaking.

Tipster   *See* Tip-off.

Touchscreen studio   A studio where all the equipment is controlled electronically by touching part of the screen of a computer.

Trail (or promo) Telling the audience about items which are to follow.

TX Shorthand for transmission.

Umbrella story A single story incorporating a number of similar items under one banner. *See also* Multi-angled story.

Uni-directional mike Microphone which responds mainly to sounds directly in front of it.

VCR Videocassette recorder.

Vérité Actuality programme or feature made without accompanying narrative or commentary.

Video-journalist Solo act by a reporter with a video-camera who shoots, interviews and edits.

Vision mixer (switcher, technical director) 1 Operator who controls, fades, wipes and dissolves in the studio control room. 2 Device used to fade, wipe, dissolve. *See also* Wipe.

Visuals The visual element of a TV report: photographs, film or tape footage or graphics.

Voice-over Commentary recorded over pictures by an unseen reader. *See also* OOV.

Voice report (voicer) Details and explanation of a story by a reporter or correspondent. More expansive than a copy story. Permits a change of voice from the newsreader.

Vox pop Latin 'vox populi' or 'voice of the people'. Refers to street interviews conducted to poll public opinion. (US – man in the street interviews.)

Visual production effects machine (VPE) Computer graphics system used in TV.

VTR Videotape recorder.

VU meter Volume unit meter. Imprecise meter for monitoring recording and playback levels. *See also* PPM.

Waveform Digital speech is displayed on a computer in the form of zig-zag waves of sound. These can be edited on-screen.

WHAT formula Essentials of story construction: What has happened? How did it happen? Amplification; Tie up loose ends.

Wildtrack Recording of ambient sound for dubbing later as background to a report.

Wipe Crossing from one picture to another, giving the impression that one is wiping the other off the screen.

Wire service News agency which sends copy out to newsrooms along landlines (wires) where it is received by teleprinters or directly into computers.

World Wide Web (WWW) Graphical interface of the global network of digitized information stored on the Internet.

WPB The ultimate destination of 90 per cent of a newsroom's incoming mail – the waste paper bin.

FURTHER READING

A-Z of Radio Production, Pat Taylor, BBC Radio Training, 1991.

An Introduction to ENG, B. Hesketh and I. Yorke, Focal Press, 1993.

Basic Editing, Nicola Harris, Spa Books, 1991.

Basic TV Reporting, Ivor Yorke, Focal Press, 1990.

Behind the Scenes at Local News, R. S. Goald, Focal Press, 1994.

Blue Book of British Broadcasting, Tellex Monitors Ltd.

Breaking the News, James Fallows, Pantheon Books, 1996.

Broadcast News, Radio Journalism and an Introduction to Television, Mitchell Stephens, Holt, Rinehart and Winston, 1980.

Broadcast News, Writing and Reporting, Peter E. Mayeux, Brown & Benchmark, 1995.

Broadcast News, Writing, Reporting and Producing, Ted White, Focal Press, 1996.

Broadcast Voice Performance, Michael C. Keith, Focal Press, 1989.

Broadcasting: Getting In and Getting On, John Miller, Newpoint, 1990.

Broadcasting in the UK, Barrie MacDonald, Mansell, 1992.

Careers in Television and Radio, Michael Selby, Kogan Page, 1997.

Careerscope – Careers in Radio, John Keats, Hamilton House Publishing.

Editing and Design, Book One: Newsman's English, Harold Evans, Heinemann, 1972.

Effective TV Production, 3rd edition, Gerald Millerson, Focal Press, 1993.

Electronic Media Ethics, V. Limburg, Focal Press, 1994.

Ethical Issues in Journalism and the Media, Belsey and Chadwick, Routledge, 1992.

Fundamentals of Radio Broadcasting, John Hasling, McGraw-Hill.

Grammar of the Edit, Roy Thomson, Focal Press, 1993.

Guide to Independent Radio Journalism, Linda Gage, Duckworth, 1990.

How to Handle Media Interviews, Andrew Boyd, Management Books 2000, 1999.

ITN, The First 40 Years, ITN, 1995.

Law and the Media, 3rd Edition, Tom Crone, Focal Press, 1995.

Lights, Camera, Action! Josephine Langham, BFI, 1993.

Local Radio Journalism, P. Chantler and S. Harris, Focal Press, 1992.

McNae's Essential Law for Journalists, Walter Greenwood and Tom Welsh, Butterworths, 1997.

Making Radio, R. Kaye and L. Popperwell, Broadside, 1992.

Mastering the News Interview, S. C. Rafe, HarperCollins, 1991.

Media Ethics, Matthew Kieran (ed.), Routledge, 1998.

Media Law, Peter Carey, Sweet & Maxwell, 1999.

News, Newspapers and Television, Alastair Hetherington, Macmillan, 1985.

On Camera, Essential Know-how for Programme-makers, Harris Watts, AAVO, 1997.

Radio Production, R. McLeish, Focal Press, 1999.

Reporting for Television, Carolyn Diana Lewis, Columbia University Press, 1984.

Research for Writers, Ann Hoffman, A&C Black, 1999.

Reuters Handbook for Journalists, Ian Macdowall, Butterworth-Heinemann, 1992.

See It Happen: The Making of ITN, Geoffrey Cox, Bodley Head, 1983.

So You Want to Work in TV? Alan Quays, Kogan Page, 1998.

The Media Guide, Steve Peak (ed.), *The Guardian* (annual).

The Spoken Word, A BBC Guide, Robert Burchfield, BBC, 1981.

The Technique of Television News, Ivor Yorke, Focal Press, 1987.

Work in Local Radio!, Geoffrey Roberts, Bradford College Print Centre.

World Communications, UNESCO, Gower Press/Unipub/The Unesco Press.

Videojournalism, Richard Griffiths, Focal Press, 1998.

Index

Focal Press

http://www.focalpress.com

Join Focal Press On-line

As a member you will enjoy the following benefits:

- an email bulletin with **information on new books**
- a bi-monthly **Focal Press Newsletter**:
    - o featuring a selection of new titles
    - o keeps you informed of **special offers, discounts and freebies**
    - o alerts you to **Focal Press news and events** such as author signings and seminars
- complete access to **free content** and reterence material on the focalpress site, such as the focalXtra articles and commentary from our authors
- a **Sneak Preview** of selected titles (sample chapters) *before* they publish
- a chance to have your say on our **discussion boards** and **review books** for other focal readers

Focal Club Members are invited to give us feedback on our products and services. Email: worldmarketing@focalpress.com – we want to hear your views!

Membership is FREE. To join, visit our website and register. If you require any further information regarding the on-line club please contact:

Emma Hales, Promotions Controller
Email: emma.hales@repp.co.uk
Fax: +44 (0)1865 315472
Address: Focal Press, Linacre House,
Jordan Hill, Oxford,
UK, OX2 8DP

Catalogue

For information on all Focal Press titles, we will be happy to send you a free copy of the Focal Press catalogue:

USA
Email: christine.degon@bhusa.com

Europe and rest of World
Email: carol.burgess@repp.co.uk
Tel: +44 (0)1865 314693

Potential authors

If you have an idea for a book, please get in touch:

USA
Terri Jadick, Associate Editor
Email: terri.jadick@bhusa.com
Tel: +1 781 904 2646
Fax: +1 781 904 2640

Europe and rest of World
Christina Donaldson, Editorial Assistant
Email: christina.donaldson@repp.co.uk
Tel: +44 (0)1865 314027
Fax: +44 (0)1865 315472

Focal Press

Also available from Focal Press ...

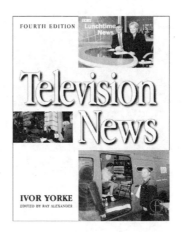

Television News
(Fourth Edition)
Ivor Yorke
Edited by Ray Alexander

Television News is a straightforward account of the editorial and production processes used by journalists to bring television news to the viewer. It is an invaluable text for students on journalism courses, print and radio journalists moving into television, and television journalists wishing to update their knowledge.

This fourth edition has been thoroughly updated to take account of the latest practices and issues in the television industry. It includes new illustrations of developments from both a technological and an editorial perspective.

September 2000 • 288pp • 26 black & white photos • 67 line drawings
246 x 189mm • Paperback
ISBN 0 240 51615 X

To order your copy call +44 (0)1865 888180 (UK)
Or +1 800 366 2665 (USA)
Or visit our website on **http://www.focalpress.com**

Focal Press

Also available from Focal Press ...

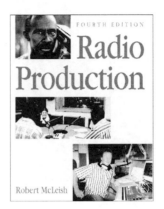

Radio Production
(Fourth Edition)
Robert McLeish

Radio Production is a complete working handbook on every aspect of producing radio programmes to a professional standard. From operational techniques to news production, conducting interviews, writing radio scripts, news-reading and presentation, making commercials, producing different types of programme formats, outside broadcasts, music recording, features and drama, and programme evaluation: everything you need to know is laid out in a clear, accessible and readable manner.

The 4th edition:

- has been updated to include the latest digital techniques: computer based editing, mini-disc, digital broadcasting
- includes practical training exercises
- features checklists, sample scripts, practical examples and case studies
- has a reader-friendly layout, with technical detail explained in simple terms
- has a comprehensive glossary

August 1999 • 288pp • 100 line drawings
246 x 189mm • Paperback
ISBN 0 240 51554 4

Focal Press

Also available from Focal Press ...

Journalism in the Digital Age: Theory and practice for broadcast, print and online media
John Herbert

This book provides the practical techniques and theoretical knowledge that underpin the fundamental skills of a journalist. It also takes a highly modern approach, as the convergence of broadcast, print and online media require the learning of new skills and methods. The book is written from an international perspective, with examples from around the world in recognition of the global marketplace for today's media.

Journalism in the Digital Age is an essential text for students on journalism courses and professionals looking for a reference that covers the skills, technology and knowledge required for a digital and converged media age. The book's essence lies in the way essential theories such as ethics and law, are woven into practical newsgathering and reporting techniques, as well as advice on management skills for journalists, providing the wide intellectual foundation which gives credibility to reporting.

November 1999 • 368pp • 234 x 156mm • Paperback
ISBN 0 240 51589 7

Focal Press

Also available from Focal Press ...

Practising Global Journalism: Exploring reporting issues worldwide
John Herbert

Practising Global Journalism is essential reading for today's practising and trainee journalists. John Herbert examines the global environment in which journalists operate and describes the latest technology and its impact on print, broadcast and online journalism practice.

From this book, you will gain an understanding of:
- the effects of the digital revolution on journalism worldwide
- the global media marketplace - the technology, the players and the issues
- news agencies, sources and networks, issues of ethics, global media ownership and control
- how journalists are using the web and even newer ways to collect and communicate information

Practising Global Journalism is a unique overview of the profession, providing a comparative study of journalism practice worldwide. Case studies are drawn from Europe, Australia, the Asia Pacific, South Asia, China, Africa and the Americas.

October 2000 • 288pp • 234 x 156mm • Paperback
ISBN 0 240 51602 8

To order your copy call +44 (0)1865 888180 (UK)
Or +1 800 366 2665 (USA)
Or visit our website on **http://www.focalpress.com**

Focal Press

Also available from Focal Press ...

Satellite Newsgathering
Jonathan Higgins

Dealing with technical theory, as well as practical aspects, **Satellite Newsgathering** is an ideal primer for anyone working, or interested, in Satellite Newsgathering (SNG).

SNG is the process that delivers 'live' and 'breaking' news to the viewer/listener as it happens. The focus of this book is the use of satellite uplinks for newsgathering (for both television and radio news reporting). Jonathan Higgins provides an insight into the technical and operational considerations in specifying and operating SNG systems around the world, the satisfaction faced in doing so successfully and the problems occasionally encountered.

April 2000 • 472pp • 30 line drawings • 25 black & white photos
234 x 156mm • Paperback
ISBN 0 240 51551 X

To order your copy call +44 (0)1865 888180 (UK)
Or +1 800 366 2665 (USA)
Or visit our website on **http://www.focalpress.com**